W9-CCK-891

Dancing in the Street

Dancing in the Street

Motown and the Cultural Politics of Detroit

Suzanne E. Smith

HARVARD UNIVERSITY PRESS
Cambridge, Massachusetts
London, England

Copyright © 1999 by Suzanne E. Smith
All rights reserved
Printed in the United States of America

Fourth printing, 2003

Library of Congress Cataloging-in-Publication Data

Smith, Suzanne E., 1964–
Dancing in the street : Motown and the cultural politics
of Detroit / Suzanne E. Smith.
p.   cm.
Includes bibliographical references and index.
ISBN 0-674-00063-3 (cloth : alk. paper)
ISBN 0-674-00546-5 (pbk. : alk. paper)
1. Motown Record Corporation.   2. Afro-Americans—
Music—Social aspects—Michigan—Detroit.   3. Civil rights
movements—Michigan—Detroit.   I. Title.
ML3792.S65   2000
781.644'09774'34—dc21   99-34399

For my parents,
Gerald and Caralee Smith,
and in memory of my grandfather,
Edward Smith (1909–1973)

Contents

Contents

Illustrations

Dancing in the Street

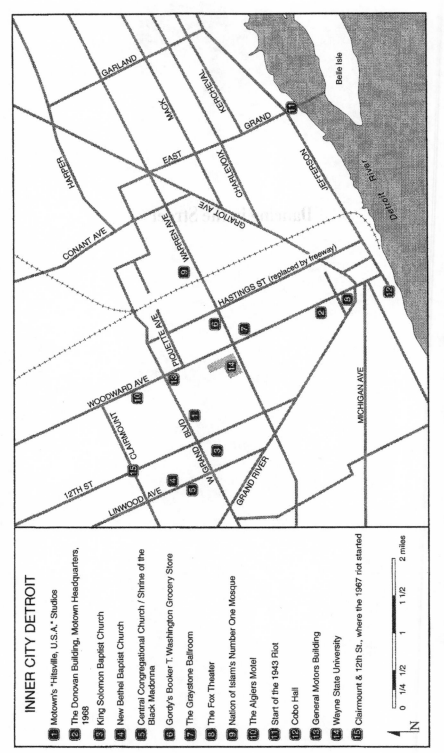

Map of inner-city Detroit. (Courtesy University of Wisconsin Cartographic Laboratory.)

INNER CITY DETROIT

1. Motown's "Hitsville, U.S.A." Studios
2. The Donovan Building, Motown Headquarters, 1968
3. King Solomon Baptist Church
4. New Bethel Baptist Church
5. Central Congregational Church / Shrine of the Black Madonna
6. Gordy's Booker T. Washington Grocery Store
7. The Graystone Ballroom
8. The Fox Theater
9. Nation of Islam's Number One Mosque
10. The Algiers Motel
11. Start of the 1943 Riot
12. Cobo Hall
13. General Motors Building
14. Wayne State University
15. Clairmount & 12th St., where the 1967 riot started

0   1/4 1/2   1   1 1/2   2 miles

Introduction:
"Can't Forget the Motor City"

On a humid July afternoon in 1967, Martha and the Vandellas stepped onto the stage of Detroit's prestigious Fox Theater as the much anticipated grand finale of the "Swinging Time Revue." The revue, based on a local television show of the same name, was a regional version of Dick Clark's *American Bandstand*. Robin Seymour, a top disc jockey in the Detroit area, hosted the television show, which was broadcast from CKLW studios in Windsor, Canada. His live stage show featured performances by many local favorites in Detroit's rhythm and blues circuit. Acts including the Parliaments, who sang their hit "I Wanna Testify"; the Dramatics, who were promoting their single "All Because of You"; and the comedy act the Li'l Soul Brothers guaranteed a spirited show. Martha Reeves and the Vandellas were, of course, the main attraction with their repertoire of Motown hits such as "Nowhere to Run," "Jimmy Mack," and—appropriately for the sweltering summer day—"Heatwave." Their biggest number, however, was "Dancing in the Street."[1]

Martha Reeves jumped into the song with her usual vigor, but she became distracted when a stage manager began to wave his hands and signal to her from the wings. Reeves finished the number and quickly went off stage to find out what was causing the commotion. The stage manager grabbed Reeves and told her that rioting had broken out on the streets of Detroit. A police raid on an illegal after-hours drinking spot, also known as a "blind pig," had ignited a burst of violence, looting, and arson that was spreading dangerously throughout the city. Young people out on the streets—as one observer noted at the time—appeared to be "dancing amidst the flames." Reeves returned to center stage and explained the situation, as calmly as possible, to her loyal fans. She advised all of them to travel to safety. Heeding her own advice, Reeves, the Vandellas, and their backup band packed up their equipment and left Detroit that night.[2]

They decided to travel to their next tour date in Newark, New Jersey. When they arrived in New Jersey, riots broke out there as well. The group then moved on to Myrtle Beach, South Carolina, but when they heard that black nationalist Rap Brown might be passing through the area, they left for Los Angeles. Years later, Reeves recalled those confusing weeks with a degree of resentment. On a television talk show, Reeves recounted that she and the Vandellas eventually ended up in England to continue their tour. The British press aggravated Reeves when someone put a microphone in her face and asked her if she was a militant leader. The British journalist wanted to know if Reeves agreed, as many people had claimed, that "Dancing in the Street" was a call to riot. To Reeves, the query was patently absurd. "My Lord, it was a *party* song," she remarked in retrospect.[3]

Reeves's insistence that "Dancing in the Street" was a party song cannot be disputed by anyone who has ever heard the infectious and buoyant tune. Yet "Dancing in the Street" was never just a party song. Music, particularly music created in Detroit's black community during the 1960s, could rarely, if ever, transcend the politically and racially charged environment in which it was produced—or, in the case of Reeves, the stage on which it was performed. The sounds, music, and "dancing" that emerged from the streets of black Detroit reflected and directly engaged with the challenges African Americans faced as they built their lives in that major industrial city. A song such as "Dancing in the Street" was only one example of how music in Detroit's black community constituted daily life rather than acted as a diversion from it. Some of this music did not emanate from Motown studios, but the songs clearly illustrate how the sounds of Detroit's streets could articulate the needs of African Americans.

Martha and the Vandellas, circa 1965. Martha Reeves stands on the right. (Courtesy Motown Record Co., L.P., a Polygram Company.)

One year after Martha Reeves's quick exit from the Fox Theater, several hundred black autoworkers gathered outside Chrysler's Dodge Main Plant located in Detroit's Hamtramck neighborhood. The workers had recently formed the Dodge Revolutionary Union Movement, more commonly known as DRUM. DRUM aimed to be the voice of black autoworkers, who felt that their needs were not being addressed either by the automobile manufacturers or the United Auto Workers (UAW). DRUM hoped to organize black industrial workers nationally and believed that "the black working class would be the vanguard of the revolutionary struggle in this country."[4]

On July 12, 1968, DRUM organizers staged a picket line outside the Chrysler plant, where strikers were demanding a black plant manager, equal pay, and job opportunities comparable to those for their white counterparts. Participants arrived in a relatively festive mood. Many wore colorful African robes and tikis around their necks. Some brought bongo drums to the demonstration—a symbol of the new militant union. Soon they began to beat the bongos while other DRUM members "danced in the street" to the sound of the African rhythms. Onlookers tied up traffic as the crowd swelled to close to a thousand.[5]

The dancing and music stopped when the factory's starting whistle blew. Tension increased as some participants began harassing workers— both black and white—who crossed the picket line to begin their shift. Soon, the police interceded in an attempt to disperse everyone. Then, suddenly, the sound of a solitary bongo drum returned. A few feet away another drummer took up the beat, then another, and another. Autoworkers who had already entered the factory could not ignore the protest music as one worker, Edward Lee, noted that "perhaps twenty bongo players rent the air with the curious, alien and slightly frightening noises." Many wondered as they gazed down at the protesters below what the sounds meant: Were they sending messages to one another? Was it a call to revolution? Gradually, the drumbeats drowned out the noise of the traffic and the murmuring of the bystanders. The sounds carried up to the factory windows and threatened the workers caught inside. To diffuse the tension, a few autoworkers retreated from the windows and started their machines. Oddly, as Lee observed, "they [did] not begin work," yet "the hum of the motors, powerful, familiar and reassuring, seem[ed] to provide an antidote to the unknown."[6]

The beat of the bongo drum, the rattle and hum of factory machinery, the boisterous rhythms of a Martha Reeves and the Vandellas song: these sounds, heard in isolation, might seem innocuous enough. But considered in context, in the charge of their historical moment, the sounds acquire new meaning. The bongos on the DRUM picket line provided both an opportunity for strikers to dance in the street and a threat to the workers inside the factory. The machines running, even without the assembly line activated, offered "an antidote to the unknown." "Dancing in the Street," performed in the eye of Detroit's worst urban storm, may not have been a call to riot but could no longer be simply a party song.

Of all the sounds that emerged from Detroit during the 1960s, the "Motown sound" was clearly the most celebrated and famous. From early hits such as Barrett Strong's "Money (That's What I Want)" and the Marvelettes' "Please Mr. Postman," to later chart toppers including the Supremes' "Reflections" and the Temptations' "Just My Imagination," the Motown Record Company completely transformed the American popular music scene. Never before had a black-owned company been able to create and produce the musical artistry of its own community, and then sell it successfully to audiences across racial boundaries.

Historically, the music industry had established and maintained these boundaries for marketing purposes. Record companies first began marketing "black" music as "race records" in the 1920s in response to the popularity of blues singers such as Gertrude "Ma" Rainey and Bessie Smith. *Billboard* magazine monitored these records on its "Harlem Hit Parade," which eventually became the "Rhythm and Blues" chart. Before Motown, most independent black-owned record companies such as Don Robey's Duke-Peacock label in Houston and Vee-Jay Records in Chicago succeeded primarily within the confines of the rhythm and blues market. Motown's music defied the internal segregation of the music industry when its records began to sell widely outside conventional black markets.[7]

Motown's achievements both as a cultural phenomenon and as a business enterprise have received considerable attention in the popular press, in the many biographies and autobiographies of Motown legends, in the record industry, and in scholarship on popular music. Over the years, these works have attempted to either recount or revise the "Motown story" for the general public. The plot of this story typically begins with the young Berry Gordy Jr. founding the company in Detroit in 1958 with a small $800 loan from his family. With this investment, Gordy managed to use his talents as an entrepreneur and a songwriter with an ear for popular hits to create the "Sound of Young America."

While the goal was ambitious, the means were modest. Motown Studios began in a small house on West Grand Boulevard in Detroit, which the staff quickly dubbed "Hitsville, U.S.A." The enterprising record label soon attracted the best local African American musicians and performers in the city—often by scouting out local talent shows and amateur singing contests. The company released its first major hit, "Money (That's What I Want)," in 1959 and by February 1961 had its first million-seller: the Miracles' "Shop Around." From this moment on, Hitsville began to live up to its bold name and succeed beyond all expectations. By the mid-1960s, Motown was producing some of the biggest acts on the charts: the Miracles, the Contours, Mary Wells, the Marvelettes, the Four Tops, Marvin Gaye, Martha and the Vandellas, Stevie Wonder, the Supremes, Kim Weston, Junior Walker and the All-Stars, Gladys Knight and the Pips, and the Temptations. This wealth of talent turned Motown into a "hit factory" that churned out one hit after another from Mary Wells's "My Guy," Marvin Gaye's "Pride and Joy," and Martha and the Vandellas' "Heatwave," to the Four Tops' "Baby I Need Your Loving," the Temptations' "Ain't Too Proud to Beg," and Stevie Wonder's "Superstition." Gordy's genius rested in his ability to attract strong talent, to control every aspect of the record production process, and to groom his artists for white "crossover" audiences.

Motown's "family" found its biggest commercial success in the Supremes, the young trio of Diana Ross, Mary Wilson, and Florence Ballard, who had their first major hit in 1964 with "Where Did Our Love Go?" A string of number-one records quickly followed: "Baby Love," "Stop! In the Name of Love," and "I Hear a Symphony." The group's overwhelming popularity—with both crossover and black audiences—opened new doors for Motown in television, in the nightclub market, and eventually, through Diana Ross's solo career, in Hollywood. The Supremes' trajectory fulfilled the company's biggest aspirations but also moved the company further and further away from its hometown roots. In 1972 Motown left Detroit to establish its headquarters in Los Angeles, in order to expand from music production into filmmaking and television.

The Motown story did not end in the early 1970s with the move to California, but much of the magic of the early years was never recaptured. Most studies on Motown and its music attempt to analyze how and why the black company achieved the success that it did—especially with white audiences. The larger historical perspective of these works usually involves the recognition that the national civil rights movement, which so tangibly heightened America's awareness of racial inequality during the 1960s, contributed to the popularity of the Motown sound. In other words, the civil rights movement created the environment in which broader cultural integration—as typified by Motown's wide appeal— could occur.[8]

Yet little historical research has been done on exactly how the modern civil rights movement influenced Motown's evolution from a small local record company into an international music industry giant. If the gains of the civil rights movement facilitated Motown's success, how did this process work? Was it mere coincidence that the music and the movement happened at the same historical juncture or were more complicated forces involved? Did Motown's economic and musical accomplishments result from or contribute to the fight for racial equality—or both? What did Motown's success mean to African American audiences during the civil rights era? Moreover, if Motown's success fostered racial tolerance in any way, why did the company maintain such an ambivalent relationship to the larger social movements that were occurring around it?

The answers to these critical questions require concrete historical evidence that most recent studies on Motown have been unable to provide. Moreover, it is difficult to move beyond broad generalization when discussing the relationship between a national social and political movement and a form of popular music that also had such widespread appeal. The detail and mechanics of how these two phenomena influenced each other remain elusive. A more specific focus can remedy these larger problems, however. The Motown story, as many people either forget or are unaware, is a story of the Motor Town: Detroit, Michigan, also known as the Motor City.[9] Situating the record company and its music within specific histories of Detroit provides clear parameters in which to analyze the complex relationships that existed among the Motown Record Company, its music, local activism, and the larger civil rights struggle.

Many writers, music fans, and scholars have argued that Detroit is *not* critical to understanding the Motown phenomenon. "Motown" could have happened anywhere, or at least in any city with a large and vital African American population—Chicago, New York, Pittsburgh, or Cleveland.[10] These arguments tend to emphasize individual ambition rather than community life, urban geography, economic structures, or race relations as factors in Motown's rise to the top of popular music. Popular legends also cast Berry Gordy Jr. as the central protagonist in the company's success story. These narratives reinforce the idea that American individualism—as exemplified by Gordy's career—explains Motown's accomplishments more than its place of origin.[11]

This book demonstrates how a focus on Detroit presents a sharper picture of Motown's cultural, political, and historical contributions throughout the civil rights era. Most significantly, this book shifts attention away from Motown's crossover success with white audiences. Many scholars and writers cite Motown's enduring appeal with white fans as clear evidence of a cultural manifestation of racial integration. I argue that Motown's relationship to African American audiences, and specifically to black Detroit, reveals an equally important story. Motown Records had a distinct role to play in the city's black community, and that community—as diverse as it was—articulated and promoted its own social, cultural, and political agendas. These local agendas, which reflected the unique concerns of African Americans living in the urban North, both responded to and reconfigured the national civil rights campaign. A close analysis of community activism in Detroit and its relationship to cultural producers such as Motown Records teaches important lessons about how "cultural politics" operated at the grass-roots level.

Cultural politics took many forms in black Detroit. Black newspapers, churches, radio stations and radio shows, nightclubs, poetry collectives, and recording studios all worked to promote the talents and to articulate the needs of the city's black community. This cultural infrastructure instigated social change and created community identity. Local activists, politicians, community leaders, business owners, autoworkers, musicians, and performers used the infrastructure to pursue a wide range of goals: campaigning for elected office, supporting community activism, forming unions, celebrating black culture and art, and preserving black history. The Motown Record Company was a product of and an agent within this unique, and distinctly urban, cultural formation.

I use, therefore, a particular type of cultural analysis to recast the history of the Motown Record Company and its music. This analysis employs the theoretical concept of cultural formation to understand the role of black commercial culture in the development of a black urban community. Cultural theorist Raymond Williams has argued that "you cannot understand an intellectual or artistic project without also under-standing its formation." He defines cultural formations as "simulta-neously artistic forms and social locations." The idea of simultaneity is key here. The constant dynamic between an "artistic form" and its place of origin or "social location" structures the analysis of a cultural forma-tion. Art, in broader and more traditional terms, cannot be separated from the society that produced it. Motown's relationship to Detroit offers a provocative example of a cultural formation, since the "artistic form" is popular music and the "social location" is an industrial city with a strong black middle class and a long history of racism. Exploring Motown's formation in Detroit reveals how the development of a strong black urban community created unique opportunities for the development of an independent black commercial culture, and how this independent commercial culture then participated in the larger struggle for racial equality.[12]

My analysis of Motown's urban origins or cultural formation in De-troit also differs structurally from the more traditional narratives about the company's history. These narratives tend to follow a straight chro-nological path as they trace Motown's founding in the late 1950s, its dominance on the popular music charts during the mid-1960s, and its decline in the mid-1970s.[13] While this book is loosely chronological—it begins in the early 1960s and ends after Motown left Detroit in 1973—its overall structure is more like a mosaic. I juxtapose each piece of the story, including Motown's emergence, local black politics, the national civil rights campaign, and other cultural movements in Detroit, in relation to one another. The resulting interplay among these multiple narratives supports my overall argument that Motown did not stand apart from its social circumstances but was the product of a complex set of historical forces. Like a mosaic, each piece of the picture or narrative could stand alone, but it is only in the overall pattern that one sees the much richer and yet more conflicted history of the company and its music.

Viewing Motown and its music as the product of a cultural formation initially might seem counterintuitive. After all, Motown Records secured and has maintained its fame not through its association with the city of Detroit but through its mastery of the mass media. Radio airplay, national record sales, and television allowed Motown music to transcend time, space, and place to become the ubiquitous "soundtrack" of its era. Motown's current, almost sacred, status in the history of American popular music exists not because its audiences have a deep affinity for Detroit and the city's musical heritage, but because songs such as the Temptations' "My Girl" or the Supremes' "Baby Love" were, through radio and record play, and continue to be, through "oldies" stations and compact-disk commemorative boxed sets, a powerful musical presence around the world.

Why, then, does Detroit matter? Reinserting Motown and its music into the political, social, racial, economic, and cultural histories of Detroit immediately disrupts the nostalgia that often obstructs critical analysis of either the company or its sound. Motown emerged from a city that was known not for racial harmony and civic peace but rather for chronic patterns of racial discrimination that often led to violent civil disorder. In response to such persistent patterns of discrimination, the city's black community forged a place for itself using every means possible.

These efforts produced not only Motown but also a host of cultural, economic, political, religious, and historical institutions. Among cultural institutions, the Broadside Press, one of the country's first black-owned publishing houses; the Concept East Theater, the first African American theater company in the urban North; and WCHB, the first radio station built, owned, and operated by African Americans, all began in Detroit. On economic fronts, black Detroiters founded the Booker T. Washington Trade Association, one of the largest chapters of the National Negro Business League; and the Dodge Revolutionary Union Movement, which became the League of Revolutionary Black Workers. In politics, Detroit activists founded in 1963 the Freedom Now Party, the first all-black political party in the country; and in the early 1970s U.S. representatives from Detroit, Charles Diggs Jr. and John Conyers, helped to organize the Congressional Black Caucus. In terms of religion, Detroit was the birthplace of both the Nation of Islam and the Shrine of the Black Madonna. Black Detroit was also at the forefront of preserving and promoting African American history. The Detroit Public Library housed the Azalia Hackley Collection of Negro Music and the Burton Historical Collection. The city sponsored an active chapter of the Association for the Study of Negro Life and History and was the site of the first African American history museum and one of the first African American bookstores, which was founded by Edward Vaughn on Dexter Avenue. All of these efforts, which first appear disparate, shared common strategies to achieve their respective goals.

This is not to claim, however, that the Motown Record Company agreed with or supported all of the political campaigns, radical organizations, and cultural movements that emerged from Detroit's black neighborhoods. On the contrary, Berry Gordy Jr. was extremely wary about affiliating his business with any organization or movement that might negatively influence his company's commercial success. Nevertheless, both Motown's music and its entrepreneurial acumen emerged from an urban black community that regularly asserted its "politics" through cultural and economic means. The Motown Record Company's status as Detroit's most famous cultural producer and eventually the country's most successful black business must, therefore, be understood in political terms regardless of whether or not the company or its artists perceived it as such.[14]

How, then, does one begin to map Motown's relationship to Detroit? The first connection between the music and the city came from the company itself. A tangible sense of place characterized the record company from its founding in 1958. The company name ensured that the music would always be linked to the industrial pride of Detroit. And the company's nickname (Hitsville, U.S.A.) asserted that, metaphorically, a separate cultural municipality existed within the geography of the city, an entity that was a part of Detroit yet distinctive and important enough to have its own name. Eventually, the company's record label featured a map of Michigan with a star highlighting Detroit. The cartographic emblem reinforced the idea that while the music, as the company's motto stated, was the "Sound of Young America," the sound was not from anywhere in America but was deeply tied to a specific locale.

Music played a central role in the history of African American life in Detroit long before Motown became a sound. Initially, blues songs helped to instigate early African American migrations to Detroit. When Henry Ford announced his wage of five dollars a day on January 5, 1914, workers from around the country flocked to Michigan in search of jobs. Blues artists played a significant role in publicizing Ford's promises among African Americans. Blues songs such as Blind Blake's "Detroit Bound Blues" broadcasted the possibilities in Detroit:

> I'm goin' to Detroit, get myself a good job
> Tried to stay around here with the starvation mob.
>
> I'm goin' to get me a job, up there in Mr. Ford's place
> Stop these eatless days from starin' me in the face.[15]

These tunes, often sung in the juke joints and byways of the South, motivated many black Americans to move North. In *Blues People* LeRoi Jones (Amiri Baraka) also noted that Ford's Model T, "the poor man's car," was one of the first automobiles many African Americans could afford to purchase. The popularity of the Model T and the promise of employment inspired many blues musicians to write songs about the Ford Motor Company.[16]

Once in Detroit, many African Americans did not find jobs as plentiful as the blues songs had described or were given the worst jobs on the line. The blues, however, offered a creative outlet from the monotony of assembly-line work. Bobo Jenkins, urban blues singer and Chrysler autoworker for twenty-six years, maintained that his hours on the line inspired his best music. Jenkins claimed, "That whirlin' machinery gives me the beat. It's like hearin' a band playing all day long. Every song I ever wrote that's any good has come to me standin' on that line." Blues songs could also speak more directly about and against the oppression of assembly-line work. Autoworker and longtime blues musician Little Junior commented, "When you're on that line, you're thinking of anything that will get you off it. You get this deep grieving feeling way down inside somewheres. Then comes the music." Several of the most famous Detroit blues songs emphasize this "deep grieving" with unmitigated candor. Blues artist Joe L. Carter wrote the famous song "Detroit, I Do Mind Dying," which includes the lyrics: "Please, Mr. Foreman, slow down your assembly line. No, I don't mind workin', but I do mind dyin'." Music tempered the constraints and regimen of industrial work and provided some relief from its rigidity.[17]

While the blues offered a creative outlet from assembly-line work, the music rarely provided a road out of the factory. In Detroit, as in many other cities, blues artists had difficulty making a living solely from their craft.[18] In 1955, when the young Berry Gordy Jr. aspired to break into the music business, he had to work briefly at the Ford Wayne Assembly

Motown Record Company label. (Courtesy Motown Record Co., L.P., a Polygram Company.)

Plant to make ends meet. He, too, would hum tunes and compose songs in his head to alleviate the drudgery of the assembly line. In his autobiography he recalled,

> Since I had no piano I had to devise another method of writing. I used "Mary Had a Little Lamb," the simplest song I could think of, to form the basis to remember songs in my head. I gave each note or tone of the scale a number from one to seven. "Mary Had a Little Lamb" turned out to be 3212333–222–355–32123333–22321 . . . As I began to create interesting melodies in my head, I would associate each note with a number. This allowed me to remember my new musical ideas.[19]

Although Gordy has never claimed his days on the line inspired his best songs, he has discussed how the efficiency of Ford's production methods influenced his ideas about mass-producing hit records. Reflecting on his brief tenure in the auto plant, Gordy wrote, "At the plant cars started out as just a frame, pulled along on conveyor belts until they emerged at the end of the line—brand spanking new cars rolling off the line. I wanted the same concept for my company, only with artists and songs and records. I wanted a place where a kid off the street could walk in one door an unknown and come out another a recording artist—a star."[20]

Gordy implemented his idea of inserting the assembly-line process into the recording studio as soon as he founded Motown. The early years flowed with creative energy as the company produced successes including Mary Wells's "The One Who Really Loves You" and the Contours' "Do You Love Me?" The Miracles' big hit, "Shop Around," boosted the hit factory's confidence and profits. By 1963 the company was consistently reaching the top ten of the rhythm and blues *and* pop charts with songs such as the Miracles' "Mickey's Monkey," Martha and the Vandellas' "Quicksand," and Stevie Wonder's number-one hit "Fingertips, Part 2." At the end of 1963 the company grossed $4.5 million in sales.[21]

Motown's music, which sold to wide audiences, completely transformed popular ideas about what "black" music was or could do. Over the years, many attempts have been made to define exactly what constituted the Motown sound. Was it the instrumental innovations of the Funk

Brothers, Motown's house band? The Funk Brothers used anything from tambourines to tire chains to create the gritty backbeat of songs such as Martha and the Vandellas' "Nowhere to Run." Or was it the playful lyrics and call-and-response style of Motown songs such as the Temptations' hit "My Girl"? For many fans, the sound was also an image—of Motown artists performing their songs in sharp matching outfits as they executed dazzling synchronized dance steps.

Deciding what the Motown sound *meant* has proved to be as complicated and contentious as defining what it was. Many Motown artists and fans have preferred to embrace the celebratory spirit of the music and its potential to bring people together. Songs such as "Dancing in the Street" do bring people out of their seats and onto dance floors. Other observers—particularly in Detroit—viewed the music as an affirmation of black culture and strength. From this perspective, Motown's sound was "Afro-American music, without apology" and never merely entertainment.

Debates about the political meanings of the Motown sound were, of course, part of a much larger question about the relationship of any form of black art to black struggle. Many scholars have sought to understand the relationship of black culture to social protest and black consciousness from slavery to the present.[22] I argue that the meaning of the Motown sound during the civil rights era cannot be separated from Motown's other identities as a successful black business and an independent producer of black culture. The local dynamics of these relationships in Detroit, moreover, spoke to larger concerns within the national civil rights campaign about the role of black entrepreneurship and culture in the movement.

During its early years, the Motown Record Company seemed to fulfill the promise that black capitalism could be a tool in the fight for racial justice—particularly in light of Detroit's larger economy. The automobile industry has dominated Detroit's economy since the invention of the horseless carriage. Stories of exploitation, racism, and betrayal pervade histories of African Americans' participation in Detroit's automobile industry.[23] The industry excluded African Americans from controlling the means of production and profited from their labor. Berry Gordy Jr.'s decision to create a hit factory of popular song recordings was a complicated response to the history of African Americans in the automobile industry. Motown's assembly-line production style imitated the auto industry, while its product, music, stood apart from the city's larger economy. In Detroit any product that did not depend on the automobile industry for its market value involved both risk and possible reward. Motown's product, the music of Detroit's black neighborhoods, became a particularly powerful example of black economic independence since it relied on black creativity and talent.

But Motown ultimately did not uphold the promise of black capitalism. This promise held that a black business, once successful, would always support the local community that produced it. If a company prospered, the wealth would be shared by all through employment and general economic growth. By the late 1960s Motown Records offered one example of how black capitalism, in practice, did not always guarantee racial, social, or economic justice for African Americans. Motown's controversial royalty practices, limited profit sharing with employees, and eventual decision to leave Detroit for Los Angeles illustrated how black capitalism did not ensure equity or preserve community. In the end, Motown's success in the record industry proved how capitalism, by definition, cannot be bound by racial agendas or community concerns.[24]

Motown's limitations on economic fronts, however, did not diminish the importance of its role as an independent producer of black culture. By recording black culture the company participated in a larger history of promoting racial equality through creative and educational endeavors. Motown's musical and spoken-word recordings contributed to a long-held practice of recognizing, preserving, and celebrating the accomplishments of black people. These traditions can be traced back to Carter G. Woodson, who founded the Association for the Study of Negro Life and History in 1915. Woodson believed in not simply recognizing the historic, artistic, and intellectual accomplishments of black people, but in recording, publishing, and distributing them to wide audiences as well. Individuals such as Woodson saw their efforts in political terms—as a means to assert the dignity and legitimacy of African American life.

In Detroit's black community independent record labels, radio shows, poetry collectives, and black newspapers all contributed to the cause. Hitsville, U.S.A., of course, took these strategies to new heights.

The company used talent shows, radio airplay, its own "Motortown Re-vue" road show, and television appearances to make its music the "Sound of Young America." Motown's accomplishments in the music industry offered a powerful example of how the mass distribution of black culture affirmed African American contributions to American culture.

Motown's success within the music industry allowed the company to experiment with other types of recording that directly addressed the civil rights movement. These recordings documented the efforts of black Americans to integrate not just popular culture but American society as a whole. In 1963 Motown produced its first spoken-word recording, en-titled *The Great March to Freedom*, which preserved Martin Luther King Jr.'s speech at the Detroit demonstration held on June 23, 1963. By the late 1960s Motown had created a separate spoken-word label—the Black Forum label—with the explicit goal of preserving black thought and cre-ative writing. Motown founded Black Forum as "a medium for the pre-sentation of ideas and voices of the worldwide struggle of Black people to create a new era . . . [and as] a permanent record of the sound of the struggle and the sound of a new era."[25] Albums included poetry record-ings by Langston Hughes and Margaret Danner, Amiri Baraka, and Elaine Brown as well as political speeches such as *Free Huey!* by Stokely Carmichael. The Black Forum label illustrated Motown's awareness that, as an independent black cultural producer, it should help preserve black history and culture.

Motown's commercial success put the record company in a unique position to promote a wide range of black cultural expression. In some ways, the situation revealed unexpected connections between black pop-ular music and other forms of black art. A Motown song may appear to have little or no relation to a Langston Hughes poem at first glance. Yet the popular song and the poem ultimately do have more in common when viewed against the backdrop of African Americans' limited access to power within the music industry or literary publishing world. The pro-duction, distribution, and publicity of black art largely determines the range of its influence—artistic or political. Artists such as Langston Hughes and Marvin Gaye understood these realities and perceived the Motown Record Company as a conduit for their work—whether poem or popular song.

Still, Motown's role as a producer of black culture and its ambitions in the business world did not coexist without conflict and contradiction. At Hitsville, U.S.A., commercial concerns about the marketability of a recording often stalled and sometimes canceled projects that management deemed too politically controversial. The political climate at Motown Records was highly variable. Throughout the civil rights era the company wavered between willingness and caution when asked to produce recordings—musical or spoken-word—that involved overt political or racial messages. Sometimes an atmosphere of race consciousness prevailed, and other times a politically conservative ethos dominated.

Motown's internal ambivalence about its relationship to the civil rights movement was, however, only one side of the story. On the other side were popular music audiences, local activists, and national civil rights leaders, who had their own ideas and disagreements about the meanings of Motown's music and commercial success for the movement. At the national level debates about Motown's role in the struggle for racial justice mirrored larger divisions within the movement itself. From 1963 to 1973, the general time frame of this study, the national civil rights campaign shifted from the unified fight for integration—exemplified by the March on Washington—to a more fractious battle for Black Power. Given these transitions, Motown could not avoid becoming a contested symbol of racial progress. Motown's music symbolized the possibility of amicable racial integration through popular culture. But as a company, Motown represented the possibilities of black economic independence, one of the most important tenets of black nationalism.

Moreover, national shifts in the civil rights movement offer only broad explanations of Motown's complicated role in the struggle for racial justice. To fully understand Motown's relationship to the civil rights movement in all of its complexity, one must begin on the streets of Detroit. Here, amateur singers, autoworkers, preachers, musicians, poets, business leaders, community activists, and politicians all participated in an elaborate "dance" to reclaim the city for African Americans. The dancers moved in unpredictable patterns but shared many of the same steps. For some, participation involved seeking public office or organizing community action groups. For others, it involved publishing a newspaper, broadcasting a radio show, or singing a song. For still others, it involved opening a business, forming a union, or buying a home. In total, Detroit's black community choreographed a distinctly urban social movement. The movement experienced defeats but also instigated social change, altered political power, and produced the Motown sound. Like the song "Dancing in the Street," it encompassed celebration, rebellion, and adversity.

In 1967, the same year that Martha Reeves found herself singing "Dancing in the Street" in the middle of a city in flames, Harold Cruse published his ground-breaking study, *The Crisis of the Negro Intellectual*. In an early chapter, "Mass Media and Cultural Democracy," Cruse argued that for any social movement to be successful, it must be "at one and the same time *a political, economic, and cultural movement*." For Cruse, such a movement was only possible in the urban North, and specifically Harlem. He wrote, "All of black America has to take Harlem's social lead because virtually no other Negro community in America has the combined political, economic and cultural features that are characteristic of Harlem."[26]

Cruse's argument was persuasive, but his assessment that only Harlem had the resources for such struggle was short-sighted.[27] As this study attests, Detroit's black community combined political, economic, and cultural movements throughout the twentieth century. The ultimate success of these movements, however, cannot be measured by only one scale. At certain moments, political efforts prevailed while economic or cultural efforts waned. At other times, cultural work excelled while economic or political campaigns floundered. At the worst times, violence and destruction overrode all other productive efforts for social change.

Motown's participation in the cultural politics of Detroit offers a critical case study about the relationship of black capitalism and popular culture to the civil rights movement. The relationship of the record company and its music to Detroit's unique history of race relations complicates more traditional narratives about both Motown's success and the scope of the national civil rights struggle. A closer analysis of Motown's origins in Detroit provides a new understanding of how black communities in the urban North actively used commercial culture and the mass media to assert their political needs during America's civil rights years. These needs differed from the southern struggle for voting rights and desegregation of public facilities. African Americans in the urban North struggled with the problems of urban renewal, de facto housing segregation, police brutality, and employment discrimination, which was often exacerbated by the automation and decentralization of industrial work. Throughout the 1960s, Motown and the other cultural work of black Detroit offered not only a symbol of what was possible but also a means to empower the city's often embattled African American community. Whether it was the beat of a bongo drum at a black autoworkers' strike or the celebratory chorus of "Dancing in the Street," the sounds of black Detroit reverberated with the history and circumstances of its producers. Motown, in other words, provided more than a soundtrack to its era. The company and its sound were active—though sometimes reluctant—agents in the politics of its time.

Over the years the national and international appeal of Motown's music has obscured the company's connection to Detroit. Yet throughout the 1960s Motown Records never lost sight of its ties to the Motor City. Company slogans and labels always asserted the connection, but these overt gestures to link the record company to its geographic coordinates were never merely clever marketing ideas. A much broader and more elaborate topography is needed to understand Motown's role in the cultural politics of Detroit and how these politics transformed the national civil rights campaign. Hitsville, U.S.A., emerged from a city in which African Americans felt they had little influence over white power structures and within an economy that was wholly dependent on the patterns and fluctuations of the auto industry. Given these circumstances, the remarkable rise of a company that was black-owned *and* whose product—music—was independent of the auto industry demands further examination.

1

"In Whose Heart There Is No Song, To Him the Miles Are Many and Long": Motown and Detroit's Great March to Freedom

On August 28, 1963, the Motown Record Company released its first spoken-word recording. The album, entitled *The Great March to Freedom*, was an anomaly for the Detroit-based label best known for its chart-topping hits. *The Great March to Freedom* was more than a deviation from the company's musical offerings. The recording marked a critical juncture in the history of Motown Records, the city of Detroit, and the national civil rights movement. For Motown, the recording represented the company's first attempt to affiliate itself publicly with the national civil rights campaign. The album, purposely released on the same day that Martin Luther King Jr. appeared at the March on Washington, commemorated King's appearance in Detroit only two months earlier. Detroit's Great March, held on June 23, 1963, raised funds for the Birmingham, Alabama, campaign of the Southern Christian Leadership Conference (SCLC) and offered King the opportunity to present an early version of his "I Have a Dream" oration.[1] He declared Detroit's march "the largest and greatest demonstration for freedom ever held in the United States." The demonstration proved an ideal forum for the leader of SCLC to articulate his vision of America—both North and South—transformed through non-violent protest into an integrated and more just society. The Motown Record Company's efforts to record King's Detroit address preserved this historic moment.[2]

Berry Gordy presents the *Great March to Freedom* album to Martin Luther King Jr. at SCLC benefit in Atlanta, August 1963. Lena Horne and Billy Taylor look on. (Courtesy Motown Record Co., L.P., a Polygram Company.)

Motown's promotion of the recording reflected its belief in the timeliness and significance of the speech. Publicity for the record went beyond mere advertising. In a small ceremony in mid-August, when Berry Gordy flew to an SCLC benefit in Atlanta to present King with a personal copy, Gordy proclaimed,

> Realizing that in years to come, the Negro revolt of 1963 will take its place historically with the American Revolution and the Hungarian uprising, we have elected to record the statements of some of the movement's leaders. We are delighted that Reverend King's Detroit speech is to be the first in this series. The June 23 Freedom Rally had all the ingredients of a historic event. In his speech Reverend King intelligently and succinctly explains the Negro

revolt, underlines its ramifications and points the way to certain solutions. This album belongs in the home of every American and should be required listening for every American child, white or black.[3]

Gordy's assertions about the historic significance of the national "Negro revolt of 1963" cannot be disputed. The assassination of Medgar Evers, the March on Washington, and the Sixteenth Street Church bombing in Birmingham were just a few of the pivotal events that shook the movement during 1963. Yet his belief that King's Detroit speech was equally historic proved less prophetic. Years after the event, King's appearance at Detroit's Great March to Freedom does not hold a prominent place in the history of the early civil rights years. Gordy obviously hoped that Motown's recording of King's speech would be "required listening" for Americans "white or black." Over time, however, King's Detroit oratory and the Great March to Freedom have been given only brief attention by civil rights scholars and have been lost to the general public.[4]

From its inception to its commemoration in the Motown recording, however, the Detroit demonstration expanded the objectives and strategies of the "Negro revolt of 1963." The civil rights movement at that time, most often considered a southern and primarily rural struggle for desegregation and political enfranchisement, had important battles to fight in the urban North. Specifically, employment and housing discrimination, de facto segregation in public schools, and police brutality plagued Northern cities such as Detroit. Moreover, as early as 1946 Detroit, like many cities in America, implemented an urban renewal program that over the course of two decades would demolish several major black neighborhoods and business districts. By 1963 these policies were having devastating social and economic consequences for Detroit's black community. The Great March to Freedom, therefore, offered Detroit's black citizens the opportunity to support their southern brethren in Birmingham *and* to articulate civil rights concerns unique to the urban North.

Ironically, Detroit's national reputation as a city with progressive race relations was growing at the time of the Great March. The city recently had become known as the "model city of race relations" after voters elected Jerome P. Cavanagh, a liberal Democrat, mayor in 1962.[5] The presence of the polished and successful Motown Record Company contributed to Detroit's image as a city of racial tolerance where African Americans could thrive. The Hitsville, U.S.A., Studios, located in a converted house at 2648 West Grand Boulevard, sat only a few blocks from the site of the demonstration on Woodward Avenue; and, by the summer of 1963, the company had firmly established itself as a gathering place of young black talent in the Motor City.

Detroit's black civil rights organizations acknowledged the cultural significance of Motown. In February 1963 the Detroit chapter of the National Association for the Advancement of Colored People (NAACP) awarded Berry Gordy Jr. a special citation for his accomplishments in the recording industry. The *Detroit News* reported that the citation was given " 'in recognition of his spectacular rise in a very competitive field,' and for his efforts in opening the field to Negroes . . . 'Through [Berry Gordy's] efforts, Detroit has become recognized as the center of the rhythm and blues recording industry.' "[6]

The company itself was not oblivious to the importance of its role as a cultural force in the fight for racial justice. The *Michigan Chronicle*, Detroit's preeminent black newspaper, published two special issues in February 1963 to commemorate the centennial of the Emancipation Proclamation. In the first installment of the series, Hitsville, U.S.A., Inc. placed an advertisement with a copy that read as follows: "Music . . . has been one of the main vehicles of Free Expression of the Negro during his long struggle for human dignity. We are proud to be a part of this industry." The remainder of the advertisement included a list of the company's current releases, including Marvin Gaye's "Hitchhike," Martha and the Vandellas' "I'll Have to Let Him Go," the Miracles' "You've Really Got a Hold on Me," and the album *The Great Gospel Stars*. In the upper left-hand corner, an anonymous epigram read,

> In whose heart there is no song
> To him the miles are many and long.[7]

The aphorism foreshadowed the spirit of the Great March to Freedom. In Detroit the miles were "many and long" for African Americans. Literally, long migratory waves brought them to the city; figuratively, prejudice and discrimination faced them once they arrived. And yet, a "song," a metaphor of cultural life in general, provided solace, sustenance, and in some cases important modes of resistance to racial oppression. Specifically, the Great March revealed how the city's black cultural life—its producers and its products—was central to black political organizing in the urban North. The demonstration succeeded largely because of the collaborative efforts of many black cultural institutions including churches, radio stations, newspapers, and companies such as Motown Records. Cultural workers used their own finances, access to the media, and mastery of modern technologies to respond to infringements on their civil rights. Both Motown's music and its efforts to record King's speech became part of Detroit's long "march" to "freedom." The entire demonstration illustrated how an urban black community could use the mass media and its technologies to support collective action.

Nevertheless, race relations in the city could not be measured through these cultural advancements alone. When Motown recorded King's address at the Great March, the speech that it preserved did not glorify Detroit's new racially progressive reputation. On the contrary, Martin Luther King Jr. came to the Motor City to acknowledge that the fight against segregation and injustice did not stop once one crossed the Mason-Dixon Line, and that even a city seen as a model of racial harmony held a different reality and history for the people who lived there.

The History behind Detroit's Great March to Freedom

Detroit's history of race relations shaped the Great March to Freedom from its inception. The demonstration marked two historic anniversaries: the centennial of the Emancipation Proclamation and the twentieth anniversary of the Detroit riot of 1943. The two events shared a history of bloodshed. In 1863 Detroit witnessed one of its first major race riots, a conflict that reflected underlying anxiety about long-term consequences of the Emancipation Proclamation. In June of 1943 racial tensions in wartime Detroit erupted into a riot that lasted several days and left many citizens dead or injured and property extensively damaged. The anniversaries of these two episodes of racial violence implicitly challenged Detroit's reputation as a model city in 1963. How much progress had Detroit made to ameliorate racial inequality one hundred years after emancipation and, more specifically, twenty years after wartime racial conflicts nearly destroyed the city?

City leaders and community activists debated openly whether the Great March marked real progress or complete inertia in Detroit's race relations. The Reverend C. L. Franklin, chair of the Detroit Council for Human Rights (DCHR), told the *Detroit News* on June 8, 1963, that the "Walk to Freedom" was "a warning to the city that what has transpired in the past is no longer acceptable to the Negro community. We want complete amelioration of all injustices." Gus Scholle, president of Michigan's American Federation of Labor and Congress of Industrial Organizations (AFL-CIO), echoed similar sentiments in his public statement endorsing the demonstration. Scholle remarked that "freedom's fight is 100 years overdue . . . The Freedom March and fight is labor's fight." The *Michigan Chronicle* printed an editorial also emphasizing that battle against racial discrimination in Detroit was ongoing and not a remnant of the past. The editors supported the Great March but expressed skepticism that one demonstration could have an "impact on the deplorable conditions that have held back the Negro in Detroit and the rest of Michigan." The editors argued that the demonstration should be followed by "a united movement to eliminate all traces of racial discrimination and segregation in the areas of housing, employment, and education."[8]

Other city leaders viewed the Great March as an opportunity to showcase Detroit's new status as a model city of race relations. Mayor Jerome Cavanagh publicly announced that the march could be "a demonstration of goodwill [that] would show that our citizens have an honest, strong, desire for equal rights for all people of this nation." The editors of the *Detroit Free Press* argued, "Detroit is different. This is not a march of one race against another, but a march of people of good will of all races, protesting injustice against their fellow men." The public rhetoric of city officials, which relied on vague platitudes of this kind, avoided any discussion about specific racial discrimination in Detroit.[9]

For the organizers of the march, however, racial discrimination—both around the country and in Detroit—was the reason for the demonstration. Police brutality in particular was a central concern of local activists. In March 1963 the Congress of Racial Equality (CORE) and the United Auto Workers organized a meeting in Detroit to protest police brutality against civil rights workers in Birmingham, Alabama. The Reverend Albert B. Cleage Jr., one of Detroit's most prominent and charismatic black leaders, attended the meeting and infused it with his own militant energy. At the gathering Cleage, a master of provocative sound bites, stood up and denounced not only the Birmingham situation but also the Detroit police force. His animosity reflected long-standing hostility and distrust between the Detroit police force and the city's black citizens. Cleage then proposed that a march be organized "down Woodward Avenue with so many tens of thousands of people that the police would be afraid to show their faces." In the following weeks Cleage and others joined forces with the Reverend C. L. Franklin to found the Detroit Council for Human Rights and plan the Great March.[10]

The more aggressive approaches of Cleage and others toward the march created internal tensions among the city's more established black organizations. Older, more conservative civil rights organizations thought that the massive demonstration was too controversial, and some distanced themselves from the event. The Detroit chapter of the NAACP, resentful that the March was raising funds for an outside organization such as the SCLC, debated its participation until the last minute and agreed to join in only when it realized the magnitude of the event. The Detroit Baptist Ministers Alliance contested Franklin's role as chief organizer of the march, claiming that he had little experience leading community events.[11]

By the time King arrived to lead the march, however, community leaders had set aside their disagreements and misgivings and a spirit of coalition infused the day. The demonstration officially began at 3:00 P.M. on June 23, 1963, when King led the procession down Woodward Avenue to Cobo Hall. An impressive phalanx of state and city politicians, union leaders, and community activists aligned themselves near the young yet already highly respected, civil rights leader. Walter P. Reuther, head of the UAW; former Michigan governor John B. Swainson; Mayor Jerome Cavanagh; U.S. Representative Charles C. Diggs Jr.; and Franklin, Cleage, and James Del Rio from the Detroit Council for Human Rights formed a unified vanguard to lead the thousands of marchers.[12]

A festive atmosphere prevailed even as the jostling crowds sometimes overwhelmed the proceedings. The throngs of Detroiters practically lifted King and the other leaders off of the pavement as they made their way down Woodward Avenue toward the riverfront. The marchers created a potent image of a northern urban community moving forward—literally and figuratively—toward a future of racial justice and civic peace. But the procession, so filled with uplift and promise, could never completely walk away from the city's past, a history scarred with racial dissension and violent conflict.

The past resonated in King's speech as he stood at the lectern in Cobo Hall. In his opening remarks King commemorated the one-hundredth anniversary of the Emancipation Proclamation with the sobering acknowledgment, "But, 100 years later, the Negro in the United States of America is still not free." Onlookers in the crowd shared King's perspective. One marcher held a placard that read, "Time is running out: 1863–1963."

Gestures linking the emancipation of 1863 with the 1963 struggle for freedom had a particular significance in Detroit. On March 6, 1863, African Americans in Detroit celebrating the Emancipation Proclamation were forced to confront their own vulnerability as a community when the violent riot erupted. In June 1963 Broadnus Butler, a local black journalist, noted the connection between the Great March to Freedom and the violence of 1863. Butler reported that "the last Freedom demonstration and parade of such magnitude in Detroit was 1863—100 years ago at the time of the announcement of the Emancipation Proclamation. That one eventuated into a riot which for sheer sadism and brutality by whites was worse than the 1943 riot." Clearly the consequences of the 1863 uprising had direct connections to the state of Detroit's race relations at the time of the Great March.[13]

The riot of 1863 reflected the strains that the end of slavery caused in the North and the South. Racial tensions started to build soon after the Emancipation Proclamation. White immigrants' fears about losing jobs to freed blacks in a city that quickly was becoming a manufacturing center ran high. Wilbur Storey, the editor of the *Detroit Free Press*, fueled the fire with claims that the Civil War was fought not to preserve the Union but to ensure "nigger domination." The city's popular press abetted racist sentiments by publishing leaflets, posters, and newspapers that pandered to whites' anxieties about interracial sexual encounters. During this period, the term "miscegenation" first came into use to describe race mixing.[14]

In Detroit cultural anxiety about racial purity, sexuality, and identity provoked the 1863 race riot. Mob violence broke out at Beaubien and Lafayette streets, as local officials led Thomas Faulkner, charged with attacking two young women, one black and one white, to jail. Many considered Faulkner, an upstanding shop owner of mixed blood, "to all intents a white man." But confusion over Faulkner's racial identity stoked the fury surrounding his alleged crime, as the poem "The Riot" by "B. Clark Sr., A Colored Man," attests:

> Now it be remember'd that Falkner [sic] at right,
> Although call'd a "nigger," had always been white,
> Had voted, and always declared in his shop,
> He never would sell colored people a drop.
>
> He's what is call'd white, though I must confess,
> So mixed are the folks now, we oft have to guess,
> Their hair is so curl'd and their skins so brown,
> If they're white in the country, they're niggers in town.[15]

Relying on the testimony of the two young women, the city tried, convicted, and sentenced Faulkner to life imprisonment.[16]

As rumors of the man's sexual crimes raced through the city, a mob gathered and descended upon him as he marched to prison. The military guard protecting Faulkner used gunfire to drive off the crowd intent on lynching him. Irish and German immigrants, undeterred and under the rallying cry "Kill all the damned niggers!" proceeded to ransack, burn, and destroy homes and businesses in the black community as well as to physically attack innocent bystanders. As the melee raged out of control, authorities called troops in from Fort Wayne and Ypsilanti to quell the disorder. When the Detroit City Council realized that such drastic measures were needed to restore and maintain peace, it resolved to organize a police department for the city. The Detroit Police Department was founded, therefore, with one central objective in mind: to contain racial unrest in the city. This policy of containment and the racial battle lines that it created in Detroit continued to be a flash point in the city's race relations for decades to come.[17]

On June 23, 1963, however, the Detroit Police Department received high praise from King for its assistance in making the Great March a nonviolent one. Early in his speech, King noted that the large event was a "magnificent demonstration of discipline" in that there was "not one reported incident of violence" throughout the day. King gave credit for the peace to city leaders, the Detroit Police Department, and particularly Police Commissioner George Edwards. Edwards, a former Michigan State Supreme Court justice and prominent liberal, had been commissioner for only two years. He had accepted the position to help Jerome Cavanagh win the mayoral election in 1961. At the time, the incumbent candidate, Louis Miriani, was receiving extensive criticism from the black community for his administration's hostile approach to police-community relations. During the election year, Miriani's Police Department instigated a "crime crackdown" throughout the city that African American citizens saw as a "reign of terror." Cavanagh made improved police-community relations the focal point of his mayoral campaign. With this strategy, he obtained an estimated 85 percent of the black vote and won the election. The victory revealed how police-community relations dominated the racial politics of the city.[18]

Once in office Edwards moved quickly to develop a rapport with black constituents by appearing before community groups and establishing formal complaint boards. Edwards's proactive approach was an improvement over the open animosity characteristic of police-community relations under Mayor Miriani. A few weeks before the Great March, an editorial appeared in the *Michigan Chronicle* reviewing Edwards's one-and-a-half-year tenure as police commissioner. The paper asserted that Edwards had indeed "met the challenge" of improving police-community relations and that his successor, former *Detroit Times* crime reporter Ray Girardin, would have to work hard to maintain the quality of Edwards's work.[19]

King echoed these sentiments in his speech in Cobo Hall and in a formal letter to Edwards and Mayor Cavanagh soon after the March. Comparing his experience in Detroit to his experiences in the South, King wrote,

> As one who bears both the physical and psychological effects of brutal and inhuman police forces in the South, I was both uplifted and consoled to be with a police force that proved to be a genuine protector and a friend indeed.
>
> Never before have I participated in a demonstration for the cause of freedom and justice that was at one and the same time gigantic and disciplined. I am sure that a great deal of the success of the march can be attributed to you and the significant leadership that you have given the Police Department of Detroit. You have proved to the Negro citizenry of your community that you are a friend rather than an enemy.[20]

While King was optimistic about Detroit's police-community relations, he was not naive about the challenges and injustices that African Americans faced in the Motor City. Near the end of his speech, King noted that many Detroiters had asked him what they could do to help the civil rights fight in Birmingham. The southern preacher reminded his audience that the most productive contribution they could make would be "to work with determination to get rid of any segregation and discrimination *in Detroit*—realizing that injustice anywhere is a threat to justice everywhere." He continued to assert that the problem of racial injustice was a national problem, not a regional one. Recognizing that racism in the North appeared in more "subtle and hidden forms," King contended that employment discrimination, housing discrimination, and de facto segregation in the public schools plagued cities like Detroit and were just as injurious as any overt segregation in Alabama or Mississippi. King reiterated these sentiments in his concluding "I Have a Dream" incantation. In a stirring crescendo, King spoke of his dream that "right here in Detroit a Negro will be able to buy a house or rent a house anywhere that their money will carry them. They will be able to get a job."[21]

King's closing avowal echoed Franklin's earlier assertion that the Great March was a "warning to the city" about black Detroit's unwillingness to endure continued discrimination, rather than a celebration of racial progress. In looking toward the future, they were both struggling to come to terms with the past and to rectify, in particular, the losses Detroit had incurred during the 1943 riot. For this reason it is important to review the historical and racial circumstances of wartime Detroit.

"Detroit Is Dynamite"

The war years transformed Detroit from the automobile capital of the world into the Arsenal of Democracy. The industrial boom in defense manufacturing drew workers from around the country to southeastern Michigan in search of jobs. The War Manpower Commission estimated that, from June 1940 to June 1943, 500,000 people migrated to the Motor City. Over 350,000 of these newcomers arrived during the fifteen months before the riot. African Americans, whites from southern Appalachia, and European immigrants—most of whom were Poles—composed the majority of the migratory wave.

All of these groups competed for work and the limited housing in the city. Persistent employment discrimination against blacks in the war plants especially agitated the racial animosities. From the black perspective, the war abroad for "democracy" only accentuated the injustices that African Americans faced in their own country. In Detroit approximately one-fourth of the city's 185 war plants did not hire blacks at all. In the spring of 1943 black workers began to channel general discontent with job discrimination into formal protests. On April 11, the NAACP and the UAW organized an "equal opportunity" rally in Cadillac Square with over 10,000 people in attendance.

White workers fervently resisted these campaigns for equality. When three black autoworkers fought for and won promotions at a Packard plant, 26,000 white employees walked out. As the protesters exited the foundry, one worker got on a loudspeaker and notoriously proclaimed that it was better to let Adolph Hitler and Emperor Hirohito win than "work beside a nigger on the assembly line."[22] The national press did not ignore Detroit's growing racial tensions. As early as August 1942, *Life* magazine published an article entitled "Detroit Is Dynamite." The magazine predicted that the city "can either blow up Hitler or it can blow up the U.S."[23]

Eleven months after this prophecy, Detroit's racial tensions erupted into violence. The first detonation occurred on the bridge leading to Belle Isle Park, which lies in the Detroit River and was one of the most popular locations for summer picnics, boating, and swimming. The heat and humidity of a summer afternoon agitated the racially mixed crowd of approximately 100,000 people. At nightfall, hundreds of visitors to the park jostled one another on the bridge leading back to Jefferson Avenue, and soon intermittent brawls punctuated the evening. Black youth fought against their white, primarily Polish American and Appalachian, counterparts and a battalion of sailors from the Naval Training Center on the island.

Rumors about the fighting traveled quickly through both black and white neighborhoods. Woodward Avenue, running north from the Detroit River, acted as the dividing line between these neighborhoods. The city's black community lived just east of the avenue, and the white community just west of it. Among blacks rumors circulated in Paradise Valley, a district located on the city's East Side in and around Hastings Street. On the first night of the riot, a young black man jumped up on the stage of the Forest Club, the largest establishment on Hastings Street, and told the audience that a white man had thrown a black woman and her baby off the bridge and killed them both. Complementary rumors that a black man raped or shot a white woman on the bridge spread throughout Cass Corridor, the white counterpart to Paradise Valley.[24]

The incendiary gossip resulted in civil disorder of unprecedented proportions. Hand-to-hand combat between whites and blacks, as well as widespread looting and arson, continued for several days. City police eventually had to seal off particularly volatile areas such as Hastings Street, and Mayor Edward Jeffries Jr. requested state troops from Governor Kelly to supplement the police efforts and restore order. The disturbance ended only after President Roosevelt volunteered an additional 6,000 federal troops to quell any further violent outbreaks.[25]

By the end of the disturbance, 34 people were dead, hundreds were injured, and property damage reached approximately $2 million. Of the dead, 25 were African American and 9 were white. The police, according to official reports, were responsible for 17 of the Negro deaths, and the Department of Public Welfare noted that blacks made up 1,300 of the

1,800 rioters arrested. National black organizations, such as the National Urban League and the NAACP, did not ignore these disproportionate statistics, which bespoke a strong racial bias on the part of the Detroit Police Department. NAACP executive secretary Walter White and special counsel Thurgood Marshall wrote an analysis condemning the department and recommending increased hiring and promotion of Negro officers. Among city officials, only councilman George Edwards urged that a grand jury investigate 15 of the riot deaths as murders, but the council and the police commissioner rejected his request.[26]

City and federal officials singled out blacks as the scapegoats for the entire disturbance. On June 30 Mayor Jeffries publicly discussed how he was losing patience with "Negro leaders" who insisted on criticizing the Police Department. He claimed that these leaders were more interested in their "caustic criticism . . . than they are in educating their own people to their responsibilities as citizens." City prosecutor William Dowling not only opposed any grand jury investigations but openly declared his opinion that the NAACP and the *Michigan Chronicle* were responsible for instigating the riot. In his postriot recommendations to President Roosevelt, U.S. Attorney General Francis Biddle went so far as to request that "careful consideration be given to limiting, and in some instances putting an end to Negro migrations into communities which cannot absorb them, either on account of their physical limitations or cultural background. This needs immediate and careful consideration. . . . It would seem pretty clear that no more Negroes should move to Detroit."[27] Biddle's comments illustrated the extent to which many saw African Americans as intruders and outsiders in northern cities, rather than as legitimate citizens who had an equal claim to the opportunities that urban life offered.

In Detroit public policy soon reflected the thrust of Biddle's recommendation. In an effort to bolster Detroit's postwar economy, Mayor Jeffries unveiled in 1946 the Detroit Plan, which was the city's—and one of the country's—first urban renewal proposal. The plan, drafted by Albert Cobo, city treasurer and entrepreneur, argued that the city should purchase and then demolish slum property in order to sell the real estate to private developers at prices well below cost. The first stages of the Detroit Plan began in 1947 and 1948. The city condemned property in black neighborhoods such as Black Bottom and Paradise Valley and then marked it for demolition. In 1949 George Edwards ran for mayor on the Democratic ticket and argued that the cleared land should be used for increased public housing for black citizens. Albert Cobo, nominated as the Republican candidate, defeated Edwards with the promise that the property would be reserved for business developers and private interests. By 1953 Mayor Cobo had overseen the demolition of 700 buildings in Black Bottom, a process that displaced over 2,000 black families.[28]

Ten years later, in March 1963, the Detroit Commission on Community Relations reported that the city's urban renewal projects had demolished or were scheduled to demolish more than 10,000 structures, and that 43,096 people, 70 percent of them black, had been displaced or were to be displaced by these plans.[29] These statistics explain how urban renewal received the nickname "Negro Removal." At the Great March King did not ignore the urgency of Detroit's urban renewal problems. Standing at the lectern in Cobo Hall—named after the former mayor who had implemented the Detroit Plan—King expressed his hope that no black citizen of Detroit would be discriminated against in the city's housing market. For many black Detroiters, the fight to turn King's optimism into substantial change had just begun. For Motown Records and the city's black cultural producers, the effort to reclaim a place for African Americans in a city that had ravaged black neighborhoods was already under way.

Fingertips, Part 1

On May 21, 1963, Motown Records released Little Stevie Wonder's "Fingertips, Part 2." The single was the first Motown recording of a live performance: Wonder's appearance in a "Motortown Revue" show at Chicago's Regal Theater. The recording opens with Wonder shouting out to the audience, "Everybody say 'Yeah!' " A rousing "call and response" of "yeahs" ensue between Wonder and his fans as the band comes in behind his harmonica solo. Wonder calls back to the crowd to give "just a little bit of soul—yeah, yeah, yeah—clap your hands just a little bit louder, clap your hands just a little bit louder." He and the band repeat the instrumental chorus as "Little Stevie" promises that "I'm going to swing the song—yeah—just a one more time." He teases out the ending with a string of "good-byes" and playfully improvises "Mary Had a Little Lamb." Bill Murray, the revue emcee, then asks Wonder to take a bow to signal his exit from the stage. Just as the song appears to be over, Wonder quickly returns to the stage for an unexpected encore. The confusion and surprise give the recording its charm. Listeners hear the baffled bass player, who was setting up for Mary Wells's next song, shout, "What key? what key?" and curse as the rest of the band backs up the chorus "just one more time."

When Berry Gordy decided to release the recording, he had to break the song into two parts owing to the seven-minute length of the entire performance. The first part was the original song, and the second part the prolonged encores and pandemonium. "Fingertips, Part 2" captivated listeners, and the record went to number one on *Billboard*'s rhythm and blues *and* pop charts in the summer of 1963. It was only the second Motown recording, after the Marvelettes' "Please Mr. Postman," to achieve this honor.

More than a hit, however, the song captured the spirit of Detroit's black community—and specifically its cultural leaders—at the time of the Great March to Freedom. The song's electricity emanates from Wonder's unwillingness to finish the number and leave the stage. He wins over the crowd and wants to enjoy the moment, but show business etiquette demands that he give the spotlight to Mary Wells. Wonder's surprise encore celebrates a desire to assert oneself in face of authority, rules, and literal displacement. His presence and talents cannot be suppressed or removed even after the emcee officially asks him to exit the stage.

A similar defiance infused Detroit's black community at the time of the Great March. In the twenty years following the 1943 race riot, black Detroiters watched the city government systematically destroy their homes and neighborhoods as well as their cultural and economic foothold in the city: the Hastings Street and Black Bottom districts. By 1963 the dire consequences of the Detroit Plan for the city's African Americans were clear. General living conditions deteriorated drastically as urban renewal dislocated large segments of the city's black population from the already constricted neighborhoods that they had inhabited in the 1940s.

The plan did some of its most serious damage to the Hastings Street business district, which had provided an economic base for black entrepreneurship. It would take years for the many black businesses that the plan destroyed to relocate and rebuild their customer base.

Detroit's urban renewal plan also paralleled a related shift toward deindustrialization and automation in the automobile industry. Deindustrialization involved the relocation of manufacturing plants outside the city to the suburbs. Automation, in which machines replaced workers on the assembly line, reduced labor costs and increased output for the automobile manufacturers. The increased unemployment, which resulted from these developments, disproportionately effected African American workers, who were often unable to travel to the suburbs to work and whose unskilled jobs were the first replaced by automation. Despite these setbacks, Detroit's black community—like Stevie Wonder—did not "exit the stage" willingly but continued to organize and rally for its rights.[30]

The Great March to Freedom gave the black community an opportunity to proclaim its presence to a city that seemed indifferent to its most basic needs. Thousands strong, participants marched down Woodward Avenue, the longtime dividing line between racial groups in Detroit. The March's astounding turnout revealed the collective power of the city's African American citizenry. Local black leaders also used the demonstration as an opportunity to gather support for their immediate efforts to fight employment discrimination. The Reverend Albert B. Cleage Jr. came to the podium after King's speech and urged Detroiters to boycott local supermarkets until they hired black managers. Cleage, an experienced activist, knew that any demonstration had to conclude with a specific task for participants. A clearly defined activity gave people a concrete way to make a difference and discover their own powers to change the system.[31]

In Detroit black leaders and activists also understood that their power to change the system rested firmly in their ability to use the mass media and its technologies to promote their causes. Independent newspapers, radio stations, and recording studios directly contributed to the success of the demonstration, but they served a much larger, and more significant, function as well. Black Detroit used the mass media to reassert a sense of community in a city that had worked hard over twenty years to physically dismantle it. Radio airwaves, newspaper columns, and independent recordings created and maintained community ties in the face of the urban renewal and freeway development plans designed to destroy community.

The Great March to Freedom illustrated how an increasingly sophisticated black cultural apparatus in Detroit could work to promote the causes of the city's black community. In the print media the *Michigan Chronicle* reported extensively on the planning and execution of the demonstration. The day after the march the paper printed an abbreviated transcript of King's speech for its readership. In subsequent issues the *Chronicle* published a series of editorials on the nonviolent demonstration, contrasting it with the riots of 1943 and 1863 and entreating black leaders in the community to continue to work together.[32]

Cleage used his own newspaper, the *Illustrated News*, which had a biweekly circulation of 35,000, to promote the Great March. The *Illustrated News* extended Cleage's pulpit beyond the sanctuary of his Central Congregational Church on Linwood Avenue. Founded in 1960, the newspaper quickly became one of the activist minister's most effective secular tools. It diligently reported on community problems including segregation in the public schools, job discrimination, and police brutality. Cleage's more confrontational style influenced the tone of the newspaper's coverage of the demonstration which was decidedly more militant than the accounts of the *Michigan Chronicle* or the white press. The front page of the issue that publicized the march featured a contentious image of angry protesters above the caption "June 1963: The moment seems to be now."

On the airwaves WCHB, the first radio station in the country built, owned, and operated by African Americans, offered its services to broadcast the march proceedings live. The history of WCHB epitomized the spirit of black cultural production in Detroit. Wendell Cox and Haley Bell, two dentists, founded the Bell Broadcasting Company in 1955. Their radio station, WCHB-AM (the call numbers created from their combined initials) went on the air in November 1956. The station soon touted itself as "the Voice of Progress," as it became an important forum for community service, public affairs, and religious programming. Because of Federal Communication Commission regulations, the station operated out of Inkster, Michigan—a suburb of Detroit—but was soon the premiere

"The Moment Seems to Be Now," *Illustrated News*, June 1963. (Courtesy Walter P. Reuther Library, Wayne State University.)

dio station for the entire Detroit metropolitan area. On June 23, 1963, WCHB's "Voice of Progress" aptly broadcast the Great March to Freedom to its listening public.

Just as WCHB volunteered its services to broadcast the march, Motown Records offered its talents to record the demonstration for future generations. While Motown artists could have performed at the rally, the company chose instead to record King's compelling arguments. Hitsville's recording studio was one of the best equipped in the city to preserve King's speech with the highest degree of audio fidelity. Significantly, the recording engineer for *The Great March to Freedom* album was not a regular Motown employee but attorney Milton Henry, an audiophile and local activist who worked with Franklin and Cleage at the DCHR. Henry's role as recording engineer illustrates that local black activists in Detroit recognized the importance of audio recordings in political organizing.[33]

Black Detroit was particularly adept at using radio broadcasting and independent record production to further its political causes and reclaim its presence in the city. No one person in Detroit better exemplified this trend than the Reverend C. L. Franklin. In 1963 Franklin's dual roles as the most celebrated black Baptist preacher of his era and the head of the Detroit Council for Human Rights proved that, within the city's black community, cultural influence—cultivated via radio airwaves and recordings—could translate into political power. In fact, Franklin's career both foreshadowed and inspired the trajectory of the Motown Record Company's own marketing genius.

C. L. Franklin, "The Jitterbug Preacher"

Born on January 22, 1915, in Sunflower County, Mississippi, Clarence LaVaughn Franklin grew up in the rural community outside Doddsville, Mississippi. His grandfather, Elijah J. Pitman, was a preacher. His father served in the military during World War I and abandoned his family after he returned from overseas. His mother, Rachel, soon remarried, choosing Henry Franklin, a sharecropper who remained indebted to white landowners throughout his life.

After witnessing the frustrations of sharecropping, the young C. L. decided that there was "no future in farming" and turned to the church. He had a vision early in his adolescence that God visited him and said, "Go and preach the gospel to all the nations." His stepfather disapproved of his religious calling, but his mother, a devout Christian, encouraged her son's career. She also influenced C. L.'s charismatic preaching style. When noisy classmates drowned out Franklin's speech at a school recital, Rachel Franklin punished the boy and proclaimed, "The next time you speak, people are going to hear you!" Franklin performed his first sermon in his midteens and, in his late teens, was ordained at Saint Peter's Rock Baptist Church.[34]

After spending a number of years preaching in rural Mississippi, Franklin moved to Memphis, Tennessee, to work at the New Salem Baptist Church. In Memphis Franklin made his first attempt to use the mass media to promote his religious calling. He contacted a local radio station manager soon after his arrival in the city and established a weekly radio broadcast of his sermons. The live broadcast from the church quickly attracted new parishioners. After three years in Tennessee, Franklin moved to Buffalo, New York, and became the pastor of the Friendship Baptist Church. Many of Franklin's northern parishioners had migrated to Buffalo from the South to work at Bethlehem Steel and found comfort in his southern Baptist preaching style. While Franklin enjoyed his congregation, he longed to leave the isolated and conservative city. In his own words, "I wanted to be in a city where there were crossroads of transportation. Trains, buses, planes, where people are coming and going, conventions of all kinds, and migrations."

In 1945 Franklin preached at the National Baptist Convention in Detroit, a city where people were "coming and going" and with a reputation for good preachers. When the New Bethel Baptist Church offered him the position as pastor, he accepted and moved to Detroit in June 1946. Franklin decided, soon after his arrival, that the church's sanctuary, "a dilapidated building that had been converted from a bowling alley," was unsatisfactory and set out to raise funds to build a new church on Hastings Street. For the next two years, the church held services outdoors and in the city's Brewster Center to save money for the financially struggling parish.

In an attempt to liquidate his church's debt and increase his congregation, Franklin turned, as he had in Memphis, to radio broadcasts. He initially broadcast his sermons from a small station in Dearborn, but in 1952 he switched to WJLB, a much larger Detroit station, which gave him airtime every Sunday night. The exposure proved beneficial. According to Franklin, "We eventually had a high-interest loan and finished rebuilding on Hastings Street. After the broadcast started, the congregation grew tremendously. People would line up outside the church ahead of time to get in for the broadcast on Sunday nights. Some nights they would have to get there an hour before the service started."[35]

Franklin's theatrical preaching and his attention to his personal appearance bolstered his local celebrity. His reputation as a snappy dresser earned him the nicknames "Black Beauty" and "Jitterbug Preacher." In 1953, as Franklin's congregation grew into the thousands, Joe Von Battle, a local record store owner and record producer, approached him about the possibility of recording his sermons. Franklin, who had become curious about recording, agreed to work with the entrepreneur. Von Battle taped Franklin's sermons live from the New Bethel sanctuary using his own Ampex portable recording equipment and then released them on his own JVB label. To promote the recordings, Von Battle broadcast the albums from loudspeakers outside his record store located on Hastings Street near Franklin's parish, and he had to call the police more than once to break up the crowds gathering around to listen. In an effort to reach a broader audience, Von Battle contacted Chess Records in Chicago and leased his recordings to the larger company.[36]

With Chess's wider distribution, Franklin's records quickly gained national attention. One radio station, WLAC-AM in Nashville, Tennessee, had a powerful nationwide radius and began to play Franklin's recordings every Sunday night. A local Nashville record store, Randy's Record Shop, sponsored the broadcast and began to sell Franklin's albums across the country. These broadcasts solidified Franklin's celebrity as the most popular black preacher of his era. Remarking on Franklin's influence, Jesse Jackson has commented, "Did not our ears perk up for years before we had a television or an elected official in America, if we could just hear WLAC, Nashville, Tennessee, Randy's, on a Sunday night? Sunday night, New Bethel, Hastings Street, was the common frame of reference for the black church. The soul of Motown was Hastings Street before Grand Boulevard."[37]

As the record sales increased, a demand arose for Franklin to tour the country and perform his sermons live before his growing followers. When Franklin met the Clara Ward Singers at the National Baptist Convention in Memphis, the gospel celebrities decided to join forces and organize a national gospel road show. The C. L. Franklin Gospel Caravan featured a roster of gospel acts including the Clara Ward Singers, the Dixie Hummingbirds, the Bradford Singers, and eventually his own daughter, Aretha, whose precocious singing talent delighted audiences. Reverend Franklin's sermon acted as the grand finale of each engagement.[38]

All participants had achieved their popularity through a combination of live performance, exposure on radio, and strong record sales. Unlike traditional evangelical revivals, Franklin staged his sermons on the tour to replicate his already popular recordings. Franklin explained his approach as follows: "I would preach whatever the deejay had been playing, and what was indicated to the deejay that the people liked most. At first I resented these requests. I had the attitude that I would have at the church, that people should be ready to listen to whatever I chose to preach on, but people are not like that. They want to hear what they have been hearing. Now you may have a better sermon on something else in your own judgment, but as far as they're concerned, they don't want to hear it."[39]

Franklin's keen awareness of his audiences' preferences served him well. He recorded over seventy albums of his sermons throughout his career. Many of these albums became the best-selling black gospel recordings of their time—earning the preacher one more nickname, "the Man with the Million Dollar Voice." Some of Franklin's most popular sermons included "Dry Bones in the Valley," "Give Me This Mountain," and "Without a Song." The last echoed the sentiments of the epigram that Motown quoted in honor of the Emancipation Proclamation centennial ("in whose heart there is no song"). In the sermon Franklin celebrated the power of song: "We have songs of confusion and trial, burden and tribulation. Then we have songs of peace and a brighter day. We have songs of promise. We have songs of God and destiny. We have songs of life and death. So that any message that you really want to get over, you can get it over in a song. Isn't it so?"[40]

By 1963 Franklin's recordings had earned him national celebrity, but his success did not save his parish in Detroit. The city demolished Franklin's New Bethel sanctuary on Hastings Street, which he had worked so hard to build. The church was just one more of the long-term casualties of Mayor Cobo's Detroit Plan. Franklin responded to the loss of his parish in two ways: he rebuilt a new church on the corner of Linwood and Philadelphia Avenues, and he became more active in political organizing. Franklin always believed that his church served a political function. He once told fellow activist Grace Lee Boggs that he hoped his church could build "a political community in Detroit to help blacks from the South cope with the isolation and individualism of city life." Yet the demolition of his church motivated Franklin to move beyond his own sanctuary and form coalitions with other local activists.[41]

The dedication of the rebuilt New Bethel Church, which took place on March 10, 1963, foreshadowed the Great March to Freedom. Reverend Franklin led his congregation in a dramatic procession from its temporary sanctuary on Twelfth Street to its new home on Linwood Avenue. A caravan of over three hundred cars traveled the route from the site of the temporary church to the new one. At the opening service Franklin spoke about the "conflict and trials" of losing the Hastings church and the "triumph" of rebuilding anew. He also noted that the Linwood church was built "wholly by Negroes . . . 'proof that as a race we can do for ourselves if we take advantage of opportunities to qualify ourselves.' " The dedication ceremony revealed Franklin's keen promotional skills. The *Michigan Chronicle* reported that the "services will be covered by several national magazines, various newspapers and one television station." It was only a few weeks after the opening of his Linwood sanctuary that Franklin founded the DCHR with Cleage and began to organize the Great March.[42]

C. L. Franklin's celebrity as a Baptist preacher did not protect his church from demolition, but the tactics he used to achieve his fame inspired the Motown Record Company as it established its place in the city. Like Franklin, Hitsville, U.S.A., sought radio airplay and organized promotional tours in an effort to reach the widest possible audiences.

These efforts proved equally successful for the fledgling record company. By 1963 Motown's music was emanating from radio waves and turntables across the country and challenging the racial categories that the music industry imposed upon it. In Detroit the Motown Record Company challenged other racial boundaries as well.

Fingertips, Part 2

One week before the Great March To Freedom, the *Detroit Free Press,* the *Detroit News,* and the *Michigan Chronicle* reported that Berry Gordy Jr. had purchased the Graystone Ballroom on Woodward Avenue near Canfield Street for $123,000. Gordy's acquisition of the ballroom represented more than a simple real estate investment. The purchase rectified the reputation of an entertainment venue that had a troublesome history of racial segregation. Moreover, in the wake of urban renewal, Gordy's takeover recovered an important landmark of Detroit's musical culture for African Americans.[43]

The Graystone Ballroom had a complicated relationship to Detroit's musical history and cultural life. Beginning in the 1920s, Detroit became an important contributor to the development of big band jazz. The city's Graystone Ballroom, along with the Arcadia, the Pier Ballroom near the Belle Isle Bridge, and the Palais de Danse provided employment for many black jazz artists, who innovated big band arrangements. McKinney's Synco Jazz Band, organized in the early 1920s, became one of the most famous of the Detroit big bands. In 1927 the jazz ensemble became the first all-black band to play at the Graystone, although not until it agreed, under management pressure, to change its name to McKinney's "Cotton Pickers."[44]

The "Cotton Pickers" broke a racial barrier for performers at the Graystone, but the ballroom's dancers remained primarily white. Throughout the 1920s racial segregation pervaded most dance halls in Detroit—although the Graystone and the Arcadia were the least discriminatory of the major ballrooms. The Graystone Ballroom designated one night a week, Monday night, for African American patrons. As a youth, Berry Gordy Jr. frequented Detroit ballrooms on these designated evenings. In his autobiography he recalled, "Graystone Ballroom and Gardens was where we went on Monday nights, the only night colored people could go. That was our night. Everybody who was anybody would be there, dressed to kill." The Graystone continued to attract major jazz talent throughout the Depression, but the proliferation of nightclubs and cabarets in the new black entertainment district of Paradise Valley drew audiences away from the ballroom circuit. Over the years, the artistry of African Americans undeniably contributed to the ballroom's legendary status, yet the popular establishment continued to discriminate against black patrons.[45]

When Berry Gordy purchased the Graystone Ballroom in 1963, he reclaimed the dance hall for African American musicians, performers, and audiences.[46] The investment established a new entertainment venue for black talent in a city that had systematically destroyed core regions of African American cultural life. Along with Franklin's New Bethel Baptist Church, city planners had demolished the majority of black establishments in and around Paradise Valley and Black Bottom by the late 1950s. The final demise of Hastings Street, the central artery of black nightlife in Detroit, came in 1960 with the construction of the Chrysler Freeway. Joe Von Battle, Franklin's loyal record producer, lost his record shop at this time. In an oral history Marsha L. Mickens, Joe Von Battle's daughter, remembered how her father communicated the loss of the Hastings Street district to her:

> [My father] walked me across the street . . . to this gigantic pit that was in the ground. It looked like a canyon to me. He looked at me and said, . . . "This is where Hastings used to be." All my life, as a little girl, I didn't know what that was. I just had this memory of this pit. As I got older, I realized that it was the initial diggings for the I-75 freeway. What my father so graphically understood and expressed with that sentence was that a way of life had been totally destroyed by the Chrysler Freeway. The street of Hastings just no longer existed . . . people talk about how Hastings was destroyed purposefully. That has always been the scuttlebutt within the community. The white man decided to get rid of Hastings because the community was becoming too strong . . . It was very purposeful and destroyed the infrastructure of the people in that area.[47]

In the Motor City the new expressways connected the city's primarily white suburbs to the downtown area. For black Detroit construction of the Chrysler Freeway razed clubs including Henry's Swing Club, the Crystal Bar, and Brown's Bar—establishments that featured artists such as John Lee Hooker, Bobo Jenkins, and Rufus "Speckled Red" Perryman.

The musicians and singers who would eventually create the Motown sound received early musical training in these clubs. Legendary bassist James Jamerson, whose innovative style shaped the distinctive beat of scores of Motown hits, got his start playing with the band Washboard Willie and the Supersuds of Rhythm in Detroit blues clubs including the Caribbean Club, the Apex, and the Calumet Lounge. The Warfield Theater also acted as an important training ground for aspiring entertainers. Many young singers caught their first glimpses of fame by winning the theater's weekly talent shows. Singing groups such as the Del-Phis, the Primes, the Primettes, and the Voice Masters, who competed against one another at the Warfield, emerged later as Motown groups—known respectively as Martha and the Vandellas, the Temptations, the Supremes, and the Originals. Detroit's black musical culture continued after the construction of the Chrysler Freeway, but it never again recaptured the cohesiveness it once knew in neighborhoods such as Paradise Valley and Black Bottom.[48]

Motown's acquisition of the Graystone not only provided one venue to replace the many lost, but also reinvented the image of black entertainment establishments. Much of the allure of nightclubs, dance halls, and blind pigs on Hastings Street originated from the district's aura of forbidden pleasure. The Graystone Ballroom, located in the heart of downtown Detroit, stood apart from the more tawdry associations of Paradise Valley.

When Berry Gordy took over the ownership of the ballroom, he immediately prepared to use the facility to spotlight Motown's promising young stars. Gordy hoped that the Graystone would imbue his young performers and their audiences with the glamour, elegance, and respectability of its former years. He employed his brother-in-law, Michigan state representative George H. Edwards, as general manager and controller of the ballroom. At the time of the purchase, Edwards argued that the name of the ballroom should be changed since, in recent years, the building had been used for boxing matches and had lost some of its prestige. The *Detroit News* reported, however, that Gordy, "[a] native Detroiter who remembers the golden days of the Graystone . . . said he would like to keep the name." Gordy hoped that memories of the Graystone's glory days would attract new audiences, who could now see their favorite black artists perform, not just on Mondays, but on any day of the week.[49]

On July 20, 1963, only a month and a half after the public announcement of Gordy's purchase, the ballroom hosted a Little Stevie Wonder concert series. The series attracted approximately seven thousand patrons and promoted Wonder's smash hit "Fingertips, Part 2." In an article on the concert the *Michigan Chronicle* emphasized how—despite overflow crowds—there were no disturbances at the concert, "[t]he young people were neatly dressed and well-behaved at the matinee and the older crowd at the evening performance was just as attractive and mannerly." The reporter's detailed description of the audiences' well-mannered behavior contributed to Gordy's goal of asserting the respectability of black entertainment. William "Mickey" Stevenson, Motown's artists and repertoire director, has recalled how the Graystone Ballroom performances positively influenced local black youth. Motown concerts at the ballroom "gave us a chance to get the youngsters off the streets and see what our image was about . . . inspiring them a little to maybe live up to that imagery."[50]

When Wonder took to the stage of the Graystone Ballroom to perform before an audience of his, primarily black, fans, he participated in a shift in the racial politics of one of Detroit's most legendary entertainment establishments. The Graystone Ballroom, with its history of white ownership and policy of limiting and often excluding African American patrons from performances, now enjoyed black ownership, featured local black entertainers, and welcomed black audiences. The success of the concert series also proved the commercial viability of black entertainment in downtown Detroit. Gordy's purchase of the Graystone Ballroom offers one—often overlooked—example of how black Detroit found ways to resist the real displacement of urban renewal.

The challenges that African Americans faced in the urban North clearly differed from the racial problems in the South. These differences reflected the unique circumstances of life in an industrial city. Cultural

Marquee for the Little Stevie Wonder concert at the Graystone Ballroom, July 1963. (Courtesy Motown Record Co., L.P., a Polygram Company.)

leaders such as the Reverend C. L. Franklin and Motown Records had opportunities to use their finances and local clout to counteract some of the devastating effects of the Detroit Plan. But Motown was not entirely removed from the fight for desegregation that dominated the civil rights struggles in the South and that eventually brought Martin Luther King Jr. to Detroit in June 1963 to raise money for SCLC.

In November 1962—eight months before the Great March to Freedom—Berry Gordy Jr. launched the first "Motortown Revue," a ten-week national road tour designed to publicize the company's latest releases. Similar to Franklin's Gospel Caravan, the revue promoted Detroit's black talent far beyond the city's limits. Publicity tours were common in the popular music industry as a means to propel a new song up the charts. Yet they were usually organized by the impresarios of the record world such as deejay Dick Clark, whose "Caravan of Stars" began in 1959. The "Motortown Revue," a road show sponsored solely by a black-owned record company, was one of the first of its kind in the music industry.[51]

Independent sponsorship gave Berry Gordy Jr. the ability to control every aspect of the tour. To ensure a degree of consistency between the recorded songs and the live musical performance, Gordy sent Motown studio musicians on the tour to back up the singers at every gig, whereas many other road shows relied on local bands. Gordy also used his authority over the tour to support other blacks in the music business. During the 1962 revue, Gordy made special arrangements with black deejays in certain cities for the mutual benefit of both parties. In Philadelphia Georgie Woods, deejay from radio station WDAS, gave Motown songs generous airplay. When the revue came to town, the company returned the favor by giving Woods and his radio station exclusive rights to promote the show at the city's Uptown Theater. These arrangements revealed how African Americans, who had access to the mass media—whether radio or recording—supported one another.[52]

These unwritten contracts and an itinerary that retraced the "chit'lin circuit" from Boston to Florida and then back to the Apollo Theater in New York guaranteed that when the "Motortown Revue" pulled into certain cities, it would be received by an audience of loyal and primarily— although not exclusively—black fans. These fans gave the tour a warm welcome at practically every stop. Of course, audience reception was not something that could be controlled or predicted at all times. Certain concerts drew audiences who reacted to the entourage of young "Negro" entertainers in unexpected and volatile ways.

On November 9, 1962, the "Motortown Revue" arrived in Birmingham, Alabama, and performed before a racially integrated audience at a local baseball field. The concert proceeded without a disturbance, but the young black performers from the North did not depart the southern town without a warning. Gunshots rang out as the singers and musicians began to board the bus to leave town. Everyone escaped without injury, but the attack left several bullet holes in bus windows. The brush with violence would leave its mark on all of the participants, many of whom had previously believed that Motown's mystique would shield them from racial attack. Reflecting on the first tour, Mary Wells commented, "Me in my little Motown star bubble. All of sudden everything kind of crushes." The revue's frightening exit from Birmingham foreshadowed the conflicts to come when Martin Luther King Jr. began his fight to integrate the southern city.[53]

Berry Gordy Jr.'s procurement of the Graystone Ballroom and the revue's attempts to perform before integrated audiences in the South provide two examples of how the company and its music participated, albeit sometimes unintentionally, in the larger campaign toward racial equality. When Motown decided to record King's speech at Detroit's Great March to Freedom, the company directly affiliated itself with the political objectives of the SCLC civil rights campaign. The album also, of course, preserved a pivotal moment in the history of Detroit's race relations.

Even in the immediate afterglow of the demonstration, however, many Detroiters debated the march's historic significance. On the one hand, the *Detroit Free Press* quoted an official of the DCHR saying, "You know, Detroit will never be the same after this day." Another marcher, Charles Denby, shared similar sentiments that he later recounted in a personal memoir. Denby remembered that at the march "the feeling and morale was so high that I felt as though I could almost touch freedom, and nothing could stop this powerful force from winning." On the other hand, this enthusiasm was qualified by citizens on the street like Jeannette Anderson, who doubted that the marchers had "gained anything. Maybe the talk helped them feel better, but no one is going to let them into Grosse Pointe." Miss Wolfe similarly commented that the march "showed that Negroes are freer in the North, but that things are not so hotsy-totsy up here, either."[54]

Skepticism clearly simmered underneath the spirit of optimism that pervaded the Great March. Unfortunately, the immediate future of race relations in Detroit after the demonstration justified the skeptics' doubts. Only thirteen days later the black community in Detroit rallied against the city's Police Department when a patrol officer, Theodore Spicher, shot and killed Cynthia Scott, a young black woman. At 3:00 A.M. on July 5, Scott was enjoying the after-hours celebrations of the Fourth of July on John R Street with Charles Marshall, an acquaintance, when a scout car stopped the pair. Six-feet, four-inches tall and a sex worker by trade, Scott, also known as "Saint Cynthia," was a formidable and easily recognized figure on the streets. According to police reports, the woman brandished a knife and attempted to slash the officers who were trying to apprehend her. As she ran to escape, Officer Spicher shot her twice in the back and then once in the stomach when he reached her collapsed body. Scott's companion, Marshall, disputed the police officers' version of the story in a special interview with the *Michigan Chronicle*. He claimed that Scott did not attack the officers with a knife and had walked—not run—away from the scout car when she told Spicher and his partner that they had no grounds to arrest her. As she proceeded to leave the scene, the officer opened fire.[55]

Within nine hours, news of the fatal shooting had traveled throughout the city's black neighborhoods, and a crowd had gathered at police headquarters to protest what was seen as an "unnecessary" killing. In the days that followed, the city prosecutor, Samuel H. Olsen, proclaimed that the slaying was justified. Black organizations throughout the city, from conservative to militant, generated an outcry against the ruling. The Detroit NAACP demanded a full and immediate investigation "to determine if this tragic slaying . . . can be justified by the rule of sound police practice."[56]

Other community organizations such as the Group on Advanced Leadership (GOAL) also planned formal protests. Richard B. Henry, president of GOAL, and brother of Milton Henry, who acted as attorney for Scott's family, organized a picket line for July 13 at the police headquarters on Beaubien Street. Henry asserted that the protest was "aimed at discrimination in hiring and upgrading in the police department and at the open season which the police and prosecutor have declared against Negro lives and rights." Approximately three thousand demonstrators stood outside police headquarters shouting, "Get killer cops" and threatening to storm the building. The young, militant group UHURU (Swahili for "freedom now"), led by its president Luke Tripp and other black students attending Wayne State University, supported the GOAL protests and supplemented them with their own street rallies and sit-ins. Unified outrage in the black community about the Scott case lingered for years. Most significantly, the Cynthia Scott case abruptly reminded Detroit's black community that the fight for racial justice would not be solved by one Great March.[57]

In the weeks and months that followed the Great March, the monumental task of turning King's "dreams" of justice into a tangible reality on the streets of Detroit proved more elusive than anyone could have anticipated on that bright Sunday afternoon. The Motor City had a long road to travel if it were ever to live up to its new reputation as the model city of race relations, and that road would not be paved smoothly. In fact, Detroit's pattern of racial conflict and urban destruction would repeat itself in a few short years with an unprecedented vengeance. Ultimately, the Great March to Freedom resonated with the unrest of the past, celebrated the present rapprochement, and foreshadowed the conflicts to come.

2

"Money (That's What I Want)":
Black Capitalism and Black Freedom in Detroit

Approximately four months after Martin Luther King Jr. appeared at Detroit's Great March to Freedom, Malcolm X came to the Motor City. On November 10, 1963, the Nation of Islam's most famous minister delivered his "Message to the Grass Roots" speech at the city's Northern Negro Grass Roots Leadership Conference. Malcolm X's trenchant oratorical style enlivened his incisive arguments—just as Martin Luther King Jr.'s powerful delivery had stirred Detroiters in June. The Grass Roots Conference organizers, like those of the Great March, wanted to preserve both the content and performance of the public address. Yet, in this instance, the Motown Record Company did not record Malcolm X's speech.

Attorney Milton Henry, recording engineer for both events, acted as a common link between the two productions, but Henry released Malcolm X's speech on his own label, the Grass Roots, L.P. Co. The album's liner notes acknowledge that Henry's efforts to record the speech are "semi-professional" but sincere. The minor "squeaks" that occur in the recording are forgiven since "a pearl dragged from the deep by unorthodox methods is still nonetheless a pearl—a gem worthy to be cherished . . . [And it] will be desired by all students of contemporary history; and particularly by those interested in the development of the Negro Freedom Movement."[1]

The recordings of both Malcolm X's speech and Dr. King's address at the Great March to Freedom had particular significance to the Negro Freedom Movement: they represented the technological evolution of the long-held tradition of valorizing oral history in African American culture. The Motown Record Company could have further participated in the Negro Freedom Movement by recording this "pearl," but it did not. Perhaps Berry Gordy Jr. did not want his company to affiliate itself with a radical leader so openly critical of King's nonviolent, integrationist approach. From a business perspective, the company needed to focus its energies on Stevie Wonder's career after the success of "Fingertips, Part 2." In September 1963 Motown Records released his next hit, "Workout Stevie, Workout." The company also may have shied away from the recording because of legal concerns. In September 1963 Motown attempted to produce a recording of Martin Luther King Jr.'s "I Have a Dream" speech from the March on Washington. Within a month King and SCLC filed a lawsuit against Motown and two other record companies for producing recordings of his speech without proper authorization. SCLC dropped the lawsuit against Motown at the end of October, and King eventually signed an exclusive recording contract with Motown Records, but the legal action revealed that civil rights recordings could lead to troublesome copyright conflicts.[2]

Motown's absence from the recording of Malcolm X's "Message to the Grass Roots" speech, however, did not diminish the company's important presence in Detroit as a successful black capitalist enterprise. In fact, Motown's prosperity as a black-owned business achieved many of the economic objectives of black nationalism espoused by leaders such as Malcolm X. Many of the ideals of black nationalism's economic philosophy can be traced back to Booker T. Washington, who was never considered a black nationalist, but whose economic "self-help" principles inspired others including Marcus Garvey.[3] The Gordy family history typified Washington's philosophy of economic self-sufficiency and encapsulated larger trends in the development of black capitalism in Detroit. Berry Gordy Jr.'s economic achievement with the Motown Record Company was never, therefore, simply an individual success story. Motown was the product of decades of black economic self-help in Detroit, a movement that was, by November 1963, a centerpiece of black nationalist thought.

But Motown's status as a successful black business that sought white as well as black consumers made the company a much easier symbol of

King's integrationist dream than of Malcolm X's black nationalist revolution. In his "Grass Roots" speech at Detroit's King Solomon Baptist Church, Malcolm X painted a harsh picture of the black struggle when he declared, "Revolution is bloody, revolution is hostile, revolution knows no compromise, revolution overturns and destroys everything that gets in its way. And you, sitting around here like a knot on the wall, saying, 'I'm going to love these folks no matter how much they hate me.' No, you need a revolution. Whoever heard of a revolution where they lock arms . . . singing 'We Shall Overcome'? You don't do that in a revolution. You don't do any singing, you're too busy swinging."[4] Malcolm X's volatile rhetoric at the Grass Roots Conference bore no resemblance to the harmonious spirit of Detroit's Great March to Freedom or to the harmonious sound of a Motown song.

From a triumphant Sunday in June to a divisive Sunday in November, Detroit's black community—including the young Motown Record Company—participated in the larger philosophical and tactical debates challenging the national civil rights movement. Detroit's Great March, which had fostered unity among the city's civil rights groups, had taken several unexpected detours in the months that followed. By November 1963 these detours had evolved into distinct crossroads as civil rights leaders within Detroit's black community became fiercely divided about what constituted the "freedom" toward which they were marching. Motown Records and community leaders such as the Reverend C. L. Franklin maintained a public allegiance to King's integrationist, nonviolent campaign. Other activists, most notably the Reverend Albert B. Cleage Jr. and Milton Henry, found Malcolm X's militant, separatist arguments for black nationalism more compelling.[5]

Franklin, Cleage, and Henry initially worked together when they founded the Detroit Council for Human Rights in the spring of 1963 and organized the Great March. The afterglow of the march inspired these community leaders to organize the city's civil rights groups into a formal network—the Northern Negro Leadership Council. This council, based on the structure and principles of the Southern Christian Leadership Conference, sought to create a coalition among Detroit's civil rights organizations and with activists from urban communities throughout the

Northeast and Midwest. Eager to launch the organization, Cleage, Franklin, and other members of the DCHR decided to sponsor a Northern Negro Leadership Conference in November to inaugurate their plans. On September 27, 1963, the DCHR held its first mass meeting at Franklin's New Bethel Baptist Church to plan the event.[6]

Almost immediately, however, the Detroit activists divided over whether the new organization should have an integrationist or a separatist agenda. On September 30, 1963—only three days after the New Bethel Baptist Church mass meeting—Cleage's family newspaper, the *Illustrated News*, published an advertisement for the "First Public Rally for a Freedom Now Party: With an All-Black Slate and a Platform for Liberation" to be held at Cleage's Central Congregational Church on Friday, October 11. Scheduled speakers included not only Cleage, but also Malcolm X's brother, Wilfred X, from the Nation of Islam's Detroit Mosque Number One. The rally for the Freedom Now campaign represented a growing community interest in the development of an all-black political party.[7]

Wary of its separatist agenda, Franklin wanted to dissociate himself and the DCHR from the Freedom Now Party organizing. Franklin felt pressure to avoid anti-integrationist rhetoric and organizing because of his close association with King and SCLC. At a DCHR board meeting in late October, Franklin expressed his concern that the Northern Negro Leadership Conference might be infiltrated by "black nationalists and other radical groups" from the East. As chairman of the DCHR, Franklin announced that he did not want to be "labeled a black nationalist like Marcus Garvey." Cleage responded that the conference should be a forum for "free and open discussion and decision by individuals representing all shades of Negro opinion." Franklin opposed Cleage's approach and insisted that the conference could not endorse the all-black Freedom Now Party or criticize the philosophy of nonviolence.[8]

Confronted with Franklin's resistance, Reverend Cleage resigned from the DCHR, and the unity that originated during the planning and execution of the Great March to Freedom fractured irrevocably. The fracture resulted in two competing conferences on the same weekend: the Northern Negro Leadership Conference, sponsored by Franklin and the

DCHR, which featured Adam Clayton Powell; and the Northern Negro Grass Roots Leadership Conference, sponsored by the Group on Advanced Leadership, with keynote speaker Malcolm X.

On the Monday following the competing conferences, the Detroit press coverage revealed which conference had won out. Reporters declared Franklin's conference a dismal failure—drawing only a handful of participants to the near empty rooms reserved at Cobo Hall. The Grass Roots Conference clearly eclipsed Franklin's efforts when over a hundred people from more than eleven northern states crowded the Grass Roots workshops held at Mr. Kelley's Lounge and Recreation Center. On Sunday night over seven hundred people attended the conference's closing rally at King Solomon Baptist Church, where Malcolm X gave his "Message to the Grass Roots" speech. Throughout the talk Milton Henry's tape recorder permanently captured Malcolm's controversial arguments and biting wit.[9]

While Motown chose not to participate in this recording, the company's success was connected to Malcolm X's ascent as a leader of black nationalism. The paths that led Berry Gordy Jr. to establish the Motown Record Company and brought Malcolm X to the King Solomon Baptist Church may appear disparate at first glance. Yet the founding of the Motown Record Company and the history of black nationalism—particularly the urban origins of the Nation of Islam—were intricately entwined. In Detroit black capitalism and its self-help strategies emerged from the same urban industrial milieu that would also produce one of the most influential black nationalist organizations in the United States. Moreover, the historical interplay between black capitalist development and black nationalist philosophy helps explain the emergence of the all-black Freedom Now political party in Detroit.

The interconnections among the economic success of Motown Records, Malcolm X's black nationalist philosophy, and the formation of the Freedom Now Party emerged from the larger history of black protest and politics in Detroit. Throughout this history, the pursuit of African American economic empowerment, independence, and solidarity energized more overt political fights for racial equality. These political fights were, however, always highly contested. The shifting allegiances that occurred from June 1963 to November 1963 between Martin Luther King Jr.'s integrationist message and Malcolm X's separatist, revolutionary rhetoric attested to the vicissitudes of black politics in Detroit.

Regardless of the debates about integration versus separatism, Detroit activists and community leaders agreed on the importance of fighting for black economic enfranchisement. Without an economic base, local black activists knew that they could not gain a foothold in the city's political system and force that system to respond to its needs. In the aftermath of the Great March, Detroit witnessed a series of civil rights demonstrations designed to address issues of economic empowerment. These rallies protested discrimination against African Americans in the city's employment lines and also formed coalitions to support local black business owners. The demonstrations reverberated with the struggles of the past and grew out of the cooperative efforts of an earlier generation of business leaders, politicians, and activists. Berry Gordy Sr., Michigan state senator Charles C. Diggs Sr., and Elijah Muhammed (Malcolm X's spiritual father), who were members of this older generation, understood the importance of the alliance of black capitalism and black political representation. They strongly believed in the power of African Americans working cooperatively to build economic and political strength.

Booker T. Washington's National Negro Business League, formed at the turn of the century, laid the foundation for subsequent efforts at economic self-help throughout the country. In Detroit these early coalitions of black economic self-help planted the seeds of several major developments in black business, religion, nationalism, and electoral politics. The founding of Motown Records, the rise of Malcolm X within the Nation of Islam, and the formation of the Freedom Now Party in 1963 were all indebted to this earlier generation of black leaders and business people and in fact interrelated.

Of Mr. Booker T. Washington and Others

Booker T. Washington's Negro Business League advanced the beliefs that laissez-faire economics were color blind and that racial prejudice could be conquered through entrepreneurial success. Indeed, black capitalism could create an economic base from which other facets of black empowerment could be pursued. Based on these principles the league avoided

addressing issues of political and civil rights throughout its early years.
Its central objective of encouraging Negro support for Negro business
implicitly acknowledged, however, that racial prejudice and discrimination negatively affected aspiring black business owners. The league's
rapid growth—establishing 320 branches within seven years of its founding—testified to the appeal of its black economic nationalism.[10]

The Detroit chapter of the Negro Business League was founded on
July 14, 1926. The original sixty members worked diligently to develop
a sense of unity among black business owners in the city and to educate
black entrepreneurs about sound business practices. The Detroit branch
represented one of the black business community's earliest attempts at
economic self-help. Soon, however, two other organizations—the Booker
T. Washington Trade Association (BTWTA) and the Housewives League
of Detroit (HWLD)—advanced these efforts even further. The Reverend
William H. Peck of the Bethel AME Church and his wife, Fannie B.
Peck, founded the BTWTA and its sister organization, the HWLD, in
1930. During their first years of existence, the organizations stated their
objectives in a joint declaration of principles:

> We emphasize and declare it to be the most desirable to own our
> own business and manage it ourselves. While we recognize as an
> act of fairness the employment of Negroes in businesses owned
> and operated by other racial groups, yet we feel that the solution
> of our economic problem is the ownership [of] business, and to
> this end we shall confine our efforts.[11]

The BTWTA and the HWLD saw their efforts to foster solidarity within
the city's black business community as distinct from traditional politics:
"we are not a political organization," they declared. But their focus on
building a strong independent black economy was a political act in and
of itself. From the time of slavery forward, African Americans had struggled to find an economic foothold in American society and were often
denied access to education and training in many professions. Given this
history, any organization such as the BTWTA or the HWLD, which sought
to support black economic advancement, engaged with the racial politics
of its era.[12]

Throughout the 1930s the BTWTA and the HWLD expanded rapidly and offered a variety of services and programs to promote economic self-sufficiency and to develop a strong black business and professional class. The BTWTA's most established program was the Noonday Luncheon Club, which met weekly and sponsored events highlighting specific professions such as "Lawyer's Day" and "Insurance Day." The Housewives League encouraged black women in the community to direct their patronage to black businesses. Fannie Peck realized that if black housewives in Detroit acted together—as black women in Harlem had begun to do—their strategic consumerism could buoy local black businesses. Members of the league also believed that their patronage could have long-reaching consequences including the potential employment of their children in the businesses that they supported. In 1938 the BTWTA and the HWLD sent the second-largest delegation to Houston, Texas, for the thirty-eighth annual convention of the National Negro Business League. By the end of the conference, the impressive efforts of the BTWTA and the HWLD had established Detroit as a "city where blacks were really doing things."[13]

The career of Charles C. Diggs Sr., a prominent member of the BTWTA, illustrated how successful black entrepreneurship could have direct political consequences. In 1936 Diggs became the first black Democrat to be elected to the Michigan state senate. Born in Mississippi in 1894, Diggs did not arrive in Detroit until 1913, after graduating from Mississippi's Alcorn Mechanical and Industrial College. Once in Detroit, Diggs opened a shoe-repair shop and saved his earnings, which he eventually used to acquire professional training as an embalmer. In 1921 he opened his own funeral home, the House of Diggs, Inc., which became the largest black funeral establishment in the city and financially one of the most successful black businesses in the country.[14]

Diggs's activism and political career began in the 1920s when he was a member of the Republican Party and the Detroit chapter of Marcus Garvey's United Negro Improvement Association (UNIA). Diggs's funeral establishment affirmed the principles of Garvey's black nationalist economic agenda, yet the young entrepreneur eventually left the UNIA to pursue more traditional avenues to political power. In 1930 he ran his first campaign for the Detroit Common Council and, though his bid was unsuccessful, he continued to pursue elected office. When Franklin Roosevelt was elected in 1932, Diggs transferred his allegiance to the Democratic Party. A coalition of blacks, white ethnics, liberal Democrats, and labor organizers supported his 1936 campaign for the Michigan state senate, which marked a new era of progressive black politics in Detroit.[15]

During the 1936 election Charles Diggs Sr. specifically enlisted the help of other black business owners and his colleagues at the BTWTA. Berry Gordy Sr., who owned his own carpentry and plastering business, volunteered to canvass votes when he met Diggs while completing a construction job for the House of Diggs Funeral Home. On election day Gordy drove voters to the polling booths and encouraged them to cast their vote for "old man Senior Diggs." Gordy believed that blacks needed political representation and that "if you get good people in office, then you don't have to worry 'bout gettin' justice." Charles Diggs Sr.'s bid for the state senate inspired Berry Gordy Sr., who admired both Diggs's progressive political agenda and his rise to prominence in Detroit's black business community. When Berry Gordy Sr. participated in the Diggs campaign, he contributed to the political agenda and spirit of cooperation inherent in the philosophy of black economic self-help. Collectively, black business owners in Detroit were a powerful force that challenged political institutions to be responsive to the needs of black constituents. Gordy, by canvassing for Diggs, contributed to and identified with the young politician's journey from a modest southern upbringing to the position of a distinguished leader in Detroit's black community—a biography that strongly paralleled Gordy's own.[16]

"Big Dogs"

Berry Gordy Sr., like Diggs, migrated to Detroit from the South. He arrived nine years later, in 1922, and hailed from Sandersville, Georgia.[17] While most African Americans migrated to Detroit from the South in search of economic betterment, Berry Sr. left Georgia because the Gordy family business in Sandersville had become too profitable in the eyes of the white citizens of Oconee County.

Berry Gordy Sr. learned his business skills from his father, also named Berry, who had been enslaved throughout his childhood. After emancipation, the elder Gordy was determined to be economically independent from white landowners and, since he was both literate and numerate, persevered in his quest for self-sufficiency. Gordy kept meticulous records and saved all of his business receipts. After much conscientious bookkeeping and saving during the 1890s, Gordy purchased 168 acres of land and ran his own farm. The Gordy plantation cultivated cotton, corn, potatoes, sugarcane, and fruit orchards and consistently reaped profits. The family's success earned them the nickname "big dogs" throughout their rural community.[18]

On May 31, 1913, a lightning bolt struck and killed the elder Gordy while he was walking the fields of his farm. The sudden death shattered the Gordy family. His son, also known as "Little Berry," was with his father when the accident occurred and immediately assumed his father's responsibilities. The young Berry Gordy, only twenty-five years old at the time, undertook the duty of administering his father's estate. Whites often acted as administrators over the estates of black landowners in the South in order to procure the newly available real estate. Berry Gordy, in accordance with his father's philosophy of self-reliance, took it upon himself to study law books and learn all of the legal intricacies of the administrator's role. Most important of these rules, Gordy "knew when to sign administrator and when not to sign administrator behind my name." Learning this distinction kept the family from losing the farm to creditors. Whenever the family needed a loan or decided to purchase anything for the business, Gordy always signed the bills in his own name, rather than as administrator for the estate. The astute young man knew that signing debts over to the estate turned the land into collateral to white creditors and risked the independence his late father had fought so hard to achieve.[19]

Berry Gordy, eventually known as "Pop," drew upon the experiences of his youth when he began his own family and chose his own life's work. In 1918 Gordy married Bertha Ida Fuller, a local schoolteacher originally from Milledgeville, Georgia, whose professional status matched the Gordy family's prestige within their community. Pop Gordy, wary of the uncertainties of farming, moved away from his father's work in agriculture and decided to concentrate on food distribution. On Saturday afternoons, payday for most blacks in the Sandersville area, Gordy sold fresh beef from a meat wagon and prided himself on outselling all of his competition.

ident that "even the president of the United States got to eat to live," Gordy soon hoped to branch out beyond meats and open a full-fledged market. In 1922 the industrious merchant sold a packet of timber stumps from his mother's land for $2,600. Gordy was well aware that the financial windfall could generate destructive envy in his white neighbors and abruptly set out for Detroit, temporarily leaving behind his wife and their three children.

The city's entrepreneurial possibilities captivated Gordy as soon as he arrived. As he would later recall, "I got up there in Detroit and I saw how things was. I saw a lotta people makin' money. But I wasn't makin' money! I just kept lookin' 'round to make money. But I liked it so well; I knew if other people were makin' good money, I was gonna be able to make some." Gordy's quest for financial security began in earnest one month later, when Bertha and the children joined him in the Motor City.[20]

In their early months in Detroit the Gordy family experienced the mishaps of other southern migrants acclimating themselves to life in the urban North. In his first attempt at employment, Gordy was hired as a blacksmith at Michigan Central with the enticing pay of seventy cents an hour. The job quickly turned sour, however, when Gordy realized he had been hired as a scab and narrowly escaped being beaten up by striking workers.

Real estate agents also duped the earnest, somewhat naive Gordy in his attempts to find housing for his growing family. For their first few months in the city, Berry, Bertha, and the children roomed at his brother's house on the East Side, but they soon were looking for their own place on the West Side, which they had been told was "the best side of town for colored people." Gordy, who was anxious to move into the neighborhood, became an easy mark for a conniving real estate agent by the name of Singleton. Mr. Singleton rushed the eager Gordy over to a house at 5419 Roosevelt, the interiors of which he had covered with new wallpaper and paint. Singleton used the classic ploy that another buyer was ready to bid on the property and convinced Gordy to put down $250—the only money he had left from his share of the family's $2,600 check from the lumber sale. Gordy realized his mistake soon after the purchase when the fresh wallpaper peeled off and revealed a building that suffered from severe internal decay. A city inspector subsequently declared the structure condemned.[21]

Gordy, frustrated but undaunted by these setbacks, quickly learned how to outwit the legerdemains of urban life and began to pursue his goal of economic independence in earnest. He, unlike most southern migrants looking for work in Detroit, resisted the enticements of the Ford Motor Company's employment office. The monotony of assembly-line work and the dependence of the autoworker on the whims of a large corporation held no allure. When Gordy realized that plasterers earned high wages, he decided to master this craft. He bungled early attempts to get hired as a plasterer when trained contractors recognized his lack of experience. After an apprenticeship, however, Gordy became a skilled and well-paid plasterer and saved his earnings to start his own business. By 1924 he had accumulated enough capital to establish the plastering and carpentry business that would eventually introduce him to Charles C. Diggs Sr. and allow him to open—at long last—his own grocery store.[22]

The Booker T. Washington Grocery Store, located on the city's East Side near the intersection of Farnsworth and St. Antoine Streets, quickly became an important fixture in the black working-class neighborhood of which it was a part. In Gordy's own words, "We had the nicest store of any colored anywhere in the city. Nicer than a lotta white folks'." In his autobiography Berry Gordy Jr. recalled that "[w]e were the only colored people in the neighborhood who owned a commercial building, and for the first time people looked up to us." To Pop Gordy, the Booker T. Washington Grocery Store was both a business and a living testament to its namesake's philosophy that hard, and often menial, work were the stepping stones to financial success.[23]

As proprietors and parents, Pop and Bertha Gordy instilled these ideals in their eight children, who all worked in the market. As Pop later recalled, "We started 'em workin' there when they couldn't see over the counter! You could go in there and see the little children there makin' change." The Gordy family work ethic knew no gender restrictions either. Mom and Pop Gordy encouraged all of the children—Esther, Fuller, George, Loucye, Gwendolyn, Anna, Berry Jr., and Robert—to be industrious and develop their own business ventures.[24]

In the Gordy marriage, Bertha Fuller Gordy was as ambitious and driven as her husband. Her work ethic affirmed that the business world was never an exclusively male domain. A former schoolteacher, Bertha Gordy pursued formal education throughout her life to enhance her business skills. She studied retail management at Wayne State University, took courses at the University of Michigan, and graduated from the Detroit Institute of Commerce. Bertha Gordy also frequently held down additional jobs in conjunction with her work at the family's Booker T. Washington Grocery Store. Over the years, she worked for the Briggs Manufacturing Company and was an agent for the Western Mutual Insurance Company. With such an impressive résumé, Bertha Gordy received many invitations to speak before Fannie Peck's Housewives League, of which she was a founding member.[25]

Throughout her business career Bertha Gordy achieved a balance between the pursuit of profits and a commitment to serving one's own community. In 1937 she assumed a leadership position in the Paradise Valley Consumers Association as a member of its public relations committee. In 1945 she founded the Friendship Mutual Insurance Company with her brother, Burton A. Fuller, and acted as secretary-treasurer. The Friendship Mutual Insurance Company was one of the many insurance companies established in Detroit to address the needs of the city's black community. Bertha Gordy was also active in social organizations such as the Elks and church work. In 1959 she helped found the Friends Club, a small philanthropic organization that raised money for the Congress for Racial Equality, the NAACP, and the Freedom Fighters in Mississippi. Like her husband, Bertha Gordy understood the interconnections between success in the business world and political empowerment and often campaigned for Democratic candidates.[26]

With both of their parents serving equally as role models, the Gordy children grew up eager to fulfill the family's high standards of achievement. The Gordy family's accomplishments were so extensive that in June 1949 *Color Magazine* featured them in an article entitled "America's Most Amazing Family: The Famous Gordys of Detroit Have What It Takes." The article recounted not only the family's business skills but their talents in a wide range of hobbies including bowling, horseback riding, and music. For *Color Magazine* readers, the Gordy family exemplified the dream of black middle-class success, as the parents' hard work had provided the children with the opportunity to explore leisure activities and personal interests. As the Gordy siblings advanced into young adulthood, their goals and accomplishments diversified. The older children, Esther, George, and Fuller, most assiduously emulated their parents' business practices. George and Fuller worked in the plastering and carpentry business and, with their sister Esther, founded the Gordy Printing Company. Loucye Gordy used her business and organizational skills to become the first woman civilian to be assistant property officer at the Michigan and Indiana Army Reserves at Fort Wayne.[27] The younger siblings, Gwendolyn, Anna, Berry Jr., and Robert, were also ambitious, but they did not always pursue the traditional family business ventures of printing, insurance, or grocery retail. Of all the children, Berry Jr., who had a passion for boxing and music, appeared the least interested in following in his parent's footsteps and establishing himself as a small business owner. Ironically, of course, Berry Jr. capitalized on his personal interest in music to become the most successful businessperson in the Gordy family. It was an achievement that would one day fulfill the highest hopes of the Booker T. Washington Trade Association and Detroit's entire black business community.

"Got a Job": The Motown "Miracle" of "Negro" Business

The Booker T. Washington Trade Association held its thirty-fifth anniversary banquet on Friday, July 15, 1965, in the city's Latin Quarter.[28] The keynote speaker for the evening was Dr. Andrew F. Brimmer, assistant secretary for economic affairs in the U.S. Department of Commerce. In his speech Brimmer proclaimed that the erosion of racial segregation was weakening the strength of the Negro middle class. The *Michigan Chronicle* reported that some audience members were dismayed with the noted economist's argument that "segregated facilities and neighborhoods have been the best things that ever happened to a lot of Negro businessmen and professionals, but they can't depend on segregation any longer. And most of them aren't prepared to change."[29]

One audience member, Berry Gordy Jr., had prepared for the change, however, and was one of the evening's honorees as the recipient of the BTWTA's business achievement award. An ideal choice for the award, Gordy's career bridged the past glory of "Negro" business in Detroit, which his parents helped to establish, with the present imperatives to market one's wares to an integrated public. Gordy's Motown Record Company, a multimillion dollar enterprise by 1965, could attribute its unprecedented success to creating a product—black popular music—that sold to a multiracial audience of consumers. Son of a founding member, Berry Gordy Jr. displayed a business savvy that was a particular emblem of pride at the Booker T. Washington Trade Association's celebration.[30]

Berry Jr.'s entrepreneurial talents were not self-evident in his youth and young adulthood. He did work in the family store and often earned extra cash shining shoes, but his dream was to be a championship boxer. Although Berry Jr.'s boxing career diverged from the traditional Gordy family business interests, it did correspond to the imperative behind any Gordy business enterprise: the pursuit of financial wealth. Gordy personally struggled with his finances throughout his young adulthood, and the allure of quick riches through boxing held particular appeal to him as it would any man without economic security.[31]

Evidence of Gordy's financial instability can be gleaned from his own autobiography and from those who knew him during these early years. In his book, *To Be Loved*, Gordy recalls in detail his years of "hustling like mad" between odd jobs to pursue his interests in boxing and songwriting. His eventual decision to start his own record label produced some anxiety when he realized that "I was twenty-nine years old and hadn't made any money yet." Gordy's second wife, Raynoma Gordy Singleton, recalled in her memoir that her most vivid memory of meeting Berry Gordy was his "ugly brown-striped shirt with both elbows worn completely through" and the eventual realization that this man had "no car, no clothes, and no money." Smokey Robinson also recounted his first impression of Gordy as "a street dude, short and plainly dressed."[32]

Gordy, like many black men in the Motor City who aspired to be boxers, had a powerful role model in Detroit's own Joe Louis. Throughout the 1930s and 1940s "the Brown Bomber" glamorized boxing as an acceptable means for African American men to achieve riches and international fame. Louis secured most of his wealth from his bouts in the ring, but he also used his celebrity to make money in endorsements and public appearances. Louis's achievements proved that boxing was more than a sport—it could also provide financial security and advance race pride. One of Detroit's most famous rhythm and blues artists, Jackie Wilson, also, like Gordy, pursued a boxing career in his youth. At the age of sixteen, Wilson won his first Golden Gloves championship.[33]

Gordy exhibited an early talent for the sport and actively competed throughout his adolescence. Five feet, six inches tall and weighing only 112 pounds, he began his boxing career as a flyweight, though he eventually had fifteen fights as a Golden Gloves featherweight. He quit Northeastern High School when he was just sixteen to turn professional. The professional boxing circuit proved more difficult and physically taxing than he had imagined, however, and he gave up the sport after winning his last bout over Joe Nelson at Detroit's Olympia in 1950.[34]

Berry Gordy in front of Hitsville, U.S.A., circa 1965. (Courtesy Motown Record Co., L.P., a Polygram Company.)

After his boxing career, Gordy entered the army for a two-year period from 1951 to 1953, which included a brief tour in Korea. When he returned to Detroit, he met and married his first wife, Thelma Louise Coleman, with whom he had two children, Hazel Joy and Berry IV. Settling down with his own family at the age of twenty-four forced Gordy to evaluate his career options and decide what vocation would best support his wife and children. Gordy had a favorite story he loved to tell people when asked about his decision to enter the music business. He recalled staring at a pillar in the Woodward Avenue Gym with two posters hanging on it after a particularly hard day of boxing practice. One poster promoted an upcoming bout between two fighters who wore all the scars of their battles in the ring. The other poster advertised a "Battle of the Bands" between Duke Ellington and Stan Kenton. The entertainers' elegance and polish dazzled him. According to Gordy, "the fighters were about twenty-three and looked fifty; the band leaders about fifty and looked twenty-three." The glamour of the music world prompted Gordy to abandon his boxing career for good.[35]

Gordy opened his own record store in his first attempt to break into the music business. In 1953 the young entrepreneur used his army discharge pay and a family loan to open the 3-D Record Mart, a store that specialized in jazz recordings. The business endeavor grew out of Gordy's enthusiasm for music he characterized as the "only pure art form."[36] Detroit's jazz scene burgeoned throughout the fifties in clubs such as the Minor Key, Baker's Keyboard Lounge, the West Inn, and Club Twenty-one. Gordy frequented these nightspots, which drew the talents of Yusef Lateef, Kenny Burrell, Elvin Jones, John Coltrane, and Charlie Parker, among others. His idea of selling the recordings of these artists seemed like an infallible plan. In an interview, Gordy explained why the plan ultimately failed: "I loved jazz—Stan Kenton, Thelonius Monk, Charlie Parker—and I wanted to let people know I was modern, so I called the place the 3-D Record Mart. People started coming in and asking for things like Fats Domino. Pretty soon I was asking, 'Who is this Fats Domino? What is this rhythm-and-blues stuff?' I listened and ordered a few records by these people and sold them. Still all my capital was tied up in jazz, but jazz didn't have the facts, the beat. I went bankrupt."[37] The local public's lack of interest in jazz recordings drove the 3-D Record

Mart out of business. The business failure eventually forced Gordy onto the assembly line at Ford's Wayne Assembly Plant. By the fall of 1955 he was earning $86.40 a week working as an upholstery trimmer on Lincoln-Mercury sedans.

The monotony of the assembly line inspired Gordy's next foray into the music business. He decided to shift from the distribution end of the industry as a record store owner to the production side as a songwriter. As Gordy later recalled, "I originated a lot of songs in my mind while I was working. They consoled me and helped me forget I was doing the same thing every day: move this, move that." When Gordy finally left Ford, he decided to pursue songwriting in earnest. His songwriting talents had been discovered in adolescence when he won honorable mention in a local talent show for his composition "Berry's Boogie." And his career change received enormous support from his sisters Anna and Gwen, who had opened up a photography and cigarette concession at the popular Flame Show Bar. The Flame Show Bar was a key meeting place for the city's black musical talents and was known for featuring top-name acts including Dinah Washington and Detroit native Della Reese. Anna and Gwen Gordy, gregarious and savvy, promoted their brother's songwriting talents to the musicians and artists whom they met at the club.[38]

The contacts Berry Gordy made at the Flame Show Bar launched his songwriting career. In 1957 Gordy met Al Greene, a local talent agent who was managing the career of "Mr. Excitement" Jackie Wilson. Shortly thereafter, Gordy convinced Greene and his associate, Nat Tarnopol, to have Wilson record the song "Reet Petite," which Gordy had written in collaboration with his sister Gwen and her boyfriend, Billy Davis—also known as Tyran Carlo. In the autumn of 1957 "Reet Petite" climbed the charts, and Gordy had his first hit. From 1957 through 1959 Gordy continued to compose with his sister and Davis, and the collaboration produced more hits for Wilson, including "To Be Loved," "I'll Be Satisfied," "That's Why (I Love You So)," and "Lonely Teardrops." The success of these tunes bolstered Gordy's confidence as a songwriter, but the limited royalties he received prompted him to seek more control over record producing. Like his father and grandfather, Berry Gordy craved financial independence and resisted job situations that left him feeling powerless.

From 1957 to 1958 Berry Gordy Jr. made several friendships that were integral to his evolution from songwriter to independent record producer. In August 1957 Gordy was auditioning acts for Jackie Wilson's show with his manager Nat Tarnopol and musical arranger Alonzo Tucker. One young group, the Matadors, consisted of four men and one woman— a gender composition similar to that of the Platters, one of the most popular singing groups at the time. Tucker dismissed the group, convinced that the Matadors could never outshine the more famous Platters. Berry Gordy was impressed, however, that the singers had performed all of their own material, and he followed them out the door to find out who was doing the composing. William "Smokey" Robinson, leader of the group, presented Gordy with his school notebook—filled with over a hundred songs.[39]

Intrigued by Robinson's talent, Gordy offered to manage the group, which included Ronnie White, Pete Moore, Bobby Rogers, and his cousin Claudette Rogers. Initially, Claudette had been singing with the Matadors' sister group, the Matadorettes, and her brother, Emerson "Sonny" Rogers, sang with the Matadors. When Emerson left the Matadors to enter the army, Robinson, who had been dating Claudette, decided his talented girlfriend's voice would be an ideal replacement. When Berry Gordy began to manage the group, he decided that the "Matadors" was an inappropriate name for a gender-integrated group and renamed the act the Miracles. With the newly rechristened group, Gordy secured his first act, and the Motown musical tradition began.

By November 1957, only four months after their initial meeting, Smokey Robinson and Berry Gordy were collaborating on the Miracles' first hit, "Got a Job." An "answer song" to the Silhouettes' hit single "Get a Job," the Miracles' "Got a Job," written by Robinson and produced by Gordy, was released on the New York–based End Records label. The song's lyrics capitalize on an edgy humor about the mundane realities of wage labor for any young black male. The song's protagonist secures a job at a local grocery store only to find himself hounded by his boss. The boss quickly tells his new hire to "get that mop and clean the dirty floor / And when you've finished, wash the windows and the doors." The tasks are also given with a stern warning, "do the job or I'll get a replacement." While the protagonist worries that his boss is "gonna drive me insane,"

The Miracles, circa 1962. (Courtesy Motown Record Co., L.P., a Polygram Company.)

he also vows that he will "never, never quit my brand new job." The song emphasizes both the drudgery and necessity of common labor.

The struggle of the song's protagonist must have resonated with Gordy and Robinson, who both felt trapped in an economically dependent relationship with the End Records label. "Got a Job" never achieved the popularity of the Silhouettes' original tune, but the single did make its mark on the record charts and received strong airplay in Detroit. The Miracles proceeded to cut another release with End Records and after recording four songs on the label received a royalty check of $3.19.

Discouraged yet again by the paltry earnings of songwriters, Gordy, with the encouragement of Robinson, started plans to found his own independent record label.[40]

In the spring of 1958 Gordy met another person who was crucial to the formation and development of Motown Records: Raynoma Mayberry Liles. Liles, a trained musician and singer, won a Monday night talent show at the popular Twenty Grand nightclub singing with her sister Alice. The club management encouraged Raynoma and her sister to contact Gordy, who—given his recent work with the Miracles and young singers such as Marv Johnson—was developing a promising reputation as a manager. After a brief audition, Gordy recognized Raynoma's impressive range of musical talent and invited her to work with some of his acts as an arranger and musician. Soon, Liles and Gordy decided to formalize their partnership and founded the Rayber Music Writing Company. The company's name was a combination of their first names and signified the merger of their two talents: Gordy's songwriting and business expertise with Liles's gifted musicianship.[41]

The Rayber Music Writing Company targeted aspiring artists and singing groups who had hopes of recording a song and needed a facilitator to polish, record, and promote their work. Clients supplied their own material: lyrics, a melody, or their own singing voice; and Gordy and Liles worked together to add whatever dimensions of the song were needed: musical arrangement, lyrical hooks, or instrumental backup. Then the Rayber Company recorded the song and helped publicize it. The total charge for their services was $100 paid in installments if necessary.

By the autumn of 1958 the Rayber Company had developed its first major release, Marv Johnson's "Come to Me," for national distribution on the United Artists record label. To finance the initial production costs, Gordy and Liles applied for an $800 loan from the Gordy family co-op, Ber-Berry. According to Liles, "Ber-Berry had been established for the purpose of purchasing real estate. Every week each family member deposited ten dollars into the fund; weekly business meetings were held with minutes, an agenda, and discussions of items that sometimes went to a vote." At first, Gordy's family was skeptical about his plans but finally agreed to provide the loan. With the Ber-Berry loan, Gordy and Liles quickly completed the production of "Come to Me." United Artists offered $3,000 for the national rights to the record and allowed the Rayber Company to retain the local distribution rights.[42]

United Artist's concession of the song's local distribution rights inaugurated the first stages of what was to become the Motown record label. In January 1959 Gordy released the local version of "Come to Me" on his own Tamla label. The "Tamla" name was a slight variation on "Tammy," which had already been registered to someone else. Gordy hoped the name would capitalize on the popularity of the Debbie Reynolds's 1958 hit song "Tammy" from the movie of the same name. The musical style of "Come to Me" foreshadowed the Motown sound. The studio band that performed on the record included Benny Benjamin on drums; James Jamerson on bass; Thomas "Beans" Bowles on saxophone; Eddie Willis and Joe Messina on guitar; and Robert Bateman, Brian Holland, and Raynoma Liles as the Rayber Voices backup vocalists. Also, in the makeshift style of early Motown recordings, Gordy and Liles cut "Come to Me" at the Rayber recording studio at 1719 Gladstone Street, a two-family dwelling in which they used a closet as a sound booth and a bathroom as an echo chamber.[43]

By the summer of 1959 the limited space on Gladstone Street was cramping the creative energy of the Tamla staff, and the company relocated to another converted house at 2648 West Grand Boulevard. Immediately dubbed "Hitsville, U.S.A.," the new location quickly lived up to its nickname when the company produced Barrett Strong's infectious song "Money (That's What I Want)" only two weeks after moving into the building. The song's urgent beat, bluesy piano riffs, and avaricious lyrics captured the ambition of the young company and its owner and embraced an optimism quite different from the tone of "Got a Job." Gordy and Motown staffer Janie Bradford wrote "Money" in a spontaneous moment. As Gordy recalled,

> I began to play some of the chords to my song, telling her [Bradford] how as a young kid I'd heard people say, *"The best things in life are free,"* but knowing how much easier that was to say when you had money I sarcastically added, *"But you can give them to the birds and bees, I need money . . ."* She laughed. I loved the

fact that she laughed so I rushed into the next verse singing the song as I played—*"Money don't get everything it's true, but what it don't get I can't use, I need money."* . . . Janie was ecstatic. Still laughing, she offhandedly threw in her own line—*"Your money gives me such a thrill, but your love don't pay my bills, gimme some money, baby."*[44]

Gordy released the record nationally on the Anna Records label, which was another example of the reciprocity among Gordy family business ventures. Gordy's sister Gwen and Billy Davis—his earlier song-writing collaborators—owned the label and named it after Gordy's other sister Anna. Locally, Gordy released "Money (That's What I Want)" on his own Tamla label. The song reached number two on *Billboard's* rhythm and blues chart, and the profits from the record soon fulfilled the lyrics' plea for the financially struggling company. With the success of "Money" Berry Gordy Jr. began his own entrepreneurial legend and, in essence, paid homage to his father's early ambitions. The song resonates with the sentiments of Pop Gordy's impressions of his first days in Detroit: "I knew if other people were makin' good money, I was gonna be able to make some."

"Buy-In": Black Business and Black Freedom

Berry Gordy Jr.'s early success in record producing upheld his family's business ethic and the self-help ideals of Booker T. Washington. As the Motown Record Company began to grow in its early years from 1958 to 1963, Hitsville, U.S.A., became both a personal achievement for the family and a public contribution to the black community in Detroit, much like Pop Gordy's Booker T. Washington Grocery Store had been during the 1930s and early 1940s. The Motown Record Company became a particular symbol of pride within the black business community in Detroit because its product—captivating rhythm and blues music—emerged from the city's unique black cultural and musical traditions. Whether it was a street corner, a gospel choir, a blues club, or a high school music class, the culturally rich environment of Detroit's black neighborhoods nurtured the artists and musicians who came to define the Motown sound. Since the Motown Record Company combined black entrepreneurial

achievement with a culturally resonant product, it was destin
a vibrant and contested symbol of African American accomplism..
Detroit—along with the rest of the country—confronted the racial politics
of the early civil rights years.

These connections between Motown's success and the larger civil
rights campaign were most evident when the record company recorded
Martin Luther King Jr.'s speech at the Great March to Freedom. Yet the
Great March album was not Berry Gordy Jr.'s first attempt at producing
a political recording. In 1957 he followed his father's example of supporting local black politicians like Charles Diggs Sr. by donating his
songwriting and record producing talents to a political campaign. Gordy
wrote the campaign song "By George, Let George Do It" for his brother-
in-law, George H. Edwards, who was running for the Michigan state leg-
islature. He persuaded Jackie Wilson to record the song and then got
local disc jockeys to play it on Detroit radio stations. The *Great March*
and the George Edwards recordings were Gordy's first overt efforts to
support political causes.[45]

While less overt, the Motown Record Company's status as a successful "Negro" business carried its own political weight. Soon after the
Great March to Freedom, the role of the "Negro" in Detroit's local economy became a rallying point for civil rights demonstrations staged
throughout the city. Local activists organized demonstrations to increase
employment opportunities for African Americans in white-owned businesses and to encourage the establishment of more black-owned businesses. These protests and picket lines, which occurred throughout the
city, were not far removed—physically and historically—from the Motown Record Company on West Grand Boulevard.

Only a few days after the Great March local civil rights activists
organized a picket line to boycott a Kroger Supermarket located near
Motown Studios. Luke Tripp, head of the student group UHURU, led the
peaceful marchers, who were drawing attention to the supermarket's discrimination against blacks when hiring for management positions. The
boycott also included members of the CORE and the DCHR, and the
unified effort led to a rapid resolution. Within two weeks, Kroger reached
an agreement with the protesters. The company implemented an active
nondiscriminatory employment policy that included the immediate hiring

of two African American management trainees. One week after the Kroger settlement, the A & P Grocery Store chain also pledged to increase minority hiring in an effort to end a seven-week selective buying campaign against their stores. Organized by the Negro Preachers of Detroit and Vicinity, the successful boycott of A & P—along with the Kroger campaign—confirmed that African Americans could combat employment discrimination through "selective patronage." Black consumers could choose where they spent their money, and these choices could contribute to the end of discriminatory practices.[46]

Selective patronage could also support black enterprise. One week after the Kroger case was settled, U.S. Representative Charles C. Diggs Jr., son of the former Michigan state senator, spearheaded a "buy-in" campaign at the local Community Supermarket at the intersection of Roosevelt and Myrtle Streets. A group of black business leaders had purchased the supermarket as a proactive approach to generate economic development in the city's black neighborhoods. Diggs rallied local leaders and civil rights groups to patronize the store in a show of support. Organizations including the DCHR, the NAACP, and the Nation of Islam's Mosque Number One joined with representatives from the Trade Union Leadership Council (TULC), the Cotillion Club, the Shriners, and the Housewives League to publicize and participate in the buy-in. Such broad-based support ensured the campaign's success. Record numbers of patrons crowded the store in just a few days, overwhelming the staff and management.[47]

Charles C. Diggs Jr.'s "buy-in" campaign for the community supermarket was not simply derivative of other contemporary civil rights demonstrations; it was an event embedded in the history and politics of black economic self-help in Detroit. Charles Diggs Jr., who was both a business owner and a politician, was an exemplary choice to coordinate the campaign. His role as organizer of the event illustrated the generational legacy of his father's business achievements and political success in the Michigan state senate. The HWLD's and the BTWTA's participation in the campaign also had historical significance. When the two organizations promoted the cause, they lent support to a strategy of economic alliance their organizations and founding members—which included Charles

Diggs Sr., Berry Gordy Sr., and Bertha Gordy—had initiated in Detroit. Finally, the decision to organize the campaign around a community supermarket recalled another era in which small stores—like the Gordy family's Booker T. Washington Grocery Store—served the city's black neighborhoods by providing goods and services to African American consumers and, most importantly, by confirming the power of black economic independence.

The goal of black economic independence and racial solidarity motivated much of the civil rights activism in Detroit during the autumn of 1963. The success of the boycotts and picket lines that fought to end employment discrimination inspired community activists like the Reverend Albert B. Cleage Jr. to begin organizing for black political enfranchisement. In October 1963 Cleage sponsored the first rally for the Freedom Now Party, which precipitated his break with C. L. Franklin and the Detroit Council for Human Rights. After his departure from the DCHR, Cleage, along with James Boggs, Grace Lee Boggs, Milton Henry, and Richard Henry—his compatriots in the Group on Advanced Leadership—decided to sponsor the Northern Negro Grass Roots Leadership Conference.

The agenda of the Grass Roots Conference illustrated the degree to which these activists were focused on economic and political goals. The conference platform included a boycott against a Cadillac Motor Dealer in Cleveland, Ohio; a general Christmas boycott of local merchants who discriminated against African Americans; and the endorsement of the Freedom Now Party. Conference organizers believed that Malcolm X's keynote speech would act as the perfect finale to the conference. Malcolm X's arguments for black revolution offered a dramatic counterpoint to Martin Luther King Jr.'s integrationist philosophy, yet the essence of Malcolm X's philosophy would not be "new" to his Detroit audience. Malcolm X's black nationalist arguments, like Charles Diggs Jr.'s political success in the U.S. Congress and Berry Gordy Jr.'s business accomplishments at the Motown Record Company, derived from a common generational legacy.[48]

These lineages illustrate how an earlier generation of Detroit's black self-help leaders produced much more than economic gain for the city's black community. They were ultimately responsible for a wide range of religious, political, and economic movements that attempted to improve conditions for African Americans in the Motor City. One genealogy of black nationalism began, as did the Gordy family history, in Sandersville, Georgia, and in the life of Elijah Muhammad (then known as Elijah Poole).

From Sandersville to King Solomon Baptist Church

In 1923, one year after Berry Gordy Sr. migrated to Detroit from Sandersville, Georgia, Elijah Poole, also a native of Sandersville, left Georgia to seek a new life in the Motor City.[49] Poole, son of a Baptist preacher of modest means, fit the standard description of an African American migrant moving north. Married with two children, Poole had been working in Macon, Georgia, for the Southern Railroad Company and the Cherokee Brick Company when he decided to move his family to Detroit in hopes of better economic opportunities. Unlike Gordy, who resisted factory work, Poole quickly sought employment at the American Copper and Brass Company. In 1925 Poole took a job on the assembly line at the Chevrolet Gear and Axle Plant where he worked until he was laid off in late 1926.[50]

The circumstances surrounding Poole's dismissal from Chevrolet were unclear, although Poole's membership in the Detroit chapter of Garvey's UNIA may have prompted the layoff. Garvey, a disciple of Booker T. Washington's advocacy for black capitalism, hoped that the UNIA could fully implement Washington's ideas as well as his own Pan-Africanist philosophy. The UNIA's Black Star Steamship Line, founded in 1919 in New York, generated national attention as a prominent company solely owned and operated by African Americans. The Black Star line combined two of Garvey's main objectives: empowering blacks through capitalism and creating a business that literally transported blacks to Africa. In his newspaper, *Negro World,* Garvey ran advertisements that encouraged potential stockholders to participate in "a direct line of steamships, owned, controlled, and manned by Negroes to reach the Negro peoples of the world." Not surprisingly, Garvey christened one of his ships the *Booker T. Washington.*[51]

Garvey's philosophy of economic self-determination enticed new members across the country including Elijah Poole. Poole received early training on the importance of black economic autonomy through this formative experience and met a network of fellow UNIA activists including Charles Diggs Sr. John Charles Zampty, former Detroit UNIA leader, commented on Poole's tenure in the Detroit UNIA: "I have to give credit to Elijah Poole of the Nation of Islam. He was a good member of the UNIA and worked with us for many years . . . [he] was wise enough in arousing Black people . . . to recognize that they must do something economic for their race, and that since they are Black Muslims, then they must work for Black people."[52]

In 1930, however, Poole left the UNIA when he met W. D. Fard, a peddler who walked the streets of Paradise Valley selling silks and wares. A merchant as well of black salvation through faith in the Nation of Islam, Fard (also known as "the Prophet") had begun to acquire a large following in Detroit's black working-class neighborhoods. Fard's religious message, which denounced whites and glorified blacks, attracted Poole. He had pursued odd jobs for three years after his release from Chevrolet and had become despondent about his employment status. Poole, like many other desperate black southern migrants looking for work, was searching for personal affirmation. In an early study of the Nation of Islam in Detroit, sociologist E. D. Beynon determined that almost all converts to the religion "were recent migrants from the rural South" who had recently "suffered their first experience of urban destitution" when they joined the organization.[53]

W. D. Fard's religion lured converts with its evocations of Mecca—a promised land far from the unforgiving urban terrain of Detroit; its critiques of oppressive white power structures; and its emphasis on black pride. Fard would introduce himself by stating, "My name is W. D. Fard and I came from the Holy City of Mecca. More about myself I will not tell you yet, for the time has not yet come. I am your brother. You have not yet seen me in my royal robes." Historian Robert Conot has argued that the "mysterious" Fard perhaps worked at the Ford Motor Company; he was familiar with Henry Ford's personal philosophies and seems to have capitalized on Ford's name by changing his name from Wali Farrad to W. D. Fard. Henry Ford believed that eating habits should be a part of religion, argued against alcohol and smoking, and was anti-Semitic. Fard included these principles when he founded the Nation of Islam.[54]

Fard preached that conversion to Black Muslim faith restored individuals to their true selves and symbolized this transformation by giving all new disciples a new name. Fard first christened Elijah Poole as Elijah Karriem but then renamed him Elijah Muhammad. The "Muhammad" surname signified Elijah's devotion to the faith and his promotion by Fard to the first chief minister of Islam.[55]

In conjunction with Elijah Muhammad's leadership appointment, Fard's burgeoning religion began to take on other formal characteristics. Initially, Fard conducted all religious meetings in private homes. By 1931, responding to popular demand for a permanent site of worship, Fard had founded his first temple, the Mosque Number One, in a storefront at 1470 Frederick Street on Detroit's East Side.[56] In 1932 Fard decided to expand the Black Muslim movement outside Detroit and sent Muhammad to Chicago to found Temple Number Two on the city's South Side. Fard remained in Detroit, although his leadership was weakened when the Detroit Police Department began investigating the organization after charges emerged that the sect practiced human sacrifice. By June 1934 Fard had vanished as mysteriously as he had arrived in the city. At the time of his disappearance, Elijah Muhammad deified Fard and began referring to him as Allah. Muhammad then designated himself the new Prophet and decided to leave Detroit. He moved to Chicago and declared the Chicago Temple Number Two the new headquarters of the movement.[57]

Under Elijah Muhammad's leadership, the Nation of Islam grew into an elaborate, multifaceted organization. True to its separatist doctrine, it founded its own educational system, the University of Islam; its own newspaper, *Mr. Muhammad Speaks;* and its own self-defense group, the Fruit of Islam. In terms of economic philosophy, the Black Muslims' business practices emulated the ideals of Booker T. Washington and Marcus Garvey. Muhammad encouraged his followers, many of whom were members of the working class, to obtain vocational training and to aspire to independent business ownership. Black Muslim members were expected to contribute 10 percent of their personal earnings to the Nation of Islam to assist in the establishment of independent Muslim businesses.

Such financial backing allowed Nation of Islam members to open restaurants, gas stations, barber shops, clothing stores, and grocery markets. Muhammad also encouraged his followers to patronize any Negro business and to refrain from contributing to the profits of white businesses.[58]

Elijah Muhammad's endorsement of selective patronage for all Negro businesses illustrated one way that the Nation of Islam participated in non-Muslim black activism. While Black Muslims pledged to put the Nation of Islam first in their lives, allegiance to the faith did not preclude their participation in other related campaigns for black empowerment. Detroit Mosque Number One exemplified the Nation of Islam's standard of cooperative activism. During the summer of 1963, this temple actively supported Representative Charles C. Diggs Jr.'s "buy-in" campaign at the Community Supermarket in Detroit.

Wilfred X, the leading minister at Mosque Number One, coordinated the Nation of Islam's efforts to support black activism in Detroit. He recruited supporters for Diggs's buy-in campaign and participated in Albert Cleage's campaign to organize the Freedom Now Party in Detroit. Wilfred X represented Mosque Number One at the first Freedom Now rally held at Cleage's Central Congregational Church, where he gave a speech endorsing the formation of the all-black political party. But Wilfred X's most significant contribution to the Freedom Now campaign was his relationship to his younger brother, Malcolm, who agreed to come speak at the Northern Negro Grass Roots Conference. Wilfred mentored Malcolm during his early years with the Nation of Islam, but by 1963 Malcolm had advanced beyond his brother's leadership position in the faith. His speech at King Solomon Church would be both revolutionary and familiar to his Detroit audience. Listeners were anxious to hear his more radical philosophy but were already well versed in fighting for black economic empowerment—one of Malcolm X's highest priorities.

Malcolm's Message and Motown's Money

Wilfred X's close relationship to his brother made Malcolm X's visit to Detroit for the Grass Roots Conference a personal homecoming. As children, Wilfred and Malcolm learned black nationalism from their father, Earl Little, who was an active member of Garvey's UNIA in Lansing,

Michigan. From his sons' perspective, Earl Little's militancy led to his untimely death in a streetcar accident in Lansing, which many people speculated was a murder by the Black Legion, a local variant of the Ku Klux Klan. As adults, both Malcolm and Wilfred Little found a surrogate father figure in Elijah Muhammad, their father's former colleague in the Michigan UNIA. Wilfred joined Muhammad's movement before his brother. In 1948, while Malcolm was incarcerated for burglary, Wilfred and Malcolm's other siblings, Philbert, Reginald, and Hilda, began to write to their brother about the Nation of Islam and encouraged him to join. Malcolm was the last of his family to convert to the faith, but he soon became one of Muhammad's most devoted followers.[59]

Upon his release from prison in 1952, Malcolm moved to Detroit to live with Wilfred and his family and learn the daily practices of the Black Muslims. Wilfred felt the move would deter his brother from returning to his former life as the streetwise hustler "Detroit Red." As he recalled, "I got [Malcolm] paroled to me because I didn't want him to get loose again in Boston or New York. I had a job for him. I wanted to keep him away from people that were in the rackets, because if he got back out there with them he would be back in it again . . . I was able to hold onto him because I stayed right with him. He worked with me. When he got off work, he had to ride with me because he didn't have a car. I took him straight home." Malcolm's job involved selling furniture at the Cut Rate Department Store, where Wilfred had been working since 1941.[60]

More interested in selling Elijah Muhammad's message than living room sets, Malcolm became an assertive recruiter for the Mosque Number One, on Frederick Street. Membership at the temple tripled within a few months. During this period Malcolm decided to quit working at the furniture store and took a job at Ford on the Lincoln-Mercury assembly line. His tenure at Ford was a brief one—as Berry Gordy Jr.'s would be when he went to work on the same assembly line as an upholster trimmer in 1955. Malcolm quit his job at Ford in June 1953 when Muhammad named him Detroit's Temple Number One assistant minister. In late 1953 Malcolm left Detroit and traveled to Chicago's Temple Number Two. In Chicago he received personal training from Elijah Muhammad and devoted himself solely to his work as a minister of Islam.[61]

Ten years later—in early November 1963—when Malcolm X returned to Detroit to give his "Message to the Grass Roots" speech, his charismatic power as a spokesperson for the Nation of Islam had made him an internationally recognized proponent of black nationalism. His celebrity advanced the cause of the Grass Roots Conference by drawing large crowds and bolstering interest in the Freedom Now Party, but it had begun to erode his relationship with Muhammad, who was increasingly envious of his disciple's growing fame. In his autobiography Malcolm recalled sensing Muhammad's jealousy as early as 1962, when his activities as a minister were no longer covered in the Muslim newspaper *Mr. Muhammad Speaks.* He remarked that "there was more in the Muslim paper about integrationist Negro leaders than there was about me. I could read more about myself in the European, Asian, and African press."[62]

The content of the "Message to the Grass Roots" speech reflected Malcolm's strained relationship with Muhammad and the Nation of Islam. In his opening remarks Malcolm downplayed his allegiance to the Black Muslims as he argued for the importance of building a black unity that transcended religious differences: "What you and I need to do is learn to forget our differences. When we come together, we don't come together as Baptists or Methodists. You don't catch hell because you're a Methodist or a Baptist, you don't catch hell because you're a Mason or an Elk, and you don't catch hell because you are an American; because if you were an American, you wouldn't catch hell. You catch hell because you are a black man. You catch hell, all of us catch hell, for the same reason." Malcolm refrained from couching his statements in Black Muslim dogma throughout the remainder of the talk and spoke instead about his belief in the need for a complete revolution.[63]

By distancing himself from Nation of Islam rhetoric, Malcolm was able to articulate the scope of the black revolution in broader terms. He had, in previous speeches, focused on bloodshed as the defining feature of the revolution. In the "Message to the Grass Roots" he acknowledged that while the revolution could bring bloodshed, it also could involve confronting the American political system through marches and nonviolent protest. In his speech Malcolm commented on the threats of southern politicians to filibuster President Kennedy's Civil Rights Bill. He focused on how some black leaders planned to react: "they were going to march on Washington, march on the Congress, and tie it up, bring it to a halt, not let the government proceed. They even said they were going out to the airport and lay down on the runway and not let any airplanes land. I'm telling you what they said. That was revolution. That was revolution. That was the black revolution."[64] In these remarks he presented a vision of revolution that involved direct, yet nonviolent confrontation with the federal government to demand that the state protect the civil rights of its citizens. His acknowledgment that black revolution could take place through direct engagement with, rather than the violent overthrow of, America's political system affirmed one of the main goals of the Grass Roots Conference: endorsement of the Freedom Now Party.

The primary goal of Detroit's Freedom Now Party was the end of racial and economic inequality through the election of black officials, who would then challenge the existing political order to respond to the needs of black constituents. The party's founders recognized that Freedom Now represented a unique opportunity in contrast to political organizing in the South, where the mere act of registering black voters involved serious physical risk.[65] Freedom Now candidates campaigned in the context of a northern urban political system that did not violently suppress the black vote or bar black candidates from the election process. Given these circumstances, party organizers were able to construct an elaborate platform that addressed constituents' concerns on a wide range of issues. The party sought not only political but also cultural and economic change, and hoped its efforts could close "the widening gulf that exists between Nationalist (separatist) and Integrationist trends among Negroes, particularly in the North."[66] Finding solutions to black economic disenfranchisement in the forms of employment discrimination and de facto housing segregation was a top priority. The party's platform sought to unify the efforts of business organizations, labor unions, and social work organizations such as the Urban League to combat these problems on a broad scale. The Grass Roots Conference acted as Freedom Now's first convention, and Malcolm X's endorsement generated much-needed publicity for the party. It planned to run candidates at the local, state, and national levels during the 1964 election year.[67]

Malcolm X supported Freedom Now's electoral strategies yet continued to maintain that black revolution included the possibility of blood-

shed. Throughout his speech Malcolm ridiculed the effectiveness of recent attempts at nonviolent protest and referred to Detroit's own Great
March to Freedom as a circus, "with clowns leading it, white clowns and
black clowns." These blunt remarks angered some in the audience, but
many of the spectators listened openly to Malcolm X's prescient arguments about the inevitability of violence in any attempt to end America's
racist practices.[68]

The willingness of the Detroit audience to consider alternatives to
King's nonviolent approaches—only three and half months after the
peaceful Great March—reflected the skepticism about civil disobedience
that grew throughout the nation by the autumn of 1963. The Sixteenth
Street Church bombing in Birmingham, Alabama, in September heightened the sense of frustration about nonviolent protest. In his "Message
to the Grass Roots" Malcolm X used the bombing to support his radical
rhetoric: "How can you justify being non-violent in Mississippi and Alabama, when your churches are being bombed, and your little girls are
being murdered?" To many in the audience at King Solomon Church, the
grim logic of his argument rang true—however frightening its consequences. By the end of his speech Malcolm X had articulated an agenda
for black revolution that included efforts such as the Freedom Now Party
as well as the possibility of violence in the name of self-defense.[69]

Malcolm's outspoken opinions about violence came to haunt him
two weeks after his appearance in Detroit. When John F. Kennedy was
assassinated on November 22, 1963, Malcolm remarked that the shooting
was an example of the "chickens come home to roost." The national press
quickly publicized the comment, and Elijah Muhammad suspended him
from the Nation of Islam. Malcolm defended his comments to the press:
"I said that the hate in white men had not stopped with the killing of
defenseless, black people, but that hate, allowed to spread unchecked,
finally had struck down this country's Chief of State."[70] The explanation
elucidated the controversial remark but did not reconcile the exiled
leader with Muhammad or the Nation of Islam. Malcolm X's suspension
led to his complete break from the religion.

As an independent black nationalist, Malcolm X was quick to set
his own political agenda, which echoed many of the objectives established at Detroit's Northern Negro Grass Roots Conference. On March

11, 1964, he held a press conference at the Park Sheraton Hotel and publicly announced the formation of the Muslim Mosque, Inc. This new organization, similar to the Freedom Now Party, would "be an action program designed to eliminate the political oppression, the economic exploitation, and the social degradation suffered daily by twenty-two million Afro Americans."[71] The founding of Muslim Mosque signaled the transformation of Malcolm X's black nationalism from a rigid separatist approach to a more inclusive strategy that involved forming political coalitions with other groups to fight for human rights.[72] In Detroit these types of coalitions were already being forged through events like the buy-in campaign at the Community Supermarket and the Grass Roots Conference. Malcolm X's new organization also sought to advance black economic empowerment—one of the major goals of both the Grass Roots Conference and the Freedom Now Party. As he noted, "It's because black men don't own and control their own community's retail establishments that they can't stabilize their own community." Malcolm X articulated a primary concern for blacks in the urban North, who did not face as much pervasive political or social segregation as their southern counterparts, but who felt marginalized in urban industrial economies.[73]

In Detroit the Motown Record Company was accomplishing what Malcolm X and the Freedom Now Party advocated: black economic independence that did not rely on the industrial base of the city—auto production—to survive. At the same time, as its music began to gain more and more white fans, Motown represented the ideal of racial integration via cultural exchange advocated by Martin Luther King Jr. and SCLC. By late 1963 Hitsville, U.S.A., was benefiting from a small, but significant change within the record industry. On November 30, 1963, *Billboard* magazine suspended its "Rhythm and Blues" category and began charting all music in the "Pop" category. *Billboard*, responding to the national climate of civil rights fervor, decided that the more neutral "Pop" classification avoided the racial connotations of the "Rhythm and Blues" category. The magazine's taxonomic change reinforced the early signs of Motown's crossover success. By November 1963 Motown hits such as the Miracles' "You've Really Got a Hold of Me," Martha and the Vandellas' "Quicksand," and Marvin Gaye's "Pride and Joy" were generating tremendous profits for the company—a formidable example of the possibilities of black entrepreneurship.[74]

Motown's business and musical achievements, a symbol of pride in Detroit's black community, served a function within the grass-roots organizing in the city that was sometimes indirect but significant nevertheless. If Motown did not record Malcolm X's "Message to the Grass Roots" nor sponsor a panel on black business at the Grass Roots Conference, the company's founding reflected the spirit of grass-roots cooperation within Detroit's black business community. Consider Mr. Kelley's Lounge and Recreation Center, where the Grass Roots Conference held its workshops. Motown Records had a close relationship to Mr. Kelley's Lounge. When Berry Gordy and Raynoma Liles were looking for capital to start their own label, George Kelley, already an established business owner in the city, offered to become a partner in the new record label. Seeking complete control over the endeavor, Gordy declined his offer (and turned to the Gordy family co-op for a loan instead). Nevertheless, Kelley's financial offer illustrated how Detroit's black business owners tried to support one another.[75]

Gordy was able to reciprocate Kelley's generosity when the Motown label began to succeed. Throughout Motown's early years Gordy used Mr. Kelley's Lounge to showcase his budding stars, which helped maintain the lounge's status as one of the most popular black nightclubs in the city. Motown acts such as the Miracles, Martha Reeves and the Vandellas, and Marvin Gaye drew large crowds to Mr. Kelley's Lounge and increased the revenues of another independent black business in the city. The popularity of the club also made it an appropriate site for the Grass Roots Conference workshops. George Kelley's assistance with the conference revealed how black business could play a supporting role in political organizing.

Motown's relationship to the political fervor in Detroit during the formation of the Freedom Now Party manifested itself in more subtle ways. Local party activists needed positive symbols of black independence and economic success to illustrate the benefits of an all-black political party. Freedom Now publicity often made an effort, therefore, to include Motown in its coverage of local news and events. The most direct examples of this phenomenon appeared in *Now! Magazine: News of De-*

troit and the World, published locally from an office on Linwood Avenue by Sterling Grey, the editor and publisher, and by attorney Milton Henry, who acted as senior editor. *Now! Magazine,* a glossy, biweekly publication, chronicled the Freedom Now Party campaign and published other articles documenting freedom struggles around the world.

In several issues *Now! Magazine* included photographs and articles about Motown artists. For example, in the November election issue an image of Albert Cleage, "a Freedom-Now Vote Getter," immediately followed a glossy photograph of the Supremes; a feature on another Motown female singing group, the Velvelettes, appeared in the same issue. In February 1965, Motown artists Diana Ross and Marvin Gaye graced the front cover of the magazine.

These images of Motown artists amid coverage of the Freedom Now campaign were not incongruous with the broader radical agenda of *Now! Magazine* or the objectives of the Freedom Now Party. The political aims of the publication and the party included a cultural dimension that celebrated efforts such as Motown. The party's platform argued for cultural revolution, which saw the "Negro creative artist and performer" as "equal participants" in the fight for racial justice.[76] Also, seen in the context and history of black politics, capitalism, and culture in Detroit, the juxtaposition of Hitsville celebrities with Freedom Now candidates was quite understandable. As a black business in Detroit capitalizing on the city's black talent, Motown affirmed, by its very existence, one of the main objectives of the Freedom Now Party: black economic independence. The Supremes were appropriate company for the Reverend Albert Cleage on the pages of *Now! Magazine* not because they shared the same tasks or even philosophy with the radical minister but because, as a symbol of Motown's success, they spoke to the changes the Freedom Now Party hoped to institute.

These hopes had to be modified when the final results of the November 1964 election came in. The Freedom Now Party did not win any of its campaigns, although it did succeed at being placed on future ballots.[77] One black candidate from Detroit, however, did taste victory in 1964 and suggested that working within the two-party system might be the most effective way to gain black political representation. Voters elected Democrat John Conyers Jr. to Congress from the newly reappor-

"Money (That's What I Want)"

Now! Magazine cover, February 20, 1965. (Courtesy Walter P. Reuther Library, Wayne State University.)

st district of Detroit. Conyers defeated Richard Austin, another black candidate, in a campaign that deeply divided the black community in the city. Conyers joined Charles C. Diggs Jr. in Washington, D.C., making Michigan the leader in black representation in the nation's capital. This milestone became more significant after the bitterness that followed the National Democratic Convention in Atlantic City. The Democratic Party refused to recognize and seat the delegates of the Mississippi Freedom Democratic Party, led by Fannie Lou Hamer. Hamer's party refused any compromise offers from Democratic Party leaders and, therefore, never received official recognition at the convention. Conyers's 1964 election from Detroit offered some solace since the victory added one more black representative to Congress.

Back in Detroit, Motown's role in the political milieu that surrounded it would become increasingly complicated. Throughout the "Negro revolt of 1963," the company and its music served multiple political interests. Motown's recording of King's speech at the Great March to Freedom publicly aligned the company with SCLC and its efforts at promoting a nonviolent and integrationist agenda. By November 1963 the company's business success also exemplified the economic philosophy of black nationalism, and Freedom Now Party organizers willingly appropriated images of Motown's success to promote its agenda of black economic and political empowerment. This appropriation had a specific resonance in 1963 and 1964 that would not be sustained in the same way in years to come. Motown's drive to attract white audiences would eventually lead the company further away from the concerns of local black activists. The work of these activists, who ranged from Great March organizers to Freedom Now Party members, revealed that civil rights organizing in the urban North involved much more than the public contrast between Martin Luther King Jr. and Malcolm X. At the grass-roots level, Detroit activists, and the city's black community in general, struggled with class, philosophical, and tactical differences as they sought to fight racial and economic inequality. These struggles often anticipated rather than reacted to the larger shifts in the national civil rights campaign.

One such shift involved the turn to black culture as a means to advance race pride and promote the civil rights cause. Black culture played an important role in the civil rights struggle from the beginning.

Civil rights workers around the country used freedom songs, poetry, plays, and photography to educate the public about racial injustice and to boost morale in the midst the movement's difficult battles. One of the more understudied aspects of this history involves how black artists got their material produced, published, or recorded and then distributed to the public. The dissemination of black culture often determined the range of its political influence. Since African American artists historically have had difficulty getting their work published or produced, the growth of independent black cultural production in the 1960s—including the Motown Record Company—gave hope that many forms of black culture would find wider audiences. With wider distribution, black culture had the best chance of showing positive images of black people to the general public and improving race relations.

The Motown Record Company's highly successful efforts to produce black popular music could not avoid being associated with the emergent cultural approaches to black empowerment. Moreover, the growing interest in the promotion of black culture caused Motown to consider producing more spoken-word recordings similar to *The Great March to Freedom* album. In Detroit's black community the embrace of black culture as a tool in the pursuit of racial "freedom" would create new and unexpected alliances among artists, business leaders, and political activists. Many of these individuals worked to organize the Great March and supported the Freedom Now Party. With the limited success of the Freedom Now campaign, these coalitions of cultural workers and local activists began to create more innovative strategies to pursue the larger goal of ending racial inequality. Their efforts, typical of the cultural politics of Detroit, continued to use the lessons of the past to plan for the challenges ahead.

3

"Come See about Me":
Black Cultural Production in Detroit

When Motown released the *Great March to Freedom* album on August 28, 1963, the company sent a complimentary copy to Langston Hughes. On September 8, 1963, the poet wrote a thank you note for the gift. In that letter Hughes expressed his delight with Motown's efforts to capture Martin Luther King Jr.'s Detroit speech and offered to "devote some space to this very stirring album in my nationally-syndicated column."[1] Hughes's commentary, entitled "Record It," appeared in newspapers in mid-September. Hughes did not mention Motown's *Great March* album specifically in the final draft of the essay, but the poet did discuss, in general, how much he valued the age of sound recordings from a historical perspective. Marveling at the ability of audio technology to preserve important voices, he wrote, "Posterity, a 100 years hence, can listen to Lena Horne, Ralph Bunche, Harry Belafonte and Chubby Checker."[2]

One month later, in October 1963, Hughes signed his own contract with Motown Records to record an album with Detroit poet Margaret Danner. The release, tentatively titled *Poets of the Revolution*, was to feature Hughes and Danner performing readings of their poems. It would offer both poets an opportunity to work together and juxtapose their poetry, which was somewhat similar in style.[3] For Motown the recording represented another manifestation of the company's newfound interest in preserving spoken work. Different from the polemics of King's speech at the "Great March to Freedom," the *Poets of the Revolution* recording would document the artistic expression of black thought and political consciousness. In their distinct roles, both Langston Hughes, the poet, and Martin Luther King Jr., the civil rights leader, reminded black Americans to pursue their "dreams"—no matter how long they had been "deferred."[4]

Motown's decision to record the poetry album and King's speech reflected important traditions of twentieth-century African American cultural life. Central to these traditions was the desire to preserve, produce, and disseminate culture, art, and history. Langston Hughes's column "Record It" expressed this imperative as it extolled audio technology's unique contribution to historical preservation. Hughes, a folklorist and historian in his own right, understood the significance of being able to capture the sounds of black America—whether speech, poem, or song—for the ages.

African American cultural production, like the history of black capitalism, cannot be separated from the racial politics of twentieth-century America. When Booker T. Washington founded the National Negro Business League in 1900, he endeavored to build a powerful network of black businesses that could empower African Americans economically. On September 9, 1915, Carter G. Woodson—hoping to replicate what Washington had accomplished with his Negro Business League—founded the Association for the Study of Negro Life and History (ASNLH). The ASNLH, a national organization with local chapters across the country, promoted the study, preservation, dissemination, and celebration of black culture and history. The founding of the ASNLH made a strong political statement in relation to another major cultural event of 1915: the release of D. W. Griffith's film *Birth of a Nation.* The controversial film, which glorified the Ku Klux Klan and perpetuated racist stereotypes, represented the growing power of mass culture to shape public opinion about black Americans. The ASNLH, organized at this historic moment, asserted the dignity and legitimacy of African American life.[5]

Detroit occupied a prominent place in the history of black cultural production and preservation. In 1938 Sylvia M. Tucker and Fannie H. Peck, who was also president of the Housewives League, founded the Detroit chapter of the ASNLH. The ASNLH's 1938 *Negro History Bulletin* reported the founding of the Detroit branch and noted, "Rarely has a branch of the organization been launched under such favorable auspices." Over the years Detroit's ASNLH became one of the most respected branches of the national organization. In October 1962 the *Negro History Bulletin*, the ASNLH's most widely distributed periodical, published a special issue on Detroit's history and culture. In a prefatory note Broadnus Butler, editor of the special issue, commended the Detroit chapter and its accomplishments, which included efforts to found two major archives in the Detroit Public Library: the Azalia Hackley Collection of Negro Music and the Burton Historical Collection.[6]

One year later, in October 1963, Detroit's ASNLH contacted Langston Hughes and asked for his assistance with its latest project. The chapter was organizing a campaign to open an African art gallery in the Detroit Institute of the Arts. The gallery would integrate one of the city's most prestigious and Anglocentric cultural institutions. Hughes agreed to support the campaign even though he was quite busy at the time with his own act of cultural integration—producing his new gospel musical *Tambourines to Glory* on Broadway.[7] Hughes made plans to come to Detroit in February 1964 to inaugurate the fund-raising drive for the African Art Gallery and the ASNLH's Negro History Week.[8]

Hughes's arrangements with Detroit's ASNLH coincided with his plans to record the *Poets of the Revolution* album with Motown Records. More than concurrent events, Hughes's recording contract with Hitsville, U.S.A., and his work for the Detroit branch shared certain goals. Motown's project with Hughes and Danner would potentially introduce the work of the two poets to new audiences. The ASNLH encouraged any efforts to bring "Negro Life" to the American public, whose cultural institutions traditionally had excluded, appropriated, or ignored the contributions of black people. The Detroit campaign to establish an African art gallery the city's Institute of the Arts advanced this cause. Similarly, Motown's efforts to take Detroit's black musical talent to the top of the popular music charts challenged the racial boundaries of the American music industry. Historically, these boundaries segregated "black" music from mainstream audiences by marketing the music primarily to African American listeners. All of these endeavors served a broader goal, first articulated by Carter G. Woodson upon the founding of the

ASNLH, to recognize "Negro Life" as an integral facet of "American Life."[9]

While Motown's music broke racial barriers in the national record industry, the means by which the company produced hit records responded to the racial politics of Detroit. Like black capitalism, black cultural production in the Motor City thrived on a self-help imperative. Independent cultural production stood apart from Detroit's larger economy. Producing and marketing the cultural work of the black community in a city economically dominated by an automobile industry, which both excluded African Americans from controlling the means of production and profited from their labor, was an inherently political act. Motown heightened the political significance of these issues through its appropriation of industrial mass-production techniques. The record company produced music independent of the automobile industry, yet it capitalized on the industrial ethos, marketing strategies, and emerging technologies of automobile manufacturing to create its music and promote its entertainers.

Motown's talent for mass-producing and selling black popular music gave the company the ability to consider smaller projects such the Hughes and Danner recording. Yet Motown faced conflicts between its role as an independent producer of black culture and its goals as a black capitalist enterprise. The company's ambitions to become a major force in the music industry always took precedence over any spoken-word projects. By early 1964 Motown's musical "assembly line" had sent one of its acts, the "no-hit" Supremes, to the top of the popular music charts. By the end of that same year, the Supremes were international celebrities, becoming the first Motown group to appear on the *Ed Sullivan Show*. The Supremes' appearance on national television was a landmark in the history of the record company, of black cultural production in Detroit, and of the promotion of "Negro Life" in America. Motown reveled in the Supremes' new fame and high record sales, but it did not sustain its initial support for the Hughes and Danner poetry recording. These production conflicts revealed how the cause of disseminating black culture and the tenets of black capitalism could be at odds with each other.

No two Motown projects seemed more distant from each other in 1964 than the promotion of the Supremes and the recording of Langston

Hughes and Margaret Danner. The Supremes represented the company's most dramatic crossover success with white audiences. The group's appeal within the predominantly white popular music market was key to Motown's continued growth as a black capitalist enterprise. In contrast, the Langston Hughes and Margaret Danner poetry album was one modest spoken-word recording that sought to preserve black culture in the tradition of the ASNLH. The stories of the two projects, when, juxtaposed against each other, reveal the true complexity of black cultural production in Detroit during the early civil rights years.

Black artists, musicians, singers, and poets maintained complicated relationships with black cultural producers such as Motown Records throughout the 1960s. Both parties—the artists and the producers—knew that their relationship was based on mutual needs, dependencies, and an often uneasy exchange of cultural and monetary capital. Exactly who benefited or profited from any arrangement or contract was not always clear or stable. Artists knew the value of their cultural wares but also knew that, without proper production and distribution, their work might never be appreciated by the public. Producers knew that, without a fresh supply of talent and material, monetary profits could run dry and their role could quickly become obsolete. The civil rights struggle confused these relationships even more. Many artists and writers felt compelled to address the "Negro revolt" in their work, but some producers were cautious about such subject matter since it might have limited marketability. At the same time, many civil rights groups and activists were beginning to seize on black culture as a new way to "market" the movement.

The contrast between the story of the Supremes and of the *Poets of the Revolution* recording reveals the many layers, unexpected alliances, broken promises, and promising moments of black cultural production in Detroit. The two stories first converged in October 1963, when Langston Hughes signed his recording contract with Motown Records. The Supremes' story begins, however, in 1960. At the time the group was several years from establishing the Motown sound as the "Sound of Young America" and not simply of black Detroit. Ironically, the Supremes' first step from a local singing group into a national phenomenon began not in Detroit or even in the United States, but in Windsor, Canada.

Primettes to Supremes

On August 1, 1960, four high school girls—Florence Ballard, Mary Wilson, Diane Ross, and Betty McGlown—stood offstage in the thick summer air. They were waiting for their turn to participate in the prestigious Emancipation Celebration amateur talent contest being held in Windsor, Canada. The crowd of over four thousand spectators from Detroit and Canada cheered from the grassy lawn of Jackson Park. The competition had drawn all types of acts including doo-wop groups, belly dancers, and ventriloquists. Florence, Mary, Diane, and Betty sang. They called their quartet the Primettes and along with their brother group, the Primes, had begun to make a name for themselves by performing at local sock hops and banquets around Detroit. The Windsor talent show was their first "international" appearance and the first time the group was to perform before such an enormous audience, which the popularity of the festival guaranteed.[10]

Anticipation had been building for weeks for the entire festival weekend, which had a long history dating back to the mid-nineteenth century. The celebration originally commemorated the emancipation of the slaves in the British West Indies on August 1, 1834. Each year, around the first week of August, the black community from Detroit traveled across the border to Canada to celebrate with the black community of Windsor the freedom of their West Indian brothers and sisters. After the U.S. Emancipation Proclamation in 1863 and the passage of the Fifteenth Amendment to the Constitution in 1870, the Windsor festivities became a multiple celebration. The Canadian location of the festival confused outside observers and the white press. For black Detroiters, Canada's status as the final refuge for fugitive slaves on the Underground Railroad explained why the celebration took place in Windsor. The Windsor Emancipation Celebration continued throughout the twentieth century to be a meaningful observance that nurtured a sense of community and race pride among blacks across national boundaries.[11]

The theme of the 1960 celebration was "The Greatest *Freedom* Show on Earth." Daisy Bates, president of the Arkansas NAACP and leader in the fight to integrate Central High School in Little Rock, was the keynote speaker for the weekend. Opening day featured a little league baseball

The Primettes, circa 1961. (Courtesy Motown Record Co., L.P., a Polygram Company.)

tournament, a pet show, and a rock and roll concert. Sunday was Spiritual and Gospel Day. The Clara Ward Singers performed with the hundred-member gospel choir from Reverend T. S. Boone's King Solomon Baptist Church. The festival also included a parade and an exposition area with booths displaying crafts and promoting local businesses. Excitement grew over the three days for the final night, which featured a beauty pageant and the long-awaited talent contest.[12]

The Primettes' wait came to an end when the emcee announced their name. As they walked onto the stage the roar of applause from the thousands of spectators charged the moment. As Diana Ross later recalled, "my heart sped up and a shot of adrenaline rushed up my spine." Leaning into the electric atmosphere, the young women began their medley singing "The Twist," "There Goes My Baby," and—a personal favorite—their rendition of Ray Charles's hit song "(Night Time Is) The Right Time." Florence captured the audience with her deep bluesy lead, and Diana responded and harmonized in the higher ranges. Mary and Betty sang the back up "night and day" lyric to complete the sound. The combination sent the crowd into a frenzy. When the judges announced the winners at the end of the show, the Primettes walked again to center stage to claim first prize and savor their first taste of fame. Later that evening, Mary, Florence, Betty, and Diana wandered among the carnival booths and, newly confident in their talents, began to think about the future. The next logical step out of the amateur singing circuit was to cut a record.[13]

Cutting a record was not a pipe dream in black Detroit—even if you were still in high school. Independent record producing thrived in the Motor City. In the mid-fifties Joe Von Battle, who had taped the Reverend C. L. Franklin's sermons live at the New Bethel Baptist Church, set an early example of successful local record producing. Von Battle released the recordings on his own JVB label and sold them in his record store on Hastings Street. As Von Battle's daughter, Marsha Mickens, remembered, "My father was the first person to record a lot of people because there was nowhere else they could be recorded. This was in the early 1950s. This was pre-Motown. It would be a big deal to go to Joe's record shop and have your voice recorded. He was open almost all night long. He always played records out of the loud speaker of the record shop so you could hear music as things went on."[14]

By the late fifties many local studios around the city including the Fortune and Sensation labels were eager to record young talent. The Primettes knew that their peers—Otis Williams, Melvin Franklin, and Richard Street, who first called their singing group "Otis Williams and the Distants"—recorded some of their songs for Northern Records. Johnnie Mae Matthews, who had her own group "Johnnie Mae Matthews and the Five Daps," owned Northern Records. The label was best known for recording Detroit groups like Popcorn and the Mohawks, which featured Popcorn Wylie on piano and Norman Whitfield on tambourine, and solo singers such as Mary Wells. Matthews, who had a reputation for spotting talented musicians, hired James Jamerson, the innovative bass player, for her Northern Records studio band.[15]

Independent labels proliferated in Detroit even though the logistics of the recording business could be daunting. New record producers often found it difficult to acquire the proper equipment. Not many individuals could afford audio equipment, but those who did often set up recording studios in their homes and basements. In her autobiography Raynoma Gordy Singleton recalled the rare privilege of owning recording equipment: "I had started writing songs when I was twelve years old and had begun making rustic recordings on a Webcor[e] Wire machine that Mama and Daddy bought for us. The Webcore was a very primitive 78 rpm disc-cutting recorder that operated along the old Edison cylinder principles. As you played music into the machine, a needle cut grooves into a piece of vinyl. In those days very few people, especially among our peers, owned equipment. So we were mighty proud of that Webcore, regardless of its simplicity."[16]

One of the most famous "basement studios" was in the house of "Senator" Bristoe Bryant, a popular black disc jockey at Detroit's WJLB radio station. Bryant was known for renting out his studio to aspiring musicians or singers who wanted to press their talent into vinyl. In the early fifties a young man came to Bryant's studio to record a song as a radio commercial for one of his family's businesses. The song was entitled "Let Gordy Be Your Printer Too," and the composer, Berry Jr., hoped the jingle—sung in Nat King Cole's style—would draw customers into his siblings' latest business venture, the Gordy Print Shop. In the late fifties Gordy and his business partner, Raynoma Liles, rented Bryant's studio when any of their clients at the Rayber Music Company were ready to cut a record. When Gordy decided to open his own Hitsville Studios, Bryant, in an effort to be supportive, sold the new record company his two-track tape recorder, one of the first pieces of audio equipment at Motown studios.[17]

On the night of August 1, 1960, Motown Studios soon became a topic of conversation, as the Primettes discussed their plans to cut a record. Marvin Tarplin, the Primettes' backup guitarist, first suggested that the girls try to audition for Gordy's company. Mary, Diana, and Betty were intrigued, but Florence was skeptical—not sure that the company would look out for the group's best interests. She had heard negative rumors about Motown's treatment of artists, but the other girls felt strongly that the label was their best option in Detroit.[18] A few weeks after winning the talent show, the Primettes decided to pursue an audition at Hitsville, U.S.A., in earnest. In their first attempt, Diana Ross asked Smokey Robinson, her former neighbor, if the Primettes could audition for the Miracles, and Robinson agreed. The group performed a short medley of their most polished songs for the Miracles at Bobby Rogers's house. The Primettes' vocal talents and Tarplin's guitar accompaniment impressed Robinson, who agreed to introduce the young women to Motown and asked Tarplin if he would like to join the Miracles.[19]

As the summer of 1960 drew to a close, Motown granted the Primettes an audition. One day after school, the group walked over to the studios on West Grand Boulevard and performed the songs that had won over the crowd at the Emancipation Celebration talent show just a few weeks earlier—including their rendition of the Drifters' song "There Goes My Baby." With guitarist Marvin Tarplin now working with the Miracles, the young women had to rely on their a cappella vocal abilities to impress Berry Gordy, recording engineer and songwriter Richard Morris, and company talent scout and producer Robert Bateman. All three of the men recognized the Primettes' talent, but Gordy told the group that he would not sign them until they completed their schooling. Gordy avoided the added responsibilities of signing artists who were legal minors whenever possible.[20] Soon after the first Motown audition, Betty McGlown decided to leave the group to get married.

Undeterred by Gordy's dismissal or McGlown's departure, Mary, Florence, and Diana began to make daily visits to the Hitsville Studios in the hopes of being signed on or asked to be background vocalists. The excitement and welcome "family" atmosphere at Motown attracted the Primettes. As Wilson remembered, "The building on West Grand Boulevard was a home away from home for many young singers and musicians then. The company was still serving hot family-style meals for everyone who happened to be around. Those of us who loved Motown remember fondly these times of special closeness and friendship."[21]

The Primettes continued to try to cut a record throughout the autumn of 1960. When they were not lingering around Motown Studios, the young women continued to perform around Detroit. Sock hops, organized by local disc jockeys such as "Frantic" Ernie Durham and Bristoe Bryant from WJLB, gave new groups exposure at more prestigious venues like the Graystone Ballroom and the Twenty Grand nightclub. The Primettes received more bookings when Richard Morris, who attended their Motown audition, offered to act as the group's manager.[22]

Morris arranged the group's first recording session at Robert West's Flick and Contour studio. Typical of independent recording in Detroit, the Flick and Contour studio was, according to Mary Wilson, a "drab little basement in a house on Forest Street." Yet what the studio lacked in glamour, it compensated for with enthusiasm and a cooperative spirit. On the day that the Primettes arrived at the studio, other artists including the Falcons and Wilson Pickett were rehearsing. Several musicians from the Falcons played backup for the Primettes when they recorded two songs: "Pretty Baby" and "Tears of Sorrow." West pressed the record on a new label, Lu Pine, and released it through his own B & H distribution company. The Primettes' recording debut ended abruptly, however, when B & H became the target of a payola investigation. The canceled record dampened the group's spirits until Barbara Martin, a regular at Graystone Ballroom sock hops, agreed to join the Primettes and complete the quartet. The reconstituted group decided to go back to Hitsville, U.S.A., and renew the campaign for a recording contract.[23]

In January 1961 the Primettes's tenacity prevailed, and Berry Gordy approached the group about signing a contract. Gordy insisted that the group find a new, more marketable name. Florence composed a list of possible alternatives including the Melodees, the Sweet Ps, and the Jewelettes. When the final contracts were drawn up on January 15, 1961, another name from Florence's list had been chosen, and "the Supremes" became the new act on the Motown roster. The name change reflected the young company's sensitivity to product development. Whether it was considering a group's name or the beat of a song, the Motown hit factory sought to manufacture the most marketable sound and image. Hitsville, U.S.A., was only beginning to live up to its name when the Supremes signed their contract, but a new milestone for the company was just around the corner.

On February 12, 1961, one month after the Supremes signed with Motown, Berry Gordy's hit factory achieved a major goal when the Miracles' song "Shop Around" became the company's first million-seller. Written and produced by Berry Gordy and Smokey Robinson in the autumn of 1960, the song, a clever tune about a mother's wisdom about young romance, reached number one on the rhythm and blues charts and number two on the pop charts by December 1960. The song's success resulted from Berry Gordy's diligent efforts to increase record sales. Toward the end of 1960 Gordy began to structure his company into separate divisions. As he later explained,

> I broke down my whole operation into three functions: *Create, Make, Sell.* I felt any business had to do that ... The *Create* phase—writing, producing, and recording—was really starting to come together as the Hitsville talent pool expanded on a regular basis. The *Make* phase—manufacturing, pressing of the records— was the process that Loucye [Gordy] oversaw. It now required a growing support staff to deal with inventories, the plants, deliveries to distribution points and the billing to the distributors. We were doing fine with the *Create* and *Make* phase but the *Sell* phase—placing records with distributors, getting airplay, marketing and advertising—was the area I needed to develop.[24]

Gordy hired Barney Ales, an aggressive and shrewd veteran in the record industry, to head Motown's sales department. Gordy knew that Ales, one of the company's first white executives, could give Motown crucial access to the broader national record market, which traditionally excluded independent black record producers. Ales quickly proved his worth. As Raynoma Gordy Singleton recalled, "Within two weeks of [Ales] joining Hitsville, 'Shop Around' started to move. Barney orchestrated the participation of all the major white distributors nationwide, and in so doing set up the machinery for us to repeat this success in the future. We had crossed over, and Barney Ales had been our navigator."[25]

The hiring of Ales revealed the challenges black record producers faced when they attempted to distribute their records to a national audience. The cooperation of white executives already established in the music business, like Ales, was key. Without it, Motown ran the risk of being shut out of mainstream radio playlists entirely. In 1960 black popular music did not crossover to white audiences on the basis of its appeal alone. This transition involved an elaborate system of marketing the artists and behind-the-scenes deal making with distributors, disc jockeys, and record store owners.

Soon after "Shop Around" became a million-seller, Gordy began to have difficulty individually coordinating all the details of his artists' careers. He created International Talent Management Inc. (ITMI) as the separate artist management division of Motown Records and put his sister, Esther Edwards, in charge. ITMI represented the first stages of Motown's development into a formal corporate structure. The new division helped performers get engagements and negotiated contracts, but it also gave Motown management more control over each artist or group. ITMI restricted access to the company records, which often made it more difficult for artists to keep track of their royalties. These practices facilitated Motown's business growth but also revealed that artists did not have as much agency in the overall production process. These changes illustrated how Motown's corporate growth counteracted the "family" ethos that had always been the pride of the company.[26]

The Supremes became one of ITMI's first clients when they signed on at Motown in January 1961. Their career at the company, however, had a slow start. Motown released their first single, "I Want a Guy," on March 9, 1961, but the song did not make a dent on the rhythm and blues or pop charts. Soon after its release, Barbara Martin decided to leave the group to get married. As a trio, the Supremes continued to know only modest success over the course of the next two years. Only two of their singles, "Buttered Popcorn," released in July 1961, and "When the

Lovelight Starts Shining Through His Eyes," released in October 1963, gained some degree of popularity. Florence Ballard sang the lead on "Buttered Popcorn," a soulful dance tune that played well around Detroit but never broke onto the national scene. In her autobiography Mary Wilson claimed that "Buttered Popcorn" never received a big promotional push because Berry Gordy felt that Ballard's voice wasn't as commercial as Ross's singing style. "When the Lovelight Starts Shining Through His Eyes" only reached number twenty-three on the rhythm and blues charts.[27]

While the Supremes searched for their first big hit at Motown in October 1963, Langston Hughes signed his contract with the label to record the *Poets of the Revolution* album with local Detroit poet Margaret Danner. The project diverged from the company's musical offerings, yet revealed how Motown's success in the music business attracted other black artists looking to promote and distribute their work. Hughes and Danner knew that a Motown recording of their poetry could preserve their work and introduce it to new audiences. For Motown the project represented another experimental venture into spoken-word recordings. While Motown was never deeply invested in the poetry recording, the story of its production deserves attention. The details reveal the challenges and promise of black cultural production in Detroit. The challenges tested artists such as Hughes and Danner, who sought innovative ways to bring black poetry to the public, and producers such as Motown Records, a company that vacillated between its obligations to preserve black culture and its goal to increase profit margins. The effort to produce the album brought talented people together and actively engaged with the struggles of the civil rights campaign.

Langston Hughes and Motown's *Poets of the Revolution* Recording

Soon after Hughes signed his contract with Motown, he and Danner began their work on the album. Production of the recording moved quickly. In mid-October Danner flew to New York City, where Hughes was rehearsing *Tambourines to Glory* on Broadway, for the recording session. On October 21, 1963, the poets went into a sound studio and performed poems including Hughes's "Of Freedom's Plow" and "Sweet Words from Liberals on Race," and Danner's "To a Cold Caucasian on a Bus." The project also sparked Hughes's interest in Motown's music. At the time of the recording session, Hughes asked Motown staffers for information about Stevie Wonder's appearance in the "Motortown Revue," which was currently on stage at Harlem's Apollo Theater.[28]

The Hughes and Danner recording session in New York did not receive much assistance from Motown's main office. Margaret Danner paid for her trip to New York City without the financial support of the company, and Hughes and Danner managed other aspects of the production on their own. Hughes arranged with his friend and professional photographer Louis Draper to shoot portraits of himself and Danner for the album jacket. In the months that followed, Hughes became disgruntled when Motown delayed payments for the photographs, which postponed the release of the recording. Moreover, Motown planned to draw on Hughes's and Danner's royalties from the recording to pay Draper. The cross-collaterization of royalty accounts, in which the cost incurred in the production of a recording could be charged against an artist's royalties, was a common practice at the company in its early years and in the record industry in general.[29]

By January 1964 these problems were on Hughes's mind as he made plans to travel to Detroit in February to commence a weekend of festivities honoring his life and work. Hughes's obligations to the Detroit chapter of the ASNLH, which included launching National Negro History Week and fund-raising for the African Art Gallery, dominated the itinerary of the trip. Nevertheless, Hughes was ready to make time to visit Motown Studios. In a letter to Danner about his schedule in Detroit, Hughes wrote, "I would love to see the Motown folks—and collect that money for the photographer!" Danner replied, "it seems quite important to me that we tour Hitsville . . . I do not want to make demands upon you but in the case where money and prestige is involved I feel that it would be wise for *us both to allow such people to be nice to us.*" In another letter Danner advised Hughes to avoid direct confrontation with Motown out of fear that "[t]he man [Gordy] might decide to cancel the record," and because "[i]f the record ever comes out we will be ahead." These sentiments reveal that while Motown was not as supportive with production of the recording as either Hughes or Danner would have liked, the poets knew that the "prestige" of the company and its marketing skills could advance other causes.[30]

Hughes and Danner planned to use the Motown recording to promote their own efforts to disseminate "Negro" poetry. Both Danner and Hughes hoped that *Poets of the Revolution* would generate interest in Hughes's latest anthology, *New Negro Poets, U.S.A.,* which was scheduled to be published in May 1964. The anthology featured the work of several Detroit poets including Danner, Dudley Randall, Oliver La Grone, and Naomi Long Madgett. In a letter to Hughes, Danner wrote that "the record may bring us some money and at least good publicity if we show an interest." Hughes hoped that, when released, the album would be played on radio stations to publicize both the *New Negro Poets* anthology and the record itself.[31]

Just as Hughes and Danner wanted to use their affiliation with Motown Records to promote their poetry, Detroit's chapter of the ASNLH wanted to capitalize on Hughes's celebrity to advance its cause, the new African Art Gallery in the Detroit Institute for the Arts. The national ASNLH was supportive of the Detroit chapter's campaign for the gallery. The February 1964 issue of the *Negro History Bulletin* was a "Special Detroit Edition," which featured a broad range of articles on the city and extensive coverage of the gallery fund-raising drive. One essay, entitled "African Art Gallery Seen as Retribution to Negro Cause," highlighted the political implications of the campaign. The author, Betty De Ramus, argued that the culture of Africa "has been dissipated, lost, and stolen through centuries of colonial occupation and rule" and described the planned gallery as "a form of compensation to Africa and to her displaced people here in the United States." These motives inspired Detroit's ASNLH to plan an entire weekend of events to honor Langston Hughes and generate funds for the gallery.[32]

Hughes traveled to the Motor City on Friday, February 7, 1964. A seven-car motorcade, which included youth groups from CORE, the NAACP, the Student Nonviolent Coordinating Committee, and Big Brothers, greeted the poet at the Detroit Airport with much fanfare and proclaimed him "the People's Poet." The motorcade then drove Hughes to a special reception at Mayor Cavanagh's office. The mayor's office presented the poet with a key to the city and officially declared Sunday, February 9, 1964, "Langston Hughes Day." At the ceremony Hughes expressed his admiration of Detroit's black artistic community, remarking that "Harlem used to be the Negro culture center of America. If Detroit has not already become so, it is well on it's way to becoming it."[33]

The Detroit chapter of the ASNLH planned two major events for the weekend: a testimonial banquet and the fund-raising gala, "An Evening with Langston Hughes," to be held at the Detroit Institute of Arts. At the banquet Hughes received special greetings from Mayor Cavanagh, Michigan Governor George Romney, and U.S. Representative Charles Diggs Jr., among others. Oliver La Grone, a local artist who had sculpted a bust of the poet, presented the statue to Hughes after the speeches. The local press reported that the series of tributes overwhelmed Hughes, who had to pause for several moments to regain his composure before responding to his audience. Approximately fifteen hundred people attended the ASNLH gala that followed the dinner at the Detroit Institute of the Arts.[34]

The presence of Hughes throughout the weekend not only raised money for the African Art Gallery but achieved one of the most important goals of the ASNLH: to generate pride in "Negro Life." Like the Great March to Freedom, the Langston Hughes weekend gave black Detroit a chance to gather and celebrate as a community. Two days after the gala evening, June McKee, corresponding secretary of Detroit's ASNLH and coordinator of the tribute weekend, wrote to Hughes and reflected, "Your BEING here has enlivened and quickened us all, and heightened our aspirations as well as awarenesses." Oliver La Grone reiterated these sentiments in a note in which he remarked, "Those three days shook Detroit to its very roots—in a most happy way—Negritude soared!"[35]

The impact of the weekend lingered for years to come. One year after the event, Detroit poet Naomi Long Madgett wrote to Hughes and continued to comment on the event. She enthused, "I wanted to tell you what a wonderful experience Langston Hughes weekend in Detroit was last year! I spread your material around (some of which you sent me several years ago) for display on bulletin boards in some schools which have never before dared to discuss a Negro writer." Madgett's comments about the resistance of some schools to discussing a "Negro writer" illustrated how crucial the work of organizations such as the ASNLH was to Detroit's black community. Hughes's visit had a special effect on the city's local poets. On the Saturday evening before Langston Hughes Day, the poet paid a special visit to the group of writers working with Margaret Danner. Describing his influence on the young black artists, Danner commented, "Your visit here was an inspiration to every boy and girl in Detroit. And as for the adults, I doubt that the poets, alone, will ever regain a calm outlook. Some are dedicating their lives to being like you."[36]

With such a full schedule, Hughes had to modify his plans to visit Motown Studios to promote the *Poets of the Revolution* recording. Hughes and Danner never found time to tour Hitsville, U.S.A., but Marvin Gaye and Diana Ross met the poet at J. L. Hudson's, the city's largest department store, at what became the most well-attended book-signing party in the store's history.[37] The encounter between two of Motown's rising stars and the country's most preeminent African American poet achieved several goals. For Motown the meeting publicly affiliated the record company with the city's Langston Hughes weekend and acted as prepublicity for Hughes and Danner's poetry recording. While this type of promotion was important to Hughes, who wanted to see the album completed, it was particularly crucial to Danner, a local poet who would receive considerable national exposure when Motown released the recording. Danner was a leader in Detroit's black arts community. Her work nurturing young poets was similar in some ways to Berry Gordy's efforts to cultivate young musical talent at Hitsville, U.S.A. Danner and her writers also used their poetry to respond to the challenges of the civil rights movement, thus fulfilling the ideals set out by Carter G. Woodson when he founded the ASNLH.

Boone House and the Rise of Black Poetry in Detroit

Margaret Danner, a Chicago native, came to Detroit in 1959 to work with fellow writers and poets at Wayne State University. By 1962 Wayne State had offered Danner the position of poet-in-residence. Danner appreciated this academic honor and accepted the position, yet she also longed to work outside the university setting where she could encourage aspiring artists throughout the city. Describing herself, Danner once declared, "I

Marvin Gaye and Diana Ross meet Langston Hughes at a book-signing party held at Hudson's department store, February 1964. (Courtesy Motown Record Co., L.P., a Polygram Company.)

am no ivory tower poet. I think poetry is written to be read aloud." She decided to establish a center for the arts that would be open to all city residents and where poetry could be "read aloud." When she discovered a small empty parish next door to the main sanctuary of King Solomon Baptist Church, she asked the Reverend T. S. Boone if he might allow her to use the space for her project. Boone approved of the idea, and Danner christened her new organization "Boone House" in honor of the minister's gesture. Danner also expressed her appreciation for his generosity in the poem "Boone House," which describes the church's "calm sanctuary" as "A balm / to those struggling through creativity's / strident, summer, city heat."[38]

Boone House's reputation as a lively center for the arts grew quickly. When the ASNLH's *Negro History Bulletin* published its special issue on Detroit writers in October 1962, the journal featured the biographies and poems of sixteen artists collaborating at Boone House and gave the organization its first national exposure. In November 1962 the *Negro Digest* featured an article entitled "A City Survey: The Arts in Detroit," which noted that Danner was a prominent figure in the "literary scene . . . [which] is at its brightest currently." The collective regularly sponsored art exhibits and jazz sessions as well as poetry readings by local artists such as Dudley Randall, Harold Lawrence, and Margaret Ford. Danner also invited established writers from outside the city—including Langston Hughes—to come to the center and perform readings of their work.[39]

Boone House artists did not take these opportunities for granted. In December 1962, only a few months after the collective began, Dudley Randall wrote the following poem, "For Margaret Danner," to express his gratitude for Danner's efforts in establishing Boone House:

> Courage banners
> Not only in battles, perils
> In scaling peaks or probing seas and caves,
> But in enduring cold and hunger,
> In nurturing,
> Through loneliness and neglect,
> The seeds of the spirit.
> May your crocuses rise up through winter snow.[40]

Reflecting on his inspiration for the poem, Randall commented that, "The purpose of [Boone House] was to bring the arts to the Black community. Since the federal government had not begun to fund community projects at this time, Margaret had to rely on membership fees and donations . . . In the winter, the place would be insufficiently heated, and we would come early to the meetings in order to break up pieces of wood to make a fire in the fireplace. It was quite hard on Margaret, and I wrote [the] poem expressing my admiration for her courage."[41]

The small cultural community at Boone House that nurtured "the seeds of the spirit" actively responded to the civil rights struggle. When a bomb exploded the Sixteenth Street Church in Birmingham, Alabama, on September 16, 1963, Randall captured the terror and anguish surrounding the murders of Denise McNair, Cynthia Wesley, Carole Robertson, and Addie Mae Collins in his poem "Ballad of Birmingham (On the bombing of a church in Birmingham)." In the poem a young girl asks her mother to allow her to participate in a freedom march. The mother refuses, "For I fear those guns will fire, / But you may go to church instead / And sing in the Children's Choir." In the final stanzas the mother hears the explosion from the church: "Her eyes grew wet and wild. / She raced through the streets of Birmingham / Calling for her child."[42]

Randall first introduced the poem to his Boone House colleagues, but the topical theme of the "Ballad of Birmingham" soon gained audiences beyond poetry circles. Grace Lee Boggs, Detroit activist and Freedom Now Party organizer, read the poem and offered to publish it in *Correspondence*, a radical newspaper that covered working-class struggles from political and cultural perspectives. Jerry Moore, a New York folk singer, set the verses to music and converted the poem into a freedom song that activists performed across the country at mass meetings, rallies, and marches. Randall's "Ballad of Birmingham" offered poetic commentary that spoke to people's heightened fears about the increasingly violent national civil rights campaign.[43]

Boone House poets also wrote about the local political organizing that was occurring in Detroit, most notably, Malcolm X's appearance at the Northern Grass Roots Leadership Conference in King Solomon Baptist Church's sanctuary, directly next door to Boone House. Grass-roots organizers initially turned to the Reverend T. S. Boone when they realized that they would need a large facility for their conference. Boone, wary of the conference's black nationalist agenda, refused to allow the conference workshops to be held in his church. His resistance can be read as simple political conservatism but should be situated in its historical moment. After the horror of the Sixteenth Street bombing, black church sanctuaries could no longer be seen as safe havens for civil rights strategizing and were in fact potential targets for the violent retribution of those who opposed the movement. These dangers may have contributed to Boone's reluctance to offer his church facilities. Nevertheless, when it became apparent that the Reverend Albert Cleage's own Central Congregational

Church was too small to accommodate the large crowds predicted for Malcolm X's appearance, Boone agreed to offer his spacious sanctuary for the conference's final rally.

In her poem "Malcolm X, a Lover of the Grass Roots," Danner memorialized Malcolm X's appearance in Detroit. In one stanza she wrote about how the rally's close proximity to Boone House caught her attention:

> I saw him with those he called his own,
> His growling laughter
> at the sinister absurdity of the thorned plan
> rumbled with such force through the window
> of a fought-for auditorium
> that it drew me from the house next door.[44]

Danner's recollection of being drawn in "from the house next door" accentuated the short physical distance between what appeared, at first glance, to be two different worlds: the cultural haven of Boone House and a contentious political rally advocating black nationalism. The figurative distance between these two spheres, however, was not that far. By the time Malcolm X spoke in Detroit on November 9, 1963, Danner had already completed her own "message to the grass roots" by recording *Poets of the Revolution* with Hughes. The recording demonstrated how artistic expression responded to the politics of its time.

Poets of the Revolution not only bridged the spheres of art and politics but also brought together two of Detroit's richest black cultural communities: Boone House and Hitsville, U.S.A. Margaret Danner's efforts to organize an arts collective in Detroit, while much smaller in scale and unencumbered by profit motives, shared certain characteristics with Berry Gordy Jr.'s endeavors to build a record company in the city. Danner's Boone House and Gordy's Motown Records, which were located within a mile of each other, both created environments that nurtured the creative energies of young black artists in Detroit—whether aspiring writers such as Naomi Long Madgett or accomplished musicians such as bass player James Jamerson.

While Hughes and Danner worked on the final details of the poetry recording, Hitsville U.S.A., channeled most of its energies into the art form it knew best: popular music that was capturing the attention of the emerging baby-boomer youth market. By early 1964 Motown songs such as Mary Wells's "My Guy," Marvin Gaye's "You're a Wonderful One," and the Temptations' "The Way You Do the Things You Do" had climbed the music charts. These hit songs emerged from the same cultural institutions that supported Detroit's black poetry community and the city's black activists. In his memoirs Otis Williams, lead singer of the Temptations, recalled how the gospel acts that appeared at King Solomon Baptist Church influenced the style of one of Motown's most famous male singing groups: "One thing Paul, Eddie, Melvin, Al, and I liked to do together was catch the gospel acts that came to Detroit. Although most gospel performers toured the South, few came to Texarkana, so I wasn't exposed to the live-performance aspect of gospel until I moved to Detroit. There, at King Solomon's Church, I saw Clara Ward, Mahalia Jackson, the Vocalaires, the Violinaires, and others. I loved them all, but I particularly liked the male gospel quartets, whose multipart harmonies left me breathless."[45]

Williams's comments provide one small example of how the urban environment outside Motown studios influenced the music that was created inside. King Solomon Baptist Church, with its multifarious roles as religious organization, concert hall, poetry collective, and site for political rallies, illustrated the knotted quality of black life in Detroit. The church clearly acted as more than a sanctuary for religious rituals. Furthermore, neither the church nor the separate activities that occurred in it could be completely understood in isolation from one another.

Similarly, the Motown Record Company cannot be understood apart from other aspects of Detroit's urban life. Hitsville, U.S.A., emerged from a city that was economically dominated by the automobile industry, yet manufactured a product completely independent of this industry. Using the technologies of automobile manufacturing to produce and market its music and applying industrial methods to record production, Hitsville, U.S.A., was able to reach the largest audiences in the history of black cultural production in Detroit. It was an achievement that had both political and racial implications. The company defied the more common and disadvantaged position of blacks within Detroit's automobile-based economy by appropriating the methods and emerging technologies of industrial manufacturing to produce black culture. As a result, Motown's hit factory was able to bring the talents of black Detroit to the attention of the American public and eventually to fans around the world.

Most notably, the Supremes' ascendance into national stardom during the summer of 1964 marked a watershed in the history of the record company and of black cultural production in Detroit and—on a national level—in the promotion of "Negro Life" in America. The Supremes' appeal broke down racial boundaries within the popular music industry more successfully than any other Motown group. They also demonstrated the effectiveness of Motown's production techniques. As soon as the group had its first major hit, the company's assembly line focused its energies on packaging and preparing the Supremes for their impending celebrity. Motown's skill at marketing the Supremes set a new standard for all of the company's performers. The group's overwhelming popularity illustrated how effectively Hitsville could use certain aspects of Detroit's industrial ethos to transform the Motown sound into the "Sound of Young America."

The Supremes and Motown's Hit Factory

One month after Detroit's Langston Hughes weekend, in March 1964, Eddie Holland, singer and songwriter at Motown, approached the Supremes and invited them to record a new song of his entitled "Where Did Our Love Go?" Holland first had asked the Marvellettes, famous for their hit single "Please Mr. Postman," if they would record the song, but unsure of its potential appeal, they turned down the offer. The Supremes, who up until this point had achieved only modest success with two other songs, "Buttered Popcorn" and "When the Lovelight Starts Shining Through His Eyes," were more willing to attempt the song—although they, too, were skeptical of the tune. In her memoirs Mary Wilson recalled: "To my ears, 'Where Did Our Love Go?' was a teeny-bopper song. It had childish, repetitive lyrics ('Baby, baby, baby, baby don't leave me . . .'), a limited melody, and no drive. It was too smooth, and I couldn't imagine anyone liking it."[46] Despite Wilson's doubts, the Supremes recorded the song and hoped for the best. If "Where Did Our Love Go?"

did not move up the charts, the group would have a harder time moving up the ranks at Motown.

In the summer of 1964, however, the Supremes' sluggish career took a dramatic turn when Motown convinced Dick Clark to take the trio on his "Caravan of Stars" summer tour. Clark initially resisted the idea since "Where Did Our Love Go?" had yet to prove itself a hit. He was more interested in signing Motown's Brenda Holloway, whose record "Every Little Bit Hurts" had received a great deal of play on his *American Bandstand* television show. Berry Gordy urged Esther Edwards in her role as director of ITMI to persuade Clark to take a chance on the Supremes. As he remembered in his autobiography, Gordy argued, "Please listen to me. 'Where Did Our Love Go' could be an out-and-out smash. The R & B guys are wailing on it already. We need Dick Clark for the white people. I gotta have that tour, and you gotta get 'em on it."[47] Clark finally agreed to take the Supremes but paid the group a modest six hundred dollars a week. With Ross's mother acting as chaperon, the money had to be split four ways. The arrangement led to a huge financial disappointment for Wilson, Ballard, and Ross. As Wilson recalled, "We couldn't wait to find out how much we'd earned, and I went to Esther Edwards' office feeling very proud. When I asked her how much each of us would get, she replied, 'There is no money . . . [the tour] probably cost the company, but you needed the exposure.' I tried to figure it out; where could the money have gone, especially when we so rarely stayed in a room anywhere."[48]

Despite their meager earnings, the Supremes received the critical exposure they needed through the "Caravan of Stars" tour. Over the course of the summer "Where Did Our Love Go?" steadily climbed the charts. By the end of August the audiences that greeted the tour were screaming for the Supremes to sing what had become the number one song in the country. At Motown the Supremes' breakthrough proved how well high-visibility national promotion worked to bring their "products" to wider and whiter audiences.

Motown's push to get the Supremes on Dick Clark's tour was only one aspect of the company's hit factory production plan. Each phase of Gordy's "create, make, sell" process replicated the manufacturing techniques of the auto industry. The creative stage involved a strict division of labor. According to Otis Williams, "When it came to what artists could and should do, Berry was very clear: artists performed, writers wrote, and producers produced."[49] Musically, songs were often broken down into discrete units—or interchangeable parts—to be pieced together at a later date. As Earl Van Dyke, bandleader and keyboardist in the Hitsville studio band known as the Funk Brothers, explained, "Sometimes we got called into the studio just to cut rhythm tracks for songs that hadn't even been written yet—no melody, nothin'. A lot of things we found out later wound up as parts of the melodies and vocal backgrounds of hit songs. On 'Baby I Need Your Lovin',' the background that the Four Tops are singing came from melodic lines I played on a rhythm track. They took that piano part out of the mix and put the lines on the voices."[50] The musicians also compartmentalized different octaves of songs within one instrument. In the studio, for instance, three guitarists broke down the different musical ranges of a song: one played high, one middle, and one low. Keyboardists used the same strategy. With this division of labor and by using a larger number of musicians—usually ten and sometimes up to twelve as opposed to the typical four or five in a rhythm section—the Funk Brothers were able to produce a more powerful sound.[51]

After a song was recorded, it moved on to the next stage of product development. Producers brought final cuts to the quality control department, headed by Billie Jean Brown, a former journalism student from Cass Technical High School. Brown decided if a recording was polished enough to be considered in the company's Friday morning product-evaluation meetings. According to Gordy, these meetings were "the life-blood of our operation." On Friday mornings producers, writers, and company leaders decided which songs would be released that week. Competition and ambition charged the atmosphere at these gatherings in which entire careers could be launched with one decision.[52]

The marketing of Motown artists also replicated the efficiency of industrial manufacturing. The company's artist development department became an increasingly important "way station" on the production line. In artist development, also referred to as the company "charm school," performers learned etiquette, deportment, choreography, and stage presence. Artist development evolved over time but was a formal entity with its own building and directors by the summer of 1964—just as the Supremes were emerging on the national scene. Harvey Fuqua headed the program from the outset. Fuqua, a former member of the Moonglows, was a show business veteran who first developed acts for the Gordys on their Anna Record label. Maxine Powell, who owned her own finishing and modeling school in Detroit, joined Motown in mid-1964. Powell taught all the courses on etiquette, stage presence, and makeup. Cholly Atkins, the legendary choreographer who began in New York as part of the Coles and Atkins dance team, took responsibility for creating the artists' dance routines. Maurice King, an accomplished band leader from Detroit's Flame Show Bar, acted as musical director of artist development. King had been musical director of the International Sweethearts of Rhythm in the late 1940s and brought years of experience to his position.[53]

The artist development department, with its team of skilled show business practitioners, proved vital to Motown's continued success and public image. Strong ideas of bourgeois respectability shaped this image—a concept of respectability that can be traced back to Booker T. Washington's and Carter G. Woodson's respective campaigns to uplift the race and dignify "Negro Life." In his autobiography *Up from Slavery*, Washington recounted how the educational mission of his Tuskegee Institute extended beyond the classroom:

> The students were making progress in learning books and in developing their minds; but it became apparent at once that, if we were to make any permanent impression upon those who had come to us for training, we must do something besides teach them mere books. The students had come from homes where they had no opportunities for lessons which would teach them how to care for their bodies. With few exceptions, the homes in Tuskegee in which the students boarded were but little improvement upon those from which they had come. We wanted to teach the students how to bathe; how to care for their teeth and clothing. We wanted to teach them how to eat, and how to eat properly, and how to care for their rooms.[54]

Carter G. Woodson shared Washington's belief that instruction in basic etiquette was essential for blacks to gain access to institutions and opportunities previously denied them. But Woodson thought that most forms of black music eroded rather than cultivated respect for the race. In 1931

Woodson critiqued the black gospel tradition as "howling, crying, singing, dancing and groveling on the floor in answer to the emotional appeal of an insane or depraved preacher." He also believed that jazz had little value, was overly erotic, and for the sake of "social progress," should be "stamp[ed] . . . out as an evil." For Woodson certain forms of indigenous black culture did not fit into his rather circumscribed vision of "Negro" edification.[55]

Motown's preoccupation with public image, proper etiquette, and general decorum stood in direct relation to these older philosophies about black respectability and black culture. The company sought to produce the black music of Detroit but also to package it in such a way as to not contribute to any racist stereotypes of African Americans as uncouth or uncivilized. Motown marketed a product that proved that black popular culture could "uplift the race" on a mass scale; it could be both "of the people" and dignified.

For the performers this dignity needed not to be learned, only refined. As Mary Wilson commented, "None of us came from homes that didn't teach manners. We were all trying to get ahead, and it's always bothered me that some people have assumed that by accepting what some consider 'white' values, we sold out. It's just not true." Wilson, Ross, and Ballard may have had proper manners when they first arrived at Hitsville, but when "Where Did Our Love Go?" reached number one, the company's interest in the women's public image and behavior heightened considerably. As Wilson recalled, "Once we got back from the Dick Clark tour, Artist Development went into overdrive working on the Supremes." Motown invested substantial time and energy coaching the group on fashion, hairstyles, posture, diction, and appropriate responses to press interviews. The company knew what was at stake: the Supremes had the potential to become the most profitable Motown "product" ever.[56]

Industrial Technologies and the Marketing of the Motown Sound

Motown's ability to produce the city's black culture and turn it into a profitable commodity had deeper political significance when set in the context of larger trends in Detroit's economy. The record company's efforts to manufacture a lucrative cultural product in the Motor City became an important symbol of independence in Detroit's black community. In the early 1960s Detroit's industrial economy did not offer the same opportunities to African Americans looking for a steady livelihood as it had in the 1940s and 1950s. Most notably, automation, in which manufacturers had replaced workers with machines on the assembly line, had become commonplace in industrial manufacturing in the late 1950s and early 1960s. By 1964, when the Supremes' "Where Did Our Love Go?" climbed the charts, automation in industrial manufacturing had replaced approximately 40,000 unskilled and semiskilled jobs a week nationwide. Moreover, as historian C. Vann Woodward noted at the time, "since Negro workers are disproportionately employed in such jobs they are bearing the brunt of technological displacement."[57]

Black workers in Detroit experienced "technological displacement" with unusual severity. The automobile industry's dominance in the city's economy left few occupational choices for those workers looking for jobs outside manufacturing. Moreover, when the automakers created new industrial jobs, they relocated the manufacturing plants outside the city limits. As historian Thomas Sugrue has observed, "Between 1947 and 1958, the three largest automobile producers, Ford, General Motors, and Chrysler, built twenty-five new plants in the metropolitan Detroit area, all of them in suburban communities, most farther than fifteen miles from the center city." Most black workers did not have the means to commute to these jobs and were not welcome in the suburban plants.[58]

Motown Records could not fight these larger economic trends, but it did offer some individuals an alternative to other forms of wage labor. As singer Mary Wells recalled, "Until Motown, in Detroit, there were three big careers for a black girl: babies, the factories, or daywork, Period . . . [My mother] scrubbed floors, did domestic work. Daywork they call it. And it was damn cold on the hallway linoleum. Misery is Detroit linoleum in January—with a half frozen bucket of Spic and Span."[59]

Critiques of the labor crises facing black workers in Detroit originated most incisively from within the city's own black community. James Boggs, Chrysler auto worker, grass-roots activist, and organizer for the Freedom Now Party, analyzed the destructive effects of automation on black workers' labor opportunities in his book *The American Revolution: Pages from a Negro Worker's Notebook*, which was published in May 1963.

Boggs saw automation as "that stage of production which carries the contradictions of capitalism to their furthest extreme, creating and sharpening inside capitalist society the conflicts, antagonisms, clashes between people that make for social progress and the inevitable struggle that goes along with it."[60]

Within Detroit's economy Motown Records participated in, profited from, and challenged many of the contradictions, aspects of social progress, and struggles that resulted from automation and technological advancements in automobile manufacturing. The company's use of audio technology to produce and sell black music offered one counterpoint to the ways in which industrial technology displaced black workers from the automotive job market. Moreover, postwar advancements in radio and automobile engineering worked to Motown's advantage as it created its sound and disseminated it to the public. Specifically, the development of the transistor radio, which made car radios more affordable and effective, influenced the style and production of Motown music. First introduced in 1953, the transistor immediately transformed the radio listening experience. The transistor made radios not only more portable but more mobile as well. The car radio first came into use in 1928. William Lear, eventual designer of the Learjet, invented the original prototype and called it the Motorola. Bulky in size and plagued by poor reception, early car radios did not enjoy widespread popularity or use. Throughout the 1950s transistors made the car radios more reliable and, by 1963, fifty million automobiles had radios.[61]

At Hitsville Studios the proliferation of the car radio was not overlooked but capitalized on. Both the musical form and the audio fidelity of Motown hits such as "My Girl" and "Shop Around" were well suited and often produced with a car radio audience in mind. Some of the first critical commentary on the Detroit sound noted that "Motown's light, unfussy, evenly stressed beat, its continuous loop melodies, [are] the ideal accompaniment for driving."[62] Songwriters at the company confirmed observations that the radio dictated musical form. In an interview Smokey Robinson discussed his songwriting techniques as follows: "I've just geared myself to radio time. The shorter the record is nowadays, the more it's gonna be played. This is a key thing in radio time. . . . If you have a record that's 2:15 long it's definitely gonna get more play than one that's

3:15, at first, which is very important." Bobby Rogers, who sang with Robinson in the Miracles, also remembered how shorter songs helped Motown build its crossover audience:

> When [the Miracles] first started to record on Motown, our music was considered race-music and white radio stations were a bit reluctant to play our material. If they did play it, they would just play a portion of it to lead into the news or a commercial. We finally decided to put a shorter time on the record than it actually lasted. If it lasted three minutes, we would print two minutes and ten seconds on the label. That way they began to play the recordings just to fill up a short period of time, but by the time they were aware of what was happening, the record was over.[63]

While Motown shortened songs to fit into radio time, the company also produced records specifically with car radio audio quality in mind. Motown recording engineers set up car speakers in the studio so that they could simulate and perfect how a song would sound emanating from a car radio. Richard Street, a member of the Temptations and a former studio engineer, described the process this way: "We'd have small to medium to large speakers. You'd put in the small one and turn the dial, and if you couldn't understand the words or it wasn't clear enough, you'd write a little memo back downstairs, like 'Turn up the drums' or 'Too much bass' or 'Can't hear the vocals loud enough.'" Hitsville Studios continued to monitor new advances in audio components for cars throughout the 1960s and marketed their products accordingly. In July 1966 a newspaper article reported that Motown Records led the field "in the first reported tabulations of sales of automobile eight-track stereo tape cartridges."[64]

Motown was also aware that the majority of its car radio listeners were baby-boomer teenagers and continued to produce music with their tastes in mind. Yet Hitsville, U.S.A., was not the only Detroit enterprise to capitalize on the consumption patterns of this new youth market. In January 1961 Lee Iacocca, another Detroit entrepreneur working across town from Berry Gordy's West Grand Boulevard studios, began to develop what was to become by 1964 the "Car of Young America": the Ford

Mustang. Motown's sound and Ford's Mustang sought the same youth market and, at times, used each other to reach it.[65]

The promotion of the Ford Mustang marked a turning point in the history of the automobile industry. The Mustang was the first car to be marketed to young adults on an unprecedented scale. Automobiles and "youth culture" have been linked since the 1920s, but the cars that young Americans drove usually were purchased by parents and borrowed for a Friday night date. In the early sixties Iacocca recognized the buying power of the growing population of baby-boomers. In a story on the young automobile executive, *Time* magazine noted that "Iacocca is one of the leading authorities on the youth market [and] the first man in the auto industry to recognize its importance and capitalize on it." Iacocca relied on new statistics about the young generation to promote the Mustang as a sporty yet inexpensive car. For instance, Iacocca knew that the population of twenty- to twenty-four-year-olds would increase by 50 percent throughout the 1960s. Also, more of these young people than ever before were college-educated and therefore, according to research, more likely to be car purchasers.[66]

In an effort to target the new market, Ford's public relations department began a massive publicity campaign to generate interest—particularly with young people—in the Mustang. The company sponsored "hootenanny" folk concerts at college campuses and gave the editors of college newspapers complimentary Mustangs to test drive for a few weeks. Both *Time* and *Newsweek* magazines simultaneously featured the new car as a cover story in April 1964. The Mustang became a "celebrity" in its own right, and 1964 proved to be a banner year for car sales. Significantly for Motown Records, 80 percent of Mustang buyers requested a car radio in their new vehicle.[67]

Motown developed other connections to the automobile industry besides having its hit songs emanate from car radios. The company appropriated images of Detroit's auto production to market its artists, and the city's auto manufacturers also used popular music at publicity events—such as Ford's "hootenanny" concerts—to associate their car models with youth culture. At Motown publicity shots often included an automobile, usually a Cadillac, as ornamentation to evoke a certain class and celebrity status to an artist or group. In these photographs the glamour of the artist

Marvin Gaye poses with Cadillac. (Courtesy Motown Record Co., L.P., a Polygram Company.)

and the elegance of the automobile complemented each other—as consumers gazed upon the best that Detroit had to offer in music and in engineering. Cadillac cars also became status symbols within Motown's company hierarchy, according to Mary Wilson:

> As soon as a writer, producer, or performer got his first check, it was as good as endorsed over to the local Cadillac dealership. Purchasers, intent on protecting whatever individuality they could enjoy when they were buying the same car everyone they knew had, would consult one another about style, colors, and options, so that no two would be alike. Of course, no one would dare ask Berry about his preferences. One day Mickey Stevenson drove up in a Caddy the same color and style as Berry's new one, a light color, like gray. *Someone* would have to exchange his car; a few days later Mickey was tooling around in a black Cadillac.[68]

Another variation of Motown's "automotive" marketing included a series of photos that highlighted the production of the automobile rather than the finished product. The factory setting reinserted Motown stars into the industrial landscape of the city.

The most extreme example of the marketing of music and motors occurred on a television broadcast one year after the introduction of the Ford Mustang. By mid-1965 over 400,000 Mustangs had been sold nationwide and Motown had a new hit climbing the charts, Martha and the Vandellas' "Nowhere to Run."[69] Murray "the K" Kaufman, one of New York City's most popular disc jockeys, hosted a television show entitled "It's What's Happening, Baby" on CBS-TV. The program encouraged youth to pursue education and summer employment and was sponsored by the U.S. Office of Economic Opportunity in cooperation with CBS-TV.[70] The show, broadcast on June 28, 1965, included performances by the hottest artists on the popular music scene interspersed with "Murray the K's" hip public service announcements. The show featured the Dave Clark Five, Herman's Hermits, Marvin Gaye, the Supremes, Tom Jones, Ray Charles, the Four Tops, the Miracles, and many others. Martha and the Vandellas opened the show with a rousing rendition of "Nowhere to Run." The producers staged the performance on the Mustang assembly line at the Ford River Rouge Plant in Detroit.

Gladys Knight and the Pips pose at automobile factory lot. (Courtesy Motown Record Co., L.P., a Polygram Company.)

As Martha and the Vandellas sang the hit song, they dodged around baffled auto workers attempting to execute their jobs. The song, which tells the story of an obsessive love that haunts the lover's mind, fit perfectly into the stark factory backdrop and musically had a connection to the industrial setting. The song's inventive percussion-based sound resulted from two sources: the prodigious talents of Motown drummer Benny Benjamin and one of the song's clever producers, Lamont Dozier, who shook car chains in the studio to accentuate the foreboding backbeat. The use of car parts to create the song's apprehensive tone complimented the "Nowhere to run, nowhere to hide" lyrics, which recount the lover's inability to free herself from a tortured romance. The staging of the television shoot on the factory shop floor accentuated the eerie quality of the song as Martha and the Vandellas tried to navigate their way through the mechanics of an unfamiliar assembly line. The performance concludes with "Murray the K" driving a fully assembled Mustang out of the auto

Martha and the Vandellas perform "Nowhere to Run" on the Mustang assembly line at the Ford River Rouge Plant for the "It's What's Happening, Baby" show, June 1965. (Courtesy Motown Record Co., L.P., a Polygram Company.)

plant while Martha and the Vandellas stay behind with the autoworkers and wave good-bye.[71]

In this television appearance one of Motown's musical products disrupted the Ford assembly line in order to promote Motown's sound, Ford's Mustang, and the summer employment campaign of the U.S. Office of Economic Opportunity. The moment exemplified James Boggs's assertion that automation and modern technologies carried "the contradictions of capitalism to their furthest extreme." "Nowhere to Run" became more than a song about a tormented love affair when Martha and the Vandellas performed it in the Ford River Rouge Plant, a performance televised to a national audience of teenage consumers. The audience of autoworkers at the filming of the song often had "nowhere to run" from the tedium of assembly-line work and nowhere to go if automation displaced them from their jobs. The U.S. Office of Economic Opportunity broadcast the show to encourage teenagers to look for part-time summer work but did not offer any long-term solutions to the employment crises that automation and deindustrialization had produced in cities like Detroit. For the Ford Motor Company, the "Nowhere to Run" segment offered free publicity for its new and popular Mustang. For Martha and the Vandellas, their appearance on the television special represented what had become a critical stage on Motown's own assembly line, which strengthened the record company's position in the larger record industry.

The Supremes, who had recently overtaken Martha and the Vandellas as the company's most prominent female group, set new standards for attaining national visibility through appearances on television. Their debut on *The Ed Sullivan Show* in December 1964, like Martha and the Vandellas' "Nowhere to Run" appearance, revealed how much Motown's efforts to gain national exposure did more than simply increase record sales. Motown's use of television responded to larger concerns about the role of "Negro Life" in American culture. The Supremes' celebrity affirmed the long-standing contributions of African Americans to American popular music, contributions that were often overlooked or completely ignored. Motown's marketing skills illustrated how African Americans could use television to serve their own ends even when the television industry tried to marginalize them.

Motown Televised

On the winter evening of December 27, 1964, three young women stood in the wings of the Ed Sullivan Theater in Manhattan waiting for their turn to perform on the country's most beloved television variety hour. *The Ed Sullivan Show*, reminiscent of vaudeville, always featured a wide array of talents and novelty acts. Other performers that Sunday evening included Leslie Uggams, impersonator Frank Gorshin, comedian Rip Taylor, and the Czechoslovakian Folk Dance Ensemble. Florence Ballard, Mary Wilson, and Diana Ross sang. The Supremes had rehearsed their latest hit, "Come See about Me," all week. Presentation was key. Cholly Atkins coached them to dance a subtle shimmy step around the one microphone provided. The women wore tasteful dresses—light-blue chiffon with an elegant tiered design. The only mishap involved makeup. The *Sullivan Show* makeup artists, inexperienced with darker skin tones, applied heavy dark pancake foundation on the singers. Horrified with the results, in which they resembled blackface minstrels, Mary, Diana, and Florence repaired their makeup themselves.[72]

No other crises befell the group the night of the live broadcast. The thrill of performing before millions around the country overpowered any other jitters. Finally, their turn arrived. Ed Sullivan introduced the "three youngsters from Detroit," and the Supremes took the stage. The lyrics of "Come See about Me" captured the significance of the moment. The three proud women from Detroit sang to the country to "come *see*" about them before a national television camera that made their request possible. Mary, Diana, and Florence had journeyed far from their initial triumph at the Emancipation Celebration talent contest in Windsor, Canada, but their main goal, stardom, remained the same. The Supremes' appearance on *The Ed Sullivan Show* was, however, more than the next step on fame's ladder. Their performance resonated within the larger history of the television industry and its relationship to the promotion of "Negro Life" in Detroit and in America.

Carter G. Woodson, ASNLH founder, died in April 1950 at the age of seventy-five. In his last years Woodson remained committed to publicizing black history and culture to mass audiences through the association's publications and programs. Television, still in its infancy at the end of Woodson's life, held tremendous potential to support the causes of the ASNLH. In June 1950, only two months after Woodson's death, *Ebony* magazine published an article about television's promise as a new venue to celebrate "Negro Life" and present it to the rest of the country. The report noted how Negro performers such as Ethel Waters, Pearl Bailey, and Billy Eckstine appear on the new medium with "great frequency . . . a sure sign that television is free of racial barriers." Moreover, "rarely have [Negro performers] had to stoop to the Uncle Tom pattern which is usually the Negro thespian's lot on radio shows and in Hollywood movies."[73]

The *Ebony* article also included a comment from Ed Sullivan, whose *Toast of the Town* variety show featured more Negro artists than any other network program. Sullivan asserted that, "Television not only is just what the doctor ordered for Negro performers; television subtly has supplied ten-league boots to the Negro in his fight to win what the Constitution of this country guarantees as his birthright. It has taken his long fight to the living rooms of Americans' homes where public opinion is formed and the Negro is winning! He has become a welcome visitor, not only to the white adult, but to the white children, who finally will lay Jim Crow to rest."[74] One year later Sullivan continued to be an outspoken advocate of television's ability to cultivate racial tolerance. In an essay entitled "Can TV Crack America's Color Line?" for the May 1951 issue of *Ebony* magazine, Sullivan argued that television provided a public service. On his show appearances by Dr. Ralph Bunche, Joe Louis, and Jackie Robinson, and other Negro celebrities "have proven that a man's heart, rather than skin, is ever the determining factor in American life." Sullivan's belief in television's power to influence public opinions about "Negro Life" and his support of black performers on his show endeared him to many but alienated others. The racial politics of early television were not as progressive as Sullivan hoped, and his own show proved this point.

Sullivan first hosted CBS-TV's *Toast of the Town* on June 20, 1948. An entertainment variety show, *Toast of the Town* was the CBS network's entry in the Sunday night 8:00 P.M. time slot, competing against shows such as Milton Berle's *Texaco Star Theater* on NBC-TV. The Emerson Radio Company sponsored the show for its first season but wanted CBS to choose another, more dynamic, host for the variety hour. Sullivan, a former newspaper columnist, was a sedate and rather unassuming presence on the screen. Sullivan's reserved on-camera personality was even the target of comics who appeared on his show. Comedian Jack Leonard once commented to a *Toast of the Town* audience, "Ed's the only man who brightens a room by leaving it." Yet, when the Ford Motor Company's Lincoln-Mercury division offered to sponsor the show, CBS decided to retain Sullivan as host.[75]

Sullivan, grateful for Ford's generosity, became an "ambassador" for the Lincoln-Mercury automobile. In 1955 *Time* magazine reported on Sullivan's allegiance to Ford in a cover story on the entertainer and his show, which recently had been renamed *The Ed Sullivan Show*. *Time* noted that,

> To further the cause of Lincoln-Mercury, Ed has addressed steelworkers in Pittsburgh, landed on Boston Common in a helicopter, gone down 20 ft. in a Navy diving suit and sailed up the Mississippi in a barge before 75,000 spectators at the opening of the Memphis Cotton Carnival. His identification with his sponsor is so strong that any Lincoln or Mercury buyer who is dissatisfied with his car is apt to drop Ed a complaining line. (Within ten days after such a complaint, the local district manager is on the phone or the car owner's doorstep, solicitously asking what he can do to help).[76]

In terms of sales, the Ford Motor Company's decision to sponsor *The Ed Sullivan Show* proved wise. As one Lincoln-Mercury dealer, Paul Pusey of Richmond, Virginia, remarked, "[Ed] does two-thirds of our selling job for us." Another Ford spokesperson noted that "Mercurys have come up fast in sales, thanks to Sullivan. Monday is now our busiest day, following his Sunday show." Sullivan also prided himself on his personal contacts with Lincoln-Mercury dealers. Once, when traveling in Paris, he sent picture postcards, addressed individually, to eight hundred Ford dealers across the country.[77]

One aspect of Sullivan's relationship to Lincoln-Mercury dealers was tense, however. Sullivan's long-term interest in promoting "Negro" entertainers often strained his ties with Ford dealers. When Lena Horne,

Ella Fitzgerald, or Pearl Bailey appeared on his program, Sullivan often made a point of greeting the singers with a handshake or a hug. Ford dealers, particularly in the South, found such on-camera affection between a white male host and a black female guest objectionable and voiced complaints to the network. Sullivan did not bow to his sponsor's requests, and the conflict continued over many years.[78]

The Ford dealers' desire to censor Sullivan's behavior reflected a growing anxiety about the visibility of black performers on television in general. In the mid-1950s the emergent civil rights movement, evident in collective action such as the Montgomery bus boycott, heightened awareness about racial injustice in America. In this climate corporations, afraid to offend viewers particularly in the South, became increasingly hesitant to sponsor television programming that showcased "Negro" performers. *The Nat King Cole Show*, which began in 1956 on NBC-TV, was the most famous casualty of the racial politics of television sponsorship. Cole's variety show received favorable ratings even in the South but was unable to secure a national sponsor and ended after only one season. Embittered by the experience, Cole commented publicly that "[r]acial prejudice is more finance than romance."[79]

When the Supremes walked on Ed Sullivan's stage in December 1964, prospects for blacks in television had not changed dramatically since the cancellation of Nat King Cole's show. *The Ed Sullivan Show* remained one of the few venues on television that consistently featured black talent.[80] The Supremes' identity as Motown artists and as "products" of Detroit distinguished them from other "Negro" entertainers who appeared on the show. The Ford Motor Company's sponsorship rescued Sullivan's show from possible cancellation in its early years. When Ed Sullivan became known as the ambassador of Ford Lincoln-Mercury in 1955, Berry Gordy Jr. was working as an upholsterer trimmer on Ford's Lincoln-Mercury assembly line. Sullivan's show sold the automobiles that both Gordy's and Malcolm X's labor had built.[81] Yet the auto manufacturer, which closely monitored the black performers who appeared with Ed Sullivan, maintained a highly conflicted relationship with the show and its role as a tool to foster racial tolerance.

Motown's relationship to the Ford Motor Company and to *The Ed Sullivan Show* complicated these racial and economic politics even further. After the Supremes' premiere appearance, Motown Records soon incorporated *The Ed Sullivan Show* as a final phase on its own production line. Berry Gordy scheduled subsequent appearances by the Supremes and other Motown artists including the Temptations, the Four Tops, and the Miracles strategically—to coincide with the debut of a new song. Motown's efforts to increase record sales through the *Sullivan Show,* and other popular variety hours such as *Hollywood Palace,* countered the Ford Motor Company's and other sponsors' efforts to censor or limit the visibility of African American entertainers on television. Sponsors tried to censor these appearances out of fear that they would hamper the sales of their own products. When the Supremes' sang "Come See about Me" on the *Sullivan Show,* they achieved one of Carter G. Woodson's goals in the promotion of "Negro Life" in America. When the record sold, Motown's profits outwitted the logic of the television industry, which seemed designed to keep black Americans from sharing in the economic rewards of the medium.

The Civil Rights "Market" for Black Culture

The Supremes' appearance on *The Ed Sullivan Show* introduced one facet of Detroit's black culture into living rooms across America. Their appeal held a unique power in a country eager for cultural symbols that racial integration was not only possible but attractive and nonthreatening. On July 2, 1964, President Lyndon Johnson signed into law the Civil Rights Act of 1964, which banned all forms of racial discrimination in public facilities. The national mandate for public integration increased the need for positive images of black Americans, which the Supremes and other Motown performers provided. Images of sophisticated Motown artists reassured the American public at a time when the inevitable racial tensions involved in implementing the Civil Rights Act of 1964 loomed ahead.

In Detroit local leaders recognized Motown's achievements as a positive cultural force. Just two months after the Supremes performed on national television, the *Michigan Chronicle* published its "Annual Brotherhood Edition," "[d]edicated to Racial Amity and Understanding." The newspaper published the special issue in conjunction with the city's annual Brotherhood Week and the ASNLH's National Negro History Week, which Langston Hughes had inaugurated one year earlier. Brotherhood Week, founded in 1933 by the National Conference of Christians and Jews, promoted tolerance among racial, ethnic, and religious groups. The newspaper selected eight individuals to honor "who have distinguished themselves in these efforts and who have provided the leadership which has made these giant strides toward better interracial understanding possible." The eight individuals included George Romney, governor of Michigan; John Conyers, U.S. representative from Michigan's first congressional district; Mrs. Foster Braun, chair of the Catholic Archbishop's Committee on Human Relations; Dr. Remus Robinson, member of the Detroit Board of Education; the Reverend John Weaver, retiring dean of the Episcopal Cathedral; Mrs. Roberta Hughes, executive secretary of the Commission on Children and Youth; Judge John Feikens, cochair of the Michigan Civil Rights Commission; and Berry Gordy Jr., "president and founder of Hitsville, U.S.A., a mushrooming entertainment organization that is making Detroit the center of an international art form."[82]

Gordy's accomplishments as a cultural producer—as the creator of an "international art form"—stood apart from the other honorees, who were government officials or community and religious leaders. Most significantly, the Brotherhood Committee recognized Gordy's management skills; his ability not only to create "art" but to record it, preserve it, and disseminate it to an "international" audience. Black cultural expression had the power to promote "interracial understanding," but only through access to institutions and industries that traditionally excluded "Negro Life." At Motown the ways in which the company's artists and music got produced, marketed, and distributed had as many, if not more, political consequences as the songs themselves. Yet the music also held potential as a social force. During the civil rights era all forms of black cultural expression had the capacity to be political tools or to be read as such.

The role of black cultural expression, in conjunction with its production, in the cause of civil rights and black empowerment was gaining currency by late 1964 and early 1965. In Detroit Berry Gordy Jr.'s selection as a Brotherhood honoree reflected this trend. Concurrently, artists started to reconsider their relationship to the racial and political turmoil that surrounded them. In December, at the time of the Supremes' debut on national television, Langston Hughes pondered these questions in an unpublished paper. Hughes wrote,

> Politics in any country in the world is dangerous. For the poet, politics in any country had better be disguised as poetry. Politics can be the graveyard of the poet. And only poetry can be his resurrection . . . Concerning politics, nothing I have said is true. A poet is a human being. Each human being must live within his time, with and for his people, and within the boundaries of his country. Therefore, how can a poet keep out of politics? Hang yourself, poet, in your own words. Otherwise, you are dead.[83]

Hughes's conflicted and urgent tone contrasted sharply with the celebratory message of his essay "Record It," which was published soon after the release of Motown's *Great March to Freedom* album one year earlier.

The optimism of October 1963, when the poet had just signed his contract with Motown and agreed to travel to Detroit for the ASNLH weekend, could not be sustained by December 1964. In July 1964 Hughes witnessed firsthand the wrath of the "dream deferred" as Harlem exploded into violence after a white, off-duty police officer shot and killed Jimmy Powell, a fifteen-year-old black boy. Hughes went to the funeral parlor to view Powell's body and listened to the gunfire within a hundred yards of his home on the night of the funeral. About the wake, Hughes later remarked, "I saw him lying in his coffin looking very small and dead." His poem "Death in Yorkville (James Powell, Summer, 1964)" addresses Hughes's outrage over the tragedy. The first stanza queries, "How many bullets does it take / To kill a fifteen-year-old kid? / How many bullets does it take / To kill me?" In the midst of the violence, Hughes struggled to restrain himself from getting caught up in the destruction around him.[84]

Margaret Danner wrote to him from Detroit during this trying time. Danner needed Hughes's advice about how to push Motown Records to finally release their *Poets of the Revolution* album. In the letter Danner warned her dear friend to stay out of the crossfire and remember the power of his poetry. She urged, *"Remember you fight best through your pen. Remember that to be alive is the first consideration. Hold on. Keep your hand on that pen and hold on.*"[85] Hughes heeded Danner's advice—though he had little for her in regards to the Motown recording. In July 1964 the Supremes' breakaway hit "Where Did Our Love Go?" dominated the company's attention, and the eventual release of the poetry recording seemed more remote than ever.

By December 1964 the Supremes were on *The Ed Sullivan Show,* and the release of *Poets of the Revolution* was postponed indefinitely. The two projects, which began with so much possibility in October 1963, had followed two different trajectories. No official company records explained why Motown decided to set aside the poetry record, but basic business principles undoubtedly motivated the decision. In comparison to the commercial potential of Motown's musical offerings, *Poets of the Revolution* would generate few, if any, profits. The poetry album also differed from Motown's *Great March to Freedom,* which also had limited marketability but at least commemorated a specific historic event. In 1964, as Motown watched the Supremes ascend to the top of the charts, the company became much less concerned about its obligations as a black record company to release one race-conscious poetry album. The fate of the poetry album revealed Motown's ambivalence about its role in preserving cultural documents about the "Negro revolt." This ambivalence would only deepen in the years to come as the record company continued to pursue white crossover audiences and the civil rights movement continued to look to "market" black culture as a tool of the struggle.

A new challenge at Motown was just around the corner as its "popular" music began to resonate with the racial and political upheavals of its time. Declarations of black consciousness could not be relegated to obscure poetry recordings and were often read into the lyrics of a Motown song. Motown's role as an "international art form" that could promote "interracial understanding" was only one of the attributes ascribed to the Detroit sound by the mid-1960s. Throughout 1965 and 1966 the violence and anger that Langston Hughes had witnessed in Harlem in the summer of 1964 began to threaten the movement's commitment to nonviolent protest across the country. In Detroit the desire to find new modes of resistance and activism through cultural expression was about to become more urgent than ever.

4

"Afro-American Music, without Apology":
The Motown Sound and the Politics of Black Culture

When Langston Hughes's *New Negro Poets, U.S.A.* anthology appeared in May 1964, it included a preface by Gwendolyn Brooks. In the essay Brooks eloquently articulated the dilemmas confronting "Negro" poets:

> At the present time, poets who happen to be Negroes are twice-tried. They have to write poetry, and they have to remember that they are Negroes. Often they wish that they could solve the Negro question once and for all, and go on from such success to the composition of textured sonnets or buoyant villanelles about the transience of a raindrop, or the gold-stuff of the sun. They are likely to find significances in those subjects not instantly obvious to their fairer fellows. The raindrop may seem to them to represent racial tears—and those might seem, indeed, other than transient. The golden sun might remind them that they are burning.

In his own writings Langston Hughes also pondered the ambivalence within the "Negro" artist between the wish to be "free" of racial politics when creating art and the poet's desire to "live within his time, with and for his people." The question of the relationship of the "Negro" artist and his or her art to black struggle extended far beyond poetry. All forms of black culture, including popular music, confronted these issues in some way during the civil rights years, and Motown music was no exception.[1]

5 to 1966 Motown's ability to produce a sound and an
ı glorified "Negro" talent and appealed to white sensibil-
_____ to grow. Yet Motown's broad popularity also paralleled
dramatic shifts and internal dissension within the national civil rights
campaign. In 1965 the country witnessed the assassination of Malcolm
X, "Bloody Sunday" during the Selma, Alabama, voting rights campaign,
and the Watts uprising. These crises caused many people to question the
viability of civil disobedience protest strategies and the goal of racial
integration itself. The violent outbreaks of 1965 renewed interest in black
nationalist approaches and self-defense against physical attacks, and laid
fertile ground for the emergence of Black Power philosophies. Against
this backdrop, the Motown company, its artists, and its music could not
avoid becoming highly contested symbols of black achievement.

Motown produced songs to entertain and sell, and therefore to avoid
controversy at all costs. Nevertheless, the music, as with all forms of
cultural expression, had a life of its own once it was released to the public.
The Motown sound always eluded simple definitions. Throughout 1965
and 1966 the songs produced on West Grand Boulevard maintained the
company's standard of consistently danceable tunes with lyrics that usually spoke about the travails of teenage romance. Yet, to the music's varied
audiences, Motown songs could be anything from the life of a party to a
call to revolution. For some, Martha and the Vandellas' song "Heatwave"
was a simple testament to the metaphorical, incendiary power of romance;
for others, it reminded them "that they [were] burning."

The tensions around what Motown's success and sound meant to the
black struggle played themselves out most immediately within Detroit's
black community. Some found in Motown's ability to reach white audiences the hope that interracial understanding was possible. Others considered Motown's music less about bridging racial divides than about
advancing race pride. Many of Motown's performers began to feel "twice-
tried"—wanting to be accepted as entertainers, but also remembering
that "they are Negroes." In the midst of these competing forces, the
company maintained its agenda of maximizing its music's commercial
potential with national and international audiences. Back in Detroit, local
Motown fans attempted to use the company and its music to promote their
own causes.

Motown Music, Afro-American Dignity, and Brotherhood

On February 14, 1965, the Motown Record Company received a Dignity Award at the First Annual Dignity Projection and Scholarship Awards Night held at Detroit's Ford Auditorium. Attorney Milton Henry, president of the Afro-American Broadcasting and Recording Company, orchestrated the event and selected seven individuals and ten companies to receive an award "to honor annually those persons and firms who have contributed most to the destruction of a vilifying stereotype and to the projection of the Afro-American as a being with hope of the future, as one of deep humanity, spiritual conviction, intellect, morality and responsibility—in short, as being of inherent dignity."[2] Henry acknowledged both local business leaders and national celebrities such as Marian Anderson, Rosa Parks, Sidney Poitier, and Jackie Gleason.[3] He also gave special mention to three of the ten companies that received an award: the Bell Broadcasting Company, for creating "the Midwest's first Negro-owned broadcasting complex, Stations WCHB & WCHD-FM"; Swift and Company, "for . . . tasteful advertisements . . . in which the Negro appears as being of dignity"; and the Motown Record Company, "for consistent presentation of Afro-American music, without apology, by Afro-American artists who project vibrant DIGNITY." Motown's selection had a personal significance for Henry, who had acted as recording engineer for the company's *Great March to Freedom* album two years earlier.

Motown's ability to produce "Afro-American music, without apology" fit nicely into the evening's theme of recognizing those who advanced racial pride. At the time of the Dignity Awards, Motown had several singles high on the charts including the Temptations' "My Girl," Martha and the Vandellas' "Nowhere to Run," the Supremes' "Stop! In the Name of Love," and Junior Walker and the All-Stars' "Shotgun." The pervasive presence of Motown songs on the radio affirmed one of the main goals of the Afro-American Broadcasting and Recording Company: to promote African American perspectives and culture on the radio, in recordings, and in the mass media. The organizers of the Dignity Awards also planned to donate 25 percent of ticket sales for the event toward the establishment of a scholarship fund at Wayne State University to stimulate "the entry of Afro-American youth into the field of mass communications." From

Motown, Marvin Gaye and his wife, Anna Gordy Gaye, contributed to the scholarship fund.[4]

The strong local support for the Dignity Awards event was primarily due to Milton Henry's reputation as an innovative activist. Henry first acquired local celebrity in 1963 when he represented Cynthia Scott's family in the controversial police brutality case. Soon after, he combined his skills as a political organizer and an audiophile to produce a weekly radio show. In 1964 Henry officially founded the Afro-American Broadcasting Company to present programming for "spiritually free black people." When the company decided to rerelease Henry's recording of Malcolm X's "Message to the Grass Roots" speech, it changed its name to the Afro-American Broadcasting *and* Recording Company and began to organize the awards night.[5]

The Dignity Awards also received support from the city's political circles. Milton Henry's prominent career as an outspoken attorney won him many allies, who supported his efforts to use the media to promote the interests of Detroit's black community. His colleagues from the Group on Advanced Leadership and the Freedom Now Party including his brother, Richard Henry, Grace Lee Boggs, and the Reverend Albert Cleage supported the fund-raising event. Among elected officials, U.S. Representative Charles C. Diggs Jr. acted as a patron of the scholarship fund, and Michigan Governor George Romney sent greetings to be read to attendees.[6]

Despite such fanfare, seven of the business honorees, including the Chrysler Corporation, which Henry selected for supporting a Negro franchise dealer and "for somewhat enlightened employment practices," and Hudson's Department Store, "for the use of Negro models in their fashion shows," declined their awards. In an effort to explain these refusals, the evening's program included a brief "Footnote to History," which speculated that the companies were "afraid . . . [and] [w]e suspect that they do not like Malcolm X." Malcolm X, fresh from his pilgrimage to Mecca and with his new Muslim name, El Hadj Malik Shabazz, was the keynote speaker for the evening.

Controversy followed Malcolm X to Detroit when he came to fulfill the speaking engagement. He arrived in Michigan less than twenty-four hours after his house was bombed in Queens, New York. Many people questioned his judgment in leaving his family immediately after the bombing. In a subsequent radio interview Malcolm explained his actions:

> The Black Muslim movement . . . had its origin in Detroit, Michigan. Now those who are in the Black Muslim movement symbolically regard Detroit as the Mecca, the root or the focal point of the origin or beginning of Elijah Muhammad's movement in this country. The fact that I was to appear at a rally in Detroit had been highly publicized in Detroit. My wife and I felt that one of the purposes of the bombing of the house was to keep me from going to Detroit. We discussed it. And she encouraged me not to delay my trip. I went to Detroit, made the speaking engagement, and flew right back here.[7]

Unlike his Grass Roots Conference appearance in Detroit in November 1963, when he stood confident and brash before hundreds of listeners at King Solomon Baptist Church, Malcolm seemed jittery and distracted at the Dignity Awards. At the beginning of his talk, he apologized for his disheveled appearance and blamed it on the fire damage to his wardrobe from the bombing. Throughout the remainder of his sometimes rambling speech, Malcolm presented a more strident critique of nonviolent protest than ever before. While he emphasized that he would not "call on anyone to be violent without a cause," Malcolm beseeched his audience to prepare for "vigorous action in self-defense." To justify his argument, Malcolm noted that the racial conditions that caused violence in 1963 and 1964 still existed; and he predicted that 1965 would be the "longest and hottest and bloodiest year of them all." Malcolm concluded by stating, "I'm for the brotherhood of everybody, but I don't believe in forcing brotherhood on people who don't want it."[8]

Two weeks after Malcolm's comments about the limits of brotherhood, the *Michigan Chronicle* published its "Annual Brotherhood Edition" on February 27, 1965. The *Chronicle*'s special front page featured articles about how to promote "racial amity" and a report on Berry Gordy Jr. and the other Brotherhood honorees. Here, only fourteen days after the Dignity Awards recognized Motown for producing "Afro-American music, without apology," the newspaper acknowledged Berry Gordy Jr.

for creating "an international art form" that promoted "interracial understanding." Motown's ability to fit the agenda of both the Dignity Awards and Brotherhood Week demonstrated how advocates across the political spectrum appropriated the company and its music as symbols of black achievement.

Unlike Motown, Malcolm X was not recognized by the *Michigan Chronicle* as an agent of brotherhood and "interracial understanding." A story about the controversial black nationalist did appear in the Brotherhood edition of the newspaper, but it was a story that reported his death at the hands of assassins on February 21, 1965, in Harlem's Audubon Ballroom—only seven days after his appearance in Detroit. The newspaper printed a second front page to cover Malcolm X's murder. This page bore no trace of the spirit of "brotherhood" but instead recounted the grim details of Malcolm's final hours. News of Malcolm's assassination not only undercut the spirit of Brotherhood Week, but also began to fulfill his own premonition that 1965 would be the "longest and hottest and bloodiest year of them all." Marvin Gaye, like many others, saw Malcolm X's assassination as ominous. He remarked, "I loved Malcolm's strength and his truth-telling. When they cut him down, I felt a loss inside my soul, and I knew that an age of terrible violence and suffering had just begun."[9]

Press coverage of Malcolm X's brutal death occupied headlines but did not dominate them. News of the death of another popular icon of black America, Nat King Cole, also filled the front pages of the national press in mid-February. Cole died of lung cancer in St. John's Hospital in Santa Monica, California, on February 15, 1965, exactly one week before Malcolm X's assassination. In Detroit the conjuncture of the two deaths did not go unnoticed. At an event in honor of Brotherhood Week held at Mackenzie High School, Richard Austin, a local politician, gave a speech that challenged students to contribute to "brotherhood" more than one week a year. Austin commented on the recent deaths of Nat King Cole and Malcolm X and remarked, "Neither their deaths nor their lives are comparable. I find only one thing in common which causes me to draw a parallel. Cole died of cancer and Malcolm died of the cancerous substance of extremism." Not everyone shared Austin's analysis of Malcolm X's demise. Moreover, Austin's claim that Nat King Cole's and Malcolm

X's lives could not be compared rested on an assumption that the realms of black culture and black politics did not intersect.[10]

Black activism in Detroit directly contradicted the assumption that a cultural figure such as Nat King Cole and a militant leader such as Malcolm X had no connection to each other. Milton Henry's efforts to recognize both Motown's "Afro-American music, without apology" and Malcolm X's revolutionary leadership at the Dignity Awards revealed that activists such as Henry understood that black culture was integral to black political organizing. The awards night precipitated the beginnings of a tactical shift in black political organizing in Detroit. The shift involved a turn from traditional electoral efforts and political rhetoric, such as the Freedom Now Party campaign, to an embrace of black culture and arts to communicate the spirit of black empowerment.

The inability of any Freedom Now Party candidates to win office in the 1964 election illustrated how difficult it was to attain black political representation in significant numbers on the city, state, or federal level—especially outside the two-party system. The 1964 election of John Conyers Jr., a Democrat, to Congress from the newly reapportioned first district of Detroit was, therefore, an important achievement. Conyers's victory was bittersweet, however, as he defeated Richard Austin to win his seat. The Conyers-Austin race deeply divided the black community and exposed the internal tensions that could emerge on the road to black political enfranchisement. Richard Austin expressed his frustration with the political process in his speech at Mackenzie High School during Brotherhood Week. He explained that he withdrew from a recent campaign for auditor general, "when it was clear that the majority of the legislators didn't feel like making me their brotherhood gesture of the week."[11]

Austin's subsequent remarks about the lives and deaths of Nat King Cole and Malcolm X ignored exactly how interrelated Austin's own political career, Malcolm X's revolutionary life, and Nat King Cole's artistry were. Campaigns for black empowerment took many forms by 1965, and these forms broke down long-held boundaries among the electoral, the cultural, and the radical approaches. The emergent permeability of these boundaries was, in part, a reaction to the unrelenting persistence of racial discrimination. As Malcolm X noted in his speech at the Dignity Awards, the racial conditions that caused violence and anger in 1963 and 1964 still existed in 1965. Even after the passage of the Civil Rights Act in July 1964, the goals to end racial discrimination in housing, education, and employment were still far from being realized. Nationally, Martin Luther King Jr. and SCLC started to organize the voting rights campaign in Selma in early 1965. The campaign brought attention to the need for federal legislation that would protect the black vote throughout the country. The deep entrenchment of all types of discrimination called for more innovative methods of resistance, methods that would use more than one strategy or would combine cultural, electoral, and radical tactics.

Motown and its music participated in the growing political interest in black culture, but not always willingly. The company wanted its music to transcend racial categories. By early 1965 Berry Gordy Jr. wanted to capitalize on the overwhelming popularity of the Supremes and reach audiences beyond Motown's standard youth market. Gordy knew that the prestigious nightclub circuit in New York and Las Vegas could introduce the "Sound of Young America" to adult audiences. Motown strategically set its sights on the Copacabana nightclub in New York City, which stood as the gateway to this new market.

When Nat King Cole died in February 1965, Motown was in the early stages of securing an engagement at the Copacabana. Press coverage about Cole's death heightened public awareness about the entertainer's lifetime achievements. Assessments of Cole's career focused on his talents as a jazz pianist and vocalist, and—most importantly—his elegant and sophisticated persona. Nat King Cole's suave image made him one of the most popular entertainers, black or white, to perform regularly at the Copacabana nightclub. The public never ignored Cole's racial identity, of course, and he faced the same frustrations and contradictions that confronted any black celebrity in a country divided by racial segregation. As Motown groomed the Supremes for the Copacabana, the company wanted both the style and the content of their performance to reflect the standards that Nat King Cole established throughout his career. As Motown pursued Cole's legacy as an entertainer, the company also inherited the internal conflicts that Cole experienced as a "Negro" artist in America. Cole's musical career, with its urban roots and commercial evolution, foreshadowed the challenges that Motown artists and their music would face in 1965 and 1966, as the civil rights struggle began to turn to black art and cultural expression to articulate its causes, and the record company began to turn to nightclubs to broaden its markets.

"Mr. Cole Won't Rock and Roll"

People think of a performer as a minstrel . . . he's there but he's not really there. They consider us a diversion; wind us up and we'll dance. Right there when you need entertainment. But when you're looking for a citizen to work with other people, whoever thinks about calling us in?

—Nat King Cole

Nathaniel Adams Coles was born in Montgomery, Alabama, on St. Patrick's Day, March 17, 1919.[12] His father, the Reverend Edward James Coles, was the pastor of the First Baptist Church and raised his family in a pious but loving home. His mother, Perlina Adams Coles, who was the choir director at First Baptist, encouraged her son's precocious musical talents. By the age of four, Nathaniel could play "Yes, We Have No Bananas" on the family piano. This same year the Coles family decided to migrate north to Chicago, Illinois, in the hopes of leading a better, less segregated, existence.

"Nat" Coles grew up on the South Side of Chicago, immersed in the jazz and blues culture that surrounded him. The Coles family lived near the Grand Terrace Ballroom. Nat and his older brother, Eddie, stood in the alley nearby and listened as the music of jazz greats such as Louis Armstrong and Fletcher Henderson rang out into the streets. Nat paid particularly close attention whenever Earl "Fatha" Hines performed. Hines's innovative piano playing inspired the young Coles, who dreamed of a career in jazz music.[13]

Nat's formal training in piano began in his youth. He received piano lessons as a teenager and learned classical works including pieces by Rachmaninoff and Bach. Each Sunday he played the organ at his father's church in Chicago, the True Light Baptist Church. He formed his first jazz band, Nat Coles and His Rogues of Rhythm, while still attending Wendell Phillips High School. When the group defeated Earl Hines and his band in a "Battle of the Bands" held at the Savoy Ballroom, Nat earned a new nickname, "Prince of the Ivories." In 1936 Nat met his first wife, Nadine Robinson, a dancer. Soon after, Robinson, Coles, and his band joined a revival tour of the show *Shuffle Along*, which was the first all-black show to debut on Broadway in 1920. When the tour arrived in southern California, Coles and Robinson decided to stay and try to establish their careers on the West Coast.[14]

Coles began playing jazz clubs throughout the region. In 1937 Bob Lewis, manager of the Swanee Inn on North La Brea in Los Angeles, asked him if he could organize a quartet to play regularly at his club. Nat found guitarist Oscar Moore and bassist Wesley Prince, and Lewis decided that a trio was sufficient. For publicity, Lewis dubbed Coles, Nat "King" Cole and asked the pianist to wear a gold-leaf crown while performing. Cole, who disliked the degrading gimmick, got rid of the crown in a few days, but the nickname stuck. His trio, the King Cole Swingsters, agreed to a one-month engagement at the Swanee Inn. Six months later, they remained the inn's top attraction.

From 1937 through the war years, the trio, officially renamed the King Cole Trio, continued to attract audiences—a particularly remarkable feat in the era of big bands.[15] During these years Cole's skills as a vocalist emerged when he decided to sing songs to break the monotony of instrumental sets.[16] In late 1940 the group recorded several songs that featured Cole's vocals for the Decca Sepia Series, including "Sweet Lorraine" and "Honeysuckle Rose." When Capitol Records was founded in 1942, the company turned to the King Cole Trio for fresh material. In late 1943 Capitol released "Straighten Up and Fly Right," a novelty song that Cole had written based on one of his father's old sermons. The song sold over a million copies by May 1944 and firmly established Cole's talents as a singer.[17] From that moment on, Cole's career as a vocalist took precedence over his work as a jazz instrumentalist. Cole felt ambivalent about the shift to vocal lead and continued to develop his piano playing over the years. He also applied the skills he developed as a jazz musician to his singing style. Cole did not have a broad vocal range, but he personalized songs with his distinctive and improvisational phrasing.

In 1946 the King Cole Trio had two more major hits, "Route 66" and "The Christmas Song," and played Las Vegas for the first time. The thrill of performing in Las Vegas ended abruptly when the management of the El Rancho, the establishment that had booked the group, informed Cole and his trio that blacks were not allowed in the casino. They only were to perform for white patrons. Cole vowed never to work under such conditions again. The El Rancho incident typified a central tension that continued throughout the remainder of Cole's career and life. This tension centered around the limits of his role as a prominent black entertainer in postwar America before the emergence of the national civil rights movement.

Particularly after his 1948 hit, "Nature Boy," which achieved more crossover success with white audiences than any of his previous work, Cole discovered that his celebrity came with a price. Broad appreciation of his music from white audiences did not translate into a more racially tolerant world. Both professionally and privately, Cole confronted racial discrimination on a regular basis. These confrontations also influenced Cole's relationship to his black public, who often felt that he was not outspoken enough about the injustices that he endured. From the late forties until his death in 1965, Cole struggled to reconcile his multiple identities as a jazz artist, a commercially successful popular singer, and a black man living in a racially segregated society.

Cole faced one of the most difficult challenges of racial segregation in the summer of 1948, when he and his second wife, Maria, decided to purchase a home in the exclusive and all-white neighborhood of Hancock Park in Los Angeles. Money was no object for the Cole family, particularly after the tremendous success of "Nature Boy." Money, however, was not the issue. When the Coles decided on an English Tudor-style house on South Muirfield Road, neighbors in the area formed the Hancock Park Property Owners Association. Members of the association quickly contacted Cole's managers, requesting that the Coles rethink their decision to move into the area. One member called Cole's road manager, Mort Ruby, and complained, "How would you like it if you had to come out of your home and see a Negro walking down the street wearing a big wide hat, a zoot suit, long chain, and yellow shoes?"[18]

When it became clear that the black entertainer and his family were not going to back down, resistance became more vigorous. The Coles' real estate agent received threatening phone calls, and the Hancock Park Property Owners association took legal action to block the purchase. Cole received an affidavit from the president of the association asserting that covenants existed in Hancock Park that restricted home ownership to "Christian Caucasians." Cole knew the association's claim had no power in the wake of the U.S. Supreme Court's *Shelly v. Kramer* decision in early 1948, which ruled that federal and state courts could not enforce restrictive covenants. In a public statement Cole declared, "I am an American citizen . . . My wife and I like our home very much and we intend to stay there the same as any other American citizens would." The Los Angeles Realty Board responded to Cole's persistence by organizing a campaign to amend the U.S. Constitution to protect restrictive covenants. The Coles moved into their home on August 28, 1948, defying the organized resistance. Active protests eventually subsided, but the Hancock Park incident was not the last highly publicized episode of race discrimination Cole would face in his lifetime.[19] The next incident occurred on stage.

On April 10, 1956, a group of white men physically attacked Cole while he performed before a segregated white audience in Birmingham, Alabama. The attackers, five members of the local White Citizens Council, jumped the stage as Cole began the second chorus of "Little Girl." The men lunged at Cole, hit him in the face with a microphone, and pushed him over his piano bench, which broke on impact. Stage hands rushed Cole off the stage as the melee continued. Police officers joined the fray and apprehended the men as Cole's orchestra, led by Ted Heath, began to play "America." Stunned, Cole walked back on stage briefly to accept an apology and an ovation from the audience, but he did not honor requests that he try to sing again. Backstage, he admitted that though he loved show business, "I don't want to die for it." Cole did return to the stage later that evening to perform his second show before an all-black audience, but it would be his last live performance in his home state of Alabama.[20]

The incident received national press coverage as the case against the attackers proceeded. Investigators discovered six men were directly involved: the five who were in the auditorium and one man who sat in a getaway car armed with two rifles, a blackjack, and brass knuckles. Police learned that a plan to attack and kidnap Cole began four days before the concert at a filling station in Anniston, Alabama, owned by a leader in the North Alabama Citizens Council. Asa E. Carter, head of the council, recently had made public statements denouncing "Negro" music. The council felt that jazz was part of an NAACP plot to "mongrelize America" and that " 'bebop,' 'rock and roll,' and all 'Negro music' [were] designed to force 'Negro culture' on the South."[21]

Press reports about Cole's response to the attack did not satisfy his black public. Privately, Cole expressed his anger and fear about the assault, but with the press he kept up a calm front. Speaking with journalists after the incident, Cole remarked that he was not "mad with anyone" in the South and that the people who offered him an ovation after the attack were "just great."[22] His apparent acceptance, rather than outrage, over the injustice rankled many. Langston Hughes wrote an essay entitled "Simple: Does King Cole Still Sing, 'Straighten Up and Fly Right'?" which questioned Cole's decision to perform before segregated audiences at all.[23] Thurgood Marshall, chief counsel of the NAACP, accused Cole of being an Uncle Tom. News stories also surfaced that Cole refused to join the NAACP. Cole published a letter of rebuttal in the May 1956 issue of *Down Beat* magazine that proclaimed his longtime support of the NAACP and announced his new lifetime membership. In the letter, Cole expressed his hope that "through the medium of my music I [have] . . . changed many opinions regarding racial equality."

The next challenge in Cole's career was not racial but generational. Cole had earned a reputation as the "King of the Copacabana" by the late 1950s. His shows at the posh New York club were high society events during its premiere fall season, which attracted a wealthy, middle-aged audience of dignitaries, celebrities, and socialites. Rock and roll music emerged at the same time that Cole's popularity as a nightclub entertainer was at its peak. Cole did not bow to the rock and roll impulse and continued to perform his signature ballads such as "Mona Lisa" and "Unforgettable." He did not appreciate the rock and roll sound and was uncertain if his popularity could sustain the musical trend. Two songwriters, Joe and Noel Sherman, penned a novelty song entitled "Mr. Cole Won't Rock and Roll" to capture his feelings. When Cole performed it at the Copacabana in the fall of 1959, he received a standing ovation from his loyal fans, who asked him to sing the song three times.[24]

Motown Records participated in the generational divide between

Cole's more adult nightclub style and the emerging market of teenage popular music. The company achieved its first major hit, "Money, (That's What I Want)," by Barrett Strong in 1959, the same year that Cole debuted "Mr. Cole Won't Rock and Roll." Hitsville, U.S.A., presented a unique variation on Nat King Cole's appeal as a "Negro" artist whose music sold to audiences across racial lines. Unlike Cole's adult sound, Motown music tapped into the burgeoning teen market. Motown's "Sound of Young America" fit nicely into what would become the spirit of John F. Kennedy's New Frontier and the nonviolent campaign for civil rights, which relied on the social commitment of young people. Like Cole, however, Motown quickly learned that the wide popularity of its music did not guarantee racial tolerance. When the "Motortown Revue" traveled through Birmingham, Alabama, in 1962, and local residents fired gunshots at the tour bus, it became clear that "Negro culture" was still seen as a threat in the South, just as it had been when Cole was attacked on stage six years earlier.

Nat King Cole remained committed to the idea that his music and his celebrity might inspire racial tolerance during the time of freedom rides and sit-ins, but he resisted being forced into the role of civil rights leader. In 1963 news reports appeared that the singer refused to lead civil rights demonstrations in Birmingham. Cole responded publicly that he had not been asked to lead any marches, but if he had, he would rather leave that task to trained civil rights activists. He claimed that his role was to be an entertainer, which involved taking his audiences "away from the cares of the day." He argued that "no one would want to listen to me—not even my fellow Negroes," if each song he sang was a "cause" song. In Cole's opinion, some celebrities participated in civil rights protests to gain publicity for their own careers. Cole also believed that his former critics, such as Thurgood Marshall, did not give him credit for the progress he did make through his music, such as bringing integrated bands and entertainment troupes into the South. However, Cole also announced, "If . . . the non-violent approach used by the NAACP and Dr. King, despite its current success, would break down and we as Negroes had to defend ourselves, I'd be right on the firing line."[25]

Cole's comment about his readiness to assume his place "on the firing line" revealed that even one of America's most beloved and nonthreatening black entertainers had a breaking point. When Nat King Cole and Malcolm X died in February 1965, broad support for the nonviolent approach to fighting for civil rights was starting to weaken. Malcolm X's assassination and the subsequent brutal attacks against voting rights demonstrators in Selma signaled that the year might be, as Malcolm had warned in Detroit, the "bloodiest year of them all."

Motown found itself in a charged position in the midst of these turbulent times. The Motown sound dominated popular music at the time of Nat King Cole's death, but fans continued to fight over its meaning in relation to the civil rights struggle. Many people felt that such Motown songs as Junior Walker and the All Stars' "Shotgun" or Martha and the Vandellas' "Nowhere to Run" captured the essence of the volatile civil rights struggle. The company and its artists did not cultivate these associations and denied them when they were suggested. Berry Gordy, like Nat King Cole, believed that "cause" music did not sell records and avoided it at all costs. Moreover, Gordy wanted to emulate the success that Cole had achieved singing popular standards. At the time of Cole's death, the Supremes were about to move into the nightclub market that had been the mainstay of Cole's career.

Nat King Cole's career could teach many lessons to the young Detroit record company about the politics of fame. The "King of the Copacabana" fought battles, both on and off the stage, to be accepted as a jazz instrumentalist, popular vocalist, and private citizen in white America. As a musician, Cole faced criticisms that he had wrongfully neglected his skills as pianist to profit from his commercial appeal as a singer. As a vocalist, Cole had to defend his decisions to sing romantic ballads rather than "message" songs for civil rights or teen-oriented rock and roll. During his ascendance as the "King of the Copacabana," he witnessed the abrupt cancellation of his television variety show in 1957. No corporations were willing to risk sponsoring a national program hosted by a black man. As a private citizen, Cole fought to be served in public restaurants and hotels and to live in any neighborhood he chose. Through it all, Cole's glamorous public image, commercial success, and lilting songs diverted attention from the real complexity of the entertainer's life.

As Motown built its reputation as the "Sound of Young America," it would learn, as Cole had, the many prices of fame. Even though they emerged in historically distinct time periods, Nat King Cole and Motown shared similar urban roots. Like Cole, Motown performers and musicians received early training from the unique configuration of musical resources that only an industrial city could provide. Like Cole, Motown had to assert its place in an entertainment industry and country that actively practiced systematic racial discrimination. And, finally, like Cole, Motown experienced strong ambivalence about its role in the increasingly contentious and violent civil rights struggle. In 1965 the Motown sound was more popular than ever. Yet determining exactly what the sound was and what it represented was also becoming more and more complicated. The music's genesis in Detroit offers some insight into why these debates arose. The origins of Motown's sound illustrate why, especially in Detroit, some individuals described the music as "Afro-American music, without apology."

The Origins of the Motown Sound

On January 30, 1965, *Billboard* magazine, gatekeeper of the music industry, reinstated its rhythm and blues chart. *Billboard* had eliminated the chart on November 30, 1963, and decided to monitor all former rhythm and blues music in the pop category. Fourteen months later, the "pop" classification no longer adequately represented the diverse markets that existed, and the rhythm and blues chart returned. Not surprisingly, the first song to reach number one on the reestablished rhythm and blues list came from Hitsville, U.S.A. The Temptations' song "My Girl" secured the number one spot for six weeks and, on March 6, 1965, earned the same honor on *Billboard*'s pop chart. "My Girl's" success on both charts proved that the Motown sound captivated listeners no matter what the classification.

While its appeal was indisputable, the recipe for the Motown sound was not easy to pin down. The Temptations' "My Girl" contained all the proper ingredients: the instrumental innovations of the Funk Brothers, Motown's studio band; the clever and playful lyrics of Smokey Robinson; and a distinctive vocal lead, in this case, David Ruffin, rounded out by the elegant harmonizing and call-and-response refrains of Otis Williams,

Eddie Kendricks, Paul Williams, and Melvin Franklin. Hitsville's *sound* was also an image, created by the matching outfits and dazzling choreography shown in live concerts.

While easy to recognize, the Motown sound eluded simple definitions, and any attempts generated constant, though usually lighthearted, debate. Some felt that the strong backbeat of Motown songs, which percussionists created with anything from wood blocks to tambourines to tire chains, made the music distinctive. Others attributed the music's unique flair to James Jamerson's imaginative bass lines coupled with the powerful drumming skills of Benny Benjamin. Still others felt that the brothers Brian and Eddie Holland, and Lamont Dozier, who eventually wrote twenty-five top-ten pop hits for Motown as the Holland-Dozier-Holland songwriting team, were most responsible for transforming Motown's music into a sound. When pressed, Berry Gordy often quipped that Motown's sound was a combination of "rats, roaches, soul, guts, and love."[26]

Gordy's definition, however fanciful, anchored the music to its urban origins. For Gordy the Motown sound was not a distinct pattern of chord changes, lyrics, or percussion sounds, but a raw ambition born in the ghetto ("rats, roaches") and achieved through emotional drive ("soul, guts, and love"). Gordy's emphasis on the material conditions that produced the music was not farfetched. The performers and musicians developed their musical skills from resources unique to their urban environment. Like Nat King Cole, who first heard the piano stylings of Earl "Fatha" Hines as they echoed in the alley next to the Grand Terrace Ballroom, Motown musicians and singers honed their talents on the streets and through the institutions of an industrial city. Public housing projects, public schools, local churches, jazz and blues clubs, and street corners all contributed to what became Motown's sound.

Housing, both public and private, provided the space to produce Motown music and also shaped its sound. Berry Gordy's and Raynoma Liles's original Rayber Music Company did not operate out of rented office space but began in a series of private residences including Gwen Gordy's home and Liles's own apartment on Blaine Street. Home production kept overhead costs low but required ingenuity. Recording the Rayber demo tapes in Liles's small apartment was always a challenge. As she recalled, "Creating an efficient routine was necessary . . . to make the most of our somewhat limited resources . . . there was, after all, only one piano and one tape recorder . . . We kept the tape recorder in the hallway. And when we were ready to do a demo, I gathered everyone around the piano."[27]

Gordy set up Studio A in the basement of the converted house on West Grand Boulevard. Referred to by Motown musicians as "the Snakepit," Studio A was notoriously small with a resonating wood floor and cramped isolation booths for singers built into the wall. The close quarters again created technical difficulties. During a recording session, the sounds of different instruments often blended into more than one microphone. To avoid these glitches, musicians often refrained from using amplifiers. The studio's fluctuating climate also influenced the sound of the music. Hitsville's heating and air conditioning systems created too much background noise and, therefore, producers turned them on and off between rehearsals and recording sessions. The studio's constantly changing temperature made it difficult to keep instruments tuned properly. Earl Van Dyke often winced in pain whenever he heard Marvin Gaye's "Try It, Baby," which was recorded without properly tuned instruments.[28]

Some of the limitations of the literally "in-house" production, such as tight quarters and less than reliable, makeshift sound booths eventually turned into musical assets. The musicians balanced the inconveniences of the tiny studio with the rewards of a warmer sound that could not be replicated in more advanced studios elsewhere. Even after technological advances made more precise recordings possible, Motown tried to maintain the sound quality that only "the Snakepit" could produce. When Motown eventually relocated to Los Angeles, the company considered dismantling Studio A and rebuilding it in California to preserve its sound qualities.[29]

Public housing projects also contributed to the development of the Motown sound. Many Motown singers received their earliest informal vocal training singing in doo-wop groups that they formed through their living arrangements. Mary Wilson, Florence Ballard, and Diana Ross first met one another at the Brewster Housing Projects. Tenants considered the Brewster complex, one of the few public housing projects built for African Americans in the 1930s, one of the nicer places to live during the 1950s. As Mary Wilson remembered, "Moving to the Brewster Projects in 1956 was a turning point in my life. . . . Many people would have considered a move to the Projects a step down. But for me, having already stepped down from a middle-class neighborhood to various apartments in the inner city, this was a step back up. I felt like I just moved into a Park Avenue skyscraper."[30] The Brewster Projects provided a strong sense of community for its residents and offered services and facilities that single-family homes and apartments could not easily provide. The Primettes used the Brewster recreation building to rehearse their early songs. According to Wilson, "We spent hours at the Brewster Center learning the intricate harmonies of the Mills Brothers and the Four Tops."[31]

Apart from the Brewster recreation center, young singers often appropriated the Brewster Projects' hallways and stairwells to hone their vocalizing skills. These concrete chambers with their "smooth hard walls and echo" offered perfect acoustics; and vocal groups often competed with one another to secure them. Competition for these makeshift sound booths extended beyond the housing projects to the cement corridors of other public buildings in the city. Otis Williams liked to practice singing in the halls of Hutchins Junior High School. The singers transformed empty pockets of city buildings—whether a stairwell or hallway—into performance sanctuaries. Through music, they personalized and transformed institutional environments and produced a distinctly urban culture in the process.[32]

Detroit's public schools provided aspiring singers with more than acoustical hallways. In the classrooms the schools offered the first formal music training to many of Hitsville's artists and musicians. Several Motown artists received early encouragement toward music and the arts from their teachers. Mary Wilson has said that in elementary school, "My first teacher, Mrs. Shufelt, encouraged me to join the glee club. When we participated in a citywide choir competition at the Ford Auditorium, I felt like the luckiest six-year old in town."[33] Martha Reeves experienced similar validation of her singing talents in school: "As early as third grade, I was chosen from among the thirty or thirty-five students in my class to sing solos by our music teacher, Mrs. Wagstaff . . . I cherish[ed] the smile that she would have on her face as I remembered the lyrics to like 'This Is My Country,' 'America the Beautiful,' and 'Only a Rose.' "[34] Smokey Robinson, Motown's most prolific songwriter, began learning both his musical and writing skills in Detroit's school programs. Mrs. Harris, his elementary school teacher and founder of the Young Writers' Club, sparked his poetic aspirations. "She encouraged us to create little stories, poems and sketches . . . she'd be displaying some of my work nearly every week in the hallway, even my drawings." Robinson's formal education in music started when he joined the glee club in the fifth grade. He recalled, "we'd be chirping everywhere—skipping down the hallways, jumping 'round the gym, joking in the bathrooms. Had me a quartet. Even wrote our eighth-grade graduation play, a musical, about the consequences of dropping out of school too soon."[35]

Many future Motown artists and musicians continued to cultivate their talents in high school. Cass Technical High School and Northeastern High School were just two of the schools that offered a performing arts curriculum. At "Cass Tech," an advanced high school that provided specialized training in a variety of fields, Raynoma Liles received her formal music training in the music program. In the intensive music classes Liles developed an understanding of music theory that "made it possible for me to pick up almost any instrument and play." Liles applied her skills on the early musical arrangements at the Rayber Music Company and at Hitsville Studios. Behind-the-scenes employees, such as Billie Jean Brown, also benefited from Cass Tech's specialized training. A student of the high school's journalism department, Brown quickly found a job at Motown when she responded to an employment notice she had seen at the school. Brown's initial duties at the record company included writing press releases and liner notes for nine dollars a week. The young journalist wrote the liner notes for the first Tamla album, *Hi! We're the Miracles,* and eventually became the head of quality control, a powerful job that involved deciding which records would be released. Diana Ross studied dress design and costume illustration at Cass Tech and practiced her talents on the Primettes' early stage outfits.[36]

At Northeastern High School, Mary Wilson and Florence Ballard—as well as Martha Reeves, and Bobby Rogers of the Miracles—found an important musical mentor in Abraham Silver, the school's choir director.

Under the direction of Silver, these young singers learned clas
and had the opportunity to perform before large audiences. In on
during her senior year, Silver featured Martha Reeves as the so
soloist when the choir performed music from Handel's *Messiah* before
audience of four thousand at Detroit's Ford Auditorium. Across town at
Northwestern High School, James Jamerson began playing the bass in
his music class taught by Dr. Helstein and eventually formed his own
jazz band. Other Motown musicians had a combination of formal and
informal musical training. Earl Van Dyke first began playing the piano
in 1935. His mother taught him to play by ear. His father wanted him to
learn how to read music and sent him to a tutor. He eventually trained
at the Detroit Conservatory of Music. By 1943 he had won first prize at
an amateur show at the Paradise Theater.[37]

Motown's studio musicians like Jamerson and Van Dyke received
their most profound musical education not in a classroom but in Detroit's
blues and jazz clubs. Throughout the 1950s jazz thrived in clubs such
as the Minor Key, Phelp's Lounge, the Flame Show Bar, the West End,
and the Stimson Hotel. Several Motown musicians played jazz at these
clubs and collaborated with artists including Charlie Parker, Grant
Green, and Dizzy Gillespie.

Jazz musicians also met informally outside the clubs and shared
ideas. Often popular street corners served as hangouts for local musicians. Earl Van Dyke remembered that on the corner of Canfield and
John R, "[t]here was a guy down there, Mr. Kennedy, who used to sell
hot sausages, tamales, outside on the corner . . . All the musicians used
to stand out there and meet and talk all night about our gigs."[38] For Van
Dyke these social exchanges developed into an informal way to teach
jazz:

> When I started getting into jazz, musicians at that time in Detroit
> used to get together socially on weekends, and teach each other
> tunes and exchange ideas. We didn't compete with each other. We
> called it the "Detroit way." Tommy Flanagan, Roland Hanna,
> [saxophonist-flutist] Yusef Lateef, [guitarist] Kenny Burrell, they
> were all part of the scene. Barry Harris was the leader of the young
> guys like myself. He taught me how to play "Cherokee," which

he had learned from another Detroit jazz musician named Hank Jones.[39]

For most of the Motown musicians, jazz was their first love, but—as Berry Gordy Jr. learned when his 3-D Record Mart failed to sell its extensive jazz collection—jazz did not provide a steady paycheck. As Van Dyke commented, "It [Motown] was just a gig to us. All we wanted to do was play jazz, but we all had families, and at the time playing rhythm and blues was the best way to pay the rent."[40]

Motown musicians sacrificed some of their devotion to jazz to play rhythm and blues and pay their bills, but these artistic compromises also contributed to the creation of Hitsville's distinctive sound. Like Nat King Cole, the Funk Brothers used their jazz expertise to transform the musical stylings of popular song. The core group included James Jamerson on bass; Joe Hunter, bandleader and pianist; Earl Van Dyke, Richard "Popcorn" Wylie, and Johnny Griffith on keyboards; Benny "Papa Zita" Benjamin on drums; Thomas "Beans" Bowles, Hank Cosby, and Mike Terry on saxophone; Robert White, Eddie Willis, and Joe Messina on guitar; Eddie "Bongo" Brown on the conga drum, and vibist-percussionist Jack Ashford. Of this group, the central figures were Earl Van Dyke, who acted as studio bandleader; James Jamerson; Robert White; and Benny Benjamin. Guitarist and music historian Allan Slutsky has described James Jamerson's inventive style as follows:

> James had . . . the ability to incorporate his jazz background into Berry Gordy's R & B influenced pop style . . . Gone were the stagnant two beat, root-fifth patterns and post–"Under the Boardwalk" clichéd bass lines that occupied the bottom end of most R & B releases. Jamerson had modified or replaced them with chromatic passing tones, Ray Brown–style walking bass lines, and syncopated eighth-note figures—all of which had previously been unheard of in popular music of the late fifties and early sixties.[41]

The Funk Brothers also appropriated and combined jazz melodies to invigorate the phrasing or transitions of a Motown song. Trombonist George Bohanon and keyboardist Earl Van Dyke inserted the melodies of "Canadian Sunset" and "Begin the Beguine" into the opening chord changes of Mary Wells's song "My Guy," which added to the record's winsome charm. The jazz improvisation sometimes emerged out of necessity and a desire to end the workday. In recording "My Guy," Earl Van Dyke recalled, "We were doing anything to get the hell out of that studio. We knew that the producers didn't know nothin' about no 'Canadian Sunset' or 'Begin the Beguine.' We figured that the song would wind up in the trash can anyway."[42]

These jazz-derived innovations emerged out of the numerous professional commitments the musicians maintained. Motown demanded long hours. An average work day included at least two three-hour studio sessions and sometimes up to three or four. After-hours, musicians headed to clubs to play in house bands and explore new jazz techniques. The Chit Chat Club, a favorite venue, promoted the Funk Brothers' performances through live broadcasts on WJLB radio hosted by disc jockey Martha Jean "the Queen" Steinberg. The more relaxed atmosphere at the Chit Chat led to musical experimentation that bled into the Motown sound. According to Earl Van Dyke, "Many of the grooves that made it to vinyl over at Hitsville actually had their origins in the Chit Chat jam sessions."[43]

A riff at a late night jam session, choir practice in a high school music class, vocalizing in the echoes of a concrete stairwell or under a corner street light—all of these experiences, typical of urban life, created the Motown sound. That sound resonated with the complicated lives the musicians and performers led and the basic economic needs that shaped their careers. While most Motown artists did not come from lives of extreme impoverishment or the "rats, roaches" existence that Gordy liked to evoke, many, if not all, of the singers and musicians had to struggle or work several different jobs to pursue their musical aspirations. Diana Ross bussed tables at the Hudson Department Store's restaurant to earn extra money. Martha Reeves was working as a replacement clerk at City Wide Dry Cleaners when William "Mickey" Stevenson, Motown's artist and repertoire director, "discovered" her as she sang one evening at the Twenty Grand nightclub. Joe Hunter, band leader and keyboardist, who played on such early hits as "Money (That's What I Want)" and "Shop Around," worked as an organist in local churches to supplement his income as a club musician. When some preachers criticized Hunter for "serving two gods" by playing secular and sacred music, he replied, "I'm serving just one God, the one who gave me talent." Earl Van Dyke and James Jamerson both worked as road musicians on the "chitlin' circuit" for entertainers such as Lloyd "Mr. Personality" Price and Jackie Wilson before they took permanent jobs at Hitsville Studios.[44]

The creativity and determination, or "soul, guts, and love," that forged the Motown sound were an important source of pride in Detroit's black community. The company's Dignity Award and Berry Gordy's Brotherhood Award in February 1965 illustrated two ways in which the community celebrated Motown's cultural achievements. The two awards reflected different interpretations of Motown music but revealed a shared belief that the music represented something more than popular entertainment. The public meanings of the Motown sound multiplied throughout 1965 and 1966. Debates about what Motown music signified reflected larger struggles within the company and the country about what "Negro" music was, should be, or could do. These debates heightened in the midst of a civil rights movement whose nonviolent approach and integrationist goals were coming into question. The Motown sound, with its urban origins and its "soul, guts, and love" spirit, could not avoid becoming a contested symbol of the power of black culture to either unite or divide the races. The company's own ambition to produce music that appealed to consumers across racial, class, and generational lines complicated its symbolic powers even further.

The Many Meanings of the Motown Sound

The melody belonged to everyone
even the ones who knocked you down.
. . . .
I disagree with a death that strikes down the makers
of songs. There are so many things waiting for silence like
the bombs waiting for doors to open
—Conrad Kent Rivers, "The Song Is Ended for Nat King Cole"

Junior Walker and the All-Stars' record "Shotgun" debuted on *Billboard*'s rhythm and blues chart on February 13, 1965. The single appeared during the week that the Dignity Awards recognized Motown. The record opens with the piercing crack of a shotgun blast and then jumps into a raucous and jagged saxophone-led instrumental, punctuated with Walker's shouts of the bluesy lyrics. The song's distance from the more ordered conventions of a Motown hit seemed to heighten its popularity. The record became the first release of the company's Soul label to reach number one on the chart on March 13, 1965, only one month after its debut; and it remained on the chart for seventeen weeks. Berry Gordy had created the Soul label in 1964 to market the company's rhythm and blues releases more overtly. "Shotgun" surprisingly also climbed to number four on the pop charts.[45]

"Shotgun's" unexpected, widespread popularity disrupted accepted definitions of what "Afro-American," "Negro," or "black" music was. The market for "race records" first emerged in the 1920s, when blues singers such as Bessie Smith and Alberta Hunter gained popularity. The music industry, monitored by publications such as *Billboard* and *Cashbox*, created the rhythm and blues chart to track the consumption patterns of black audiences. The "Harlem Hit Parade," the first *Billboard* chart to monitor black music, ran from October 1942 to February 1945. From 1945 to 1949 it ran under the name "Race Records." In 1949 *Billboard* renamed the category "Rhythm and Blues" and continued it throughout the 1960s with the exception of the brief hiatus from November 1963 to January 1965.[46]

Alternatively, the pop music chart implicitly monitored white consumption patterns. The distinction between "pop" and "rhythm and blues" reflected the distribution strategies of major record labels. As music industry scholars Steve Chapple and Reebee Garofalo have explained,

The division between pop and r & b, at a time when much r & b material was moving into the pop market, reflected differences in the distribution systems for the two types of music. Pop music was marketed by the major companies through their main distribution systems, which were national. R & b music was marketed by independent labels with independent regional distributors. Where major labels had r & b subsidiaries, the music was segregated in their catalogue listings and contracted out to independent distributors. R & b songs were first distributed to exclusively black retail outlets and radio stations. If they sold well enough the songs might be picked up by white stores and stations, and crossover into the white market. The black audience was separated as a secondary market, with different and inferior promotion budgets. Even today the distinction between r & b and pop is based less on music than on the race of the performing artists.[47]

Record producers, including Motown, responded to these categories by replicating the distinctions in their marketing strategies. Motown created the Soul label to signal to consumers that the music was rhythm and blues. The company marketed the Motown, Gordy, and Tamla labels to crossover consumers. Audiences tended to define "black" music as music created by African Americans that aesthetically emphasized African American musical traditions such as the blues, gospel, rhythm and blues, or jazz. When "Shotgun," distributed on Motown's Soul label, ascended the pop charts, the anomaly revealed how tenuous, ineffectual, and dubious these racial music categories were.

The stakes involved in defining "black" music, determining its marketability, and assessing its role in American culture rose as the civil rights movement fractured into competing factions and increased violence throughout 1965 and 1966. The week after "Shotgun" debuted on the rhythm and blues charts, Malcolm X was shot down at the Audubon Ballroom in Harlem. The song's opening gunshot crack lost its novelty in that instant. The real violence of the historical moment transfigured the playful violence in the song.[48] The music could not escape the meanings that historical circumstance pressed upon it. Nat King Cole learned this lesson when he was beaten on stage in Birmingham, as he tried to sing and take his audience "away from the cares of the day." To his attackers Cole's identity as a "Negro" artist singing "Negro" music before a white audience threatened the social order of the community. The singer's presence in segregated Birmingham represented a "care of the day" not an escape from it. No matter how innocuous Cole tried to make his music and public image, he could not avoid the racial conflicts of his time.

When Cole died of cancer in February 1965, Motown had begun to inherit the paradoxes of the famous balladeer's illustrious career. Commercially, the company made conscious attempts to transcend the categories of and stereotypes about "Negro" music. These attempts included Motown distancing itself, at times, from the indigenous musical style that it had created. At the same time, Hitsville, U.S.A., continued to produce its own music—songs such as "Nowhere to Run" and "Shotgun"—which often became infused with political meanings owing to historical events that no record company could control. Moreover, Motown always was implicated in the hidden histories of discrimination that lay behind "black" music and entertainment, as exemplified by Nat King Cole's career. In short, Motown's "Sound of Young America" was embedded in the cultural, racial, and political conditions that produced it.

The Supremes, more than any other group, represented Motown's commercial potential to overcome any barriers that racial identity might pose, to conquer any musical genre, and to capture the widest spectrum of fans. The company's ambitions involved artistic compromises, as Gordy was willing to abandon the Motown sound at times in order to reach larger audiences. In October 1964, when Motown released what was to become the Supremes' third number-one single, "Come See about Me," it also released their album *A Bit of Liverpool*, which featured Beatles hits including "I Want To Hold Your Hand" and "A Hard Day's Night." In February 1965 the single "Stop! In the Name of Love" hit the airwaves and eventually became the group's fourth consecutive number-one pop single. Concurrent with the single, Motown released the album *The Supremes Sing Country, Western, and Pop*, which featured songs such as "Tumbling Tumbleweeds" and "(The Man with the) Rock and Roll Banjo Band." When "Back in My Arms Again" became the Supremes' fifth consecutive number-one hit in the spring of 1965, the trio toured Britain. On the tour the group started to incorporate show tunes such as "You're Nobody 'Til Somebody Loves You" and "Tea For Two" in their live performances.[49]

Motown had several objectives when it diversified the Supremes' repertoire in the midst of their record-breaking streak. In Gordy's view the more musically versatile the group was, the more marketable it became. Motown defied popular assumptions that "Negro" artists only sang "Negro" music. The strategy also advanced Gordy's plan to bring Motown into the older nightclub market. Gordy had the Supremes sing "Put on a

The Supremes, circa 1966. (Courtesy Motown Record Co., L.P., a Polygram
Company.)

Happy Face" to prove that "teenage stars" could perform adult-oriented fare. The decision to release these efforts on albums rather than as singles also reflected a marketing push toward adult audiences. As scholar Gerald Early observed, "[t]he LP [was] the adult record of the market . . . [and] [t]he 45 single became the format in which Rock and Roll was presented to the public."[50] Ultimately, Gordy hoped that Motown would not be known for mastering Broadway songs, but that Broadway would perform Motown music. In his autobiography Gordy expressed his belief that having his artists sing the standards "could break down other stereotypical barriers . . . I had visions of Motown songs on Broadway. Motown songs in movies, clubs, everywhere." When the Supremes sang "Tea for Two" right after "Baby Love," the gesture equated both the songs as American standards.[51]

Still, the Supremes always negotiated, rather than transcended, their racial identity. No matter how often they conquered different musical genres and appealed to new audiences, they always contended with larger cultural assumptions about race and music. In May 1965 the Supremes reaffirmed their place at the forefront of "rock 'n' roll" when their fifth single, "Back in My Arms Again," went to the top of the pop and rhythm and blues charts. The achievement did not go unnoticed. *Ebony* magazine proclaimed that the Detroit trio "topped the rock 'n' roll field" in a June 1965 cover story. The group also appeared prominently in a photo montage on the cover of *Time* magazine in May 1965. The related article declared that, after ten years on the American cultural scene, rock and roll was officially the "sound of the sixties." *Time* traced the music's origins to " 'rhythm and blues'—played by Negroes for Negroes." The article also credited rock's appeal to white audiences to the popularity of Elvis Presley and of the music's champion disc jockey, Alan Freed. The Beatles "made it all right to be white," and Motown, led by the Supremes, was the "best of the brown sound."[52]

Time magazine's racial taxonomy of the best of "rock 'n' roll" perpetuated the popular idea that race, rather than specific musical techniques, defined a musical style. The Motown sound was always "brown," regardless of the company's diverse musical output and its popularity with multiracial audiences. The racial origins of Motown music were cause for celebration among some. Detroit's Dignity Awards acknowledged that Motown's "Afro-American" music generated pride that supported the continuing struggle for racial equality. But Motown considered the racial identity of the company's sound malleable and packaged it according to circumstance.[53] The company's success in multiple markets proved the profitability of its flexible approach. Hitsville's command of the rhythm and blues market did not wane while the Supremes dominated the pop charts. From January 30 to July 31, 1965, five of the seven number-one hits on *Billboard*'s reinstated rhythm and blues chart came from Motown Studios, including Marvin Gaye's "I'll Be Doggone" and the Four Tops' "I Can't Help Myself."[54]

While Motown controlled the marketing and quality of its product, it could not control the many, and often conflicting, meanings that audiences attributed to the music or the historical events that shaped these interpretations. At times, although the Motown sound seemed far removed from the fight for racial justice, the increased violence of the civil rights struggle was never far from anyone's mind. Motown was busy grooming the Supremes for the Copacabana when the Selma voting rights campaign captured the nation's attention in the spring of 1965. The Selma campaign reminded the nation how terrifying racial conflict could be. On March 7, 1965, the country witnessed "Bloody Sunday," when Alabama state troopers attacked nonviolent demonstrators attempting to march across the Edmund Pettus Bridge. Days later two civil rights workers, Viola Liuzzo, a Detroiter, and James Reeb, a Boston minister, were killed while participating in the Selma efforts. The two deaths prompted the federal government to act quickly. President Lyndon Johnson went before Congress to argue for the passage of the Voting Rights Act. When Johnson closed his speech with the phrase "And we shall overcome," many wanted to believe, but doubts grew that the movement could avoid any further violence.

At Motown the Supremes' success—worlds away from the civil rights battle lines—represented what appeared to be infinite commercial possibilities. On July 29, 1965, the Supremes debuted at the Copacabana in New York City. To Berry Gordy the evening stood as the final threshold into the prestigious nightclub circuit. Consequently, he orchestrated the entire performance to uphold standards set by role models like Nat King Cole.[55] The trio opened with "Tea For Two" and proceeded to sing and dance through a majority of show tunes interspersed with a sampling of the Motown hits that made them famous. The limited presentation of Motown songs reflected Gordy's fears that the company's sound might not please the Copacabana clientele. Contrary to such expectations, songs such as "Baby Love" and "Come See about Me" thrilled the audience, which included celebrities such as Ed Sullivan and Sammy Davis Jr. The older crowd might not have wanted Mr. Cole to "rock 'n' roll," but it expected the Supremes to perform their popular hits.[56]

The Supremes' premiere at the Copacabana took place only a few days before the national Voting Rights Act passed through Congress on August 6, 1965. Celebration of the civil rights victory was short-lived. Five days later, on August 11, 1965, a routine drunk driving arrest in Watts, California, ignited large-scale civil disorder. Los Angeles police officer Lee Minikus asked Marquette Frye, a twenty-one-year-old black man, to pull over for driving under the influence. Frye cooperated, but as the arrest proceeded a crowd gathered, and the young man suddenly turned belligerent. He lunged for Minikus's nightstick just as additional police officers arrived on the scene. When the officers began to beat and apprehend Frye as well as his brother, Ronald, the crowd yelled in outrage, "We've got no rights at all—it's just like Selma!" and "Come on, let's get them!" What began as a small skirmish quickly erupted into a massive disturbance that spread over a 150-block area. Over the course of ten days, thirty-four people were killed, over one thousand people were injured, and approximately four thousand people were arrested. Officials estimated property losses at approximately $45 million.[57]

The rebellion that raged in the streets of Los Angeles occurred far from Detroit's Hitsville Studios or New York City's Copacabana, but its impact influenced the Motown sound. As Marvin Gaye once recalled,

> I remember I was listening to a tune of mine playing on the radio, "Pretty Little Baby," when the announcer interrupted with news about the Watts riot. My stomach got real tight and my heart started beating like crazy. I wanted to throw the radio down and burn all the bullshit songs I'd been singing and get out there and kick ass with the rest of the brothers. I knew they were going about it wrong, I knew what they were thinking, but I understood an anger that builds up over years—shit, over centuries—and I

felt myself exploding. Wasn't music supposed to express feelings? No, according to [Berry Gordy], music's supposed to sell. That's his trip. And it was mine.[58]

Gaye condemned Gordy's and his own desire to produce "commercial" music rather than songs with a social conscious, but he also recognized that some of Motown's most profitable records could "express feelings." Like many others, Gaye thought that Martha and the Vandellas' music communicated the urgency of the times: "Funny, but of all the acts back then, I thought Martha and the Vandellas came closest to really saying something. It wasn't a conscious thing, but when they sang numbers like 'Quicksand' or 'Wild One' or 'Nowhere to Run' or 'Dancing in the Street,' they captured a spirit that felt political to me. I liked that. I wondered to myself, 'With the world exploding around me, how am I supposed to keep singing love songs?' "[59]

Unlike the polished elegance of the Supremes, Martha and the Vandellas always projected a grittier, less refined, more defiant image. The group's publicity tended to accentuate these associations. Press releases and magazine articles often claimed that the name "Vandella" was the feminine term for "vandal." Martha Reeves consistently refuted this legend. In her autobiography she said that she derived the group's name from a combination of the "Van" from Van Dyke Avenue in Detroit and "Della" in honor of the singer, Della Reese, a role model and fellow Detroiter. Reeves's explanation of the name highlighted the urban origins of the music. Reeves wanted the reference to Van Dyke Avenue because "[i]t would always identify us with Detroit, for it's a street that goes from east to west and connects you to north and south as it curves and winds through the heart of my neighborhood."[60]

Musically, Martha and the Vandellas' songs typified the Motown sound. The group's early hits "Come Get These Memories," "Heatwave," and "Quicksand," all released in 1963, established their style. Ostensibly, their songs recounted the trials of adolescent romance or, as in their 1965 album, *Dance Party*, celebrated the joys of youth culture. Yet, as Gaye noted, these songs possessed an immediacy and edge that communicated more than youthful exuberance or advice to the lovelorn. "Dancing in the Street," written by William "Mickey" Stevenson, Marvin

Gaye, and Ivy Hunter, became the group's signature song and exemplified the duality of Martha and the Vandellas' music. The song's theme, not simply about the joys of summer dance parties, but a specific celebration of their expression on city streets, made the music ripe for broader interpretations.

When the Watts rebellion took over the streets of Los Angeles, many people felt that songs such as "Dancing in the Street" expressed the emotions of the moment.[61] In October 1965, only a few months after Watts, an essay entitled "Rhythm and Blues as a Weapon" appeared in the *Liberator*, a black radical magazine published in New York City. Author Ronald Snellings invoked Martha and the Vandellas' music to argue that rhythm and blues music had a clear role in the black revolution:

> We sing in our young hearts, we sing in our angry Black Souls: WE ARE COMING UP! WE ARE COMING UP! And it's reflected in the Riot-song that symbolized Harlem, Philly, Brooklyn, Rochester, Patterson, Elizabeth: this song of course, "Dancing in the Street"—making Martha and the Vandellas legendary. Then FLASH! it surges up again: "We Gonna' Make It" (to the tune of Medgar Evers gunned down in Mississippi: POW! POW! POW! POW!) "Keep on Trying" (to the tune of James Powell gunned down in Harlem: POW! POW! POW! POW!) "Nowhere to Run, Nowhere to Hide," "Change is Gonna' Come" (to the tune of Brother Malcolm shot down in the Audubon: POW! POW! POW! POW! POW! POW! POW! POW!) ... OUR songs are turning from "love," turning from being "songs," turning into WAYS, into WAYS, into "THINGS."[62]

Snellings's essay testified to the degree to which some activists saw Motown songs as a "weapon" in the increasingly violent struggle for racial equality.

By the fall of 1965, however, Motown had no interest in producing music that might evoke revolutionary sentiments or provoke radical action. In November 1965 Motown released two albums: *The Supremes at the Copa* and Marvin Gaye's *Tribute to the Great Nat King Cole*. The two recordings did not engage in the type of social commentary simmering in the lyrics and tempo of "Heatwave" or "Nowhere to Run." Yet both albums paid homage to the legacy of Nat King Cole, a legacy fraught with racial conflict. Nat King Cole's career had demonstrated that no matter what the song, if it was sung by a black person, it could be implicated in the racial politics of its time. It was lesson that Motown was only beginning to learn, but one that would have increasing relevance as the national civil rights movement witnessed the emergence of Black Power and the increased use of black culture and arts to promote the cause. The shift to embrace black art as a tool in the struggle against racial inequality was international in scope but also was particularly active in Detroit. By 1966, it was taking root both in the far reaches of Africa and on the streets of the Motor City.

Black Art in a Troubled World

The Negro writer in the United States has always had—has been *forced* to have in spite of himself—two audiences, one black, one white. And, as long has been America's dilemma, seldom "the twain shall meet." The fence between the two audiences is the color bar which in reality stretches around the world. Writers who feel they must straddle this fence, perforce acquire a split personality. Writers who do not care whether they straddle the fence of color or not, are usually the best writers, attempting at least to let their art leap the barriers of color, poverty, or whatever other roadblocks to artistic truth there may be. Unfortunately, some writers get artistic truth and financial success mixed up, get critical acclaim and personal integrity confused. Such are the dilemmas which the double audience creates. Which set of readers to please—the white, the black, or both at once?

—Langston Hughes, "Black Writers in a Troubled World"

Langston Hughes presented his speech "Black Writers in a Troubled World" at the First World Festival of Negro Arts held in Dakar, Senegal, in April 1966.[63] The festival, organized by Léopold Sédar Sengor, president of Senegal, was endorsed by the United Nations and attracted over two thousand visitors and delegates from approximately fifty countries. President Lyndon Johnson appointed Langston Hughes as an official American representative to the event. Dakar hosted three weeks of cultural events. From the United States Duke Ellington and his orchestra, the Alvin Ailey dance troupe, and Marion Williams and her gospel singers all went to perform.[64]

Hughes spent most of the festival attending official functions, socializing with friends such as Margaret Danner, and giving poetry readings. His address "Black Writers in a Troubled World" was part of a one-week colloquium on the role of art in the lives of black people. In the speech Hughes criticized young black writers who used obscenity and other language of racial hatred in their writing; argued for more independent black publishing; and posed the Negro writer's "double-audience" dilemma. Hughes invoked *Négritude,* or its American equivalent, soul, as the central principle to guide the Negro writer. Soul, "a synthesis of the essence of Negro folk art redistilled," revealed "to the Negro people and the world the beauty within themselves." Hughes's address, and the Dakar festival as a whole, signaled the growing international interest in not only celebrating black arts but seeing black culture as a tool of black empowerment. Perhaps black art could both soothe and remedy "a troubled world."

The First World Festival of Negro Arts took place on African soil, but the philosophy of the gathering had many followers in the United States and, specifically, in Detroit. Black activists in the city were exploring the role of art in black life several years before international festivals were organized on the topic. As early as 1962, the Reverend Albert B. Cleage Jr. sponsored a lecture at his Central Congregational Church entitled "Black Nationalism in Jazz." Jazz vocalist Abbey Lincoln and her husband, jazz drummer Max Roach, appeared at Cleage's church to discuss the role of jazz in the development of black nationalism.[65] Cleage's interest in promoting political change through culture continued in the Freedom Now Party campaign. When the party drafted its national platform in 1964, the document contained an entire section on cultural revolution. The party sought to bring "cultural affairs into politics for the first time" and to involve "the Negro creative artist and performer—the singer, dancer, writer, dramatist, poet, musician (jazz and classical), actor, composer" as equal partners in the fight for justice. In February 1965 Motown's Dignity and Brotherhood Awards confirmed that local leaders viewed the record company's cultural achievements as a source of racial uplift.[66]

Detroit activists' embrace of black popular music as a part of the black arts movement was more inclusive than the Dakar festival. Several critics took issue with festival organizers for not including rhythm and blues artists. In an editorial for the *Liberator* magazine, K. William Kgositsile, a South African writer, noted the absence of rhythm and blues at the Senegal gathering: "Where was James Brown! Contemporary Black artists were supposed to be represented. By this I mean that rhythm and blues is the most contemporary art form in Black America. To omit rhythm and blues at any festival or carnival where contemporary art in Black America is supposed to be represented is as questionable as the omission of Nknimah's ideas in any serious discussion on the dangers of neo-colonialism."[67]

By 1966 Detroit's black artists and activists were developing several projects that sought to use popular music, literature, and the arts to express political ideas and to act as a new forum for grass-roots community organizing. One of the most exciting developments was the Broadside Press, one of the first black publishing houses in the country. Dudley Randall, former Boone House poet, officially founded the press in September 1965. Randall's own poem "The Ballad of Birmingham" was the press's first publication. Randall wanted to use the Broadside Press to protect the copyright of his work and that of others.[68]

Randall's impulse to found the Broadside Press in order to protect his work and control its dissemination was similar to the impetus behind the Motown Record Company. Like Randall, Berry Gordy Jr. began publishing songs in order to copyright and protect them. In his autobiography Gordy recalled, "Songwriting was my love, and protecting that love, in many ways, was the motivation for everything I did in the early years of my career . . . Protecting my songs was also the reason I got into the publishing and eventually the record business." Gordy founded the Jobete Music Publishing Company in 1958 to oversee the licensing of Motown songs. Melba Joyce Boyd, scholar and Broadside poet, has also drawn connections between Berry Gordy's hit factory and Dudley Randall's Broadside Press. She writes, "Their [Gordy's and Randall's] understanding of [industrial] production and the political and economic progress of black Detroiters during the 1950s and 1960s provided a home-based market to purchase and promote their products." Randall did not share Gordy's drive toward profits, however. He once commented: "I admit I am not well qualified to operate in a capitalistic society. I came of age during the Depression and my attitude toward business is one of dislike and suspicion. Writers who send me manuscripts and speak of 'making a buck' turn me off."[69]

In May 1966 Randall attended the first black writers' conference at Fisk University. The conference brought together many esteemed black poets including Robert Hayden and Margaret Walker. And it inspired Randall to take on two new publishing projects. The first was to be a series of poems by writers such as Hayden, Walker, and Gwendolyn Brooks entitled "Poems of the Negro Revolt," published individually as broadsides. Randall wanted the inexpensive leaflets to be disseminated widely so that the poems could become a part of everyday life—posted on refrigerators.[70] The second project, a book, would pay homage to Malcolm X and his revolutionary influence. *For Malcolm: Poems on the Life and Death of Malcolm X* would be a permanent anthology of poems celebrating the leader's life and accomplishments.[71] Both projects established Randall's Broadside Press as a new concept in independent black publishing. The press illustrated how black art could raise political and racial awareness in "a troubled world." To Randall poetry's social and political functions were self-evident: "Poetry has always been with us. It has always been a sustenance, a teacher, an inspiration, and a joy. In the present circumstances, it helps in the search for black identity, reinforces black pride and black unity, and is helping to create the soul, the consciousness, and the conscience of black folk."[72]

Community projects such as Dudley Randall's Broadside Press inspired Detroit activists to organize in June 1966 what became known as the Black Arts Convention. The idea for the convention grew out of biweekly forums on black history and culture that Edward Vaughn hosted at his black-oriented bookstore on Dexter Avenue. The discussion group became known as Forum 66, "the Voice of Black Unity," dedicated "to the active support of Black Nationalism throughout the world." The Black Arts Convention took place on June 24–26, 1966, at Cleage's Central United Church of Christ and, unlike the Dakar World Festival, expanded its agenda beyond the arts. Forum 66 sponsored panels on literature, music, art, and drama but also on education, religion, and Negro history. At the literature panel Dudley Randall encouraged others to develop their own media and publishing houses. Grace Lee Boggs, former Freedom Now Party candidate, discussed at the session on politics how citizens should work together to fight local grievances and exercise control over their own communities. The convention also paid homage to Malcolm X.

Organizers designed a pictorial exhibit of the slain leader's life at the church, and Malcolm's wife, Betty Shabazz, attended Saturday's events. The diversity of the gathering built bridges among previously separated groups to the inspiration of many. The *Negro Digest* reported that "[t]he convention as a whole had the fervency of a religious revival."[73]

Difficult challenges faced the larger civil rights movement during the time of the Black Arts Convention. Impatience with the nonviolent campaign for integration grew dramatically during the summer of 1966. When a sniper shot down James Meredith on June 6, 1966, the second day of his "March against Fear" in Mississippi, the nonviolent strategy came under renewed attack. In the hospital Meredith expressed regret that he had not armed himself for the march. When reminded that his remark did not uphold the nonviolent philosophy, Meredith rebutted, "Who the hell ever said I was nonviolent? I spent eight years in the military and the rest of my life in Mississippi."[74]

Martin Luther King Jr. from SCLC, Stokely Carmichael from the Student Nonviolent Coordinating Committee (SNCC), and Floyd McKissick from CORE all gathered at Meredith's bedside and decided to continue his march, though they disagreed on the goal of the demonstration. King held steadfast to the philosophy of civil disobedience and integration, while Carmichael and McKissick argued for self-defense and separatism. These disagreements continued to cause friction as the revived march got underway. When participants began to sing "We Shall Overcome," many fell silent at the stanza "black and white together." When King asked the marchers why they ignored the verse, they voiced their disenchantment with the song and argued that they should be singing not "We Shall Overcome" but "We Shall Overrun." King later wrote, the retort "fell on my ears like strange music from a foreign land."[75]

Detroit and the Black Arts Convention participated in the tensions that threatened the unity of the national civil rights struggle. On Sunday, June 19, 1966, Martin Luther King Jr. left the Meredith march temporarily and flew to Detroit to lead a Freedom Day rally at Cobo Hall. Like the Great March to Freedom in 1963, Freedom Day was a fund-raising event for SCLC.[76] Organizers raised donations for the voter registration drive in Mississippi and Alabama. By the time King departed for Detroit, Stokely Carmichael had begun leading the "March against Fear" participants in his new Black Power rallying cry. The separatist phrase disturbed King, who along with other SCLC leaders favored the more inclusive "Freedom Now" slogan, which Detroit's Freedom Day promoted. King expressed his dismay with black nationalism before a large crowd of over 15,000 at Cobo Hall and argued for the continued use of nonviolent resistance. Many in the audience embraced King as "our Moses," and the event raised $60,000.[77]

Stokely Carmichael was also scheduled to appear in Detroit on Friday, June 24, as the keynote speaker at the Black Arts Convention. Carmichael was unable to attend owing to injuries he sustained on June 23 when Mississippi state and local police fired tear gas and physically attacked the Meredith marchers. One month later, on July 30, 1966, Carmichael did speak in Detroit at Cobo Hall as part of a series of Black Power rallies.[78] His appearance drew a crowd of only 600—much smaller than King's Freedom Day rally—but received considerable press attention. Rumors circulated in the city that local radicals planned a riot in conjunction with Carmichael's visit. The SNCC leader's incendiary rhetoric at the rally validated many of his critics' suspicions. Near the end of his talk, Carmichael lashed out at public outcry for more law and order and remarked, "I've seen so much law and order that I want to see just a taste of chaos."[79]

Could chaos come to Detroit? Speculation increased throughout the summer of 1966. To many Detroit seemed the least likely target of racial unrest. The city's reputation as a model city of race relations strengthened under the mayoral leadership of Jerome Cavanagh. Detroit received national attention for its progressive racial policies. Newspapers and magazines including *Fortune, Newsweek, Harper's, Look*, the *Wall Street Journal*, and the *Los Angeles Times* all praised the city's race relations.[80] Others, particularly in the black community, were more skeptical of Detroit's ability to remain unscathed by racial violence. On July 23, 1966, the *Michigan Chronicle* ran the front page story "Can It Happen In Detroit?" which considered the possibility of a race riot occurring in the city. The article cited low unemployment and youth summer programs as preventive measures but warned that "ghetto dwellers, troubled by police brutality and aware of youth's restlessness, fear the city is sitting on a powder keg."[81]

City-appointed committees also monitored Detroit's race record closely. The Citizen's Committee for Equal Opportunity issued its report, "Race Relations in Detroit, Summer 1966," in July. The committee pointed to the city's positive economic outlook and relatively open communication between white and black leadership as hopeful signs, but it also warned that racial peace was not guaranteed. The report especially noted that police-community relations "must be kept under very close surveillance," if Detroit was to remain riot-free. The Michigan Civil Rights Commission (CRC) agreed with the Citizen's Committee recommendation. The CRC had received 114 complaints of civil rights violations on the part of Detroit police officers since January 1964. The commission recommended "adequate discipline for those officers who commit civil rights violations" and the "recruitment of a higher number of Negro officers" to the Detroit police force.[82]

The volatility of Detroit's police-community relations surfaced on August 9, 1966, when a "Big Four" police cruiser, manned by an all-white crew, stopped seven black males for "loitering" and allegedly blocking traffic on Kercheval Avenue. Four of the men left the scene when asked, but three remained and shouted, "We won't be moved. Whitey is going to kill us." When the officers called two more scout cars to the scene, the men began to fight off the officers who were attempting to apprehend them. Crowds gathered at the scene. Soon, bystanders began throwing bottles at passing motorists and shouting, "Black Power!"

The Police Department mobilized quickly to stifle what became known as the Kercheval incident. The "miniriot" lasted only two days. During that time, participants hit seventy-three police and civilian cars with rocks, broke forty-eight windows, and engaged in small incidents of looting. Ten officers and eleven civilians were injured, but no one was killed. Mayor Cavanagh and the Police Department's quick response to ending the disorder enhanced the city's "model" reputation across the country.[83]

Again, the black community's evaluation of the incident differed from the publicized praise. Early on during the disturbance, Coleman

Young, who had recently completed his primary campaign for state senator, attended his father's funeral. Young's family held the wake at his father's house on Harding Street near Kercheval. In the midst of the wake, a police officer called Young and advised him to clear his family and friends out of the area. Young complied but felt anger at the intrusion. Young called his political colleague, U.S. Representative Charles C. Diggs Jr., as well as other elected officials, ministers, and community leaders. Within a matter of hours, fifty or sixty of these leaders had gathered and were marching arm in arm down Kercheval Avenue to protest the police occupancy of the area. Officers in police cruisers taunted the protesters, but they continued marching. As Young described the scene, "[t]he officers inside [the cruisers] just glared at us, and before they moved on, one of them snarled, 'You goddamn niggers get your black asses off the street.' "[84] The demonstration indicated that the "peace" that city officials thought they had "restored" was tenuous at best.

The Kercheval incident revealed that Detroit was far from immune to the racial strife that had already scarred other communities. The city was a participant in rather than an observer of "a troubled world." Detroit activists maintained their belief that "black art" could address these troubles as Langston Hughes had suggested in his speech at the Dakar festival. At Motown Studios the company continued to confront what Hughes so eloquently described as the dilemma of the double audience. Not sure whom to please, "the white, the black, or both at once," Motown "straddled the fence" of its many markets with a certain degree of trepidation. On June 28, 1966, the company released its first "message" song: Stevie Wonder's rendition of Bob Dylan's "Blowin' in the Wind." Wonder's interpretation of lyrics such as "Yes, and how many years can some people exist / Before they're allowed to be free" captured the frustration and concern that many people felt about a civil rights struggle that was plagued by internal division and increased violence. By the end of the summer, the record had reached number one on *Billboard's* rhythm and blues chart and number nine on its pop chart.[85]

Motown also continued its pursuit of the older, white-oriented, nightclub market during the summer of 1966. Marvin Gaye made his debut at the Copacabana in July to mixed reviews. Gaye, who had so admired

Nat King Cole's ease in such venues, had a difficult time stepping into the balladeer's shoes. Moreover, Gaye remained torn between his desire for popular celebrity and his social consciousness, which demanded another form of artistic expression unencumbered by commercial motives. Neither Marvin Gaye, nor Motown as a whole, resolved its double-audience dilemma in 1966, and the conflict would not dissipate in the future.[86]

Langston Hughes closed his speech at the First World Festival of Negro Arts with the affirmation "how mighty it would be if the black writers of our troubled world became our messengers of peace."[87] Many Detroiters hoped that black art would bring "peace" and, perhaps, revolutionary change. The success of the Black Arts Convention inspired plans for a second gathering in June 1967. With effort, the forum for the city's black culture and black political organizing could become an annual and nationally recognized event. Detroit did gain the nation's attention in the summer of 1967, but not for the Black Arts Convention or for being a "model city" or a "messenger of peace." The violence of July 1967 communicated another message about exactly how "troubled" the world was—a message of destruction that no Motown song or Broadside poem could easily repair.

5

"The Happening": Detroit, 1967

The song "The Happening," released on March 20, 1967, marked a turn-ing point for the Supremes. The record, which reached number one on the pop charts by May 1967, was the group's last single as the Supremes. When Motown released their next record "Reflections" on July 24, 1967, the group's name had been changed to Diana Ross and the Supremes. The name change mirrored the internal tensions building within the group. Diana Ross's ambition and intimate relationship with Berry Gordy had cemented her place at center stage and ensured her top billing. Florence Ballard, buckling under the stress of celebrity life—always in the public eye and in Ross's shadow—had begun to miss shows or arrive to engagements late and intoxicated. Marlene Barrow, member of the Andantes, one of Motown's most dependable backup groups, covered for Ballard's absences, but persistent unreliability was not tolerated for long.[1]

The song "The Happening" musically captured the discrepancy be-tween the group's public harmony and its private dissension. The first few bars of the song begin in an ominous minor key and then shift into a bouncy, up-tempo, major key. The upbeat sound of the music belies the song's lyrics, which tell the painful story of a "tender love" suddenly gone wrong. Singing lead, Diana Ross adopts the persona of the song's scorned lover, who warns listeners to learn from her tragic mistakes. The lover, "[r]iding high on top of the world," lost touch with her beloved and then abruptly "woke up" to find herself abandoned and alone. As her dreams were torn apart, she cautions others with the refrain, "when you got a tender love / You don't take care of / Then you better beware of The

Happening." Ironically, the cheerful sound of the song distracts the listener from the lyrics' foreboding message and, consequently, perpetuates the flightiness about which the lover cautions. The moral of the song, a warning that self-absorption and negligence can destroy personal relationships, reverberated in the discord that haunted the Supremes. Diana Ross's drive overpowered Mary Wilson and especially Florence Ballard, who was gradually being phased out of the group. In mid-April 1967 Cindy Birdsong, a member of Patti LaBelle and the Blue Belles, signed on as Ballard's permanent replacement.

Motown selected Birdsong not only for her talents as a singer but also for her striking resemblance to Ballard. On April 29, 1967, Birdsong made her first appearance as a Supreme when the group performed at the Hollywood Bowl. The benefit concert supported the United Negro College Fund and was sponsored by KHJ Radio in Los Angeles. At the Hollywood Bowl, an outdoor amphitheater, the stage is located farther from the audience than in traditional concert halls. The added distance between the audience and the stage facilitated Motown's effort to use "interchangeable parts" and replace one singer with another without startling fans. As Mary Wilson recalled, "it was even harder [at the Hollywood Bowl] for people to see that Cindy was not Flo, and in fact many reviewers were fooled."[2]

Not everyone would be fooled, however, particularly the Supremes' loyal followers in Detroit, who took a personal hometown pride in their rise to fame. For this reason Motown continued, throughout the spring of 1967, to employ Ballard, who made public appearances on a limited basis.[3] Ballard's presence was particularly important when the company agreed to have the Supremes act as spokespersons for Detroit's United Foundation annual fund-raising campaign, the Torch Drive. Founded on the motto "Give Once for All," the Torch Drive, raised money for the central United Fund and then distributed the contributions to many causes throughout Detroit. Henry Ford II and a group of Detroit's corporate and industrial leaders founded the United Fund in 1949. When the organization raised $19.5 million in contributions in 1961, it became the largest individual community charity in the country. The fund distributed donations to the physically disabled, families in need, and inner-city social programs.[4]

Beginning in 1965, the United Foundation enlisted famous entertainers who were Detroit natives to participate in the Torch Drive. Celebrity spokespersons provided strong publicity for the fund-raising campaign. Actor Efrem Zimbalist Jr. and actress Julie Harris were the first two entertainers to volunteer to lead the drive. In the early spring of 1967 John Fisher, the United Foundation's public relations director, approached Esther Gordy Edwards at Motown about the possibility of the Supremes' participation in the annual event; Edwards agreed. The Supremes' involvement affiliated the record company with the most prestigious charity organization in the city. And their international fame and local appeal guaranteed public interest in the drive. Motown offered the Supremes' latest single, "The Happening," to the United Foundation to use as the fund-raising campaign's theme song and to maximize publicity opportunities for both parties. In turn, the United Foundation decided to spend $1,000 to produce a promotional film entitled *It's Happening*, starring the Supremes.[5]

The Supremes' role as spokespersons for the United Foundation's Torch Drive appeared to be a simple philanthropic gesture, but it was quickly complicated by historical circumstance and race relations in Detroit. The United Foundation's history as a charity fund founded by Detroit's white corporate elite to serve those in need—many of whom were African Americans—created a situation ripe for tension and misunderstanding, particularly in 1967 as the separatist Black Power movement began to strain interracial coalitions across the country. The Supremes' participation in the drive had the potential to diffuse complaints from black Detroit that the foundation was out of touch with its community. The *It's Happening* film would use the Supremes' triumphant rise from the streets of Detroit to international stardom to appeal to white contributors and connect with black citizens.

Production of the sixteen-millimeter promotional film began in April. The United Foundation used the Supremes' personal success story and their music to frame the narrative of the film, the body of which presented the organization's charity projects. For this reason Florence Ballard participated even though the filming occurred after Cindy Birdsong had joined the group. The film opens with Ross, Wilson, and Ballard singing "The Happening" on a flashy nightclub stage. The song, with its

buoyant music and foreboding lyrics, introduces the film with an optimistic, yet serious tone. After a few choruses of the song, the scene
changes and the young women are shown walking up to the Brewster
Projects, their former home. Diana Ross leads the narration, which high-
lights the group's warm memories of living at Brewster and growing
up in Detroit. Throughout the remainder of the film, the song's opening
bars preface each new segment. The minor key and the lyrics, "Oooh,
oooh, and then it happened . . . ," introduce stories of personal tragedy
and eventual triumph over a physical disability or other type of disad-
vantage.

The personal stories explain who benefits from the United Fund. A
family with a child who is physically disabled, a Detroit executive recovering from cancer of the larynx, a stroke victim, and a blind woman
are all shown conquering their disabilities through the financial support
of the United Foundation. Near the end of the film Diana Ross briefly
mentions that funds are also given to several of Detroit's inner-city social
programs. Significantly, the segment on inner-city programs is one of the
most abbreviated moments in the film. The segment includes a quick
montage of the signs of various organizations including the Detroit Urban
League and the Sophie Wright Settlement. A fourteen-year-old boy, Steve,
expresses his appreciation for the Sophie Wright "club" in a voice-over.
He comments, "If it wasn't for Sophie Wright's . . . instead of us being a
big club, it would be a gang." The film closes on an encouraging note
and a new song. Back on the nightclub stage, the group sings their triumphant hit single "I Hear a Symphony," as Diana Ross's voice-over
announces, "Life is happening . . . health is happening—through our own
Torch Drive!"[6]

Although film production ended in late April, *It's Happening* did not
gain any public attention until July 1967. The *Detroit Free Press* ran a
story about the film on July 30, 1967. The article announced the United
Foundation's plan to use the Supremes as spokespersons for the Torch
Drive campaign and the organization's eagerness to uphold Berry Gordy's
high standards of performance. In an eerie coincidence, the first major
publicity for the Torch Drive appeared in the major city newspaper as
Detroit itself burned. At approximately 3:45 A.M. on July 23, 1967, the
Detroit Police Department raided an illegal after-hours drinking estab-

The Supremes in front of the Brewster Projects from the United Foundation fund-raising film *It's Happening*, 1967. (Courtesy Walter P. Reuther Library, Wayne State University.)

lishment—known in Detroit as a "blind pig"—located on Twelfth Street. Twelfth Street had replaced Hastings Street as the hub of black nightlife after "urban renewal" had demolished Paradise Valley and Black Bottom. Detroit's predominantly white, and frequently racist, police force was always an unwelcome presence in the Twelfth Street neighborhood.[7] Similar to events in Watts, California, in 1965, what began as a routine arrest took a quick and violent turn in the sweltering heat of the summer night. The police raid on July 23 unleashed a backlash of hostility, violence, and destruction unlike Detroit or the country had ever seen before.

What began as a rather small outburst of violence against the arresting officers—bottles and cans thrown at the paddy wagons—quickly spread, like wildfire, into a citywide disorder characterized by extensive looting, arson, and sniper attacks. Unlike Detroit's 1943 race riot, in which blacks and whites physically attacked one another, the 1967 uprising had a distinctly different character and objective. As one observer would later recall, "It was so clear to my own eyes that white people were out there looting, too. Not to say that racial tensions didn't exist, but it wasn't black against white. It was the propertied against the non-propertied." Massive looting and arson, which dominated the week's events, supported claims that the disturbance reflected deep-seated anger on the part of participants about economic inequality, which for many was directly connected to issues of racial injustice.[8]

As with to the city's 1943 riot, the magnitude of the 1967 "civil disorder" could not be contained by local and state officials alone. On Monday, July 24, Governor Romney and Mayor Cavanagh contacted President Johnson and requested that federal troops be sent in to quell the violence. High-stakes political maneuvering complicated the deployment of federal troops to Detroit. President Johnson hesitated in his response to Governor Romney's request. As historian Sidney Fine has noted, "The manner in which [Johnson] was to respond to Romney's request for troops reflected his concern about race relations at that time of racial turbulence, the mounting criticism directed at him because of the war in Vietnam, and, not the least of all, the fact that Romney was a leading contender for the 1968 Republican presidential nomination." Federal paratroopers did not arrive in Detroit until 1:00 A.M. on Tuesday, July 25.[9]

Another week passed before the troopers left, on August 2, when

Cyrus Vance, leader of the federal assessment team, declared that "law and order have been restored to Detroit." In the end 7,231 people were arrested, well over 700 people were injured, 43 people were dead—33 blacks and 10 whites—and property damage was estimated at approximately $50 million.[10] Detroit, which had prided itself on its reputation as the model city of race relations, stood in shock in the wake of the overwhelming devastation. Like the scorned lover in the Supremes' song "The Happening," Detroit "suddenly . . . woke up" to a reality of bitter discontent that it had never fully comprehended before.[11]

The United Foundation's Torch Drive acquired new meaning during the immediate aftershocks of Detroit's civil unrest. Early publicity for the autumn fund-raising campaign quickly incorporated the city's recent tragedy as a part of the cause. A promotional article, entitled "Supremes' Pitch Is in Tempo with the Torch Drive," appeared in the *Michigan Chronicle* on August 12, 1967—only ten days after the federal troops had withdrawn from the city. The news report described the regular demands of the United Foundation, which annually raised funds that were subsequently distributed to over two hundred health and social agencies in the Detroit metropolitan area. To respond to the city in crisis, the United Foundation placed $1 million "in a special fund to provide emergency relief for affected residents." The finances provided food and shelter to individuals displaced or left homeless and assisted people searching for missing persons during the first confusing days of the uprising. The press interviewed the Supremes for the article, and the singers interjected their own plea for support for the fund-raising drive. As Diana Ross commented, "Let's face it. No one can afford not to be involved in the problems of the community. We live in an inter-dependent society where each person's talents and needs must be shared responsibly." The article concluded with the comment, "Understandably, Berry Gordy and Motown Recordings as well as all of Detroit are proud that this year Diana Ross and the Supremes are the 'special ambassadors' of the Torch Drive."[12]

The 1967 campaign, which ran from September through October, raised $27.5 million dollars—breaking all of its previous records.[13] The United Foundation held a victory dinner on November 16, 1967, and invited Berry Gordy as an honored guest. At the banquet Robert P. Semple, chair of the Torch Drive, gave Gordy a special plaque that commemorated "his generosity, civic spirit, and public service" and Motown's participation in the record-breaking campaign. In his acceptance speech Gordy expressed "deep gratitude" for the recognition and his "respect and admiration for the foundation and its success in demonstrating that all races and religions not only can work together, but must work together to achieve heights previously limited by lack of understanding and lack of communication." In Gordy's opinion "lack of communication" contributed to the "racial problems that we are having, or have had in the past summer." The United Foundation representatives expressed mutual admiration for Gordy as someone who "has won a special place in the hearts of the people in this community" and especially thanked him for allowing Diana Ross and the Supremes to star in the organization's appeal film.[14]

Unbeknownst to most of the twelve hundred attendees at the banquet, however, the Torch Drive film with the Supremes had had little, if anything, to do with the unprecedented success of that year's campaign. In an internal memorandum to the United Foundation's central committee—written only days before the victory dinner—Fred Campbell, a fund-raising coordinator, reported on the difficulties he had experienced during the campaign drive. Campbell stated that during fund-raising meetings, he witnessed "considerable resentment in almost every speech I made where $1,000,000 was allotted to the riots in the Detroit area. As you know, for the most part Macomb County has an extremely limited negro population." In regard to the Supremes' *It's Happening* film, he continued,

> One other comment I would like to register before closing, and I
> do not register this in the vein of criticism because I am sure that
> if the timing had been different, the situations would also have
> been different. However, the United Foundation appeal movie,
> "It's Happening," in my opinion, hurt more than it helped due to
> the times. Wherever possible in my work in the Campaign and in
> Macomb County I did not show the movie, but instead took the
> allocated time talking and for question and answer periods.[15]

Campbell's report revealed that, despite the public praise, the Supremes' participation in the campaign did not achieve its intended goal, and the film perhaps hurt more than it helped. The image of three young black women from the Brewster Projects singing the praises of charitable giving did not appeal to many white Detroiters and suburbanites, who—"due to the times"—harbored "considerable resentment" toward the community from which the Supremes emerged. No matter how famous the Supremes had become around the world, they could not avoid, given their racial identity, becoming implicated in the racial politics of Detroit. The United Foundation's stated mission of assisting those in need and, specifically in 1967, facilitating Detroit's healing process in the aftermath of its "civil disorder," could not remedy the deep racial divisions that had so visibly scarred the city.

The Supremes' song "The Happening"—so infused with its own contradictions and foreboding undertones—foreshadowed what became the latent, racially charged subplots of the Torch Drive. The song functioned equally well as an anthem for a troubled "model" city that, like the song's lover, had so recently been torn apart by an unexpected and violent "happening." In either case, as Fred Campbell's memorandum attested, the song illustrated how quickly a form of black culture could become contentious when it converged with larger historical and political forces.[16]

As the Supremes' Torch Drive episode proved, Detroit's black cultural life had a more complicated relationship to the city's civil unrest than most observers or participants immediately realized. Socially, black culture and nightlife had always been an important refuge and outlet for the city's African American citizens, many of whom spent the majority of their days working in the automobile factories. Politically, throughout the summer of 1967, black activists in Detroit continued to champion "black arts" as a means to empower the black community. Plans for Detroit's Second Annual Black Arts Convention in late June drew interest from national Black Power advocates and generated concern with local police authorities, who saw the gathering as a hotbed of black radical activity. For these reasons black cultural life in Detroit could not avoid becoming a battleground and casualty of the city's "happening."

Detroit's Backlash Blues: Black Culture and the Great Rebellion

Mister Backlash, Mister Backlash,
Just who do you think I am?
Tell me, Mister Backlash,
Who do you think I am?
You raise my taxes, freeze my wages,
Send my son to Vietnam.

You give me second-class houses,
Give me second-class schools,
Second-class houses
And second-class schools.
You must think us colored folks
Are second-class fools

. . . .

Tell me, Mister Backlash,
What you think I got to lose?
I'm gonna leave you, Mister Backlash,
Singing your mean old backlash blues.

You're the one,
Yes, you're the one
Will have the blues.

—Langston Hughes, "The Backlash Blues"

Langston Hughes died on May 22, 1967. His poem "The Backlash Blues" was written in 1966 and published posthumously in 1967 in his collection *The Panther and the Lash.* The book contained Hughes's most overt commentary on the continuing racial crises confronting his country. Hughes wrote some of the poems including "Black Panther," "Stokely Malcolm Me," and "The Backlash Blues" during his last years in response to contemporary racial issues. Hughes had recorded three of the poems, "Merry-Go-Round," "Junior Addict," and "Sweet Words from Liberals on Race," in 1963 for the *Poets of the Revolution* album, which Motown Records still had not released.

Langston Hughes did not live to see his Motown recording completed, but his beliefs about the "revolutionary" role of poetry and art in the racial struggle lived on in Detroit's black community. At the time of Hughes's death, Motown Studios seemed to have forgotten about *Poets of the Revolution* altogether, but the city's other cultural communities and political activists continued to see black art as an important tool in the fight for racial equality. The Forum 66 organization planned the Second Annual Black Arts Convention for June 29–July 2, 1967, to be held again at Cleage's Central United Church. The church was an appropriate setting for the conference. On Easter Sunday 1967, Cleage had unveiled there an eighteen-foot mural of the Black Madonna painted by Detroit artist Glanton Dowdell. The painting marked the beginning of what would become the Shrine of the Black Madonna, a denomination that venerated black culture and espoused a theology of Christian black nationalism. Black nationalism was the central theme of the Second Annual Black Arts Convention, which organizers dedicated to the memory of Malcolm X.

The four-day conference offered a wide range of activities and events. The first day, Thursday, featured an Afro-American Trade Fair, followed by a Youth Conference on Friday. Over the weekend organizers held workshops on religion, literature, Vietnam, jazz, theater, black women's issues, community organizing, and economic self-help. Many prominent activists and cultural workers participated in the workshops. The Reverend C. L. Franklin, Cleage, and Milton Henry spoke at the religion panel. The literature workshop featured Dudley Randall, Nikki Giovanni, and John O. Killens and included a special dedication of *For Malcolm*, the first book of poetry by Randall's Broadside Press. Edward Vaughn, whose bookstore founded Forum 66, led the economic self-help discussion. Daniel Watts, editor of the *Liberator* magazine in New York City, presented a keynote address on Friday night, which was followed by an appearance by H. Rap Brown, the newly elected chair of SNCC.[17] Just as Malcolm X's speech at the Grass Roots Conference in 1963 had, H. Rap Brown's seditious rhetoric caught everyone's attention. As he shook his fist in the air, Brown declared, "Let white America know that the name of the game is tit-for-tat, an eye for an eye, a tooth for a tooth, and a life for a life . . . Motown, if you don't come around, we are going to burn you down!" Brown's use of "Motown" as a synonym for Detroit indicated how thoroughly the record company had popularized a new nickname for the city.[18]

Brown's volatile pronouncement disrupted the celebratory focus of the Black Arts Convention. His threat of violent revolution reflected the political fervor of the gathering but also diverged from the convention's cultural themes. Yet when Detroit's streets burned three weeks after the convention, Brown's warning seemed prophetic, rather than tangential to the cultural politics of Detroit. The blind pig where the conflict broke out was a highly contested cultural venue in Detroit. In fact, blind pigs had been important economic and cultural fixtures in Detroit's black community since Prohibition. At that time, Detroit's close proximity to the Canadian border made the city a convenient destination for the transfer of illegal liquor into the United States. As a youth, Coleman Young participated in this subterranean economy and the blind pig culture it spawned. As he recalled,

> It was said that eighty-five percent of the Canadian liquor that came over the border during Prohibition passed through Detroit, where the bootleg industry employed as many as fifty thousand people—not to mention kids like me—and was second only to the manufacturing of automobiles. The unlawful conveyance of booze was so common that the Detroit Tunnel was known locally as the Detroit Funnel ... Turning the whiskey into cash was no problem: all over the city, there were literally thousands of blind pigs—Prohibition saloons—that would buy our booty.[19]

After Prohibition, blind pigs continued to be an important facet of black cultural life in Detroit. The clubs offered an outlet for leisure for workers in an industrial city—many of whom devoted long hours to the unrelenting assembly-line labor. As scholar Paul Gilroy has noted, black working people "see waged work as itself a form of servitude. At best, it is viewed as a necessary evil and is sharply counterposed to the more authentic freedoms that can only be enjoyed in nonwork time. The black body is here celebrated as an instrument of pleasure rather than an instrument of labor. The nighttime becomes the right time, and the space allocated for recovery and recuperation is assertively and provocatively occupied by the pursuit of leisure and pleasure."[20] De facto segregation in Detroit, which barred blacks from most white entertainment venues in the city, created a shared black cultural life that was not divided by class distinctions. Both working-class and middle-class blacks enjoyed the blind pigs, nightclubs, and cabarets located in and around the Paradise Valley and Black Bottom districts. During the postwar years, Mayor Cobo's Detroit Plan demolished these regions, but many of the clubs, businesses, and general nightlife relocated to Twelfth Street.[21]

By the mid-1960s, Twelfth Street's commercial strip, which ran north from West Grand Boulevard to Clairmont Avenue, developed a reputation as "Sin Street" with an economy centered around blind pigs and prostitution. Civil rights gains, throughout the fifties and early sixties, altered the composition of the street's clientele. Most black middle-class patrons gradually abandoned the region as they gained increased access to white establishments, but Twelfth Street continued to be a social center for working-class blacks.[22] Many blacks who frequented Twelfth Street deeply resented intrusions on the area by Detroit's police force. In April 1967 Errol Miller, a representative of the U.S. Justice Department, visited Detroit to report on race relations. Miller cited police raids on blind pigs as "one of the chief sources of complaints" among blacks and concluded that the pigs were "an important part of life in Detroit's ghetto." He also warned that police raids on blind pigs were "an unwise attempt by a white middle class to foist its morals on the lower class." Miller's warning about the white middle class's moral righteousness could have been extended to the black middle class. On July 11, 1966, the *Michigan Chronicle*, newspaper of the city's black middle class, wrote an editorial denouncing the existence of blind pigs and calling for increased law enforcement against them. But whenever the police raided a blind pig, they transgressed important boundaries of race and class in the city, which exacerbated already tense police-community relations. As historian Sidney Fine has noted, the raids may "very well have been seen by some ghetto blacks not as a simple problem of law enforcement but as an event with both racial and symbolic significance."[23]

The blind pig that the police raided on July 23, 1967, was located at 9125 Twelfth Street and had existed since 1964. When it first opened, the owners identified the club as a local political organizing group, the

United Community League for Civic Action, as a front for the establishment's illegal activities. Here, the owners used the illusion of black political organizing to divert attention from the actual cultural and social activities that took place—a complete inversion of the approach of the Black Arts Convention, which used cultural celebration to mask political organizing. By 1967 the United Community League for Civic Action was a well-known blind pig, and the police had attempted to raid the club nine times in the preceding year.

On July 23 an undercover officer gained entrance to the pig by mingling with several women visiting the club. Soon after, the commanding officer, Sergeant Arthur Howison, and his crew broke down the door with a sledgehammer and charged in. Once inside, the officers discovered an unusually large crowd of eighty-five people, and the raid quickly became chaotic. Several people attempted to hide in the kitchen and the bathrooms, and some jumped out the back second-story window. The owners of the pig were hosting a party for two men who had recently returned from Vietnam and one other man who was soon to leave for the war. Given the size of the party, Sergeant Howison could have opted to arrest only the club owners, but he decided to apprehend everyone present. It took over an hour for the police to locate and fill the four paddy wagons needed to transport all the participants to jail.[24]

Over the course of the delays, a crowd, beginning at about twenty people and growing to two hundred, gathered in the streets outside the pig. The onlookers initially appeared jovial—some observers joked with arrestees—but became hostile when they witnessed the police's increasingly rough treatment of the party-goers. Several eyewitnesses claimed that they saw officers beat certain prisoners as well as push, kick, and twist the arms of some others. Two young men in the crowd began to shout for action. One yelled, "Black Power, don't let them take our people away; look what they are doing to our people . . . let's get the bricks and bottles going." Another chimed in, "Let's have a riot." Quickly, beer cans, bricks, and rocks showered the street. One bottle smashed through the rear windshield of the last police cruiser to leave the scene and incited the crowd. Detroit's "civil disturbance," as it was identified by government officials, or "Great Rebellion," as it became known as on the streets, had begun.[25]

The naming of the event was always highly contested. Many participants and members of the black community referred to the week as the
"Great Rebellion" or the "July Rebellion of 1967." Most press coverage
and historical accounts used the more common "Detroit Riot of 1967."
The distinction between "riot" and "rebellion" revolved around motive.
Black community leaders preferred "rebellion" since it implied that people were consciously reacting to economic oppression and racial inequality. The term "riot," by contrast, evoked a sense of randomness and irrationality, which many critics of the term believed placed too much
emphasis on the behavior of participants rather than the material conditions that generated the outrage. The government's "civil disturbance"
label had political and economic implications. Insurance companies determine coverage costs in relation to the definition of a catastrophic event.
As Sidney Fine observed, "The Insurance Bureau was anxious that no
responsible official in the state refer to the riot as an 'insurrection' since
policies with extended coverage normally covered the 'perils of riot and
civil commotion' but excluded losses resulting from insurrections."[26]

In the days that followed, the local press and national media focused
attention on the violence, looting, and arson that overwhelmed city officials, the Detroit police and fire departments, and the National Guard.
Press reports were quick to speculate that the disturbance was strategically planned by militant activists in the black community. News coverage that suggested a black nationalist conspiracy also displaced
broader analyses of the economic inequality and tense police-community
relations that propelled the violence and looting. Several stories specifically targeted individuals who attended or spoke at the Black Arts Convention three weeks earlier. The *Detroit News* ran a five-part investigative
series by Louis E. Lomax, author of the book *The Negro Revolt*. Lomax's
third article, "Organized Snipers in Riot Given Help by Residents," accused six individuals of encouraging and leading the rebellion: "attorney
Milton Henry and his brother, Richard; Edward Vaughn, a book store
owner and a Black Power advocate; the Reverend Albert B. Cleage, pastor
of the Central United Church of Christ; and James Boggs and his Chinese
wife, Grace Lee Boggs." Lomax cited the six activists' participation in
organizations such as the Group on Advanced Leadership, the Freedom

Now Party, and the Malcolm X Society as evidence of their subversive leadership.[27]

The accused activists denied any direct involvement in starting the uprising but seized the media attention as an opportunity to publicize community concerns. Milton and Richard Henry, who founded the Malcolm X Society several months before the rebellion, created the most public controversy. The Henry brothers' society advocated self-defense, espoused a pan-Africanist philosophy, and demanded that land in the United States be turned over to blacks for the establishment of a separate nation. On July 25, 1967—two days after the blind pig raid, Milton Henry sent a telegram to President Johnson, Governor Romney, and Mayor Cavanagh that read,

> Regarding insurrection in Detroit, speaking for Malcolm X Society, we will ask for cessation of all hostilities by insurrectionists by 7 P.M. today provided following eight points are accepted as basis of discussion by 1 P.M. today:
>
> 1. Withdraw all troops
> 2. Release all prisoners
> 3. Give amnesty to all insurrectionists
> 4. Set up district police commissioners
> 5. Agree to urban renewal veto by residents
> 6. Divide city council and school board by districts
> 7. Provide funds for community owned businesses
> 8. Institute compensatory and compulsory equal employ-
>   ment enforcement.[28]

Mayor Cavanagh and other city officials dismissed the demands as "ridiculous." But the Malcolm X Society continued to publicize its concerns and, two weeks after the disorder, presented a plan to revitalize Twelfth Street. The plan proposed that housing and shopping cooperatives and a community center be built to replace the destroyed sections of Twelfth Street. The community center would provide classrooms, business offices, and "several auditoriums and a recording studio, which people in the community may use to further their creative talents . . . [and] TV-movie production areas, to further the development of our literature and art." The proposal's emphasis on creating sites of cultural production reflected the activists' belief in the importance of these activities and their renewed awareness, after the city's uprising, that efforts to preserve and celebrate black culture were in danger in Detroit.[29]

One incident that occurred during the rebellion exemplified exactly how threatened Detroit's black cultural centers were. In the early morning of July 27, 1967, several Detroit police officers vandalized and fire-bombed Edward Vaughn's Forum 66 bookstore on Dexter Avenue as eye-witnesses looked on. The group of police officers arrived at the bookstore at approximately 4:00 A.M. Using rifle butts, the officers smashed the store's windows and continued inside to mutilate and destroy Vaughn's extensive book and art collection. They slashed several paintings and damaged photographs including a framed picture of Stokely Carmichael. Surprisingly, as some observers noted at the time, the portrait of Carter G. Woodson, founder of the Association for the Study of Negro Life and History, was left untouched. The vandals ripped books off of the shelves and left the faucets in the back room running. When Vaughn came to the store the next morning, hundreds of books were floating in a large pool of water, 75 percent of them completely destroyed.[30]

Vaughn recognized the malicious intent of the attack. As he commented during the cleanup, "They [the police vandals] tried to destroy an idea, but they can't do it." Vaughn referred, of course, to the symbolic importance of his business: the only bookstore in Detroit—and one of the first in the country—devoted to the promotion and dissemination of black culture and history. When *Detroit News* special reporter Louis Lomax stopped by to survey the damage, Vaughn waved a water-soaked copy of Lomax's book *The Negro Revolt* at the author and commented, "You told them; Martin King told them; everybody who cares, white and black, told them. They did not listen."[31]

The perpetrators did not deny their involvement and instead defended their actions as necessary. A sergeant from the city's Tenth Precinct admitted firebombing the building and justified it as a response to reports that guns were being stored inside. Witnesses, who saw the attack in progress and heard the officers cursing angrily, maintained their belief that the incident was a hate crime. The firebombing was also similar to the violent tactics the Federal Bureau of Investigation (FBI) used, particularly in its Cointelpro (Counterintelligence program) operations against black nationalist organizing across the country. According to scholar Nelson Blackstock, the FBI used Cointelpro to "expose, disrupt, misdirect, discredit, or otherwise neutralize the activities of black nationalist, hate-type organizations . . . [and] urged and initiated violent acts . . . including bombings." The July 27 police attack on Vaughn's bookstore was clearly motivated by these strategies. Before the firebombing, the bookstore had not been harmed by any acts of looting or arson. Vaughn and many others believed that the bookstore's reputation as a community business that promoted race pride initially had protected it from the vandalism that befell many white-owned establishments.[32]

Whether through race pride or pure luck, Motown Studios, the city's most famous black-owned business, escaped physical damage and looting. Motown's survival was quite remarkable considering its close proximity to Twelfth Street. As one Detroit resident who lived in the neighborhood recalled, "If you looked towards West Grand Boulevard, it was burning. Everywhere you turned and looked you could see nothing but flames. It was like they were just leaping in the sky, at night, and then that was when I really got terrified."[33]

Motown sidestepped the arson and vandalism that occurred only blocks from its recording studios, but it was not completely untouched by the uprising. Recall that on the evening of July 23, 1967, Martha and the Vandellas were performing "Dancing in the Street" on stage at Detroit's Fox Theater on Woodward Avenue when news came from the wings to stop the show. Reeves advised the audience to go home to safety. During the entire six days of unrest, Motown Studios remained open and continued to record in the midst of what Berry Gordy later recalled as "sirens . . . bursts of gunfire . . . flames jumping, broken glass and debris from shattered windows and looted stores." For the Motown studio band, the Funk Brothers, the Great Rebellion marked the end of a musical era. The Chit Chat Club, where the musicians moonlighted as the house band and created many of Motown's musical innovations, did not survive the uprising—it burned down in an arson fire.[34]

Another cultural fatality of the rebellion was Joe Von Battle's record store. The store had been a fixture in the city's black community since its early days on Hastings Street, when Von Battle broadcast his own recordings of the Reverend C. L. Franklin's fiery sermons on loudspeakers outside. In the late fifties Mayor Cobo's Detroit Plan demolished the store's Hastings Street location, but Von Battle relocated to Twelfth Street. Throughout the sixties Von Battle's store continued to offer the latest rhythm and blues, gospel, and pop recordings, as well as tickets to local musical events.

During the first days of the rebellion, Von Battle closed his business and posted "Soul Brother" signs in the windows in the hopes that looters would pass by the store. As the melee continued, Von Battle got a pistol and stood guard in the doorway of the shop. He retreated from his vigil when the National Guard moved into the area. At the end of the week, he returned to the store as the troops began to depart. The building was still standing—saved from arson attacks—but looters had completely ransacked the business. Amid the glass and rubble, the recordings and tapes that Von Battle had saved for a generation lay smashed and strewn on the ground. Marsha Mickens, Von Battle's daughter, witnessed her father's first trip back to the record store after he gave up his vigil. She remembered, "He just said, 'Oh, Lord.' . . . It was like his whole life's work had been destroyed. I remember that feeling of witnessing my father witness that, of seeing him powerless over the situation, of the chaos because the firemen and guardsmen were still running around." In the weeks that followed, he tried to salvage what was left and start over, but he could not make up for the extensive loss and eventually went out of business.[35]

The demise of the Chit Chat Club and Von Battle's store illustrated how the Great Rebellion created its own "backlash blues" for Detroit's black community—and specifically, for its cultural life. Looting and arson, which initially appeared to be directed at perceived "outsiders" or "enemies" of the community, soon spiraled out of control and did not discriminate between the outsider "whitey" establishments and the familiar, community-based "Soul Brother" businesses and nightclubs. The Chit Chat Club and Von Battle's store were two casualties of this pernicious entropy. When the Detroit police firebombed Edward Vaughn's bookstore, the crime conformed to a certain logic. The police destroyed the African American bookstore because they perceived it as a threat, as a site of black nationalist organizing. The burning of the Chit Chat Club and the looting of Von Battle's archive of recordings defied any such logic. The unbridled anger of the moment recoiled back on itself and consumed that which the community valued and celebrated. The burning of the Chit Chat Club, so significant to Motown's musical history, and loss of Von Battle's store, which marked the end of an era in the history of black cultural production in Detroit, did not make any newspaper headlines. Another event, what became known as the Algiers Motel incident, did capture considerable media attention, however, and revealed how Detroit's racial and cultural politics shaped not only the Great Rebellion but its aftermath as well.

The Algiers Motel Incident and Other Aftershocks

The Algiers Motel incident was another example of police aggression against a black business that was a fixture in the city's black cultural life. The Algiers Motel, located on the corner of Woodward Avenue and Virginia Park, served a primarily black clientele and, like Von Battle's record store, was a part of the Twelfth Street neighborhood. The motel had a reputation among law officials as "a haven for pimps, prostitutes, drug pushers and addicts, gamblers, numbers operators and other criminal element[s]." Within the black community, the motel—with its African-inspired name—was known as a convenient, inexpensive establishment for those whose livelihoods depended on the cultural economy of the Twelfth Street neighborhood. The Dramatics, a male rhythm and blues singing group, had sought refuge at the Algiers Motel once the rebellion began. The group had been performing with Martha and the Vandellas in the "Swinging Time Revue" at the Fox Theater. When the show closed abruptly in response to the chaos in the streets, the Dramatics decided to stay at the Algiers Motel until the situation calmed down.[36]

Unexpectedly, however, the motel became one of the most dangerous places to be in the city of Detroit. In the early morning of July 26 three black men, Carl Cooper, Auburey Pollard, and Fred Temple, were shot to death at the motel and several police officers beat and threatened other motel guests. Conflicting testimony and cover-ups shrouded the murders. Law enforcement officials circulated rumors that the three victims were snipers, who were shot by unknown assailants. Witnesses and leaders in the black community argued that three Detroit police officers, Ronald August, Robert Paille, and David Sendak, had murdered Cooper, Pollard, and Temple in another vicious episode of police brutality.[37]

Participants from the Black Arts Convention led the public outcry about the Algiers attack. H. Rap Brown returned to Detroit for a rally in late August and urged his audience to hold a "people's tribunal" about the case and "carry out an execution," if the tribunal found the police officers involved guilty. Several Detroit radicals started to plan a "mock trial" at the Dexter Theater, but the theater's management, concerned about possible risks, decided not to stage the trial at the last minute. Cleage's Central United Church, site of the Black Arts Convention, volunteered its facilities for the event. The executive board of Cleage's church made the following public statement:

> We love our church and the building in which we worship. But even if granting permission for the People's Tribunal to be held here means the destruction of the building, as churches have been destroyed in Birmingham and all over the South, we still have no choice. We serve the Black Messiah, Jesus of Nazareth, who came to unite and free an oppressed black nation. Our brothers have been brutally slain, and it is only right that the voice of truth, silent in the corrupt halls of justice, should ring out in the House of God.[38]

The mock trial's location at Cleage's church—with its towering image of the Black Madonna—had more political significance than the Dexter Theater location could have had. One woman, who attended the People's Tribunal, remarked, "The Black Madonna is our Statue of Liberty." The activists wanted the mock trial to dramatize their outrage about the murders and to emphasize their belief that justice would not be served in an official court of law.[39]

The People's Tribunal exemplified the philosophy of the Black Arts Convention. A staged cultural event, the trial acted as the black community's political statement about the Algiers case. Over two thousand people gathered at the Central United Church on August 30, 1967, to witness the event. The three Detroit police officers, August, Paille, and Sendak, were named as "defendants" in the murder case. Milton Henry acted as prosecuting attorney. Rosa Parks and novelist John O. Killens sat on the jury. Ken Cockrel, a young radical just out of law school, presided as judge. After testimony and evidence was presented, the jury handed down a guilty verdict, and Cockrel ruled that a sentence should be decided and carried out "by the people."[40]

The theatrics of the People's Tribunal galvanized public outcry within the city's black community about the Algiers Motel case but had little influence in the actual prosecution of the police officers. It would take three more years before each of the accused officers stood trial in a court of law for the murders. In the end, all-white juries acquitted August, Paille, and Sendak of any charges of murder or misconduct. The only battle that the black community won in the Algiers case was the preservation of the motel itself. In response to the Algiers incident, city prosecutor William Cahalan filed suit in October 1967 to have the motel declared a public nuisance and shut down. The motel survived but under a new name: the Desert Inn.[41]

The Algiers Motel incident reverberated with many of the central tensions that pervaded Detroit's Great Rebellion from the moment that the police raided the blind pig on Twelfth Street. The controversial case reinforced the battle lines between the Detroit Police Department and the city's black community—battle lines often drawn around or near sites of black cultural life. The incident also demonstrated how black activists could use cultural events like the People's Tribunal to assert public opinions in a city that often did not allow for their expression in more traditional political arenas. City officials did not offer Detroit's black citizens many opportunities to voice their concerns in public forums during the immediate aftermath of the rebellion. Moreover, the firebombing of Edward Vaughn's bookstore temporarily eliminated one of the more prominent venues for black political organizing in the city. For these reasons, Detroit's black community was skeptical that its needs would be addressed when the official government response to Detroit's "civil disorder" began.

Both federal and local government agencies sought to examine the socioeconomic causes of the uprising and repair its extensive damage. President Johnson appointed the National Advisory Committee on Civil Disorders (NACCD), also known as the Kerner Commission, to investigate the root causes of the destruction that overtook Detroit and so many other communities across the country. Governor George Romney, Mayor Jerome Cavanagh, and Detroit's corporate leaders, including Joseph L. Hudson Jr. of Hudson's Department Store, formed the New Detroit committee within days of the disturbance. The committee replicated the objectives of the NACCD but on a local level. The broad purpose of New Detroit was "to address itself to the problems of the disadvantaged and alienated people in this urban area." Most important, the New Detroit committee set out to build bridges between community groups and leaders who previously worked independently of one another. The initial committee consisted of individuals who represented a wide range of constituencies, including the automobile industry, the city's public school system, the NAACP, and city government.[42]

The committee focused its efforts on outreach to black leaders and the black community, but early attempts to build interracial coalitions were weak at best. The New Detroit campaign, from its outset, starkly illustrated the distance between city leaders' "good intentions" and actual effects on the community level. New Detroit organizers were forthright in their goal of aiding Detroit's black population. The committee's original statement of purpose acknowledged that while it directed its attention to all minority groups, "it is particularly concerned with the solution of the problems relative to the black minority." Early on, however, black community leaders openly criticized New Detroit as being elitist and out-of-touch with the concerns of the inner city.[43]

The Reverend Albert Cleage was one of the most outspoken critics of the committee and the Cavanagh administration in general. Cleage led a meeting at Detroit's City-County Building on August 9, 1967, which was attended by over a thousand black citizens. Strategically, the meeting was scheduled one day before the New Detroit leaders were to hold their first meeting at the same location. The venue gave Cleage the opportunity to make his point about black disenfranchisement from local government. After a series of speeches in which leaders such as Milton Henry proclaimed the need for blacks "to control our lives in all its activities," Cleage remarked that "[t]here has been more truth spoken in this chamber today than in all the days since the building was erected." He concluded, "We have the power! Now we have to organize it! The Hudson

[New Detroit] Committee will take orders from us. We will set up a committee here that represents us and we will tell Hudson, Cavanagh, LBJ, etc., what we want done with the city of Detroit."[44] In response to Cleage's suggestion, participants at the gathering decided to organize their own City-Wide Citizens Action Committee to fight for their concerns. Cleage's influence as spokesperson for the city's black constituents continued to grow in the weeks after the rebellion and during the Algiers Motel controversy. Strong evidence of Cleage's power as a local leader came when the *Michigan Chronicle,* which had traditionally shied away from militant black nationalist perspectives, offered him a weekly column to express his views. Cleage used the column to criticize and offer alternatives to Mayor Cavanagh's strategies for the city's recovery.[45]

One of the most striking examples of the postrebellion chasm between Detroit's city hall and the black community occurred in November 1967. On the first of that month Mayor Cavanagh gave a speech at the annual meeting of the National Association of Independent Insurers held in Florida. The theme of the meeting was "the Urban Crisis." Cavanagh had been asked to discuss "[t]he War at Home—Civil Disorders," and specifically, the insurance "risk potentials as they relate to inner cities." In the speech Detroit's mayor noted that "the insurance industry is a direct beneficiary of urban peace and a leading casualty of urban war" but urged insurers not to completely abandon cities because of the recent civil unrest. One possible solution to the current problems facing blacks in the cities, Cavanagh argued, was that "more emphasis should be placed on making rural life more attractive" to Negroes—"even if it requires a back-to-the-land movement."[46]

These comments received heavy criticism from Detroit's black leadership and local civil rights groups. They were an uncanny echo of Attorney General Francis Biddle's argument after Detroit's 1943 race riot that "no more Negroes should move to Detroit"—an argument that fostered postwar, urban renewal (or "Negro removal") policies. Both Cleage and Frank Joyce, director of Detroit's People against Racism—a white civil rights organization—spoke out publicly against what they called the "Cavanagh Reservation Plan." Also, black organizations such as Milton and Richard Henry's Malcolm X Society had already proposed alternatives to "rural relocation" including the Twelfth Street Revitalization

Plan, which emphasized the improvement of life for blacks in the city through better housing and community centers—fully equipped with educational facilities and recording studios. As these different proposals surfaced during the fall of 1967, the larger vision of what a "new" Detroit might look like was still unclear and highly contested.[47]

Motown Studios had a unique and highly ambiguous role to play in the aftermath of Detroit's rebellion. In one respect, the company had begun to develop alliances with the city's white power elite as exemplified by its affiliation with the United Foundation's Torch Drive. Here, Motown cooperated with Detroit's white corporate establishment in what appeared to be a unified philanthropic effort that transcended racial boundaries. Yet, the Supremes' participation in the fund-raising drive revealed that even the most innocuous efforts at interracial coalition—a black singing group promoting a primarily white, corporate, fund-raising campaign— could miscarry. The *It's Happening* film, produced to dazzle and entice citizens to "give once for all," never achieved the goals that the United Foundation publicly claimed it had. Once the Torch Drive coordinators realized that the Supremes' presence in the film seemed to remind some white audiences that they did not want to "give once for *all*," the highly publicized film was shelved. The decision revealed more about Detroit's post-rebellion racial politics than any "community study" could have.

Motown Studios was also aware by the fall of 1967 that the current state of race relations in Detroit and in the nation had placed new expectations on its role as a black-owned, internationally renowned business. Specifically, the growing interest in the Black Power and Black Arts movements placed greater pressure on Motown to support black causes and promote race pride. In response, Motown publicly announced its plans to initiate its own philanthropic and creative projects to benefit black people. In late October 1967 Detroit's local black press reported stories about Motown's new goals to diversify its mission to "includ[e] public service." In early November *Jet* magazine publicized the story to black readers across the country.

The national and local press coverage explained how Gordy planned several different projects to benefit black causes. One involved a Motown scholarship for musical excellence via the United Negro College Fund. Another entailed the founding of the Loucye Gordy Wakefield Business Career Clinic, named in honor of Gordy's late sister. The clinic would be operated through the facilities of the Interracial Council for Business Opportunity and "would make it possible for bright young Negroes to pursue a rewarding career in business." Another project harkened back to Motown's 1963 *Great March to Freedom* album, as Gordy described his hopes to develop a line of educational recordings. According to Gordy, "[i]f our artists can make special educational records to be used in schools throughout the nation—and even abroad—we will be making a significant contribution to a way of life we are all seeking." In total, Gordy hoped that these projects would prove Motown's commitment to public service. In press statements he asserted, "All of these things obviously could not be done without the existence of Motown which is highly respected in all communities, not only as a successful organization, but as an enlightened one. This is a real moment of truth in our business and our way of life. Make your own success work [to] help others achieve their measure of success, and hope they, in turn, will do likewise. This kind of wonderful chain reaction would be music to my ears, and is indeed the motto of Motown."[48] Gordy's drive to create a more "enlightened" public image for Motown reflected the increased expectations many people began to place on the record company to support the black struggle.

Gordy had difficulty, nevertheless, reconciling his entrepreneurial ambitions with his efforts to promote black causes. He was often preoccupied with Motown's latest record promotion or television appearance and was unable to directly oversee the company's educational or public service projects, instead hiring executives who would. The press coverage about Motown's new commitment to public service included, therefore, the announcement that the record company had hired two new executives: Ewart Abner as director of International Talent Management, Inc., and Junius Griffin as director of publicity at ITMI. Abner, former president of Vee-Jay Records in Chicago, was known for his outspoken advocacy for blacks within the record industry. He had worked for years with the National Association of Radio Announcers (NARA), which was the national organization of black disc jockeys; had founded the American Record Manufacturing and Distributing Association (ARMADA); and was also on the board of the Chicago Urban League. Griffin came to Motown directly from serving with Martin Luther King Jr. as the director of public relations of SCLC. Griffin began his career as a journalist and acted as one of the first black reporters to work for *Stars and Stripes*, the Associated Press, and the *New York Times*. His early coverage on the civil rights struggle in 1963 was nominated for a Pulitzer Prize. He first came to the attention of Motown in 1966, when he convinced Esther Gordy Edwards to let Stevie Wonder perform at Soldier's Field in Chicago at a fund-raiser for SCLC. Griffin's professionalism impressed Edwards, who encouraged Gordy to hire him at Motown.[49]

The national publicity about Motown's hiring of Abner and Griffin bolstered Motown's public image as a "race-conscious" and politically aware company. The actual, rather than the publicized, political orientation of Motown as a corporation has always been the subject of much debate. Gordy's decision to hire individuals such as Abner and Griffin, who never kept their political activism a secret, complicates any simple dismissal of Motown as a company devoid of political energy. By their very presence, Abner and Griffin changed the company's political atmosphere. Berry Gordy discussed the hiring of Griffin and Abner in his own memoirs. He wrote that the two men, along with George Schiffer— Motown's "white Jewish liberal" contract lawyer—"were the most outspoken at Motown when it came to social causes."[50]

The *Jet* article concluded with another statement by Gordy about the historic significance of Motown's role as a black business: "It is true that we have been able to substantially increase our activities and our profits each year since we started in business some eight years ago, but the important thing to me personally is that we are in a stronger position to employ more artists, creative talent, executive, clerical and secretarial personnel than any other firm headed by a Negro, in the annals of the entertainment world."[51] The *Jet* article enhanced Motown's image as a harmonious and socially conscious black business. Yet, like the company's participation in the United Foundation's Torch Drive, the public image did not coincide with the actual tensions and growing pains simmering just under the surface at Hitsville Studios. Gordy's final remark in the *Jet* piece proclaimed, "Happy people work for us and that is the way it will always be as long as I am head of Motown." Gordy's optimistic view of his employees' contentment was soon to be challenged. Disputes over royalties and other business practices would cause several bitter estrangements within the Motown "family." These behind-the-scenes battles also accentuated the strain that Motown's business objectives put on its other goals to appear progressive and in touch with its own employees and the black struggle.

Hitsville's internal conflicts represented, of course, only one small facet of the larger challenge that faced Detroit as it began the enormous task of rebuilding itself from the ashes of 1967. Beginning in 1968 Motown, Detroit, and the country as a whole confronted an increasingly violent and divided civil rights campaign and an escalating public outcry against the United States's involvement in Vietnam. For Motown, the country's political upheavals—both in the civil rights campaign and in foreign policy—would continue to place more pressure on the record company to produce music that spoke to and engaged with these political issues. In Detroit, where the city's own civil unrest had been compared to the fighting in Southeast Asia, a new campaign to elect a black mayor began. And, as was always the case in the Motor City, these larger questions—whether race relations or Vietnam or leadership of city government—played themselves out in the city's black cultural life, which was becoming more inseparable from political ideas and social movements.[52]

6

"What's Going On?"
Motown and New Detroit

On February 16, 1968, Martin Luther King Jr. returned to Detroit to appear again—as he had on June 23, 1963—at Cobo Hall. He did not come to lead any "great" marches or rally the cause of civil disobedience in the face of an increasingly violent movement. King came to the Motor City in a surprise visit to participate in what Mayor Cavanagh had proclaimed "Aretha Franklin Day." Similar to Langston Hughes Day in 1964, Aretha Franklin Day was a citywide celebration of black life that coincided with Black History Month and Detroit's Brotherhood Week. In 1968 the cultural extravaganza acquired more significance in the wake of Detroit's turbulent summer of the past year. Mayor Cavanagh and other city officials were eager to support an event that could promote their vision of New Detroit—a city wounded, but not defeated, by racial division; a city, in other words, capable of recognizing the talents and hopes of black Detroit, which Aretha Franklin so powerfully represented. Franklin, who had sung in her father's New Bethel Baptist Church and toured as a child in the C. L. Franklin Gospel Caravan, had achieved local celebrity at a very young age, but, by February 1968, she was a national cultural phenomenon: the Queen of Soul.[1]

By 1968 Franklin's celebrity matched and competed with that of the Supremes, but her singing style and rise to fame differed dramatically from Detroit's prize trio. Aretha first broke with her gospel roots in 1960 at the age of eighteen, when she moved to New York and signed a five-year recording contract with John Hammond at Columbia Records.

Franklin's first album at Columbia, entitled simply *Aretha,* consisted of twelve songs including "Over the Rainbow" and "Rock-a-Bye Your Baby with a Dixie Melody." Hammond produced the songs with jazz arrangements, and Franklin's vocals kept to the strictures of popular song stylings.[2] For the next six years Franklin's recordings for Columbia remained within the genre of popular ballads and Broadway standards, such as "If Ever I Would Leave You" from *Camelot,* and stagnated there. Ironically, the same show tunes that secured the Supremes' status as international nightclub stars almost ended Aretha Franklin's early efforts to reach a popular audience. When, by late 1965, none of the nine albums she had recorded with Columbia had shown large profits, the company released her from her contract.

In early 1966, however, Jerry Wexler, an Atlantic Records producer, approached Franklin, offered her a contract, and, when she accepted, quickly sent her to the Fame recording studio in Muscle Shoals, Alabama. The Muscle Shoals recording sessions proved to be a watershed in Aretha's singing career. Wexler encouraged Franklin to return to her unique gospel style. As he later claimed, "I took her to church, sat her down at the piano, and let her be herself." She and the studio band recorded "I Never Loved a Man (The Way I Love You)," a song written by Ronnie Shannon that Aretha had brought from Detroit. Wexler released the record on February 10, 1967, and the song sold a quarter of a million copies within its first two weeks of release.[3]

Franklin's rise to the top of the charts, which occurred against a backdrop of urban revolts and protest, was never merely a record industry success story. When her hit single "Respect" climbed the charts in July 1967, some fans declared that the summer of 1967 was "the summer of 'Retha, Rap [Brown], and Revolt."[4] Her songs became anthems—the soulful sound of a movement that increasingly seemed propelled by black pride and power rather than earlier "dreams" of racial integration.

Detroit's Aretha Franklin Day, held exactly one year after the smash release of "I Never Loved a Man," celebrated the singer's talents as a performer and as a symbol of black political consciousness. The Friday night gala concert at Cobo Hall demonstrated Franklin's broad appeal. Franklin received eleven different awards from local groups and record industry publications such as *Cashbox* and *Billboard,* as well as a special award from SCLC presented by King. Local disc jockey Martha Jean "the Queen" Steinberg acted as one of the hosts of the evening and declared Aretha "everybody's soul sister." After the presentation of awards and several speeches, Franklin took to the stage to perform for her adoring fans—her first local appearance in over two years. As she sang hits including "Natural Woman" and "Respect," the audience crowded the stage, some clamoring just to touch her dress. The ABC network filmed the entire evening for a television special that it was producing on Franklin's rise to superstardom.[5]

Aretha Franklin Day, more than a celebration of the singer's talents, illustrated how much black culture had gained tangible political clout by the late 1960s. King's presence at the event attested to the rising power of cultural figures such as Franklin in the freedom struggle. The head of SCLC had traveled to Detroit to honor Franklin and to affiliate himself with her undisputed popularity and public influence. King's status as the leader of the nonviolent civil rights movement had changed markedly since his earlier appearance in Detroit at the Great March to Freedom in 1963. He faced his first major defeat in 1966 when SCLC's campaign to desegregate Chicago and fight for open housing ended with little progress and much frustration. SCLC's protest strategies, which had worked so effectively in rural southern communities, were not well suited for the intricacies and power structures of the urban North. SCLC's defeat in Chicago also coincided with the rising popularity of leaders such as Stokely Carmichael and H. Rap Brown, who advocated black nationalism and separatism—a clear challenge to all that King's leadership represented. In April 1967 King spoke out against the war in Vietnam and regained the admiration of leaders such as Carmichael, but he lost the crucial support of the Johnson administration. The SCLC leader morally opposed the Vietnam conflict and was concerned that the United States's involvement in the war was weakening support for domestic programs that could aid the poor and ameliorate race relations.[6]

King came to the Motor City for Aretha Franklin Day beleaguered by all of these concerns. His place as the undisputed leader of the civil rights struggle was not as secure as it once was—weakened both by black nationalist challenges and his break with the Johnson administration. King was also deeply troubled about the growing violence tearing at

American society, of which Detroit stood as its most devastated victim. Moreover, King's and SCLC's new project, the Poor People's Campaign, was having some difficulties gaining early, broad-based support. The campaign represented an effort to move beyond the issues of racial integration and voting rights to confront, instead, the broader concern of economic injustice, which many acknowledged as the true source of the rage that burned so many cities—including Detroit—in 1967. At the Franklin gala, King, suffering from laryngitis and exhaustion, spoke very briefly to the crowd at Cobo Hall, who greeted him with a warm standing ovation. As the civil rights movement's most powerful orator rested his voice, the Queen of Soul exercised hers. The momentary contrast between King's silence and Franklin's multioctave range embodied the shifts that were transforming the face of black struggle in America. Aretha's rendition of "Respect" was the crown jewel of her repertoire, an anthem of the dispossessed, and expressed the spirit of King's agenda as no speech could have.

"Respect"

On March 1, 1968—just a few weeks after Aretha Franklin Day—the sentiments of "Respect" and the goal of the Poor People's Campaign received validation when the federal government published the Kerner Report of the National Advisory Commission on Civil Disorders. The report's indictment that "our nation is moving toward two societies, one black, one white—separate and unequal" corroborated King's and SCLC's belief that the civil rights struggle needed to focus its energies on the economic causes of this pandemic inequality. The findings of the Kerner Commission argued for more government programs to remedy social and economic inequality, but President Johnson did not act decisively to implement the report's recommendations.[7] Given Johnson's reluctance, King and SCLC leaders became more certain that the Poor People's Campaign was not only necessary but urgent to keep the issues of economic injustice in the forefront of public debate.[8]

For cities like Detroit, President Johnson's reluctance to support the findings of the Kerner Commission with legislative action would have devastating repercussions for years to come. "New" Detroit had experienced little recovery in terms of race relations or economic growth when the federal government released the Kerner Report. For this reason, the city was searching for any sign of economic strength or improved race relations. In mid-March 1968 Motown Records offered a glimmer of hope when the company announced that it was expanding its business "deeper into [Detroit's] inner city." Motown declared that, owing to its enormous growth, it needed to move into a larger office facility and had purchased the ten-story Donovan Building on Woodward Avenue across from the Fisher Freeway. The building would be renamed the "Motown Center" and would house close to three hundred employees. The original recording studios at Hitsville, U.S.A., would remain in operation on West Grand Boulevard, but the majority of the company's business administration would move to the new location.[9]

Detroit welcomed the news of Motown's expansion. The *Michigan Chronicle* ran a story that commended the record company for giving "many young Detroit Negroes . . . the opportunity to fill positions previously considered 'off limits' to black youths." The article continued to describe Motown's evolution into an international record industry giant. By 1968 Motown had offices in New York, Los Angeles, Tokyo, Paris, and London. Yet the newspaper release emphasized that "Berry Gordy Jr. has insisted that the nerve-cell of the ever increasing Motown activity remain in Detroit's inner city." The *Michigan Chronicle* proclaimed, moreover, that Motown's move to the Donovan Building would "play a vital role in the rebuilding of a New Detroit." The *Chronicle* proudly reported that the Motown Center "will be one of the largest buildings housing a business owned and operated by Negroes in the country."[10]

To some, Motown's relocation to the "inner city" breathed life into a battered city; to others, it marked the end of an era. Certain Motown loyalists felt that the company's move away from the West Grand Boulevard neighborhood that had, in many ways, created its sound was more abandonment than progress. The sterile ten-story Donovan Building shared more with the towering corporate headquarters of General Motors down the street than with homey Hitsville, U.S.A.[11] For city leaders, however, Motown's announcement about the Donovan expansion was, for the moment, similar to Aretha Franklin Day. Both events inspired public hope of civic rebirth. If Detroit was going to create a future of racial harmony and economic prosperity for itself, perhaps the city's famous black artists and businesses could lead the way.

Although Aretha Franklin or Motown might inspire hope, Detroit's future was much more complicated than any song could express or any one business decision could easily remedy. From 1968 to 1973 the Motor City's struggle to create itself anew from the wreckage of 1967 involved many competing interests and ongoing debate over who could best lead the city. Many of Detroit's black citizens felt the only way to improve the city was through black political control. Detroit's black activists, buoyed by Carl Stokes's election as the mayor of Cleveland in 1967, began their early campaign to elect a black mayor.

The Motown Record Company maintained an ambivalent relationship to Detroit and black politics during these years. The company's move to the Donovan Building, though publicly presented as a gesture of commitment to Detroit's revitalization efforts, was actually the first step of the more traditional process of corporate decentralization. Hitsville, U.S.A., with its offices around the world, was becoming increasingly invested in expanding its operations in Los Angeles with the hopes of breaking into the film industry and television production. Musically, Motown confronted an internal clash between, on the one hand, the management's desire to produce music that maintained the company's popular and commercial standards and, on the other, the artists'—especially Marvin Gaye's and Stevie Wonder's—desire to produce music that was socially and politically relevant.

Artists' interest in having creative freedom to produce their own music was only one of the conflicts beginning to divide and weaken the Motown "family" in 1968. Behind the scenes, the record company was about to face the most serious challenge to its highly cultivated image as the dream of black capitalism realized. Royalty disputes instigated the crisis and brought into question the long-held belief that black capitalism was somehow more equitable toward African Americans than any other form of capitalism. Externally, the political upheavals of 1968 tested Motown Records—along with the rest of the country. On March 31, 1968, Lyndon Johnson, responding to heightened criticism of his foreign policy in Vietnam and his domestic policy on race relations, announced that he would not seek another term as president of the United States. The announcement startled many and inaugurated one of the country's most volatile election years. Five days later, on April 4, Martin Luther King Jr. was assassinated at the Lorraine Motel in Memphis, Tennessee. The death of the leader of the nonviolent struggle generated a wave of civil unrest and violent outbreaks in cities across the country—including Detroit. At Motown, the tragedy of King's death renewed the record company's commitment to the national black struggle and to Detroit's efforts to reinvent itself as a model city.

"I Care about Detroit"

The assassination of Martin Luther King Jr. stunned the nation. King had traveled to Memphis to support a strike by the city's sanitation workers. His involvement in the strike furthered efforts to shift the focus of the civil rights struggle onto economic issues. The Memphis sanitation workers' strike revitalized the national civil rights movement and foreshadowed a new era of black labor organizing. King knew that the strike supported the goals of the Poor People's Campaign. As historian William Chafe has noted, "The call from Memphis, though on the surface a diversion of his energies, in fact spoke eloquently to the heart of his concerns. Here, class and race operated together, dramatically illustrating the principle objectives of the entire Poor People's Campaign. When King was killed, many people wondered if the campaign would continue without his leadership, but the cause of economic justice was too urgent to abandon.[12]

Plans were already under way to proceed with the Poor People's Campaign as thousands gathered in Atlanta for King's funeral. As the Reverend Ralph Abernathy proclaimed, "For any of you who linger in the cemetery and tarry around the grave, I have news for you. We have business on the road to freedom ... We must prove to white America that you can kill the leader but you cannot kill the dream." Berry Gordy Jr. attended the funeral and pledged his continued support of the Southern Christian Leadership Conference.[13]

Coretta King quickly enlisted Motown's assistance with a Poor People's March soon after the funeral. She asked Gordy if Motown artists

Black Forum's Grammy-winning release, *Why I Oppose the War in Vietnam*, 1970. (Courtesy Motown Record Co., L.P., a Polygram Company.)

would perform a benefit concert in Atlanta in support of the campaign. Junius Griffin, who had worked so closely with King at SCLC before coming to Motown, organized the details of the concert. Within a matter of days, Gordy sent Stevie Wonder, Gladys Knight and the Pips, the Supremes, the Temptations, and a special eleven-piece Motown band to perform before more than thirteen thousand at the Atlanta Civic Center. The concert raised over $25,000 for SCLC, which did not hesitate to express its gratitude. At the end of the performance, Ralph Abernathy and Coretta King presented Gordy with a special plaque and a set of leather-bound books of King's speeches to acknowledge his support. After the concert, Gordy and the Motown performers joined other celebrities including Harry Belafonte, Sidney Poitier, Sammy Davis Jr., and Nancy Wilson to officially inaugurate the march. Motown's assistance with the Poor People's March stood out as the company's most overtly political gesture since its recording of King's speech at Detroit's Great March to Freedom in 1963.[14]

The Poor People's March was reminiscent of the Great March to Freedom in other ways as well. At the Great March King articulated some of his first public criticism of the injustices that African Americans confronted in the urban North in housing and employment discrimination. The wave of civil unrest that shocked the country during the summer of 1967 (as well as the sobering conclusions of the Kerner Report) proved that little progress had been made to meet the economic needs of many black Americans. The 1968 Poor People's March brought renewed attention to these needs and issues. And on April 11, 1968, only days after King's death, Congress passed and President Johnson signed into law the Civil Rights Act of 1968. The legislation sought to expand equal employment and, most important, end housing discrimination—goals of both marches.

Motown's participation in the Poor People's Campaign generated much-needed publicity but did not guarantee its ultimate success. The Poor People's March began in Marks, Mississippi. When marchers reached Washington, D.C., on May 13, they set up an encampment known as "Resurrection City," which stood in the shadow of the U.S. Capitol. The early days of the protest were hopeful. Detroit's own Reverend C. L. Franklin traveled to Washington and preached to the demonstrators— rousing the crowd as few others could. As witness Charles Fager later recalled,

> Franklin's delivery crossed the line between speaking and singing as he rose toward a crescendo, and the responses from the crowd became tumultuous and almost continuous, beyond hope of reproduction in print. The roots of his famous daughter's vocal style could be heard reverberating in his voice. At the climax he suddenly turned and sat down, leaving the crowd in mid-cheer. But it was only a flourish; he was on his feet again in a few seconds, shouting and singing to them and with them, finally leading the church in the hymn, "I'm Gonna Trust in the Lord until I Die," and then sitting down exhausted, dramatically wiping his streaming face with a large white handkerchief. It was a magnificent performance, unequaled during the campaign in brilliance of delivery or frenzy of response. It was the closest the Washington mass meetings ever came to the kind of exultation that makes a

movement the center of a community's attention the way it was in Selma.[15]

Yet, in the end, the Poor People's Campaign suffered from a lack of direction, poor organization, and horrible rainy weather, which turned Resurrection City into a muddy swamp. Unexpectedly, regional tensions arose between the demonstrators from the urban North and the rural South. The SCLC organizers had not predicted, as Charlayne Hunter noted, "that poor people do not automatically respond positively to one another." The campaign officially ended when the Resurrection City organizers dismantled the settlement in late May 1968.[16]

Motown's participation in the Poor People's Campaign was not the only time that the record company lent its musical talents to a public cause in 1968. During the summer Motown participated in Detroit's efforts to avoid a repeat of the "long, hot summer" of 1967. The mayor, community activists, and corporate leaders wanted to prevent any situations that might lead to another summer uprising. Detroit revisited some of the unrest of July 1967 in the days immediately following King's assassination in April 1968 but quickly contained the violence and vandalism. City hall and law enforcement officials implemented new "riot control" tactics that they developed after the many mistakes of July 1967.[17] But city officials wanted more preventive measures to ensure that the summer of 1968 would be peaceful. In February 1968 the U.S. Department of Housing and Urban Development (HUD) awarded $60,000 to Detroit's Youth Opportunity Program. The funding allowed city leaders to plan a summer program that would provide jobs, recreation, and educational projects for Detroit's young people. The United Foundation offered its financial support, and Motown agreed to assist with publicity. Organizers officially named the program "Detroit Is Happening," a variation on the "It's Happening" theme of the 1967 Torch Drive, based on the Supremes' hit single.[18]

The "Detroit Is Happening" program immediately received widespread support. The United Foundation, the New Detroit Committee, and the federal government, as well as private individuals, raised more than $1 million in funds for the campaign. Motown Records produced two theme songs for the summer program. The first recording, "Detroit Is Happening," was an adaptation of the Supremes' hit "The Happening" and included a motivational voice-over by Willie Horton, star outfielder for the Detroit Tigers. Smokey Robinson and the Miracles recorded a second song, "I Care about Detroit," on June 28, 1968. Motown distributed both "Detroit Is Happening" and "I Care about Detroit" throughout the city as a part of the summer-long efforts to promote civic peace. Over 100,000 people bought "I Care about Detroit" buttons, bumper stickers, shopping bags, and records.[19]

The lyrics of "I Care about Detroit" reflected the themes of the "Detroit Is Happening" campaign. In the song's opening preface, Smokey Robinson addressed listeners with the following remarks:

> There are many reasons why one cares about a city—why you care about its problems, its people and indeed its very future. Is it friendly, warm, hospitable? And are there good job opportunities, educational facilities, and a cultural center? Are you proud to call it your hometown? When you come right down to it I'd venture to say that you'd all come down to a resounding "yes!" when you are talking about Detroit, my hometown.[20]

As the song mentions, the "Detroit Is Happening" program sought to provide "good job opportunities, educational facilities, and a cultural center" for the city's youth. The program created 30,000 summer jobs, and 30,000 students enrolled in summer school classes, with an additional 70,000 enrolled in remedial education classes. Detroit's Parks and Recreation Program launched its most ambitious summer activity schedule including "playmobiles" that transported portable play equipment to inner-city locations. In addition, 50,000 inner-city children participated in a camping program, and black arts and culture workshops taught city youth about black history and culture.[21]

Unlike the Poor People's Campaign, the "Detroit Is Happening" program ended on an optimistic note. Near the end of the summer-long effort, Mayor Cavanagh proclaimed that, " 'Detroit Is Happening' proved—if it ever really needed proving—that Detroit is a good place to live and to work and to have fun. Many Detroiters had forgotten how the city was before July 23, 1967. 'Detroit Is Happening' reminded them and they, in turn, gave the city a chance to live again." Cavanagh also specifically cited Motown's participation in the program as an example of the generosity Detroiters have toward their city. In the final report on "Detroit Is Happening," organizers suggested that Motown Records might expand its participation in the program in the future: "Motown Records and the radio industry should sponsor a city-wide band and vocal competition with a recording contract as first prize."[22]

Motown's contributions to "Detroit Is Happening" and to the Poor People's Campaign illustrate how the record company affiliated itself with various public causes in 1968.[23] Yet the larger objectives of these two campaigns also reveal how Motown's gestures toward "public service" were often quite contradictory. Motown's benefit concert for the Poor People's March aided SCLC's efforts to disrupt Capitol Hill and force the federal government to recognize the economic plight of America's poor. The company's recordings for "Detroit Is Happening" supported federally funded programming to prevent any such "disorder" on the streets of Detroit. In these two cases Motown used its celebrity both to support the black movement and to align itself with government programming and Detroit's white corporate establishment. The divergent objectives of these efforts reflected the tightrope that the company walked between its allegiance to the black struggle and its desire to establish itself in corporate America. The tension that these competing goals created would soon begin to erode Motown's relationship with some leaders in Detroit's black community and with its own employees. Specifically, the black labor movement, which gained momentum during the Memphis sanitation workers' strike, was starting to challenge Detroit's automobile industry. These challenges were also about to resonate at Hitsville, U.S.A., as the record company faced its first major labor dispute.

"Our Thing Is DRUM"

A distinct black labor movement emerged in Detroit during the spring of 1968. On May 2, 1968, a racially integrated group of four thousand autoworkers staged a wildcat strike at Detroit's Dodge Main plant. A recent speedup on the assembly line sparked the strike, but many long-term grievances also motivated the job action. The wildcat strike, which by definition started without union authorization, began as an interracial effort but soon divided along racial lines. White workers dominated the picket lines, but black workers disproportionately received disciplinary action from the Chrysler Corporation. Several black workers, including one strike leader, General G. Baker Jr., were fired.[24]

General Baker rose to prominence as a black militant leader soon after the Great Rebellion of July 1967. He, along with a core group of about thirty activists, began publishing their own newspaper the *Inner City Voice (ICV)* in October 1967. The *ICV*, subtitled *Detroit's Black Community Newspaper* and the *Voice of Revolution*, quickly became a catalyst of black political activity. When Chrysler punished the black leaders of the wildcat strike, all of whom were active participants in the *ICV* network, they decided to form their own caucus to represent the needs of black workers. The Dodge Revolutionary Union Movement (DRUM) was born. DRUM planned to organize workers nationally and believed that "the black working class would be the vanguard of the revolutionary struggle in this country."[25]

The DRUM movement grew rapidly during the summer of 1968 and directly challenged the upbeat image of the "Detroit Is Happening" campaign. Organizers used the *ICV* newspaper, which had a circulation of ten thousand, to promote their cause. A front page story, published in June 1968, explicitly described the plight of the black auto worker:

> black workers are tied day in and day out, 8–12 hours a day, to a massive assembly line, an assembly line that one never sees the end or the beginning of but merely fits into a slot and stays there, swearing and bleeding, running and stumbling, trying to maintain a steadily increasing pace. Adding to the severity of working conditions are the white racist and bigoted foremen, harassing, insulting, driving, and snapping the whip over the backs of thousands of black workers, who have to work in these plants in order to eke out an existence. These conditions coupled also with the double-faced, backstabbing of the UAW have driven black workers to a near uprising state. The UAW with its bogus bureaucracy is unable, has been unable, and in many cases is unwilling to press forward the demands and aspirations of black workers.[26]

The militant style of the *Inner City Voice* appealed to workers throughout the city and inspired more labor unions in the spirit of DRUM. Over the course of several months, new organizations formed, including UPRUM (among United Parcel Service workers), HRUM (among health workers), and NEWRUM (among *Detroit News* workers). By June 1969 these locals had founded the League of Revolutionary Black Workers to unite and protect all the local RUMs.[27]

The DRUM movement relied on cultural expression and independent forms of cultural production to communicate its political message. As mentioned in the Introduction, at one wildcat protest some DRUM activists "danced in the street" and beat bongo drums outside the Dodge Main Plant to draw attention to their cause and intimidate their opponents. The League of Revolutionary Black Workers also produced a documentary film, *Finally Got the News*, to promote their cause. In the opening sequence several autoworkers carpool to work as the blues song "Detroit, I Do Mind Dying" plays on the radio. Both the film and the music featured in the soundtrack reflected the league's creative political energy. The *Inner City Voice* newspaper also published local poetry, cartoons, original artwork, and photography to juxtapose against and enhance its written articles.[28]

Publication of the *ICV* was never a simple task, however. The FBI attempted to stop the presses soon after the *ICV* started publishing. FBI agents visited local print shops that produced the newspaper and questioned the owners about their participation in subversive activities. Because of these tactics, the *ICV* was never printed in the same location twice; and eventually copy had to be shipped to Chicago, where it was published by the same firm that produced the Nation of Islam's *Muhammad Speaks*. The *Inner City Voice* staff faced outside resistance with determination. Their efforts to publish the newspaper emulated a long history of independent black cultural production in Detroit that ran from Joe Von Battle's recordings of the Reverend C. L. Franklin, to the Reverend Albert B. Cleage's newspaper the *Illustrated News*, Milton and Richard Henry's *Now! Magazine*, and Dudley Randall's Broadside Press.[29]

Significantly, however, the *ICV* activists did not perceive Motown Records, Detroit's most famous black cultural producer, as a compatriot in their struggle. In December 1967 the *ICV* ran an article entitled "How U Sound Motown" by John Cosby Jr., in which Cosby asked, "what has Motown done for the environment that put it on the map?" He continued, "if some of the better than 15 million per annum doesn't funnel back to some lay blackies, it really shouldn't matter about Motown. And talk of being a source of pride, to the serious minded, is nonsense."[30] The *ICV* article voiced a growing sentiment among black activists in Detroit that Hitsville, U.S.A., was more interested in its own profit margins than in the fight to improve economic opportunities for everyone. Motown's international success in the record industry and its ambitions in film and television had begun to alienate the company from the community that had produced it.

The *Inner City Voice*'s critique of Motown stood out against the public praise that the record company usually received. Few publications, locally or nationally, had an unkind word to say about Hitsville during the fall of 1967. In September 1967 *Fortune* magazine published a feature about Motown that praised the company as a "model" black business—just as it had praised Detroit as a model city of race relations a few years earlier. In early November Berry Gordy also received glowing local press for the Supremes' contribution to the United Foundation's Torch Drive. And, in that same month, *Jet* magazine published its press release about Motown's contributions to the United Negro College Fund, its plans for an educational record label, and—according to Gordy—his "happy" staff. With the exception of the *Inner City Voice,* all of these reports painted a convincing picture of black capitalism at its best—financially successful and yet always in touch with the betterment of the race and the common good.[31]

Back in Detroit, however, Motown's reputation continued to suffer when the company began to use aggressive business tactics to weaken its competition within the city's local recording industry. In 1968 the company bought out its major rival in Detroit, Golden World/Ric Tic Records. Eddie Wingate, owner of the popular Twenty Grand nightclub, and Joanne Jackson, a local businesswoman, founded Golden World Records in 1964. Golden World soon merged with Ric Tic Records, another local label started by LeBaron Taylor, a popular disc jockey at WCHB radio. Golden World/Ric Tic had several major hits over the years including the Parliaments' "(I Just Wanna) Testify" and Edwin Starr's "Agent Double-0 Soul." Motown's rivalry with the company ran deep. Throughout 1965 and 1966 Motown's prized studio musicians, the Funk Brothers, periodically moonlighted at Golden World/Ric Tic when the label offered to pay them union scale. At the time, Gordy sent out Mickey Stevenson, Motown's artist and repertoire director, to put an end to the late-night recording sessions, but he got final revenge when he bought out Golden World/Ric Tic for an estimated $1 million. To some in Detroit, Motown's efforts to overtake its competition destroyed the cooperative spirit of the city's black business community, the very spirit that had made Hitsville, U.S.A., possible in the first place.[32]

Outside criticism about Motown's takeover of Golden World/Ric Tic Records paralleled the beginnings of the record company's most serious internal crisis about its own labor practices. In late 1967 Motown's celebrated songwriting team of Eddie Holland, Lamont Dozier, and Brian Holland—officially known as Holland-Dozier-Holland, or H-D-H—began a work slowdown to protest what they perceived as Motown's inequitable royalty system. H-D-H was without question the most successful writing collaboration Motown had ever produced. From 1963 to 1967 the trio wrote twenty-five top-ten pop records, twelve of which hit the number-one spot, as well as twelve other songs that made the top-ten on the rhythm and blues chart. Some of their early successes included the Marvelettes' "Please Mr. Postman" (1961), Martha and the Vandellas' "Heatwave" (1963) and "Nowhere to Run" (1965), and Marvin Gaye's "How Sweet It Is to Be Loved by You" (1964). When H-D-H started its collaboration with the Supremes, beginning in 1964 with "Where Did Our Love Go?" they became an indispensable creative force in Motown's hit factory. H-D-H's songs perfectly matched the Supremes' singing style and polished image. The combination produced a string of number-one hits including "Baby Love," "Come See about Me," "Stop! In the Name of Love," "I Hear a Symphony," and "The Happening." By late 1967, however, Holland-Dozier-Holland had stopped writing new songs in protest. The songwriting team felt that they deserved more compensation for their role in creating the Motown sound and making it the "Sound of Young America."[33]

Holland, Dozier, and Holland were not the first Motown employees to express discontent with the company's policies and minimal profit-sharing. In its early years, many of Hitsville's youngest stars were initially quite naive about the intricacies of their recording contracts. In 1964 Mary Wells left Motown in search of a better contract. As she later recalled, "I was quite young when I signed with Motown and the contract I signed paid me nothing compared to the revenue my records were bringing in for the company. My contract ran out in 1964 and when another record company offered me a much more lucrative contract, I took it. I know a lot of people feel I made a mistake but I'm glad I made the move because I was finally paid a decent salary for my work."[34] Also, Motown's cross-collateralization policies, in which the cost of record production was charged against artists' royalties, reduced many performers' final earnings on any song. Mary Wilson's first contract as a Supreme reflected these policies. As she recounted,

> for the records sold in the United States (and not returned) I was to be paid 3 percent of 90 percent of the suggested retail price for each record, less all taxes and packaging costs. What was especially interesting about that was the 3 percent royalty applied only when I cut solo records . . . Based on my figures, this meant that as a solo artist I would get approximately 2 cents for every 75-cent single sold. So, if I or any of the other Supremes recorded a million-seller as a solo, that person's net would be around $20,000 *before* other expenses were deducted.[35]

In the end, Motown's ITMI division, founded in 1961, always maintained more control over performers' earnings than most of them would have liked.

By the mid-1960s many artists and musicians had begun to question the company's contracts, specifically its royalty policy. As early as 1966 Clarence Paul, Motown's assistant artist and repertoire director, held a meeting at his house in an attempt to organize Motown artists and producers collectively. The effort ended quickly when participants discovered Motown management monitored the meeting from parked cars outside Paul's house—taking photographs of all who entered.[36] In January

1967 Mickey Stevenson, who was instrumental in developing Motown's large pool of talented artists, left the company along with his wife, singer Kim Weston. Ostensibly, the departure was motivated by an offer to run a record division for MGM on the West Coast, but many insiders felt that Stevenson had grown disenchanted with Motown's miserly business practices.[37] Even the Temptations, one of Motown's most successful groups, contemplated going on strike in the hopes of negotiating a better contract. In his autobiography Otis Williams recalled, "Maybe ignorance is bliss, because it wasn't until many of us learned through a wider circle of acquaintances in all areas of the business that our contracts with Motown were substantially below industry standards ... No matter how much money we were making, Eddie (Kendricks) thought that Motown was giving us a raw deal ... Eddie's solution was simpler: the Temptations would go on strike—no more tours, no more records."[38] H-D-H's work slowdown began soon after the release of the Supremes' hit "Reflections" in September 1967. Their next song, "In and Out of Love" reached only number nine on the pop charts and, by February 1968, the songwriting team was offering no new material.

The Holland-Dozier-Holland job action began in late 1967 and early 1968 but did not become a legal battle until the summer of 1968—about the time DRUM was gaining strength in Detroit's automobile industry. In August 1968 Motown sued H-D-H for $4 million for breach of contract and damages resulting from their lack of productivity. The suit also attempted to prevent the writers from working for any other record company. Holland, Dozier, and Holland refused to return to work regardless of the lawsuit. Then, in November 1968, the team countersued the corporation for $22 million, charging "conspiracy, fraud, deceit, overreaching, and breach of fiduciary relationships." The countersuit received extensive press coverage in Detroit and in national publications such as *Jet* magazine and *Rolling Stone*.[39]

Motown's happy family was beginning to crumble. *Jet* magazine reported that in the lawsuit Holland, Dozier, and Holland charged "that Gordy 'throughout the period of association [with] the plaintiffs ... represented to the plaintiffs that he was their true friend and in effect *their father* who would look out for their best interests and should be given their complete trust and confidence' and that he betrayed both their trust and confidence in him" (italics mine).[40] The songwriters' accusation went to the heart of a central contradiction at Motown Records between its desire to be a family and its urge to be a hit factory. The family ethos was easy to maintain in Motown's early years, when the company ran on a shoestring and offered hot lunches to whoever helped out. By 1968, however, Hitsville, U.S.A., had grown into an international corporation with hundreds of employees, offices around the world, and gross annual profits of approximately $25 million. The corporate growth, while profitable for Motown's top executives and stars, quickly dispelled any illusions that a business functions like a family.[41]

Motown's hit factory, in other words, shared more than efficient production techniques with Detroit's larger automobile industry. The company's internal labor crisis revealed that the promise of black capitalism—the long-held belief that it would provide racial and economic justice for African Americans—was more myth than reality. A black cultural worker at Motown might have as much need to strike as a black autoworker at Detroit's Dodge Main Plant.[42]

The initial stages of Motown's legal battle with H-D-H, which continued for years, were particularly tense. By late 1968 the daily management of the company was increasingly separated from the daily routine at the recording studios on West Grand Boulevard. The company's recent expansion to the Donovan Building on Woodward Avenue created a distance between the creative staff at the Hitsville studios and the executive offices located in the sterile high-rise building downtown. Moreover, when H-D-H refused to return to work, Berry Gordy promoted Ralph Seltzer, one of the company's white executives, to take over as director of artists and repertoire, which Eddie Holland had been heading after Mickey Stevenson left for MGM. Seltzer, who came from a legal background, had a reputation for being difficult. Many people who had been with Motown since the early years did not feel that he was the best person to run the company's creative division and saw the promotion as misguided. According to Raynoma Gordy Singleton, Berry Gordy "had appointed people who had no history with the company, people with little or no experience making music and with little or no respect for those who knew how, to prominent positions in the company. They were business people, pure and simple. That they were given power in creative decisions was insulting to the Motown veterans. The fact that they were white only aggravated the situation, and the whole thing resonated deeply among the black ranks who were being pushed to the rear guard."[43] Then, in the fall of 1968, Berry Gordy purchased a home in Los Angeles—a clear sign of his growing interest in the company's projects on the West Coast.[44]

Without question, Motown Records was becoming less and less connected to the Motor City as it grew and diversified. Diana Ross and the Supremes' farewell concert reflected this trend. On January 14, 1970, the group performed its final show as "Diana Ross and the Supremes" at the Frontier Hotel in Las Vegas. The curtain went up around midnight as an exuberant crowd greeted Diana Ross, Mary Wilson, and Cindy Birdsong for their final appearance together. They opened with a medley of their top hits, including "Stop! In the Name of Love," "Baby Love," and "Come See about Me." Ross, eager to acknowledge her close relationship to Berry Gordy, sang two solos, "Didn't We" and "My Man," in his honor. The finale began with the first few chords of their current hit "Someday We'll Be Together" and ended with a rendition of "The Impossible Dream." After several standing ovations, Frank Sennes, the entertainment director of the Frontier Hotel, presented the women with flowers and a plaque for the hotel's "Wall of Fame." He also read two telegrams of greetings from Ed Sullivan and the mayor of Las Vegas. Mary Wilson, Cindy Birdsong, and Jean Terrell, a replacement for Diana Ross, continued as the Supremes, but the departure of Ross, who wanted to pursue a solo career, marked the end of an era.[45]

The concert's location in Las Vegas seemed appropriate, yet odd. The Las Vegas venue accurately represented how far the group had come as nightclub entertainers, but it was quite removed, literally and figuratively, from the Supremes' beginnings in Detroit. The evening's tributes also ignored the contributions of Florence Ballard, who—by 1970—was struggling to save her professional career.[46] A farewell performance at the Motor City's Twenty Grand or the Roostertail Club might have pleased local Hitsville loyalists, but Motown chose the Las Vegas location instead. The Supremes' final concert at the *Frontier* Hotel in Las Vegas accurately symbolized the company's "westward expansion" out of Detroit. In her autobiography Mary Wilson noted that the violence that occurred after King's assassination marked a turning point at Motown: "Back in Detroit

... the rioters had done incredible damage, and this event marked a turning point for Motown. The Supremes had been recording so frequently in Los Angeles that I was spending more time there than at home, and I had considered moving there. After the riots my decision was firm. Every time I was on the West Coast, I'd scout around for the perfect house."[47]

Just a few months before Diana Ross and the Supremes' farewell performance, Motown debuted what became the last major "product" of its Detroit assembly line: the Jackson 5. The five young brothers—Jackie, Tito, Jermaine, Marlon, and Michael Jackson—impressed Berry Gordy with their precocious professionalism, discipline, and raw talent at their audition in the summer of 1968.[48] By October 1969 they had released their first single, "I Want You Back," which began a string of top-ten pop hits that eventually included "ABC," "I'll Be There," and "Never Can Say Goodbye." The group's youthful charm recaptured the spirit of Motown's earliest years, when teenagers such as Diane Ross, Mary Wilson, and Florence Ballard sang and hung out on the steps of Hitsville, U.S.A., after school. The Jackson 5 were not, however, from Detroit, though their own hometown—the steel town of Gary, Indiana—shared the Motor City's midwestern, industrial ethos. Moreover, though their audition was in Michigan, the Jackson 5 moved to Los Angeles soon after they signed their contracts—yet another sign of Motown's shift away from West Grand Boulevard.

Motown based the "artist development" program for the Jackson 5 in California. In the true Hitsville tradition, the company controlled every aspect of the Jackson 5's public image and performance. Motown writers and producers designed songs specifically for the new group and trained the young boys in choreography, etiquette, and grooming. Whenever the press interviewed the Jacksons, Motown representatives were on hand to monitor their responses. On one occasion a reporter asked the group if they supported Black Power. Before the boys could answer, a Motown spokesperson interjected that the group did not think about such matters because they were a "commercial product." Describing the scene, Michael Jackson recalled, "I guess they were worried about the possibility of our sounding militant the way people were often doing in those days. Maybe they were worried after they gave us those Afros that they had created little Frankensteins." The incident encapsulated a growing tension at the record company between the artists and management about the relationship of the company's music to the political and social milieu that surrounded it. The company's interest in the production of commercial products overrode any artist's desire to create work that engaged in political or social commentary. By 1970, however, the "commercial" and the "political" aspects of any black cultural product could no longer be mutually exclusive—even at Motown.[49]

"The Sound of the Struggle"

In October 1970 Motown Records finally released the Langston Hughes and Margaret Danner poetry album—exactly seven years after the company originally recorded it. The recording of the poets' "revolutionary" verse became one of the first offerings of Motown's Black Forum spoken-word label.[50] The Black Forum project was decidedly race-conscious from the outset. The label's credo, published on album covers, stated that "Black Forum is a medium for the presentation of ideas and voices of the worldwide struggle of Black people to create a new era. Black Forum also serves to provide authentic materials for use in schools and colleges and for the home study of Black history and culture. Black Forum is a permanent record of the sound of the struggle and the sound of a new era."[51]

Ewart Abner, Junius Griffin, and George Schiffer were in charge of the label and shaped its political orientation. Abner and Griffin befriended George Schiffer when they were hired at the company in the spring of 1967. Schiffer, Motown's long-time contract lawyer, worked concurrently as a civil rights attorney for the Congress of Racial Equality in New York City. Each of these men had a commitment to the civil rights struggle that extended beyond the confines of Motown Studios on West Grand Boulevard. They perceived the Black Forum project as an opportunity to record subjects and issues often ignored by the musical offerings of the company.

The first Black Forum albums reflected the political agenda and creative interests of the label's producers. Both Abner and Griffin were friends of Stokely Carmichael, and they invited him to come to Motown to record a speech on the subject of his choice. Carmichael accepted and recorded *Free Huey!* in honor of imprisoned Black Panther Huey Newton. The label's second album was a recording of Martin Luther King Jr.'s speech "Why I Oppose the War in Vietnam." Junius Griffin, who had worked closely with King at SCLC, produced the album, which eventually won the Grammy Award for best spoken-word recording in 1970.

Black Forum's literary offerings evolved from George Schiffer's involvement with the black arts movement, including his associations with Woodie King and Amiri Baraka (Leroi Jones). Woodie King, a leader in the black theater movement, began his career in Detroit during the years that Margaret Danner's Boone House was thriving. He agreed to help produce the Black Forum poetry releases. The Hughes-Danner album was the first poetry release, produced when Griffin and Schiffer found the master tapes in Motown's recording archives. Over time, the label also produced *It's Nation Time*, featuring the poetry of Amiri Baraka; *Elaine Brown: Until We're Free*, featuring songs by Black Panther Elaine Brown; and *Black Spirits*, which was recorded live at the Apollo Theater in Harlem and featured the work of Baraka, Clarence Major, the Original Last Poets, and David Henderson, among others.[52]

The Black Forum project never shied away from provocative and politically charged subjects. In February 1972 the label produced *Guess Who's Coming Home: Black Fighting Men Recorded Live in Vietnam*, based on the research audio tapes of Wallace Terry, a black journalist who traveled to Southeast Asia and collected the personal and often brutal stories of black soldiers.[53] Also, in April 1972, Black Forum released *The Congressional Black Caucus*, which featured the keynote speeches of Ossie Davis and Bill Cosby at the first annual banquet of the caucus. Detroit's own Charles C. Diggs Jr. and John Conyers founded the coalition of black congressional representatives.

The Black Forum label allowed Motown to engage with political ideas and activities usually not associated with the company. This engagement did not, however, gain much public notice owing to the label's poor distribution and publicity. Martin Luther King Jr.'s recordings achieved more success than the others. Motown mounted special advertising campaigns after King's death, particularly in *Ebony* and *Jet* magazine, to promote these recordings as a memorial to his life. The other

Black Forum albums were often forced on record distributors. Berry Gordy told the distributors that they could not receive Motown's latest musical release unless they also agreed to take the Black Forum recordings.[54]

While the Black Forum label failed to attract large audiences, it was nevertheless significant that the company created an outlet for controversial ideas and black poetry. Motown strategically decided, of course, to produce this "forum" of the black struggle on an obscure label clearly separate from the company's popular musical offerings. The separation bespoke the apprehension that existed within the company between its commitment to present "ideas and voices of the worldwide struggle of Black people" and its desire to avoid conflict and maintain its commercial appeal with the widest possible audiences.

Motown's ambivalence about its obligation to record the "sound of the struggle" heightened when several of the company's artists and producers began to create music that addressed social and political issues. Stevie Wonder was the first artist to record such material in his June 1966 release of Bob Dylan's "Blowin' in the Wind." Many listeners embraced Wonder's rendition of the folk song as a poignant commentary about the embattled civil rights movement. He quickly followed the hit single with his album *Down to Earth* in November of 1966, which included the song "A Place in the Sun"—a continuation of some of the sentiments expressed in "Blowin' in the Wind." These recordings were quite successful on the music charts, but they did not dramatically alter the content of most Hitsville releases, which continued to be dominated by love songs and dance tunes. Motown remained hesitant in 1966 and 1967 to produce songs that could be interpreted as social commentary or what were later referred to as "message" songs.

By 1968, however, Hitsville, U.S.A., began to experiment with producing songs for the Supremes and the Temptations that addressed social issues. Ironically, the Holland-Dozier-Holland work slowdown resulted in the company's first major "message" song: the Supremes' "Love Child." When H-D-H refused to write any material for the group, Berry Gordy organized another team of writers to compose a new song for the Supremes. Gordy decided to call the new writing team—comprised of Deke Richards, Frank Wilson, R. Dean Taylor, and Pam Sawyer—the "Clan."

Initially, the group resisted the name and its resonance with the Ku Klux Klan. Gordy persisted, in light of the H-D-H legal battle, claiming, "I wanted to take a so-called negative word, and use it positively . . . I didn't want to use individual names because I wanted to keep egos at a minimum." Gordy's insistence on the name reflected his desire not only to "keep egos at a minimum" but to ensure that the writers would remain anonymous. This tactic would fend off any legal disputes in the future about who owned the songs that the Clan wrote and their earnings. The H-D-H lawsuit clearly had an immediate influence on how other songwriters were treated at the company.[55]

The Clan's first effort was "Love Child," a song that describes the trials of unwed motherhood in the ghetto. The lyrics tell a moral tale that warns listeners to avoid premarital sex and the potential burdens of an unplanned pregnancy ("This love we're contemplating / Is worth the pain of waiting / We'll only end up hating / The child we may be creating.") Motown released "Love Child" in September 1968. The record rapidly went to number one on the pop charts and eventually outsold every Supremes record before it.

The song proved the appeal of social commentary songs and Motown's astute marketing skills. As the single climbed the charts, Motown went to work to produce a follow-up album. The album cover featured a photograph of the three glamorous women in an uncharacteristic setting—leaning on the brick wall of a ghetto alley in sweatshirts and tattered jeans. Stevie Wonder's 1966 album *Down to Earth* had been the first Motown album cover to feature an urban ghetto landscape. With both albums, it was obvious that a change in the visual presentation of the artists accompanied the musical change of addressing social topics. When the Supremes appeared on *The Ed Sullivan Show* to promote the song, they abandoned their glittering ballgowns for new "ghetto" costumes. Their tattered jeans and natural hairdos acted as an effective marketing tool to package and sell the unconventional song. With "Love Child," Motown Records transformed one of the central policy concerns of America's War on Poverty—inner-city unwed mothers—into a profitable musical product.

The Temptations' "psychedelic phase," which coincided with the Supremes' "Love Child" hit also participated in Motown's new, yet cau-

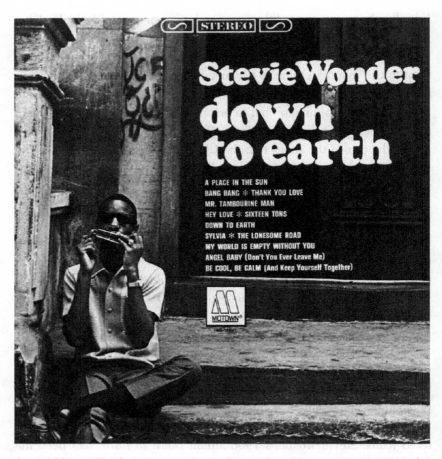

Cover of Stevie Wonder's *Down to Earth* album, 1966. (Courtesy Motown Record Co., L.P., a Polygram Company.)

tious, shift to "message" music. Beginning with the release of "Cloud Nine" in October 1968, the Temptations started performing songs that addressed politically charged subject matter including experimental drug use, racial segregation, and the plight of blacks living in the inner city. Norman Whitfield, Motown's new star producer, masterminded the Temptations' shift from songs such as "My Girl" to "Psychedelic Shack" and "Ball of Confusion (That's What the World Is Today)." These songs also departed musically from the traditional Motown sound. Whitfield had Motown's Funk Brothers experiment with a heavier use of electric guitar, wah-wah pedals, and different rhythms. The Temptations broke down their background vocal arrangements. Each singer sang different lines and parts rather than keeping to their usual unified call-and-response style.[56]

These new styles influenced Whitfield when he began to compose the militant anti-Vietnam song "War!" with Motown songwriter Barrett Strong. The song, with its pounding beat and shouted lyrics (*"War—Uh! What is it good for? / Absolutely nothin'!"*), made a militant statement against the Vietnam conflict. Whitfield wrote "War!" for the Temptations, but Motown's management deemed the song too controversial for the famous singing group. As a compromise, Motown gave the song to solo artist Edwin Starr, who had recently joined the company as a result of the Golden World/Ric Tic buy-out. "War!" quickly reached number one on the pop charts during the summer of 1970. Motown's decision to give Starr, a lesser-known artist, rather than the Temptations the opportunity to sing a song as polemical as "War!" reflected the company's vigilance

Diana Ross and the Supremes perform "Love Child," 1968. (Courtesy Motown Record Co., L.P., a Polygram Company.)

about its political affiliations. Motown hoped that Edwin Starr's relative obscurity as a singer would keep the contentious song out of the limelight. Ironically, of course, Starr's rendition of the song was so powerful that it received attention and commercial success beyond what the Temptations' version might have achieved. The popularity of the tune with pop audiences confounded the company's decision to use Starr to detract publicity from the song's angry content. The unexpected success of "War!" did not, however, make Motown more receptive to artistic freedom. The company continued to attempt to control the creative process at Hitsville Studios. This control, however, was about to face its greatest challenge.[57]

"What's Happening, Brother?"

I always knew I was an artist . . . and not the cog in some machine. To be an artist is a blessing and a privilege. Artists must never betray their true hearts. Artists must look beneath the surface and show that there is more to this world than meets the eye.

—Marvin Gaye

Marvin Gaye's career at Motown mirrored the larger ambivalence within the record company about its relationship to the turbulent political milieu of the late 1960s and early 1970s.[58] Gaye first began singing during the mid-1950s, when he performed with the Rainbows and the Marquees at gigs in his hometown of Washington, D.C. In 1958 Harvey Fuqua, a talented songwriter and producer, arrived in Washington looking for new talent for his own group, the Moonglows. Fuqua recruited Gaye, and the group traveled to Chicago to record on the Chess label. Fuqua and Gaye arrived in Detroit in 1959 and became involved with Berry Gordy's early efforts to start his own record label. Gaye was one of the first artists to sign on the Tamla label and initially worked as a backup musician on several of Motown's first records. Soon, however, Gordy realized that Gaye, a shy man with a captivating stage presence, had potential as a solo artist. His first single, "Let Your Conscience Be Your Guide," was released in May 1961. One year later, Gaye had his first hit with "Stubborn Kind of Fellow" in July 1962. A string of hits soon followed, including "Hitch Hike," "Pride and Joy," and "Can I Get a Witness." In the midst of this success, Gaye became an official member of the Gordy family when he married Berry's sister Anna, in 1963.[59]

Marvin Gaye enjoyed being on the top of the pop charts but longed to move beyond the teen market. As a young singer he idolized Frank Sinatra and hoped one day to match Sinatra's success as an elegant balladeer.[60] Many of Gaye's solo efforts, such as his tribute album to Nat King Cole in 1965, did not sell well, but his romantic duets with Mary Wells, Kim Weston, and Tammi Terrell, including "Your Precious Love" and "You're All I Need to Get By," proved his talent with ballads. By the late 1960s, however, Gaye found it increasingly difficult to perform music that seemed utterly removed from the social concerns of the day. He struggled to reconcile his artistic and commercial success as a singer with his political ideas and beliefs. In an interview Gaye once commented, "Suffering and injustice are things which I've always felt deep in my soul, and I wondered what I was doing singing rock and roll in some dive instead of leading the marchers. I know I had that ability, but that wasn't my role. My role was to sing. Years later when Bob Marley came around, I saw that both things were possible. His music caused political change, and that's why he'll occupy a high place in history."[61]

In 1966 Gaye's brother, Frankie, returned from serving in Vietnam. Frankie Gaye had a difficult time finding work and eventually had to accept a job as a hotel doorman. Marvin, moved by his brother's courage and sacrifice, vowed that he would one day write a song in honor of him. In 1971 he fulfilled his promise with the poignant song "What's Happening, Brother?" one of the movements in Gaye's masterwork: the *What's Going On?* album. Marvin Gaye composed the album over the course of several years. When completed, the work addressed not only the senselessness of the Vietnam war, but also ecology, racism, and urban violence. Berry Gordy initially resisted the project. Gordy felt Gaye's subject matter had little, if any, commercial potential and would damage Gaye's image as a balladeer. Moreover, Gordy wanted to maintain a clear division of labor within Motown's creative process and continued to believe that performers should not be given much artistic freedom. Despite these obstacles, Gaye pursued the project and was encouraged by friends and Motown songwriters such as James Nyx, who cowrote "What's Happening, Brother?"[62]

Musically, *What's Going On?* broke new ground. The recording re-fined the idea of a concept album in which all the songs on a long-playing record are interwoven and unified by a cohesive theme. On *What's Going On?* nine individual and highly textured songs, among them "What's Going On?" "What's Happening, Brother?" "Save the Children," "Mercy Mercy Me (The Ecology)," and "Inner City Blues (Make Me Wanna Holler)," were presented as a seamless whole. As the lyrics of one song ended, the instrumental backup melted into the subsequent song with no sound breaks or fade-outs between sets. This continuity gave the record-ing a musical unity and thematic completeness that had never been at-tempted before in popular music. Gaye layered the musical arrangements in a lush, orchestrated, yet improvisational style. The finished songs of-fered a stark contrast to the regulated structure, rhythm, and syncopation of standard Motown hits such as the Temptations' "My Girl."

These musical innovations heightened the political impact of Gaye's lyrics. The music created a spiritual atmosphere and stage on which Gaye could portray his drama about poverty, violence, racial discrimination, and social injustice. The combination captivated audiences and music critics—contrary to all of Berry Gordy's initial misgivings about the pro-ject. The "What's Going On?" single was released in January 1971, and by early March the song had reached number two on the pop charts and number one on *Billboard*'s "Soul" chart. When audiences embraced the album, the company had to acknowledge that there was, in fact, a market for socially conscious music and that this music should not be delegated to lesser-known artists, such as Edwin Starr, or released on a more ob-scure label like Black Forum.[63]

The astonishing success of Marvin Gaye's *What's Going On?* also renegotiated the terms on which Motown music participated in political organizing. In September 1972 the album inspired the theme of Jesse Jackson's first Operation PUSH (People United to Save Humanity) Expo in Chicago. Jackson founded Operation PUSH in December 1971. The expo, like Detroit's Black Arts Convention, brought together black po-litical leaders, businesses, community activists, and entertainers to share ideas, participate in workshops, organize grass-roots efforts, and cele-brate black culture and music. Jackson entitled the first annual fund-raiser "Save the Children," quoting the title of Gaye's song from *What's*

Going On? Motown artists including Gladys Knight and the Pips, the Temptations, and Gaye came to the four-day event and performed in support of the expo. Paramount Pictures filmed the festivities and released *Save the Children* as a feature film to the general public. At most charity benefits, Motown artists performed their hit songs as entertainment. In Chicago, Marvin Gaye's music did more than entertain when it inspired the entire theme of the Operation PUSH Expo. *What's Going On?* and specifically "Save the Children," poetically captured the gathering's political agenda, which sought to address the concerns facing black America—particularly in the urban North. In 1972 this agenda was quite pertinent to Detroit, as the city headed toward an election year and Motown began a critical transition.[64]

"Ball of Confusion"

> People movin' out, people movin' in,
> Why—because of the color of skin,
> Run, run, run, but you sho' can't hide.
> An eye for an eye, A tooth for a tooth,
> Vote for me and I'll set you free.
> Rap on brother, rap on.
> —The Temptations, "Ball of Confusion (That's What the World Is Today)"

In June 1972 the Motown Record Company officially announced its plan to move its headquarters from Detroit to Los Angeles. The pronouncement came as a tremendous blow to the Motor City and as a particular betrayal to the city's black community. Yet local press coverage of the announcement was straightforward and factual. The *Michigan Chronicle* ran a front page story about the decision on June 24, 1972. The article briefly recounted Motown's history in Detroit and then quoted Amos Wilder, a company vice president and general manager, who explained the departure as "simply a matter of sound business judgment, economics and logistics." The only hint of editorial comment came from the reporter, Rita Griffin, who responded to Wilder's dry economic explanations with the final words, "Sounds almost apologetic." Reaction on the streets of black Detroit was a bit more emotional. Soon after Motown's announcement, a rumor began to circulate at local black radio stations that Berry Gordy allegedly had remarked, "If a black disc jockey [in Detroit] never played one of my records, I wouldn't give a damn." The comment was most likely pure fabrication, but gossip about its existence did reveal the anger felt by many about Motown's decision. Many black disc jockeys boycotted Motown songs, with the exception of Stevie Wonder's music, for months after the rumor began. The silencing of Motown music from the airwaves that first brought it fame powerfully expressed the acrimony that the company's move engendered.[65]

The relocation of corporate headquarters to California was a logical business decision for Motown in light of the company's recent inroads into the film industry. In early 1971 Berry Gordy set up a movie deal to produce a film depicting Billie Holiday's life story. Gordy, a long-time admirer of Holiday, first met the singer at Detroit's Flame Show Bar in the 1950s. His film project, *Lady Sings the Blues,* allowed him to honor the great singer and simultaneously nurture Diana Ross's solo career by offering her the starring role. *Lady Sings the Blues* went into production in December 1971 and was released in October 1972, only a few months after Motown's relocation announcement. The film received critical acclaim and eventually four Academy Award nominations including a best actress nomination for Diana Ross. Although Ross did not win the award—losing to Liza Minnelli for her work in *Cabaret*—the film's many nominations suggested that Motown could become a real force in Hollywood, just as it had risen to the top of the record industry.[66]

As Motown pressed ahead with its Hollywood projects and packed up its offices in the Motor City, black Detroit turned its political energies to gaining control of city hall. The first drive to elect a black mayor gained momentum in the wake of the destruction of 1967. Deep-seated skepticism existed within the city's black community about the largely white and corporate-run New Detroit committee, which led the city's efforts to rebuild itself. Many local activists, in light of these doubts, believed that only a black mayor could adequately address the needs and protect the rights of the city's black citizens. Also, the rise of DRUM in 1968 and the subsequent formation of the League of Revolutionary Black Workers in 1969 confirmed that black coalitions could instigate radical change and raise political consciousness. For these reasons, Richard Austin, an experienced local politician, organized a campaign in 1969 to become Detroit's first black mayor.

The Austin campaign had a promising start but was quickly mired in the racial politics of the city. Austin, a black moderate Democrat who believed in building biracial coalitions, won in the primary elections with 45,856 votes but came up against his main competitor, Wayne County Sheriff Roman S. Gribbs, in the final election. Sheriff Gribbs campaigned on the theme of law and order, which attracted many white voters. Local polls revealed that while black voters were open to voting for both black and white candidates, white voters tended to vote only for white candidates. White voters were a bit more receptive to black candidates running for smaller offices such as city council seats but were highly opposed to the idea of a black mayor. During the election the *Detroit Free Press* conducted a voter survey which discovered that the main concerns of white voters were welfare, crime, and "the colored taking over." Austin had difficulty campaigning when it became clear that many white voters were going to vote against him solely on the basis of race. In his weekly column in the *Michigan Chronicle*, the Reverend Albert B. Cleage Jr. acknowledged that Austin's chances of winning without the white vote were slim; and he argued that more black citizens needed to register to vote if Austin were to have any chance at all. Without the much-needed coalition of black and white voters, Austin lost the election by a slim margin—only 6,184 votes. Sheriff Gribbs became Mayor Gribbs and the new law-and-order administration set the stage for the next battle for city hall in 1973.[67]

"Inner City Blues (Makes Me Wanna Holler)"

In his song "Inner City Blues (Makes Me Wanna Holler)," Marvin Gaye sings about how "crime is increasing" and laments that because of "[t]rigger-happy policing / panic is spreading / God knows where we're heading." At the time of the song's release in 1971, tensions between the Detroit police force and the city's black citizens were high. Police brutality or "trigger-happy policing" against black Detroiters had been a volatile political issue since the Detroit Police Department was first founded after the race riot of 1863. In the late 1960s and early 1970s, police-community relations were perhaps the most contentious issue in Detroit city politics. The election of Sheriff Gribbs in 1969 proved that a majority of white Detroiters preferred a city administration that would maintain law and order on city streets. For black Detroit, law and order came at a high price, and many felt that only a black mayor could ease the tensions between the city's primarily white police force and its black citizens. Richard Austin's narrow loss to Mayor Gribbs encouraged others to begin planning a new campaign to elect a black mayor in 1973.

Local political organizers knew that they needed a strong candidate and a sound platform to elect Detroit's first black mayor. Coleman Young and Detroit's continuing struggles with police-community relations provided the last pieces in the puzzle. Young, a Michigan state senator, had built his political reputation as a radical leader. As a young man, Young worked at Ford, but he was fired after an altercation with a white racist foreman. He flew as a second lieutenant with the Tuskegee Airmen and fought against Jim Crow segregation within the military. In 1951 he participated in the founding of the National Negro Labor Council (NNLC), the most radical black labor organization of its time, and was eventually elected executive director. Because of his involvement with NNLC, Young was ordered to testify about his relationship to the Communist Party before the House Committee on Un-American Activities in 1952. When he appeared before the committee, Young boldly defied his accusers. In his testimony he proclaimed: "I am part of the Negro people . . . I am now in the process of fighting against what I consider to be attacks and discrimination against my people. I am fighting against un-American activities such as lynchings and denial of the vote. I am dedicated to that fight, and I don't think I have to apologize or explain it to anybody." Young's bravado won him many fans in Detroit. Local supporters circulated phonograph recordings of his testimony throughout the city's black community.[68]

These legends about Young's combative personality and lifelong commitment to fighting racism and supporting labor unions made his candidacy for mayor a striking contrast to Richard Austin's 1969 campaign, which relied on a more moderate platform. Moreover, Young's militant approach was well suited to the issues that came to dominate the

1973 election—most notably, the continuing struggle over police brutality. In January 1971 Detroit's police commissioner, John Nichols, formed a new elite undercover police operation called STRESS, which stood for "Stop the Robberies, Enjoy Safe Streets." The majority of the officers assigned to the STRESS squads were white and were trained to use decoy techniques to entrap criminals in Detroit's "high-crime" neighborhoods—most often black neighborhoods. The STRESS units quickly became a notorious and violent presence in black Detroit. By the end of 1971 Detroit's Police Department was leading the country in the number of civilian killings per capita—at a rate of 7.17 civilians per 1,000 officers. More than one-third of the killings were committed by STRESS officers, who represented only 2 percent of the entire police force. Public protests against STRESS began as early as September 1971, when over 5,000 people attended a rally to abolish the unit, and continued throughout 1972 and into the election year of 1973.[69]

Coleman Young used the STRESS controversy as the focal point of his campaign platform. With Police Commissioner John Nichols as his main opponent, the issue was difficult to avoid. Nichols beat Young in the primary election winning 33.8 percent of the vote to Young's 21.1 percent. In the final election both candidates had to win voters across racial lines. Nichols attempted to capitalize on white fears of black crime by emphasizing his law-and-order approach. Young, an experienced politician, broadened his platform to include economic redevelopment and won the support of several business organizations. Young's combination of a forceful attack against STRESS, a promise to increase minority hiring in the Detroit Police Department, and economic revitalization plans won the election. On November 6, 1973, Detroit voted in its first African American mayor.

> I hope you hear inside my voice of sorrow
> And that it motivates you to make a better tomorrow
> This place is cruel nowhere could be much colder
> If we don't change, the world will soon be over
> Living just enough, stop giving just enough for the city!!!
>
> —Stevie Wonder, "Living for the City"

Motown Records had already left Detroit for Los Angeles when Coleman Young won the mayoral election. Coincidentally, however, the record company released Stevie Wonder's single "Living for the City" during the election month of November 1973. Wonder's song, inspired by the success of Marvin Gaye's *What's Going On?* album, directly engages with social issues as it tells the tale of a young black man who migrates from the South to the urban North. Once in the city, the protagonist confronts the struggles, temptations, and despair of urban life in the ghetto.[70] In the song's closing refrain Wonder makes an urgent plea for change— a plea that had particular relevance to Detroit, which was on the verge of black political control. Coleman Young's election, by its very uniqueness, created tremendous excitement and speculation about what this "new" era could bring to an increasingly enervated city.

By 1973 Detroit's economic base had deteriorated, as many companies and white citizens left the city for the suburbs after the devastation of 1967. Motown's departure for California in 1972 participated in this trend, and the cultural loss to the black community was equally difficult. J. L. Hudson, founder of the original New Detroit committee and corporate leader, commented on the possibility of black political rule in Detroit on the fifth anniversary of the uprising in 1972. Hudson remarked, "The black man has the feeling he is about to take power in the city . . . but he is going to be left with an empty bag." Coleman Young somewhat similarly admitted, "I knew that this had only happened to me because, for once in my life, I was in the right place at the right time, and that my fortune was the direct result of my city's misfortune—of the same fear and loathing that had caused all my problems and Detroit's problems in the first place. I was taking over the administration of Detroit because the white people didn't want the damn thing anymore. They were getting the hell out, more than happy to turn over their troubles to some black sucker like me."[71]

The Motor City's economy was also hit hard in 1973 as a result of the OPEC oil embargo. According to historian William Chafe, "[p]rior to [1973], America had exercised virtually unchallenged economic and military dominance in the world. Afterward, it became a dependent nation." The national energy crisis reverberated with particular intensity in Detroit. The city's entire identity and economic base revolved around the automotive industry—an industry completely dependent on the international oil market.[72]

With all of these pressing concerns, Young's inauguration in January 1974 became a critical moment for the new mayor to proclaim his agenda and for his supporters to celebrate their victory. Young's backers, many of whom had participated in Detroit's Great March to Freedom or voted for a Freedom Now candidate in 1963, never imagined that the city would one day elect a black mayor. The inaugural gala held on January 2, 1974, captured much of the enthusiasm surrounding Young's new administration.

Motown Records sent Diana Ross in from the West Coast to perform at the gala. Esther Gordy Edwards, cochair of the inauguration festivities, arranged the concert, and Ross agreed to perform free of charge. When the evening finally arrived, Ross had to overcome several major setbacks, and the concert was almost canceled. Ross did not want to leave California when both of her children got sick with a virus days before the engagement. Then, on the trip to Michigan, the airlines lost her luggage, which held her costumes, makeup, and the complete musical arrangements for the show. Yet the singer pressed on. A costume was thrown together, and the orchestra rehearsed new arrangements. Ross credited Coleman Young and her local fans for her persistence. She told the press that normally under such difficult circumstances, "I wouldn't go on . . . I wouldn't be here if it weren't for the mayor . . . and for all the people who have paid their money and expect to see a show."[73]

Ross's dedication in the face of adversity, widely covered in the local press, captured the spirit of Coleman Young's inauguration. Detroit had suffered many blows to its model-city image over the years, but Young believed that his new administration could persevere despite the setbacks and lead the city into a better future. Young's immediate agenda involved fulfilling campaign promises such as his vow to dismantle the STRESS unit in an effort to combat police brutality. Yet the new mayor did not want to appear "soft" on criminals in a city with a serious crime problem. In his inaugural speech Young boldly announced his intentions: "I issue a warning to all dope pushers, rip-off artists and muggers. It's time to leave Detroit—hit the road. Hit Eight Mile Road. I don't give a damn if they are black or white, or if they wear Superfly suits or blue uniforms with silver badges. Hit the road."[74] Young believed that his comments would reassure his constituents that he could promote law and order and also eliminate police brutality. But his brazen language and his reference to Eight Mile Road, the dividing line between the city and its surrounding, primarily white suburbs led many people to wonder if the new black mayor was going to agitate rather than calm the racial tensions that plagued Detroit's entire metropolitan area.

Coleman Young's "hit the road" remark unfortunately tapped into dominant fears that a black mayor would increase racial polarization between blacks and whites in Detroit and between the city and its suburbs. The long-fought struggle to elect a black mayor did not appear to ensure that Detroit was any closer to becoming a model of harmonious race relations than it was in 1963. The dream of black political power, like the myth of black capitalism, was more elusive in practice than in the imagination. In Detroit Young's election did lead to the end of the STRESS unit and an increase in minority hiring in the city's police force. But it did not bridge Detroit's entrenched racial divides or alter the basic configuration of economic power in the city, which was still maintained by white-owned private corporations.[75]

Only Motown Records, which was the most profitable black business in America in 1973, could have reconfigured the racial composition of Detroit's corporate economy, but this possibility disappeared when the company left the city in 1972. In the end, black political control ascended in the Motor City only to be defined and circumscribed by its relationship to white corporate power. Motown's music—Stevie Wonder's "Living for the City" or Marvin Gaye's "What's Going On?"—did make eloquent statements about the plight of black Americans left with the "empty bag" of urban America. Yet, without Motown's cultural presence and financial profits invested in the city, the songs could only passively speak about, not actively participate in, Detroit's continuing struggle to create itself anew.[76]

Conclusion:
"Come Get These Memories"

The year 1998 marked the fortieth anniversary of Motown Records. The milestone was not ignored. Motown/Polygram, Incorporated, issued a special commemorative compact disc boxed set—a compilation of the classic Motown standards. ABC-TV broadcast a special two-part, four-hour, documentary miniseries on the history of the company and its music, entitled *Motown 40: The Music Is Forever.* And America's most-watched television event of the year, the Super Bowl, featured Motown artists in the halftime show. In between halves of the annual football extravaganza, a range of Motown artists from the old guard, including Smokey Robinson, to its one contemporary hit group, Boyz II Men, performed a series of quick medleys. Martha Reeves occupied center stage for the grand finale—a rousing rendition of her biggest hit, "Dancing in the Street." Reeves's voice sounded strained at times and quickly got lost in the fanfare surrounding the number as troupes of dancers began high-kicking across the field, the Grambling State University marching band blasted backup music, and a panoply of fireworks shot off from above and below to completely overwhelm the scene. By the time the song reached one of its most famous lines, "Can't forget the Motor City," nothing seemed more forgotten than Detroit, Michigan, Motown's birthplace.

This amnesia, of course, was exactly what the Super Bowl performance celebrated. Forty years after Berry Gordy scraped together enough funds to start his own record label on the streets of Detroit, the country stood up and cheered an American musical institution that seems to have transcended all barriers of race, generation, and geography. Motown's magic is no longer simply that it is the Motown sound or the "Sound of Young America," but that it is the "Sound of All of America and the World"—young, old, black, white, Hispanic, and Asian. No one can deny Motown's popularity or argue with the Super Bowl producers' decision to feature it in the halftime show. Yet, one is left to wonder if this type of cultural transcendence should always be so prized and glorified. What gets lost when a cultural phenomenon such as Motown drifts further and further away from its historical moorings and deeper and deeper into the sea of cultural mythology?

What gets lost are those details and facts which do not fit easily into the more streamlined narratives that constitute the American Dream. The belief that with a little luck, pluck, and hard work anyone—regardless of race, class, or gender—can rise to the top of his or her field and succeed will always have a strong hold on American consciousness. The Motown story embodies the myth of the American Dream in powerful ways. Specifically, Berry Gordy's role as founder of the company and all of the individual artists and musicians who got to live their dreams through his efforts offer inspiration to many young, especially African American, entrepreneurs and aspiring entertainers.

As this book has argued, however, the Motown story involves much more than a reenactment of the American Dream. A closer historical analysis of the Motown Record Company and its origins in Detroit reveals a complicated story and one that, in fact, offers a critical tale of the limits of that myth—particularly for African Americans. The history of Motown's origins in Detroit teaches important lessons about the limits of black capitalism and black culture to institute significant social, political, and economic change. Motown's economic success illustrates how capitalism operates by rules that cannot be held to a racial or local community agenda and how easily the enduring appeal of the company's music obscures this fact.

What, then, is Motown's historical legacy? What can be learned from the Motown story, which on the surface appears so triumphant, yet upon closer inspection discloses more conflicted and problematic consequences? To answer these questions, one must begin by acknowledging that Motown has multiple legacies: to the history of popular music, to the history of black capitalism, and to the history of the civil rights movement and race relations. Moreover, Motown's relationship to Detroit grounds these legacies in specific historical circumstances.

Motown's most dominant and unambiguous legacy is its contribution to American popular music. Songs such as the Four Tops' "Baby I Need Your Loving," the Miracles' "The Tracks of My Tears," Marvin Gaye's "I Heard It through the Grapevine," and the Supremes' "Baby Love" are just a few examples of the scores of Motown hits now considered quintessential popular music standards of the 1960s. Motown's role in the 1998 Super Bowl halftime show was only one manifestation of the music's ongoing popularity. The Motown songbook also acts as a mainstay playlist at most oldie radio stations across the country—many of which feature weekly "Motown Monday" marathons. Hollywood films have also played a major role in securing Motown's status as the soundtrack of its era. The film *The Big Chill* (1983), started the trend of featuring Motown hits to attract baby-boomer audiences. Since *The Big Chill*, hundreds of films have chosen to use Motown music in their soundtracks and some, such as *My Girl* (1991), have used a Motown song to frame the entire plot. Perhaps the most telling evidence of the revered status of Motown songs is their dominance in the wedding industry music business. Most, if not all, wedding bands and deejays advertise their ability to offer the Motown sound at receptions. This marketing strategy reflects a consumer demand for the music, which clearly has become a key musical element of the standard American wedding. Forty years after it began, Motown music still consistently brings "life" to any party or life passage.

The steadfast popularity of Motown's music represents a testament to all those musicians, songwriters, performers, and producers who brought the "sound" to life. Ironically, however, it is the very appeal of the music and its continued marketability as a profitable commodity that creates the distance in the public's mind between the music, on the one hand, and the people and circumstances that created it, on the other. For many listeners, "Motown" has become simply a generic term for any type of black popular music from the 1960s. "Motown" is no longer about the specific accomplishments of a Detroit-based record label but about a musical moment in time. The conflation of Motown's specific sound with an entire era of black music does a disservice to the individual artists who created the music but can be profitable for those invested in using the music for other trade purposes. In the late 1990s the Motown sound primarily acts as a commercial trademark used by corporations to evoke a nostalgia for the 1960s in the consumer marketplace.

The 1998 Super Bowl halftime show provides strong evidence for this argument. The primary objective of the show, according to executives at NFL Properties, "is to provide entertainment to keep our audience" during the lull between halves. The Super Bowl audience traditionally draws 65 percent of all television viewers and millions of advertising dollars. In 1998 the NBC television network, which broadcast the game, estimated an audience of 130 million viewers and charged $1.3 million dollars per thirty-second commercial. Each year the National Football League and the network that broadcasts the game must find entertainers for the halftime show who will appeal to a wide range of viewers in order to maintain the game's overall high ratings.

These marketing strategies can produce a big payoff. In 1993 the Super Bowl show featured Michael Jackson, another former Motown star, and drew in 102 million viewers for a 45.5 rating, which was *better* than the game's 45.1 rating. Networks use these statistics to entice future advertisers to invest in the Super Bowl broadcast. In 1998 Royal Caribbean Cruise Lines paid $5 million for the exclusive sponsorship of the "Motown 40" halftime show. *Newsweek* magazine also reported that EMI Music Publishing, which acquired a half-interest in the rights to the Motown song catalog in July 1997, would also profit immeasurably from the Super Bowl exposure. The short ten-minute performance broadcast to "the world's largest TV audience, [would] undoubtedly [stoke] demand for more commercial uses of the music." One of the major legacies of the Motown sound, therefore, is the undeniable fact that Motown *sells*. In the commerce of public memory, Motown's music makes money.[1]

Motown music's relationship to public memory needs to be emphasized in any discussion of the music's market value since the record label no longer dominates the popular music charts. In Motown's forty-year history, the company created the bulk of its canon of popular music standards in only its first fifteen years. By the mid-1970s, Motown's music was suffering from the standard blows of corporate decentralization. The company's move from Detroit to Los Angeles in 1972 included a shift in focus from strictly music production into television and film production. This diversification weakened the company's ability to produce music of the same consistent quality and quantity of the Detroit years. Throughout the late 1970s and early 1980s the company continued to produce top-name acts including Stevie Wonder, Marvin Gaye, and the Commodores, but it could not sustain the same overall level of productivity. In the 1990s Motown's biggest act has been Boyz II Men, which has created a string of number-one hits but has not drawn a large number of comparable talents to the label. The legacy of Motown's music leads, therefore, to two very different conclusions. One involves the abiding popularity of the original sound, which will only continue to rise in cultural and economic value over time. The other involves the persistent inability of the current Motown label to produce new music that captures its era in the same way that Hitsville, U.S.A., did throughout the 1960s.

How, then, does one account for these two opposing outcomes? Why does the "magic" of Motown's early years continue to captivate audiences around the world while the label's current offerings have a more limited appeal? Several explanations are possible, but the most compelling one involves Motown's fate as an independent black capitalist enterprise, a fate that was always tied to larger trends in Detroit's automobile industry and the national recording industry. The automobile industry and the record industry have followed similar trajectories of advanced capitalism. These trajectories created the economic conditions that both made the Motown Record Company possible and ultimately led to its demise as an independent black record label. In its early years Motown's business achievements seemed to prove that the civil rights movement had made tangible gains. Berry Gordy Jr., an African American entrepreneur, had risen to the top of his field in an industry that traditionally had profited from the talents of black Americans while tending to exclude them from upper management and full ownership. Throughout the 1960s and early 1970s Hitsville, U.S.A., came to symbolize the true promise of black America when the doors of opportunity were open to all regardless of race.

Yet, forty years after it began, the Motown story can teach only rather sobering lessons about the limits of black economic empowerment. Foremost, one learns how the rise of multinational capitalism and the era of corporate mergers in the late twentieth century can devastate local urban communities. These types of communities can provide fertile soil for any number of cultural, economic, and political movements to grow. As this book has shown, Motown was always more than one man's dream. The company and its music emerged from a vibrant African American community that grew throughout the first half of the twentieth century as a result of Detroit's strong industrial economy. From the day Henry Ford announced his five-dollars-a-day wage in 1914, the city's thriving automobile industry created an economic base in the city that attracted African Americans looking for a better life. This prosperity gave an earlier generation of the city's black community a chance to develop a strong and productive middle class, which then established many businesses independent of the city's automobile industry. This generation of black business leaders, which included individuals such as Berry Gordy Sr. and Charles C. Diggs Sr., used their economic security to win political representation and power. They knew that economic empowerment was not enough, that black people also needed a voice in government to get the state to respond to their needs.

In the second half of the twentieth century Detroit emerged from World War II as the Arsenal of Democracy, the industrial hero of the global conflict. The postwar era brought an economic boom as Americans could now shed the worries and rations of wartime and instead purchase new homes, appliances, and cars. Detroit's automobile manufacturing flourished during the 1950s. At the same time, as historian Thomas Sugrue has shown in his book *The Origins of the Urban Crisis*, the postwar era in Detroit marked the first stages of the deindustrialization of the city. Automakers started to move manufacturing out of the city and rely more heavily on automation, which displaced unskilled workers. African American autoworkers were among the first to feel the effects of the initial stages of corporate decentralization and automation.[2]

Berry Gordy Jr.'s brief stint on the Ford Lincoln-Mercury assembly line in 1955 occurred during this period. As the son of one of Detroit's most successful black entrepreneurs, Gordy knew that owning his own business could provide more security than relying on employment in automobile manufacturing. Gordy's decision to found Motown Records in

1958 coincided, then, both with the first stages of the deindustrialization of Detroit and with the last stages of an earlier black economic "self-help" movement, which his parents had helped to establish. This earlier era of black self-help profited from a more racially segregated market and Detroit's industrial strength, both of which would begin to recede by the 1960s. Motown's founding, therefore, marked a critical shift in the range of economic possibilities for African Americans in Detroit. The beginning of Hitsville, U.S.A., signaled the beginning of the end of an era of employment and business opportunities for black Americans in the major industrial city.

The Motown Record Company was also the product of the heyday of independent record labels in the history of the record industry. In the 1950s independent record labels brought the emergent sounds of rock and roll to the public when major labels such as Capitol and Columbia largely ignored the musical trend. From 1954 to 1959 record sales in the United States jumped from $213 million to $603 million according to statistics compiled by *Billboard* magazine. In his book *The Sound of the City*, historian Charlie Gillett notes that a large percentage of these profits can be attributed to independent labels that worked to bring the rhythm and blues and rock and roll music of urban America to baby-boomer youth. According to Gillett, independent labels "doubled their top ten hits from 1955 to 1956 and then doubled them again in 1957."[3] Independents were able to challenge major labels such as Victor because their product—rhythm and blues and rock and roll—was the indigenous sound of urban America. Independent record companies, which were located in cities across the country, could more readily tap into the sound of the streets and bring that sound to the teenage market that craved it. Berry Gordy's decision to start the Motown Record Company in 1958 participated in this larger trend within the record industry.

Motown began, therefore, at a critical juncture in Detroit's history and in the history of the record industry. The company was independent of Detroit's automobile industry when manufacturers were beginning to move out of the city and into the suburbs—taking jobs and opportunity with it. Motown's economic success gave hope, especially to African Americans in Detroit, that there were avenues outside industrial labor that could lead to financial security. Moreover, the company's product—

black popular music that appealed to audiences across racial boundaries—proved to be a profitable formula in the burgeoning independent record business and in the emergent musical revolution that was rock and roll. The historical context of Motown's origins explains why the company's early music continues to attract audiences around the world. The music evokes a time of youth, opportunity, and urban community that comforts audiences in today's era of aging, corporate downsizing, and individual isolation.

While Motown's music embodies the hopes of the past, its present status as a record label discloses the fate of black capitalism in the age of multinational corporate conglomerates. Like Detroit's automobile industry, the Motown Record Company, as it has evolved within the record industry, has followed a gradual process of corporate decentralization, relocation, merger, and buy-out. For its first ten years Motown grew into a major force in the record industry while maintaining its small hometown structure in the Hitsville, U.S.A., studios on West Grand Boulevard. Then, in 1968, Motown took its first steps away from these roots when it moved its corporate headquarters to the Donovan Building on Woodward Avenue in Detroit, and Berry Gordy moved to Los Angeles to begin expanding operations in California. After the entire company relocated to Los Angeles in 1972, Gordy maintained ownership and control of Motown for the next sixteen years and oversaw the company's diversification into film and television production. In June 1988, however, Gordy made the momentous and controversial decision to sell his company to MCA, Incorporated, in partnership with Boston Ventures, a financial investment group, for $61 million. In his autobiography Gordy openly acknowledged the economic circumstances that motivated his decision to sell the company: "as I gazed from my office window across the forest of corporate buildings to the Capitol Records tower, I realized that many of them, too, were in the process of being taken over. Everybody was either buying or selling . . . Technology was moving faster than the speed of light . . . Conglomerates were taking over. These multicorporate entities, with their dominating distribution capabilities and their powerful foothold in a radically changing world economy, had the edge. A big edge."[4]

As a part of the MCA deal, Gordy maintained ownership of the Jobete Music Company, Motown's music publishing division, and Motown's film and television company. Yet, in the ten years since the MCA deal, Motown has changed hands two more times. In 1993 Polygram Records bought out the label from MCA/Boston Ventures. Then, in 1998, the Seagrams Corporation bought out Polygram and, thereby, took over ownership of the Motown label. In 1997 Berry Gordy also decided to sell a half-interest in the Jobete Music Company to EMI Music Publishing and in so doing divested himself of 50 percent of perhaps the most profitable dimension of the Motown enterprise—the licensing of the entire Motown songbook.[5]

What, then, is Motown's legacy to black capitalism? More pointedly, what does Motown's fate as an independent black record label reveal about the role of black capitalism in the larger history of civil rights and race relations in America? The historical record tells the basic facts. By 1973, the year that Motown left Detroit, the *New York Times* reported that the company was the most successful black business in the United States with $40 million in sales. By 1998 only a small fraction of the original company, 50 percent of the Jobete Music Publishing Company, still belonged to Berry Gordy. The Motown Record Company, perhaps the most successful black capitalist enterprise of the twentieth century, will enter the twenty-first century as a wholly owned subsidiary of a white-owned corporate conglomerate.

But what do these facts mean in the larger picture of economic empowerment and race relations? The false promise of black capitalism originates in the faulty assumption that capitalism can be enlisted to remedy racial inequality. Improving the racial conditions of society has never been capitalism's primary objective. On the contrary, as Sugrue stated succinctly in his history of postwar Detroit: "Detroit's postwar urban crisis emerged as the consequence of two of the most important, interrelated, and unresolved problems in American history: that capitalism generates economic inequality and that African Americans have disproportionately borne the impact of that inequality."[6] Motown's accomplishments as a black capitalist enterprise emerged from Detroit's postwar urban crisis and, therefore, both complicate and, in the end, affirm Sugrue's assertion.

Motown's achievements complicate discussions about capitalism and race by suggesting other alternatives: what if African Americans, who have disproportionately suffered in free-market economies, are given the opportunity to succeed in capitalism's game of unequal rewards? In its early years Motown seemed to be the perfect case study to explore such a question. But the outcome was no different from any other capitalist endeavor in which the profit motive takes precedence over all other concerns. On the most immediate level, the company's profits were not shared equally among all who participated in the venture. The Holland-Dozier-Holland lawsuit over royalties, which dragged on for years, offers one example of how the company's business fortune benefited some more than others. On a more global level, Motown's decision to leave Detroit and the community that nurtured it not only participated in the larger process of the deindustrialization of the city but ultimately created the circumstances that would leave the company vulnerable to corporate takeover in years to come. As Motown decentralized and diversified, it lost its distinctive edge in the recording industry and could no longer compete in the same way against the dominance of the major record labels. Motown's business history proves how difficult it is for black capitalism to survive in the global economy, let alone thrive enough to be able to address or promote the needs of black America.

The story of black capitalism did not end, however, with the corporate buy-out of the Motown Record Company. In the late 1990s black entrepreneurship has a new leader in former basketball star Earvin "Magic" Johnson. Since his retirement from the National Basketball Association in 1991, Johnson has invested in businesses designed to bring money back into the inner city and to the minority communities that will benefit from the economic growth. His most successful venture thus far has been the Magic Theaters multiplex movie franchise, now operating in Los Angeles, Atlanta, and Houston. He has also developed partnerships with the Starbucks and the T. G. I. Friday's franchises to bring these companies into urban neighborhoods. In Los Angeles Johnson, along with Janet Jackson and Jheryl Busby, music executive and former president of Motown MCA, have bought control of the Founders National Bank in the city's predominantly black Crenshaw-Baldwin district. Business analysts applaud Johnson's ability to recognize the economic possibilities of the inner city. Michael Porter, head of the nonprofit Initiative for a Competitive Inner City, estimated in 1998 that the inner-city retail market totaled $100 billion a year and has stated publicly that Johnson has been a major catalyst in proving that the inner city can be a viable market.[7]

Even as Johnson's efforts have begun to bring some hope to inner-city communities, they cannot alter the larger economic shifts in the global economy and general employment trends. Most notably, the rise of the postindustrial service-sector economy of the late twentieth century has brought with it the loss of full-time salaried jobs with benefits. Many of the jobs in restaurants, movie theaters, sports stadiums, and casinos, which promise to bring life back to the inner city, actually bring urban citizens, many of whom are African American and Hispanic American, only part-time, hourly work with no benefits. Without the ability to secure a stable long-term income, many of those individuals in the poorest segments of urban America will continue to have difficulty creating a better future for themselves. Magic Johnson's own success in the business world, like Berry Gordy's, was inspired by the more consistent employment opportunities and local urban communities that Michigan's industrial economy used to provide. Johnson grew up in Lansing, Michigan—only a few hours from Detroit—and has claimed that his work ethic comes from his father, who worked steadily for thirty years at the General Motors Lansing plant. Johnson did not work for General Motors and instead developed his basketball skills at Michigan State University in East Lansing, skills that would eventually earn him the financial capital to found the Johnson Development Corporation.[8]

While Johnson and others can be commended for investing in the inner city, these efforts will not have long-term effects if they do not provide alternatives to temporary employment for urban residents. Many of these individuals are already suffering from the public assistance cutbacks of the Welfare Reform Act of 1996. Officially entitled the "Personal Responsibility and Work Opportunity Reconciliation Act of 1996," this legislation replaces social welfare entitlements with alternative "workfare" programs, while cutting other sources of funding such as food stamps. These measures have made the "working poor" of inner cities such as Detroit more dependent on low-paying hourly wage labor and less able to pursue the education and training needed to move into salaried, white-collar work. Detroit, like many Rustbelt cities, has had extreme difficulty recovering from the economic consequences of deindustrialization over the course of the forty years since Motown began. Michigan was also one of the first states in the country to systematically dismantle its welfare system, an effort that eventually became a model for the Welfare Reform Act of 1996. Like many other cities in America, Detroit has decided to rest its revitalization hopes on the construction of new sports stadiums and the casino industry, which will profit outside corporate interests more than local citizens. Neither the memory of the magic of Motown's early years nor Magic Johnson himself can alter these larger economic forces, which continue to perpetuate racial inequality in urban America.[9]

Martha Reeves and the Vandellas' most famous song will always be "Dancing in the Street." It is, as Reeves has always asserted, a marvelous party song and also one that celebrates a time when the streets of America's cities offered people opportunities to dance, to gather, to march, and to struggle for a better life. The song resonated quite differently when Reeves sang it on the stage of Detroit's Fox Theater in July 1967 and when she sang it thirty-one years later, in the 1998 Super Bowl halftime show. The difference between those two performances accentuates how far Motown has traveled from its beginnings on the streets of Detroit. The disparity between Motown's urban past and its present status as an American popular music institution lies at the heart of larger debates about the historical significance of Motown's role in American culture. These debates are perhaps best captured by another Martha Reeves and the Vandellas song, "Come Get These Memories." For, in the end, it is the slippery way in which Motown's music plays with public memory that creates confusion about what the company achieved and what it lost over time.

The theme of "Come Get These Memories" captures the essence of the argument I have made throughout this book about Motown's relationship to the cultural politics of Detroit. In the song Martha Reeves adopts the persona of a scorned lover, who acknowledges the power of memories in an effort to reassert her dignity in the wake of a failed romance. She sings about the love tokens of the relationship: the friendship ring, the teddy bear, and the love letters. These artifacts, which had previously commemorated happier days, now can only evoke the pain of abandonment. In a gesture of self-affirmation, the scorned lover offers the artifacts and memories to her ex-boyfriend so that they may haunt him instead. The song plays with the idea that memories are more than simply ways of recalling the past. Memories are contested and change over time. A fond memory can turn into an albatross when it is tainted by a subsequent injustice. And a new memory of being wronged can inspire one to act for one's own empowerment.

These ideas about the changing roles of memory are relevant to Motown and the significance of its relationship to Detroit. In this book I have sought to "come get" some of the forgotten memories of Motown's past in Detroit, many of which do not fit easily into the more recent celebrations of the company's achievements. My goal was to pull back the veil of nostalgia that enshrouds the Motown sound to gain a more clear and, at times, unsettling view of Motown's accomplishments and limitations. The accomplishments show us the range of what is possible when an urban community is able—economically, politically, and culturally—to grow and thrive. The limitations reveal the long-term consequences of advanced capitalism and the ways in which it can damage these urban communities and eliminate the possibility of creative solutions that might ameliorate economic and racial inequality.

In the broadest view, Motown's relationship to the cultural politics of Detroit teaches that place matters—that productive social, cultural, economic, and political change emerges from distinct communities. Even Berry Gordy Jr., the one individual most credited with Motown's success, acknowledged in his autobiography how much the urban community of his youth contributed to his ability to create Hitsville, U.S.A. He devotes the entire first quarter of his memoir, *To Be Loved*, to his Detroit roots. Perhaps the most telling comment about Gordy's personal sense of connection to Detroit comes in an aside about his childhood home on the corner of Farnsworth and St. Antoine Streets, which was where his father established his Booker T. Washington Grocery Store. In a parenthetical remark Gordy writes, "So much would happen to me at this new home I would later buy the actual pole on top of which are those two street sign markers—one reading 'Farnsworth' and the other 'St. Antoine'—and plant it in a corner of my backyard in California."[10]

Years after Gordy founded Motown and left Detroit for Los Angeles, he felt compelled to literally purchase a piece of his Detroit past and plant it in California soil. The street sign, of course, like the friendship ring and teddy bear in "Come Get These Memories," is only an artifact. It cannot recreate the dynamism of the community and the human relationships that it represents. Nostalgia, after all, obscures the past more than it reveals its true complexity. The Motown sound has become one of the most powerful instruments to evoke nostalgia about America during the 1960s. At the end of the century the music does more to help people forget the real struggles of that era than to bring them into sharp focus. History, however, is nostalgia's worst enemy. The history of Motown and its origins in Detroit vividly recall those struggles of the past, even the ones that failed, and *these* memories can inspire the work required to create a more egalitarian future.

Notes
Acknowledgments
Index

Notes

Introduction

1. " 'Swinging Time' Comes to the Fox," *Michigan Chronicle*, July 22, 1967. Martha Reeves with Mark Bego, *Dancing in the Street: Confessions of a Motown Diva* (New York: Hyperion Press, 1994), p. 147.

2. The comment about young people "dancing amidst the flames" appeared in the official transcripts of the Kerner Commission Report. See *Report of the National Advisory Commission on Civil Disorders* (New York: Bantam Books, 1968), p. 91.

3. Gerri Hirshey, *Nowhere to Run: The Story of Soul Music* (New York: Penguin Books, 1984), pp. 145–146; Reeves, *Dancing*, p. 147.

4. "The Split in the League of Revolutionary Black Workers: Three Lines and Three Headquarters," Dan Georgakas Collection, box 4, folder 4-11, p. 4, Walter P. Reuther Library, Wayne State University. For more background on the DRUM movement, see Dan Georgakas and Marvin Surkin, *Detroit: I Do Mind Dying* (New York: St. Martins Press, 1975); and James A. Geschwender, *Class, Race, and Worker Insurgency: The League of Revolutionary Black Workers* (Cambridge: Cambridge University Press, 1977).

5. Edward Lee, "Whoever Heard of Bongo Drums on the Picket Line?" James and Grace Lee Boggs Papers, box 5, folder 4, Walter P. Reuther Library, Wayne State University. In his eyewitness account of the wildcat demonstration, Edward Lee uses the phrase "danced in the street"—an unintentional echo of Reeves's song.

6. Lee, "Whoever Heard," p. 4.

7. For further discussion of the history and racial politics of *Billboard*'s charting system, see Steve Chapple and Reebee Garofalo, *Rock and Roll Is Here to Pay: The History and Politics of the Music Industry* (Chicago: Nelson-Hall, 1977), pp. 236–237; and "Billboard Adopts 'R&B' as New Name for Two Charts," *Billboard*, October 27, 1990. For more history on independent rhythm and blues labels, see Charlie Gillett, *The Sound of the City: The Rise of Rock and Roll* (New York: Pantheon, 1983); Nelson George, *The Death of Rhythm and Blues* (New York: E. P. Dutton, 1989).

8. For examples, see Gerald Early, *One Nation under a Groove: Motown and American Culture* (Hopewell, N.J.: Ecco Press, 1995); Nelson George, *Where Did Our*

Love Go? The Rise and Fall of the Motown Sound (New York: St. Martin's Press, 1985); Berry Gordy, *To Be Loved: The Music, the Magic, the Memories of Motown* (New York: Warner Books, 1994); Gerri Hirshey, *Nowhere to Run: The Story of Soul Music* (New York: Penguin Books, 1984); Reeves, *Dancing;* Diana Ross, *Secrets of a Sparrow: Memoirs* (New York: Villard Books, 1993); Raynoma Gordy Singleton with Bryan Brown and Mim Eichler, *Berry, Me, and Motown: The Untold Story* (Chicago: Contemporary Books, 1990); William (Smokey) Robinson with David Ritz, *Smokey: Inside My Life* (New York: McGraw-Hill, 1989); David Ritz, *Divided Soul: The Life of Marvin Gaye* (New York: Da Capo Press, 1991); Otis Williams and Patricia Romanowski, *Temptations* (New York: G. P. Putnam's Sons, 1988); Peter Benjaminson, *The Story of Motown* (New York: Grove Press, 1979); and J. Randy Taraborrelli, *Motown: Hot Wax, City Cool, and Solid Gold* (New York: Doubleday, 1986).

9. For one version of this argument, see Gillett, *Sound of the City,* p. 212.

10. As Gordy explained, "Because of its thriving car industry, Detroit had long been known as the 'Motor City.' In tribute to what I had always felt was the down-home quality of warm, soulful country-hearted people I grew up around, I used 'town' in place of city.' " *To Be Loved,* p. 114.

11. At Motown's twenty-fifth anniversary show, Richard Pryor performed one of the most famous and funny versions of the Motown legend, entitled "The Motown Story: A Fairy Tale." The skit began with the line "Once upon a time in a kingdom known as Detroit there lived a young warrior named Berry." For the complete text, see Gordy, *To Be Loved,* pp. 369–370. For the performance, see the video *Motown 25: Yesterday, Today, Forever* (Motown Productions, 1983).

12. Raymond Williams discusses the concept of cultural formation in two essays, "The Future of Cultural Studies" and "The Uses of Cultural Theory," both in *The Politics of Modernism* (London: Verso, 1996). For an example of cultural formation analysis, see Michael Denning, *The Cultural Front: The Laboring of American Culture in the Twentieth Century* (London: Verso, 1996).

13. Nelson George's book *Where Did Our Love Go?* offers one example of this style.

14. My interpretation of the political meanings of Motown's cultural work corresponds to the theoretical work of C. Wright Mills, who wrote: "the politics of cultural work is not to be identified with the explicit political views or activities of the cultural workman ... The political choices of individuals must be distinguished from the political functions, uses and consequences of the cultural work they do." Mills, *Power, Politics, and People* (New York: Ballantine Books, 1963), p. 403.

15. Paul Oliver, *The Meaning of the Blues* (New York: Collier Books, 1960), p. 53, and *Blues Fell This Morning: Meaning in the Blues* (Cambridge: Cambridge University Press, 1990).

16. See also Lars Bjorn, "From Hastings Street to the Bluebird: The Blues and Jazz Traditions in Detroit," *Michigan Quarterly Review,* 25, no. 2 (Spring 1986): 257–

267; LeRoi Jones, *Blues People: Negro Music in White America* (New York: William Morrow, 1963), p. 97.

17. William Barlow, *Looking Up at Down: The Emergence of Blues Culture* (Philadelphia: Temple University Press, 1989), p. 286, and Paul Hendrickson, "Singin' the Detroit Blues: A Ballad of Broken Dreams," *Detroit Free Press*, September 30, 1973, section A, pp. 1, 12–13; "Detroit Blues: Assembly Line of Dreams," *Rolling Stone*, February 14, 1974, p. 14; Georgakas and Surkin, *Detroit*, p. 130. For another example of the influence of industrial work on music, see Brenda McCallum, "Songs of Work and Songs of Worship: Sanctifying Black Unionism in the Southern City of Steel," *New York Folklore*, 14, nos. 1–2 (1988): 9–33.

18. For a more detailed discussion of the commercial hardships faced by Detroit blues musicians, see Paul Hendrickson's article "Singin' the Detroit Blues"; Pat Halley, " 'All These Blues': Detroit Blues—Old Timers Testify," *Fifth Estate*, August 18–31, 1973, pp. 14 and 18; and Sheldon Annis, "Blues? In Detroit? You Mean That They Actually Still Play Blues in Detroit?" *Creem Magazine*, 2, no. 2 (July 8, 1969): 16–18, 20.

19. Gordy, *To Be Loved*, p. 70.

20. Ibid., p. 140; see also Michael Goldberg, "Interview with Berry Gordy," *Rolling Stone*, August 23, 1990, p. 71.

21. David Bianco, *Heatwave: The Motown Fact Book* (Ann Arbor, Mich.: Popular Press, 1988), p. 137.

22. For examples of this scholarship, see Lawrence W. Levine, *Black Culture and Black Consciousness* (New York: Oxford University Press, 1977); Tricia Rose, *Black Noise: Rap Music and Black Culture in Contemporary America* (Hanover: University Press of New England, 1994); William L. Van Deburg, *New Day in Babylon: The Black Power Movement and American Culture, 1965–1975* (Chicago: University of Chicago Press, 1992); Brian Ward, *Just My Soul Responding: Rhythm and Blues, Black Consciousness, and Race Relations* (Berkeley: University of California Press, 1998).

23. For more background on African Americans in the automobile industry, see August Meier and Elliot Rudnick, *Black Detroit and the Rise of the UAW* (New York: Oxford University Press, 1979); James Boggs, *American Revolution: Pages from a Negro Worker's Notebook* (New York: Monthly Review Press, 1963); Charles Denby, *Indignant Heart: A Black Worker's Journal* (Detroit: Wayne State University Press, 1989); Georgakas and Surkin, *Detroit;* and James A. Geschwender, *Class, Race, and Worker Insurgency: The League of Revolutionary Black Workers* (Cambridge: Cambridge University Press, 1977).

24. For more background on capitalism and race, see Manning Marable, *How Capitalism Underdeveloped Black America* (Boston: South End Press, 1983).

25. See liner notes, Stokely Carmichael, *Free Huey!* Black Forum BF452 (Detroit: Motown Record Corporation, 1970).

26. Harold Cruse, *The Crisis of the Negro Intellectual* (New York: Quill, 1984), pp. 86–87.

27. William Eric Perkins, "Harold Cruse: On the Problem of Culture and Revolution," *Journal of Ethical Studies*, 5, no. 2 (Summer 1977): 3–25. Perkins offers a thorough critique of Cruse's neglect of the black industrial working class in cities such as Detroit.

1. "In Whose Heart There Is No Song"

1. "Motown Releases Reverend King Recording," *Michigan Chronicle*, August 31, 1963, section B, p. 11. King had begun to use the dream metaphor in his speeches and writings as early as 1960. His speech at Detroit's Great March gave King his first opportunity to present his powerful "I Have a Dream" incantation to such a massive audience. For transcripts of King's earlier writings, see James Melvin Washington, ed., *A Testament of Hope: The Essential Writings and Speeches of Martin Luther King, Jr.* (San Francisco: HarperCollins, 1986).

2. In his recent work, *Just My Soul Responding*, Brian Ward argues that Motown released the Detroit recording only to capitalize on the national publicity surrounding the March on Washington. Ward writes that Motown produced the Detroit speech on an album "cleverly entitled *The Great March to Freedom*. Gordy had also christened a portion of King's untitled Detroit address 'I have a dream.'" Ward also cites a claim by King that Motown used the "I Have a Dream" subtitle in the Detroit recording "only after Motown 'saw the widespread public reception accorded said words when used in the text of my address to the March on Washington.'" I disagree with both Ward's interpretation and King's claim. Motown did not "cleverly" title the album *The Great March to Freedom*. The organizers of the demonstration, most notably the Reverend C. L. Franklin and the Reverend Albert Cleage, decided to call the march the Great March to Freedom in March 1963. Motown's album title reflects that historical fact. In regards to the claims about the "I Have a Dream" subtitle, Motown completed the album in mid-August and in time for Gordy to deliver to King a personal copy a week or so before the March on Washington. It would have been impossible for Gordy to know ahead of time that the "I Have a Dream" speech would catch on as it did after the March on Washington. It is also important to note that Motown subtitled all eleven bands of the recording to reflect the content of the speech. Ward's interpretation implicitly reinforces what I believe to be an underestimation of the historical significance of Detroit's Great March to Freedom, which this chapter seeks to rectify. The March on Washington has always overshadowed Detroit's Great March, which was historic not only in its size (which some estimate as larger than the March on Washington), but also in its content. For Ward's discussion, see *Just My Soul Responding: Rhythm and Blues, Black Consciousness, and Race Relations* (Berkeley: University of California Press, 1998), pp. 268–275.

3. *Michigan Chronicle,* August 31, 1963, section B, p. 31.

4. In his book on King and SCLC, David Garrow mentions King's appearance in Detroit only in passing. David Garrow, *Bearing the Cross: Martin Luther King, Jr., and the Southern Christian Leadership Conference* (New York: Vintage Books, 1986), p. 274. In *Parting the Waters: America in the King Years, 1954–63,* (New York: Simon and Schuster, 1988), pp. 842–844, Taylor Branch briefly describes the Detroit demonstration but does not fully explore its significance to the history of race relations in Detroit.

5. Sidney Fine, *Violence in the Model City: The Cavanagh Administration, Race Relations, and the Detroit Riot of 1967* (Ann Arbor: University of Michigan Press, 1989), pp. 1, 17–37.

6. David P. Welsh, "NAACP Honors Three, Then Takes the Ford Foundation to Task," *Detroit News,* February 13, 1963.

7. *Michigan Chronicle,* February 9, 1963, section B, p. 10.

8. "Detroiters Poised for Bias March," *Detroit News,* June 23, 1963; William Allan, "Michigan AFL-CIO Urges Full Support to Freedom March," *Worker,* June 16, 1963; "Action Must Follow June 23 March," *Michigan Chronicle,* June 15, 1963.

9. "King, Cavanagh to Head March Down Woodward," *Detroit Free Press,* June 23, 1963.

10. Grace Lee Boggs, *Living for Change: An Autobiography* (Minneapolis: University of Minnesota Press, 1998), p. 124.

11. *Detroit News,* June 8, 1963; *Illustrated News,* June 10, 1963; *Michigan Chronicle,* June 1, 1963.

12. The governor at the time, George Romney, a practicing Mormon, was unable to attend the event for religious reasons. As a rule, Romney did not make public appearances on Sundays. He did issue a special proclamation about the day, however, and sent two special representatives in his place. When his message of greeting was read during the introduction of dignitaries, the *Detroit Free Press* reported that "[t]he audience booed Romney lustily." Jerome Hansen and Jack Mann, "125,000 Walk Quietly in Record Rights Plea," *Detroit Free Press,* June 24, 1963, section A, p. 2.

13. Allan Blanchard and Earl Dowdy, "125,000 in March for Freedom Down Woodward," *Detroit News,* June 24, 1963, section A, pp. 1–2; Broadnus N. Butler, "Freedom March in Perspective," *Michigan Chronicle,* July 6, 1963. For more on Detroit's response to the Emancipation Proclamation, see John Chavis, "Detroit and the Emancipation Proclamation," *Detroit Courier,* August 17, 1969.

14. Robert Conot, *American Odyssey* (New York: William Morrow, 1974), p. 73. For more on labor and race relations during the Civil War, see Williston H. Lofton, "Northern Labor and the Negro during the Civil War," *Journal of Negro History,* 34, no. 3 (July 1949): 251–273; Albert A. Blum and Dan Georgakas, *Michigan Labor and the Civil War* (Lansing, Mich.: Civil War Centennial Observance Commission, 1964); and Norman McRae, *Negroes in Michigan during the Civil War* (Lansing, Mich.: Civil War Centennial Observance Commission, 1966).

15. *A Thrilling Narrative from the Lips of the Sufferers of the Late Detroit Riot, March 6, 1863,* (Detroit, 1863, and Hattiesburg, Miss.: Book Farm, 1945), pp. 2–24.

16. Six years later the young women confessed that their accusations had been fabrications, and Faulkner was released. Conot, *American Odyssey,* p. 74.

17. David M. Katzman, *Before the Ghetto: Black Detroit in the Nineteenth Century* (Urbana: University of Illinois Press, 1973), p. 47; Conot, *American Odyssey,* p. 75.

18. *Michigan Chronicle,* June 1, 1963; Fine, *Violence in the Model City,* p. 107.

19. At the time of the March, Edwards had announced his resignation from the position in order to accept a federal judgeship in the Kennedy administration. *Michigan Chronicle,* June 1, 1963.

20. *Michigan Chronicle,* July 6, 1963, pp. 1–2.

21. For a transcript of King's speech, see *Michigan Chronicle,* June 24, 1963.

22. Dominic J. Capeci Jr. and Martha Wilkerson, *Layered Violence: The Detroit Rioters of 1943* (Jackson: University Press of Mississippi, 1991); Conot, *American Odyssey,* pp. 378–379; Walter White and Thurgood Marshall, *What Caused the Detroit Riot? An Analysis by Walter White and Thurgood Marshall* (New York: National Association for the Advancement of Colored People, 1943), p. 15.

23. Conot, *American Odyssey,* p. 379.

24. Janet L. Langlois, "The Belle Isle Bridge Incident: Legend Dialectic and Semiotic System in the 1943 Detroit Race Riots," *Journal of American Folklore,* 96, no. 380 (1983): 185; Earl Brown, "Why Race Riots? Lessons from Detroit," *Public Affairs Pamphlets,* 87 (1944): 14.

25. For a firsthand account of the violence, see Charles Denby, *Indignant Heart: A Black Worker's Journal* (Detroit: Wayne State University Press, 1978), pp. 110–119.

26. White and Marshall, *Detroit Riot,* p. 15; Brown, "Why Race Riots?" p. 22; Conot, *American Odyssey,* p. 386.

27. Brown, "Why Race Riots?" pp. 22–23.

28. For more details about the Detroit Plan, see Steve Babson, Ron Alpern, Dave Elsila, and John Revitte, *Working Detroit: The Making of a Union Town* (New York, Adama Books, 1984), pp. 157–159; Fine, *Violence in the Model City,* p. 61; and Conot, *American Odyssey,* pp. 400–405.

29. Fine, *Violence in the Model City,* p. 62; Detroit Commission on Community Relations, "A Look at the Changing Face of Detroit," March 8, 1963, box 112, Jerome P. Cavanagh Papers, Walter P. Reuther Library, Wayne State University.

30. For more on automation, deindustrialization, and race relations in Detroit, see Thomas Sugrue, *The Origins of the Urban Crisis: Race and Inequality in Postwar Detroit* (Princeton, N.J.: Princeton University Press, 1996), pp. 125–152; and Steven Meyer, "The Persistence of Fordism: Workers and Technology in the American Automobile Industry, 1900–1960," in Nelson Lichtenstein and Stephen Meyer, eds.,

On the Line: Essays in the History of Auto Work, (Urbana: University of Illinois Press, 1989).

31. Jerome Hansen and Jack Mann, "Negroes Hail King Speech," *Detroit Free Press,* June 24, 1963. Grace Lee Boggs, "Malcolm's Message to the Grassroots," speech to the Detroit Remembers Malcolm X Conference, Wayne State University, July 24, 1993, p. 1.

32. *Michigan Chronicle,* June 29, 1963; Broadnus N. Butler, "Freedom March in Perspective: Parts I and II," *Michigan Chronicle,* July 6, 1963, and July 13, 1963.

33. Liner notes, *Great March to Freedom,* Gordy Records G-906 (Detroit: Motown Record Corporation, 1963).

34. Jeff Todd Titon, ed., *Give Me This Mountain: Life History and Selected Sermons of the Reverend C. L. Franklin* (Urbana: University of Illinois Press, 1989), pp. 4–9.

35. Ibid., pp. 20–23.

36. Ibid., p. 37, n. 18; Elaine Latzman Moon, *Untold Tales, Unsung Heroes: An Oral History of Detroit's African American Community, 1918–1967* (Detroit: Wayne State University Press, 1994), p. 362. Franklin's interest in recording his sermons was not new. As a child, he listened to the sermons of the Reverend J. M. Gates from Atlanta, who recorded over one hundred short sermons on 78s in the late 1920s. Gates was the most popular recorded preacher of his era. The majority of his sermons (unlike Franklin's) were produced by white-owned labels such as Columbia Records. See Viv Broughton, *Black Gospel: An Illustrated History of the Gospel Sound* (New York: Sterling Publishing, 1985), pp. 40–42; and Titon, *This Mountain,* pp. 4, 35.

37. Titon, *This Mountain,* p. vii.

38. In his autobiography, Smokey Robinson recalls seeing his young friend Aretha after these tours and realizing how the road gave her an emotional maturity beyond her peers. See William (Smokey) Robinson with David Ritz, *Smokey: Inside My Life* (New York: McGraw-Hill, 1989), pp. 47–48.

39. When asked in an interview if he thought his tour was unusual, Franklin replied, "Yes, it was unusual at first. It was unusual because no other preacher at that time had acquired that status in terms of recordings. I considered it a challenge. It was different from the traditional evangelistic thing, revivals. The fact that people were hearing me and demanding to see me and to hear me preach in person, all that kind of thing, it became a challenge." Titon, *This Mountain,* pp. 27–28.

40. Ibid., pp. 89–97.

41. Boggs, "Malcolm's Message," p. 126.

42. Robbie L. Crump, "New Bethel Enters New Church Home," *Michigan Chronicle,* March 16, 1963.

43. *Michigan Chronicle,* June 15, 1963, p. 3; *Detroit Free Press,* June 11, 1963, section D, p. 4; *Detroit News,* June 11, 1963, section B, p. 10.

44. Lars Bjorn, "Black Men in a White World: The Development of the Black

Jazz Community in Detroit, 1917–1940," *Detroit in Perspective: A Journal of Regional History,* 5, no. 1 (Fall 1980): 3–6.

45. Berry Gordy, *To Be Loved: The Music, the Magic, the Memories of Motown* (New York: Warner Books, 1994), p. 42. Forrester B. Washington, *The Negro in Detroit: A Survey of the Condition of a Negro Group in a Northern Industrial Center during the World Prosperity Period* (Detroit: Research Bureau, Associated Charities of Detroit, 1920), p. 16.

46. In his autobiography, Gordy describes his purchase of the ballroom in relation to the establishment's racist history. He writes, "I'd never dreamed as a kid that I'd be able to buy the Graystone Ballroom, where black people were only allowed in on Monday nights." Gordy, *To Be Loved,* p. 173.

47. Latzman Moon, *Untold Tales,* pp. 361–362.

48. Allan Slutsky, *Standing in the Shadows of Motown: The Life and Music of Legendary Bassist James Jamerson* (Milwaukee: Hal Leonard Publishing, 1989), pp. 10–11; Martha Reeves with Mark Bego, *Dancing in the Street: Confessions of a Motown Diva* (New York: Hyperion, 1994), p. 45.

49. "Comeback for Graystone Planned by New Owner," *Detroit News,* June 11, 1963, section B, p. 10.

50. The matinee concert also included a contest for "best looking attire," which reinforces this emphasis on appearance. *Michigan Chronicle,* July 27, 1963. J. Randy Taraborrelli, *Motown: Hot Wax, City Cool, and Solid Gold* (New York: Doubleday, 1986), p. 11. For more background on the "politics of respectability" among Detroit's black bourgeoisie, see Sugrue, *Urban Crisis,* pp. 205–207.

51. Ben Fong-Torres, *The Motown Album: The Sound of Young America* (New York: St. Martin's Press, 1990), pp. 32–36. Dick Clark with Richard Robinson, *Rock, Roll, and Remember* (New York: Thomas Y. Crowell, 1976), p. 230.

52. Nelson George, *The Death of Rhythm and Blues* (New York: E. P. Dutton, 1988), p. 88.

53. Gerri Hirshey, *Nowhere to Run: The Story of Soul Music* (New York: Penguin Books, 1984), p. 144; Mary Wilson, *Dreamgirl: My Life as a Supreme* (New York: St. Martin's Press, 1986), pp. 146–147. In her autobiography, Martha Reeves offers a slightly different version of this story. Reeves remembers the gunshots being fired as the tour bus left Savannah, Georgia, on its way to the Birmingham, Alabama, engagement. In all variations on the narrative, Birmingham is the scene in which the tour members recognize their vulnerability. Reeves, *Dancing,* pp. 71–72.

54. Frank Angelo, "Freedom March: A Giant Political, Economic Force" *Detroit Free Press,* June 25, 1963, section A, p. 2; Denby, *Indignant Heart,* p. 196; "Detroiters Hail Lack of Violence in 'Freedom Walk,' " *Detroit Free Press,* June 25, 1963, section A, p. 3.

55. In his autobiography former Detroit mayor Coleman Young writes, "At six feet and nearly two hundred pounds, Saint Cynthia had become a landmark around Twelfth Street, which had assumed Hastings Street's old role as Detroit's avenue of

iniquity." Coleman Young and Lonnie Wheeler, *Hard Stuff: The Autobiography of Coleman Young* (New York: Penguin Books, 1994), p. 163; "Olsen Clears Officers on Their Version of the Slaying," *Michigan Chronicle*, July 13, 1963.

56. *Michigan Chronicle*, July 13, 1963.

57. Ibid., Boggs, "Malcolm's Message," p. 126. Evidence of the lingering anger over the Scott case can be found in Barbara Tinker's 1970 novel, *When the Fire Reaches Us*, in which one of the characters says, "there is damned few black people around Detroit who have forgot" the killing of Cynthia Scott. "The cop didn't get so much as a slap on the wrist for killing her." Fine, *Violence in the Model City*, pp. 106–107.

2. "Money (That's What I Want)"

1. In the liner notes, Henry describes the technical aspects of the recording in great detail. The speech was recorded by "a semi-professional Sony 600 tape-recorder, supplemented by a Tangberg unit, fed by a Shure 55SW mike operated at low impedance." Liner notes, *Message to the Grass Roots from Malcolm X* (Detroit: Grass Roots L.P. Co., 14951 Schaefer Road, 1963).

2. For more details on the lawsuit, see *King v. Mister Maestro, Inc.*, 224 F. Supp. 101, 103 (S.D.N.Y. 1963). For discussion of the lawsuit in relation to the history of civil rights recordings, see Brian Ward, *Just My Soul Responding: Rhythm and Blues, Black Consciousness, and Race Relations* (Berkeley: University of California Press, 1998), pp. 268–275.

3. The connection between Booker T. Washington's economic philosophy and black nationalism will be elaborated later in this chapter. For further background, see Harold Cruse's essays "The Economics of Black Nationalism" and "Behind the Black Power Slogan," both in *Rebellion or Revolution?* (New York: William Morrow, 1968), and "Postscript on Black Power," in *The Crisis of the Negro Intellectual* (New York: Quill, 1984); Raymond L. Hall, *Black Separatism in the United States* (Hanover, N.H.: University Press of New England, 1978), pp. 225–227; and C. L. R. James's essay "Black Power" in Anna Grimshaw, ed., *The C. L. R. James Reader* (Oxford: Blackwell Publishers, 1992), pp. 362–374.

4. Malcolm X, "Message to the Grass Roots," in George Breitman, ed., *Malcolm X Speaks* (New York: Grove Press, 1966), p. 9.

5. For more on the history of black nationalism, see John H. Bracey Jr., August Meier, and Elliot Rudwick, *Black Nationalism in America* (Indianapolis: Bobbs-Merrill, 1970).

6. Nadine Brown, " 'Response Favorable' to Call For Leadership Confab," *Detroit Courier*, September 28, 1963.

7. *Illustrated News*, September 30, 1963, p. 2. For more background on the tension between separatist and integrationist philosophies in the history of black protest, see August Meier, Elliot Rudwick, and Francis Broderick, eds., *Black Protest Thought in the Twentieth Century* (Indianapolis: Bobbs-Merrill, 1971).

8. "Reverend Albert B. Cleage Resigns from DCHR," *Illustrated News,* October 28, 1963. For more on Franklin's position, see Grace Lee Boggs, *Living for Change: An Autobiography* (Minneapolis: University of Minnesota Press, 1998), pp. 126–127. In an article several days after the Detroit press declared Franklin's conference a "failure," Franklin modified his views claiming that he agreed with "aims of the black nationalists and Freedom Now party advocates, but he did not agree with their methods." "Northern Negro Leadership Conference 'a Failure,'" *Detroit Courier,* November 16, 1963.

9. "Conference Failure Laid to Franklin," *Detroit Courier,* November 16, 1963; Nadine Brown, "Negro Impatience Growing: 'Grass Roots' Confab Backs 'Self-Defense,'" *Detroit Courier,* November 11, 1963.

10. W. E. B. Du Bois first proposed the idea of a Negro Business League in 1899 at an Atlanta University conference entitled "The Negro in Business." One year later Washington put the idea into practice. See Louis R. Harlan, "Booker T. Washington and the National Negro Business League," in Raymond W. Smock, ed., *Booker T. Washington in Perspective: Essays of Louis R. Harlan* (Jackson: University Press of Mississippi, 1988), pp. 98–109. Ironically, while the National Negro Business League promoted self-help and black economic self-sufficiency, it was partially funded by Andrew Carnegie, who gave $2,700 each year until 1911 and $1,500 annually for three more years. August Meier, *Negro Thought in America, 1880–1915: Racial Ideologies in the Age of Booker T. Washington* (Ann Arbor: University of Michigan Press, 1966), p. 124. For a complete overview of the National Negro Business League, see Booker T. Washington, *The Negro in Business* (Chicago: Afro-Am Press, 1969; orig. ed., 1907).

11. "Constitution and By-Laws of Housewives League of Detroit" and "Declaration of Principles of the Constitution and By-Laws of the Booker T. Washington Trade Association 1937," box 1, folder "Constitution and By-Laws," Burton Historical Collection, Detroit Public Library.

12. Richard W. Thomas, *Life for Us Is What We Make It: Building Black Community in Detroit, 1915–1945* (Bloomington: Indiana University Press, 1992), p. 214.

13. Ibid., pp. 215–219.

14. Ibid., p. 265.

15. Ibid., pp. 264–266.

16. Berry Gordy Sr., *Movin' Up: Pop Gordy Tells His Story* (New York: Harper and Row, 1979), p. 125.

17. For more on black migration patterns, see Daniel M. Johnson and Rex R. Campbell, *Black Migration in America: A Social Demographic History* (Durham, N.C.: Duke University Press, 1981).

18. Gordy, *Movin' Up,* pp. 10, 53. Nelson George notes that the elder Gordy's relatively high education can be credited to his father, slave owner Jim Gordy, who "because of real Christian conviction, genuine affection for [his] sexual partner, or

as part of a general philosophy of helping blacks, took steps to support [his] bastard children, though [he] didn't grant them any . . . land." Nelson George, *Where Did Our Love Go? The Rise and Fall of the Motown Sound* (New York: St. Martin's Press, 1985), p. 1.

19. Gordy, *Movin' Up*, pp. 36–37.

20. Ibid., pp. 80–86.

21. Ibid., pp. 87, 95–99. The family's move to the west side of Detroit left an impression on the children. In his autobiography Berry Gordy Jr. wrote, "Later I came to understand that Pop's bringing us to the Westside was a major factor in who I became." See Berry Gordy, *To Be Loved: The Music, the Magic, the Memories of Motown* (New York: Warner Books, 1994), p. 16.

22. "Guide to the Gordy Family Papers," Michigan Historical Collections, Bentley Historical Library, University of Michigan.

23. See Gordy, *Movin' Up*, p. 100, and Gordy, *To Be Loved*, p. 24. At the time of his death at the age of ninety, Berry Gordy Sr. was remembered for his lifelong contributions to Detroit, including the grocery store, which became "a neighborhood social service center." See Rita Griffin, "Motown Family Head Laid to Rest," *Michigan Chronicle*, December 2, 1978, pp. 1, 4. When the Gordys opened the market in the early 1920s, they were participating in the heyday of the local neighborhood grocery before the rise of the chainstore market in the 1930s and 1940s. Throughout the early twentieth century, the local, independently owned grocer functioned to maintain ethnic and racial communities within larger metropolitan areas. For more on these shifts, see Lizabeth Cohen, *Making a New Deal: Industrial Workers in Chicago, 1919–1939* (Cambridge: Cambridge University Press, 1990) pp. 106–120.

24. Gordy, *Movin' Up*, p. 102.

25. "Matriarch of Motown Empire Is Stroke Victim," *Michigan Chronicle*, February 8, 1975, pp. 1, 4.

26. "Guide to the Gordy Family Papers"; "Helping People in Need: Friends Club President Says Its Only Reason for Being Is to Aid Worthy Causes," *Michigan Chronicle*, February 27, 1965, section C, p. 3. Bertha Gordy's accomplishments and political connections extended beyond Detroit. On July 21, 1949, Eleanor and Anna Roosevelt awarded Bertha Gordy their Woman of the Day honor. See "Mother Debunks Work Excuse," *Michigan Chronicle*, April 13, 1957. Bertha Gordy's stature in Detroit's black community was also evident at her funeral when political and religious leaders including Mayor Coleman Young, the Reverend Jesse Jackson, and the Reverend C. L. Franklin all attended. Detroit city council members Erma Henderson and Nicholas Hood, along with state representative Daisy Elliot and state senator Arthur Cartwright, introduced resolutions at the local and state level to honor the memory of Bertha Gordy. See Samuel Brooks Jr. and Brian Flanigan, " 'Mother' of Motown's Dynasty Mourned by Thousands Here," *Michigan Chronicle*, February 15, 1975, p. 1; George, *Where Did Our Love Go?* p. 11.

27. "Guide to the Gordy Family Papers"; When Loucye Gordy Wakefield died suddenly of a stroke on July 24, 1965, at the age of thirty-six, thousands of people crowded the funeral—evidence that, like her mother, the young woman was widely respected in her community. "At Services for Gordy Kin: Estimated 4,000 Mourn," *Michigan Chronicle*, August 7, 1965, pp. 1, 4.

28. By 1965 the Booker T. Washington Trade Association had changed its name to the Booker T. Washington Business Association. For consistency, I refer to the organization by its original name throughout.

29. Betty De Ramus, "A Victim of Integration???: Speaker Sounds Doom of 'Negro' Business," *Michigan Chronicle*, July 24, 1965. The argument that racial segregation can benefit black business enterprises has a long history. In the early to mid-twentieth century, the National Negro Baseball League provided the most clear-cut example of how segregation could bolster black entrepreneurs, as an elaborate economic system of black baseball teams, promoters, advertisers, and other cottage industries arose to support the Negro League. When Jackie Robinson joined the Dodgers in 1947 and integrated major league baseball, this network of independent black businesses soon lost its reason for existence, and the entire league was disbanded in 1960. Negro baseball also had close ties to other forms of black entertainment. In 1931 Louis Armstrong partially financed a seventeen-member New Orleans baseball team called Armstrong's Secret Nine. In 1976 Motown produced the film *The Bingo Long Traveling All-Stars and Motor Kings*, based on the novel by William Brasher. The film chronicles the story of an all-black baseball team traveling through the country in 1939. Significantly, Berry Gordy chose to pay homage to an earlier era of black entrepreneurship and sports entertainment in his first feature film that did not star Diana Ross. For further discussion on the National Negro Baseball League, see Nelson George, *The Death of Rhythm and Blues* (New York: Pantheon Books, 1988), pp. 12, 57–58; Bruce Chadwick, *When the Game Was Black and White: The Illustrated History of Baseball's Negro Leagues* (New York: Abbeville Press, 1992); Robert Peterson, *Only the Ball Was White* (New York: Oxford University Press, 1992).

30. "BTWTA to Salute Graves, Gordy," *Michigan Chronicle*, July 17, 1965. The Gordy family were members of the Reverend Willam Peck's Bethel AME Church. As the founder of the BTWTA, Peck served as a role model for the young Berry Gordy Jr. In his autobiography Gordy remembers Peck with respect and admiration. Gordy, *To Be Loved*, p. 29.

31. For more on Gordy's boxing career, see Gerald Early, *One Nation under a Groove: Motown and American Culture* (Hopewell, N.J.: Ecco Press, 1995), pp. 43–48.

32. Gordy, *To Be Loved*, pp. 72, 107; Raynoma Gordy Singleton with Bryan Brown and Mim Eichler, *Berry, Me, and Motown: The Untold Story* (Chicago: Contemporary Books, 1990), pp. 20, 26; and William (Smokey) Robinson with David Ritz, *Smokey: Inside My Life* (New York: McGraw-Hill, 1989), p. 65.

33. Rita Griffin, "City Mourns Favorite Musical Son," *Michigan Chronicle*, February 4, 1984.

34. Earl B. Dowdy, "The Amazing Empire on West Grand Boulevard," *Detroit News*, July 25, 1965, section G; George, *Where Did Our Love Go?* p. 13.

35. Gordy, *To Be Loved*, p. 49. See also Singleton, *Berry, Me, and Mowtown*, p. 23.

36. Gordy, *To Be Loved*, p. 59.

37. Stanley H. Brown, "The Motown Sound of Money," *Fortune*, September 1, 1967, p. 104; Dowdy, "The Amazing Empire," p. 1.

38. "Triumph of a Stay-at-Home," *Ebony*, 21, no. 4 (February 1966): 33; Brown, "The Motown Sound of Money," p. 104.

39. Robinson, *Smokey*, p. 66.

40. Ibid., p. 78. For more on "Got a Job," see Dave Marsh, *The Heart of Rock and Soul: The 1001 Greatest Singles Ever Made* (New York: Penguin Books, 1989), pp. 359, 433; and Ward, *Just My Soul Responding*, pp. 86, 205, 259, 369.

41. This professional collaboration had personal dimensions as well. By the time Berry Gordy's first marriage to Thelma Coleman officially ended in 1959, he had a new relationship with Liles. They had one child together, Kerry Gordy, in June 1959 and were married in the spring of 1960. Singleton, *Berry, Me, and Motown*, pp. 80–95.

42. Ibid., pp. 49, 70.

43. Ibid., pp. 69–71; George, *Where Did Our Love Go?* p. 29.

44. Gordy, *To Be Loved*, pp. 111, 121–122.

45. Ibid., p. 170.

46. "CORE Moves Out: Local Police Check UHURU Picketing," *Michigan Chronicle*, July 6, 1963, p. 1; "Picketing Ends: Kroger, CORE Agree," *Michigan Chronicle*, August 3, 1963, p. 1; "A&P, Kroger Target of Job Pickets," *Michigan Chronicle*, June 22, 1963, pp. 1, 3.

47. " 'Buy-In' Campaign a Success: Representative Diggs Leads in Newest Phase in Economic 'Push,' " *Michigan Chronicle*, August 10, 1963, p. 1.

48. " 'Grassroots' Group Slates Chicago Meet," *Detroit Courier*, November 23, 1963. In his essay "Black Power," C. L. R. James argues that young black activists, such as Stokely Carmichael, must be understood in relation to their predecessors. In James' words, "They [Black Power advocates] stand on the shoulders of their ancestors." These ancestors include Booker T. Washington, Marcus Garvey, W. E. B. Du Bois, Franz Fanon, and others. James continues: "too many people see Black Power and its advocates as some sort of portent, a sudden apparition, as some racist eruption from the depths of black oppression and black backwardness. It is nothing of the kind. It represents the high peak of thought on the Negro question which has been going on for over a half a century." See *The C. L. R. James Reader*, p. 369.

49. As natives of Sandersville, Gordy and Poole shared many common experiences growing up in rural Georgia, but direct evidence of any interaction between

the two is limited. Gordy, ten years older than Poole, spent his youth working on the Gordy farm and attending the family church, the Gordy Grove Church of God in Christ, which was built on Gordy property when Berry's mother, Lucy Gordy, donated the land. Poole attended his father's Baptist church. Also, the Poole family moved away from the immediate Sandersville community when Elijah was still a young child. Nevertheless, the Poole and Gordy families maintained ties to the Sandersville area long after Elijah and Berry migrated to Detroit in the early 1920s. See Mary Alice Jordan, *Cotton to Kaolin: A History of Washington County, Georgia, 1784–1989* (Sandersville: Washington County, Georgia, Historical Society, 1989), p. 265.

50. Elijah Muhammad, *Message to the Blackman* (Chicago: Muhammad Mosque of Islam Number Two, 1965), p. 178.

51. Karl Evanzz, *The Judas Factor: The Plot to Kill Malcolm X* (New York: Thunder's Mouth Press, 1992), p. 134. See also Federal Bureau of Investigation HQ Files on Elijah Muhammad (Elijah Muhammad 100-469601; Elijah Poole 105-24822), Washington, D.C.; *Negro World*, August 21, 1920; E. David Cronon, *Black Moses: The Story of Marcus Garvey and the Universal Negro Improvement Association* (Madison: University of Wisconsin Press, 1955), pp. 50–56, 122.

52. Jeannette Smith-Irvin, *Footsoldiers of the Universal Negro Improvement Association (Their Own Words)* (Trenton, N.J.: Africa World Press, 1989), p. 49; Some scholars also have speculated that Poole met Malcolm X's father, Earl Little, during his days in the UNIA. Malcolm X's sister has claimed in interviews that she first met Poole at UNIA meetings she attended with her father; see Evanzz, *Judas Factor*, p. 341, n. 16.

53. E. D. Beynon, "The Voodoo Cult among Negro Migrants in Detroit," *American Journal of Sociology*, 43 (July 1937–May 1938): 896–899.

54. Ibid., pp. 896; Robert Conot *American Odyssey* (New York: William Morrow, 1974), p. 278.

55. Louis Lomax, *When the Word Is Given: A Report on Elijah Muhammad, Malcolm X, and the Black Muslim World* (Cleveland: World Publishing, 1963), p. 52.

56. Clifton E. Marsh, *From Black Muslims to Muslims: The Transition from Separatism to Islam, 1930–1980* (Metuchen, N. J.: Scarecrow Press, 1984), p. 71. See also Alex Haley, *The Autobiography of Malcolm X* (New York: Ballantine Books, 1991), p. 194.

57. On November 21, 1932, a prominent member of the sect, Robert Harris, renamed Robert Karriem, was accused of murdering a roommate, John J. Smith, as a human sacrifice for the faith. W. D. Fard was investigated in 1932 in relation to the alleged murder or "sacrificial killing." The investigation of this murder and other practices of the sect resulted in Fard's arrest. In Elijah Muhammad's view, Fard "was persecuted, sent to jail in 1932, and ordered out of Detroit, on May 26, 1933. He came to Chicago in the same year and was arrested almost immediately on his arrival and placed behind prison bars." Muhammad, *Message to the Blackman*, pp. 24–25; see also Beynon, "Voodoo Cult," p. 903.

58. For a more detailed discussion of the influence of Washington and Garvey on the Nation of Islam's economic practices, see Raymond L. Hall, *Black Separatism in the United States* (Hanover, N.H.: University Press of New England, 1978), pp. 140, 225–227. In his essay "Postscript on Black Power," Harold Cruse argues, "in terms of economics, Elijah Muhammad carried out Booker T. Washington's philosophy of economic self-sufficiency and self-help more thoroughly than any other movement, the Black Power theorists accept the Nation of Islam, yet reject Booker T-ism." Cruse, *The Crisis of the Negro Intellectual*, p. 558; Muhammad, *Message to the Blackman*, p. 171. For more on the working-class aspects of the Nation of Islam, see Robin D. G. Kelley, *Yo' Mama's Disfunktional: Fighting the Culture Wars in Urban America* (Boston: Beacon Press, 1997), p. 86, and E. Eric Lincoln, *The Black Muslims in America*, 2d ed. (Boston: Beacon Press, 1973), p. 142.

59. Haley, *Malcolm X*, pp. 10, 155–162.

60. See Elaine Latzman Moon, *Untold Tales, Unsung Heroes: An Oral History of Detroit's African-American Community, 1918–1967* (Detroit: Wayne State University Press, 1994), pp. 273–277; see also Haley, *Malcolm X*, p. 191. Malcolm's nickname "Detroit Red" was a bit of a misnomer. Malcolm Little cultivated his skills as a numbers runner in the Roxbury neighborhood of Boston and in Harlem, not on the streets of Detroit. While in Harlem, he competed with other hustlers using the nickname "Red"—including "St. Louis Red" and "Chicago Red," eventually known as Redd Foxx. To end the confusion, Malcolm took the nickname "Detroit Red," because when people asked him what city he was from in Michigan, many had never heard of Lansing. Haley, *Malcolm X*, p. 112. For an analysis of the cultural politics of this phase of Malcolm X's life, see Robin D. G. Kelley, "The Riddle of the Zoot: Malcolm Little and Black Cultural Politics during World War II," in Joe Wood, ed., *Malcolm X: In Our Own Image* (New York: St. Martin's Press, 1992).

61. According to his Federal Bureau of Investigation file, Malcolm began his employment at Ford in January 1953. Clayborne Carson, *Malcolm X: The F.B.I. File* (New York: Carroll and Graf, 1991), p. 60; Haley, *Malcolm X*, pp. 199–211.

62. Haley, *Malcolm X*, p. 292.

63. Breitman, *Malcolm X Speaks*, pp. 3–4.

64. Ibid., p. 14.

65. Interview with Grace Lee Boggs, conducted July 12, 1994, Detroit, Michigan.

66. "Freedom Now Party: Draft National Platform," *Liberator*, February 1964, pp. 4–5.

67. For a more complete discussion about the need for an all-black Freedom Now Party, see Albert B. Cleage Jr., "Why We Need the Freedom Now Party," *Illustrated News*, March 9, 1964, pp. 3–7.

68. Breitman, *Malcolm X Speaks*, p. 16.

69. Ibid., pp. 7–8.

70. Haley, *Malcolm X*, p. 301.

71. Ibid., pp. 315–316.

72. For more on this shift, see Patricia Hill Collins, "Learning to Think for Ourselves: Malcolm X's Black Nationalism Reconsidered," in Joe Wood, ed., *Malcolm X: In Our Own Image* (New York: St. Martin's Press, 1992).

73. Haley, *Malcolm X*, p. 313.

74. David Bianco, *Heatwave: The Motown Fact Book* (Ann Arbor, Mich.: Popular Press, 1988), p. 137. For more on the history of the *Billboard* charts, see "Billboard Adopts 'R&B' as New Name for Two Charts," *Billboard*, October, 27, 1990.

75. Singleton, *Berry, Me, and Motown*, p. 69; Gordy, *To Be Loved*, p. 118.

76. "Freedom Now Party: Draft National Platform," *Liberator*, February 1964, pp. 4–5.

77. When discussing the Freedom Now Party defeats, the Reverend Albert B. Cleage blamed fears within the black community that Barry Goldwater would be elected over Lyndon Johnson. Cleage commented, "They [black voters] were convinced if Goldwater was elected he'd build concentration camps for Negroes and there'd be atomic destruction . . . Why a lot of them didn't even bother to vote for Jackie Vaughn for Council—they just didn't want to touch any of the levers." "New Freedom Now Party Blanked but Not Broken," *Detroit News*, n. d., Ernest Smith Collection, box 1, folder 1-6, Walter P. Reuther Library, Wayne State University.

3. "Come See about Me"

1. Letter to Raymond McCann, September 8, 1963, Langston Hughes Correspondence, James Weldon Johnson Collection, Beinecke Library, Yale University.

2. Since the column was nationally syndicated, different newspapers changed the headline of the essay. In the *New York Post*, the essay was entitled "Record It," in the *Chicago Defender*, "Long Gone, Still Hear the Voices." In most cases the essay appeared during the second week of September 1963. See Langston Hughes, "Long Gone, Still Hear Voices," *Chicago Defender*, September 7–13, 1963.

3. June M. Aldridge argues that "[t]he most successful poems of both poets are usually short with a sharp delineation of a situation and an often ironic perception couched in fresh and vivid imagery." Aldridge, "Langston Hughes and Margaret Danner," *Langston Hughes Review*, 3, no. 2 (Fall 1984): 8.

4. After Martin Luther King Jr. presented his "I Have a Dream" oration at the March on Washington, many of Hughes's friends noted that the speech echoed the spirit of the poet's "dream" poems. Arnold Rampersad, *The Life of Langston Hughes*, Vol. 2, *1941–1967: I Dream a World* (New York: Oxford University Press, 1988), p. 367.

5. Woodson's biographer, Jacqueline Goggin, has no direct evidence that the release of *Birth of a Nation* inspired the formation of the association. Nevertheless,

she does claim that Woodson would have been aware of the controversies surrounding the film. Goggin, *Carter G. Woodson: A Life in Black History* (Baton Rouge: Louisiana State University Press, 1993), pp. 32–34.

6. "Negro History Campaign of 1938," *Negro History Bulletin,* 1, no. 9 (June 1938): 7; Broadnus N. Butler, "Prefatory Note on This Issue," *Negro History Bulletin,* 26, no. 1 (October 1962): 3.

7. *Tambourines to Glory* was Hughes's attempt to create a show celebrating black gospel music. Hughes received criticism for producing a show that did not directly address racial problems. He defended the play as entertainment and, according to Arnold Rampersad, felt "that the show had a better chance of success with a public presumably weary of politics and race." For further discussion about the play, see Rampersad, *Langston Hughes,* pp. 255, 358–359, 368.

8. Negro History Week was one of the ASNLH's most important annual projects. Woodson first organized the event in 1926 to increase awareness of black history among the black masses and to recruit new members to the organization. He selected the second week of February for the observance to commemorate the birthdays of Abraham Lincoln on February 12 and Frederick Douglass on February 14. If the two birthdays fell in two different weeks, the week of Douglass's birthday was chosen. In *Dusk of Dawn,* W. E. B. Du Bois argued that National Negro History Week was the greatest single accomplishment to emerge from the artistic fervor of the 1920s. *Program for "An Evening with Langston Hughes,"* February 9, 1964, sponsored by the ASNLH, Detroit branch, p. 3, Burton Historical Collection, Detroit Public Library. Goggin, *Woodson,* pp. 84–85, and Du Bois, *Dusk of Dawn: An Essay toward an Autobiography of a Race Concept* (1940; rpt. New York, 1971), p. 203. Letter to Hughes from June McKee, October 5, 1963, box 6, Langston Hughes Correspondence.

9. For further commentary on this topic, see Ralph Ellison's essay "What America Would Be Like without Blacks," in *Going to the Territory* (New York: Vintage Books, 1987), pp. 104–112.

10. Until mid-1965, Diana Ross was known as Diane Ross. Her decision to adopt the stage name "Diana" was a surprise to Mary Wilson and Florence Ballard and caused some tensions. As jealousy grew within the group, the name change often became a distancing mechanism among the women. At one point Ballard remarked, "Honey, I am not working myself to death to make Diana Ross a star." Wilson commented, "We always referred to Diane as Diane, and when Flo said 'Diana' the bitterness cut through me like a knife." Mary Wilson, *Dreamgirl: My Life as a Supreme* (New York: St. Martin's Press, 1986), pp. 61, 204, and 234. For consistency, all subsequent references are to Diana Ross.

11. Observers also were confused as to why blacks would celebrate historic holidays on dates other than those on which they occurred. The simplest explanation was that the summer season provided the most amenable climate for this type of

outdoor activity. Richard W. Thomas, *Life for Us Is What We Make It: Building Black Community in Detroit, 1915–1945* (Bloomington: Indiana University Press, 1992), pp. 8–9.

12. "Entries Still Accepted in Emancipation Affair," *Michigan Chronicle*, July 16, 1960.

13. Diana Ross, *Secrets of a Sparrow: Memoirs* (New York: Villard Books, 1993), p. 100; Wilson, *Dreamgirl*, p. 39.

14. Elaine Latzman Moon, ed., "Marsha L. Mickens," in *Untold Tales, Unsung Heroes: An Oral History of Detroit's African American Community, 1918–1967* (Detroit: Wayne State University Press, 1994), p. 362.

15. Raynoma Gordy Singleton with Bryan Brown and Mim Eichler, *Berry, Me, and Motown: The Untold Story* (Chicago: Contemporary Books, 1990), p. 49; Otis Williams with Patricia Romanowski, *Temptations* (New York: G. P. Putnam's Sons, 1988), pp. 31–32.

16. Singleton, *Berry, Me, and Motown*, p. 14.

17. Berry Gordy, *To Be Loved: The Music, the Magic, the Memories of Motown* (New York: Warner Books, 1994), pp. 51–52, 118.

18. According to Wilson's recollection, when Motown was mentioned as a possible option for their recording aspirations, Florence remarked, "Isn't Motown the record company that cheats its artists?" Ballard continued to bring up rumors of Motown's reputation at the Primettes' first audition. See Wilson, *Dreamgirl*, pp. 62, 65.

19. William (Smokey) Robinson with David Ritz, *Smokey: Inside My Life* (New York: McGraw-Hill, 1989), p. 87.

20. "Little Stevie Wonder" was one of the few exceptions to Gordy's resistance to child performers. Stephen Hardaway Judkins signed with Motown Records at the age of eleven. See Gordy, *To Be Loved*, p. 148.

21. Wilson, *Dreamgirl*, p. 69. Many artists at Motown have reiterated countless times these sentiments about the company's family atmosphere. Otis Williams recalls, "Joining Motown was more like being adopted by a big loving family than being hired by a company." Others saw the gestures at community building as a means to control employees. Studio musicians remember Gordy hiring a company cook to keep them from leaving for lunch and losing studio time. Williams, *Temptations*, pp. 50–51, and Jack Ryan, *Recollections—The Detroit Years: The Motown Sound by the People Who Made It* (Detroit: Whitlaker Marketing, 1982), section 20.

22. Wilson, *Dreamgirl*, p. 71.

23. Of the payola incident, Wilson commented, "Years later, I would learn that B&H's problems with payola investigators were the product of racism; only black distributors had been harassed. I was still too young to fully comprehend the significance of this." Ibid., pp. 82–86.

24. Gordy, *To Be Loved*, p. 140.

25. Singleton, *Berry, Me, and Motown*, p. 99.

26. For more on ITMI and Motown's business practices, see Nelson George, *Where Did Our Love Go? The Rise and Fall of the Motown Sound* (New York: St. Martin's Press, 1985), pp. 27–32; Gordy, *To Be Loved*, p. 144.

27. Wilson, *Dreamgirl*, p. 116.

28. It is unclear as to whether Hughes attended the "Motortown Revue" performance, but he received information about the concert and Stevie Wonder's hotel arrangements in New York. Telegram to Hughes from Raymond McCann, October 16, 1963, Langston Hughes Correspondence.

29. Louis Draper did not receive final payment for his work until June 1964, nine months after he took the photographs. Letter to Langston Hughes from Margaret Danner, June 1964, and letter to Margaret Danner from Langston Hughes, June 2, 1964, Langston Hughes Correspondence; George, *Where Did Our Love Go?* p. 29.

30. Letter to Margaret Danner, January 30, 1964; letter to Langston Hughes from Margaret Danner, January 1964; letter to Langston Hughes from Margaret Danner, June 1964; Langston Hughes Correspondence.

31. Letter to Langston Hughes from Margaret Danner, January 1964; letter to Edward Pollock, May 6, 1964; Langston Hughes Correspondence.

32. Betty De Ramus, "African Art Gallery Seen as Retribution to Negro Cause," *Negro History Bulletin*, 27, no. 5 (February 1964): 127, 131.

33. Letter from June McKee, October 22, 1963, Langston Hughes Correspondence; "Langston Hughes Visits: For a Poet—Sirens, Key to the City," *Detroit Free Press*, February 8, 1964; *Daily Collegian* (Wayne State University), 54, no. 75 (February 10, 1964): p. 1. Woodie King Jr., leader of the Black Theater Movement and founder of Detroit's Concept East Theater, remembered Hughes's sharp wit about Detroit's elaborate efforts to honor him. When King and his friend Ron Milner went to meet Hughes at his hotel suite, Hughes commented, "Man, I wish I had one of these [suites] permanently. This is something, isn't it? Wow! Hey, they gave me the key to the City . . . Brought me in the motorcade! I wish I had the money they spent on me!" Woodie King Jr., "Remembering Langston: A Poet of the Black Theater," *Negro Digest*, 18, no. 6 (April 1969): 27–32, 95–96.

34. "1500 Pay Tribute to Langston Hughes," *Michigan Chronicle*, February 15, 1964.

35. Letter from June McKee, February 11, 1964; note from Oliver La Grone; Langston Hughes Correspondence.

36. Letter from Margaret Danner, March 18, 1964, Langston Hughes Correspondence.

37. Rampersad, *Langston Hughes*, p. 374.

38. Margaret Danner, "Introduction," in Rosey E. Pool, ed., *Beyond the Blues: New Poems by American Negroes* (England: Hand and Flower Press, 1962), p. 86; Margaret Danner, "Margaret Danner," *Negro History Bulletin*, 26, no. 1, special issue on Detroit writers (October 1962): 53.

39. Langston Hughes met many of the Boone House poets for the first time in January 1963, when he appeared at Wayne State University. Hughes came to inaugurate the university's emancipation centennial celebrations and to promote the publication of a new anthology of African American poetry, *Beyond the Blues*. For more on Danner and Boone House, see June M. Aldridge, "Margaret Esse Danner," in *Dictionary of Literary Biography*, vol. 41, *Afro-American Poets since 1955*, ed. Trudier Harris and Thadious M. Davis (Detroit: Gale Research, 1985), p. 85; "Margaret Danner and Boone House," in Dudley Randall, *Broadside Memories: Poets I Have Known* (Detroit: Broadside Press, 1975), pp. 36–37.

40. Dudley Randall and Margaret Danner, *Poem Counterpoem* (Detroit: Broadside Press, 1966).

41. A. X. Nicholas, "A Conversation with Dudley Randall," *Black World*, 21, no. 2 (December 1971): 26–34.

42. For the complete text of the poem, see Randall and Danner, *Poem Counterpoem*, p. 4.

43. For more on *Correspondence*, see Paul Buhle, *C. L. R. James: The Artist as Revolutionary* (New York: Verso, 1988), p. 119. For more background on the role of freedom songs in the civil rights movement, see Bernice Johnson Reagon, *Voices of the Civil Rights Movement: Black American Freedom Songs, 1960–1966* (Washington, D.C.: Smithsonian Institution 1980; rereleased 1997).

44. Margaret Danner, "Malcolm X, a Lover of the Grass Roots," in Dudley Randall and Margaret G. Burroughs, eds., *For Malcolm: On the Life and Death of Malcolm X* (Detroit: Broadside Press, 1967), p. 7.

45. Williams, *Temptations*, p. 63.

46. Wilson, *Dreamgirl*, pp. 171–177.

47. Gordy, *To Be Loved*, pp. 198–202.

48. Wilson, *Dreamgirl*, p. 178.

49. Williams, *Temptations*, p. 76.

50. Allan Slutsky, "Motown: Anatomy of a Hit-Making Sound," *Keyboard*, 19, no. 5, issue 205 (May 1993): 94.

51. Allan Slutsky (Dr. Licks), *Standing in the Shadows of Motown: The Life and Music of Legendary Bassist James Jamerson* (Milwaukee: Hal Leonard Publishing, 1989), p. 32.

52. Gordy, *To Be Loved*, p. 151.

53. George, *Where Did Our Love Go?* p. 35. For more on Cholly Atkins, see Jacqui Malone, *Steppin' on the Blues: The Visible Rhythms of African American Dance* (Urbana: University of Illinois Press, 1996), pp. 122–125. For more on Maurice King, see D. Antoinette Handy, *The International Sweethearts of Rhythm* (Metuchen, N.J.: Scarecrow Press, 1983); and George, *Where Did Our Love Go?* pp. 93–95.

54. Booker T. Washington, *Up from Slavery*, in *Three Negro Classics* (New York: Avon Books, 1965), p. 96.

55. Goggin, *Woodson,* p. 161. For further discussion of how notions of "class" shaped Motown's public image, see Phillip Brian Harper, "Synesthesia, 'Crossover,' and Blacks in Popular Music," *Social Text: Theory/Culture/Ideology,* Fall–Winter 1989; pp. 102–121.

56. Wilson, *Dreamgirl,* p. 181.

57. C. Vann Woodward, "After Watts—Where Is the Negro Revolution Headed?" *New York Times Magazine,* August 29, 1965. The topic of automation and "technological displacement" received a great deal of national press coverage at this time, for example, see Charles E. Silberman, "The Real News about Automation," *Fortune,* 71, no. 1 (January 1965): 124–127, 220–228.

58. Thomas Sugrue, *The Origins of the Urban Crisis: Race and Inequality in Postwar Detroit* (Princeton, N.J.: Princeton University Press, 1996), p. 128.

59. Gerri Hirshey, *Nowhere to Run: The Story of Soul Music* (New York: Penguin Books, 1984), pp. 140–141.

60. James Boggs, *The American Revolution: Pages from a Negro Worker's Notebook* (New York: Monthly Review Press, 1963), p. 38.

61. Peter Fortunale and Joshua E. Mills, *Radio in the Television Age* (New York: Overlook Press, 1980), pp. 19–20; George, *Where Did Our Love Go?* p. 114; Gerald Early, *One Nation under a Groove: Motown and American Culture* (Hopewell, N.J.: Ecco Press, 1995), pp. 60–63.

62. David Morse, *Motown and the Arrival of Black Music* (New York: MacMillian, 1971), p. 23.

63. Michael Lydon, "Smokey Robinson," *Rolling Stone,* September 28, 1968, p. 21; Ryan, *Recollections,* section 18.

64. Hirshey, *Nowhere to Run,* p. 188; George, *Where Did Our Love Go?* p. 114; David Ritz, *Divided Soul: The Life of Marvin Gaye* (New York: Da Capo Press, 1991), p. 98; "Conquering New Field: 'Detroit Sound' Leads Auto Cartridge Sales," *Michigan Chronicle,* July 9, 1966.

65. Lee Iacocca's relationship to Berry Gordy as a fellow Detroit entrepreneur continued into the 1990s. When Gordy published his autobiography in October 1994, the dust jacket included an endorsement by Lee Iacocca, who commends the book and Berry Gordy's "innovative thinking and groundbreaking business practices." In recent years Iacocca's role as the sole creator behind the Mustang has been questioned. As journalist Doron Levin noted, "Several Ford engineers and planners could have been singled out for their roles in creating the Mustang. However, only Iacocca, then the general manager of Ford's automobile division, had the savvy to dispatch his tireless PR man, Walter Murphy, to spread the word. In fact, Murphy was instrumental in getting his boss on the covers of *Newsweek* and *Time.*" See Levin, "The Real Iacocca: Why Detroit Isn't Cheering the Former Chairman's Comeback Bid," *Newsweek,* May 1, 1995, pp. 62–62A.

66. "Ford's Young One," *Time,* April 16, 1964, p. 100; Lee Iacocca with William Novak, *Iacocca: An Autobiography* (New York: Bantam Books, 1984) p. 64.

67. "The Mustang—A New Breed out of Detroit," *Newsweek*, April 20, 1964, pp. 97–101; "Ford's Young One," pp. 92–102; Iacocca, *Autobiography*, p. 74.

68. Wilson, *Dreamgirl*, p. 180.

69. Iacocca notes that, by the Mustang's first birthday on April 17, 1965, Ford had sold 418,812 cars—a new record. The goal had been 417,000, to fit the company's sales slogan "417 by 4/17." See Iacocca, *Autobiography*, p. 74. Motown released "Nowhere to Run" in February 1965; the flip side was a song entitled "Motoring." "Nowhere to Run" reached number five on the rhythm and blues charts and number eight on the pop charts. See Martha Reeves with Mark Bego, *Dancing in the Street: Confessions of a Motown Diva* (New York: Hyperion Books, 1994), pp. 123, 260.

70. For a detailed discussion of the history of the Office of Economic Opportunity and its role in President Johnson's War on Poverty, see Nicholas Lemann, *The Promised Land: The Great Black Migration and How It Changed America* (New York: Vintage Books, 1991), pp. 157, 165–170.

71. "It's What's Happening, Baby," TV special, Museum of Television and Radio, New York City, call number T88:0027.

72. Mary Wilson's recollection of the *Sullivan Show* appearance reveals just how important presentation was. Wilson describes wardrobe, makeup, and choreography in detail but makes no mention of what song they sang. Wilson, *Dreamgirl*, pp. 188–189.

73. Goggin, *Woodson*, p. 179; "Television: Negro Performers Win Better Roles in TV Than in Any Other Entertainment Medium," *Ebony*, 5, no. 8 (June 1950): 22.

74. *Ebony*, June 1950, p. 23.

75. Eleanor Harris, "That 'No Talent' Ed Sullivan," *Look*, 19 (April 5, 1955): 32.

76. "Big as All Outdoors," *Time*, October 17, 1955, p. 72.

77. Eleanor Harris, "He Smiles Back at Fortune," *Look*, 19 (April 19, 1955): 86.

78. See J. Fred MacDonald, *Blacks and White TV: Afro-Americans in Television since 1948* (Chicago: Nelson-Hall, 1983), p. 13; Jerry Bowles, *A Thousand Sundays: The Story of the Ed Sullivan Show* (New York: G. P. Putnam's Sons, 1980), p. 44; John Leonard, *A Really Big Show: A Visual History of the Ed Sullivan Show* (New York: Sarah Lazin Books, 1992), p. 46.

79. Cole, "Why I Quit My TV Show," *Ebony*, 13, no. 4 (February 1958): 29–34. For more history of *The Nat King Cole Show*, see McDonald, *Blacks and White TV*, pp. 57–64.

80. The relationship between black entertainers and *The Ed Sullivan Show* was not always smooth. In February 1961 Nat King Cole refused to appear on the show when producers insisted that he perform one of his standard hits such as "Mona Lisa" instead of a new song, "Illusion," which he wanted to promote on the show. Cole canceled his appearance rather than sing the requested songs. He justified his

decision as follows: "When a variety show begins to dictate what songs an artist of recognition and stature can or cannot do, it is time for that artist to call a 'halt' to the proceedings . . . I feel that my integrity as an artist has been questioned. I will not be dictated to by the producer of any variety show as to what the content of my repertoire is to be." See "Nat Cole Bows Out of Date with Ed Sullivan," *Michigan Chronicle,* February 4, 1961, section B, p. 4.

81. The Ford Motor Company was sole sponsor of the show until June 1957. Multiple sponsors supported the show for the subsequent fourteen seasons it was on the air. Ford's sponsorship was unique in the show's history, however, in that it saved the program from early cancellation. See "Guide to the Ed Sullivan Papers," State Historical Society of Wisconsin, Madison, p. 10.

82. Albert J. Dunmore, " 'Bridge Builders' Cited for Service to the Community," *Michigan Chronicle,* February, 27, 1965.

83. Langston Hughes, "Draft Ideas," December 3, 1964, Langston Hughes Papers, Beinecke Library, Yale University.

84. For more background on the 1964 Harlem race riot, see Arthur I. Washkow, *From Race Riot to Sit-In, 1919 and the 1960s: A Study in the Connections between Conflict and Violence* (New York: Anchor Books, 1967), pp. 255–257; Truman Nelson, *The Torture of Mothers* (Boston: Beacon Press, 1965); and Fred C. Shapiro and James W. Sullivan, *Race Riots, New York 1964.* (New York: Crowell, 1964). For more on Hughes at this time, see Rampersad, *Langston Hughes,* pp. 378–379. The poem "Death in Yorkville (James Powell, Summer, 1964)" can be found in Langston Hughes, *The Panther and the Lash* (New York: Alfred A. Knopf, 1967), p. 15.

85. Letter to Langston Hughes from Margaret Danner, July 25, 1964, Langston Hughes Correspondence.

4. "Afro-American Music, without Apology"

1. Langston Hughes, ed., *New Negro Poets, U.S.A.* (Bloomington: Indiana University Press, 1964), p. 13; Langston Hughes, "Draft Ideas," December 3, 1964, Langston Hughes Papers, Beinecke Library, Yale University.

2. Program for the Afro-American Broadcasting and Recording Company First Annual Dignity Projection and Scholarship Awards Night, February 14, 1965, p. 3, Detroit Commission on Community Relations Collection, part 3, box 18, folder "Black Muslims," Walter P. Reuther Library, Wayne State University.

3. Jackie Gleason was one of the few white honorees. The awards committee recognized him, "for continuing to afford a nationwide television showcase for Afro-American thespians in non-racially specialized settings." Program for Dignity Awards, p. 8.

4. The scholarship fund was officially named the Charles P. Howard Scholarship Fund, and the awards given for the evening were called "Howards." Howard, a syndicated writer for the Afro-American Newspaper chain and a columnist for the

Muhammad Speaks newspaper, inspired the award. Among Howard's accomplishments, he was the first "fully accredited American Negro correspondent at the United Nations"; he founded a news syndicate to newspapers in Africa and Latin America; and he was a pioneer in radio news. Program for Dignity Awards, pp. 1–3.

5. When Henry first produced Malcolm X's *Grass Roots* album, he released it on his Grass Roots, L.P. Co. label. The "Afro-American Recording Label" did not appear until late 1964. Today, the album is still in circulation through the Africana World Recording Co., a Detroit label, located on Livernois and owned by Edward Vaughn.

6. Program for Dignity Awards, pp. 2–5.

7. Panel discussion, WINS Radio, February 18, 1965, in Steve Clark, ed., *February 1965: The Final Speeches of Malcolm X* (New York: Pathfinder, 1992), p. 200.

8. Malcolm X was upset that he had to appear before the audience in "inappropriate attire." At the beginning of the speech, he said: "So I ask you to excuse my appearance. I don't normally come out in front of people without a shirt and tie. I guess that's somewhat a holdover from the Black Muslim movement, which I was in. That's one of the good aspects of that movement. It teaches you to be very careful and conscious of how you look, which is a positive contribution on their part. But that positive contribution on their part is greatly offset by too many other liabilities." Malcolm also mentioned that soon after the bombing he had been given some medication that made him drowsy and explained that the drug might cause him to "stutter or slow down" throughout his speech. Clark, *February 1965*, pp. 76, 86–88, 101–105.

9. David Ritz, *Divided Soul: The Life of Marvin Gaye* (New York: Da Capo Press, 1991), p. 106.

10. Austin's entire remark was, "We've still a long way to go before Brotherhood Week is a Celebration and not a Confessional. We have good reason to be wary of people who go about all year in their private lives making hay, often resorting to shameful exploitation and then get very pious about charity during the Torch Fund Drive or very strong about brotherhood during Brotherhood Week once a year." "Austin Speaks on Brotherhood," *Michigan Chronicle*, March 6, 1965, section A, p. 7.

11. Ibid.

12. Cole's comments appeared in one article in a series that eulogized his life in the *Chicago Defender* in February 1965. The article sought to defend Cole's reputation as a concerned citizen. Near the end of his life, Cole contributed at least $25,000 to the construction of the Los Angeles Music Center, the cultural complex first proposed by Dorothy Chandler. Cole's remarks reflected his belief most people do not expect entertainers to exhibit "civic pride" by contributing monetary gifts to assist in the construction of cultural institutions. Cole commented that people only "expect the doctors, lawyers, the businessmen to be there." The article interpreted

Cole's generosity as evidence that he, contrary to some criticisms he received throughout his life of being an Uncle Tom, cared about social causes, contributed to organizations such as the NAACP, and supported musical culture in Los Angeles by giving to the Music Center fund. The article also included another quote from Cole: "I walk in the world, but I'm not usually in it, a nonentity once off-stage. That's why I'm delighted to work with The Music Center. To take time. Take pride. Prove that entertainers would like to be involved citizens and—maybe most of all—advance the appreciation of all music." A. S. "Doc" Young, "Singer's Legacy," *Chicago Defender,* February 27, 1965, p. 2. As to his biography, the exact year of Cole's birth has been disputed by different sources and has ranges from 1915 to 1919. For details, see Leslie Gourse, *Unforgettable: The Life and Mystique of Nat King Cole* (New York: St. Martin's Press, 1991), p. xi.

13. James Haskins with Kathleen Benson, *Nat King Cole* (New York: Stein and Day, 1984), p. 17.

14. Ibid., pp. 17–22.

15. For more background on Cole's musical contributions to the swing era, see David W. Stowe, *Swing Changes: Big Band in New Deal America* (Cambridge, Mass.: Harvard University Press, 1994), pp. 191–194.

16. A legend surrounding the inception of Cole's singing career held that a drunken patron at the Swanee Inn demanded that Cole sing "Sweet Lorraine." Cole's second wife, Maria, cleared up the rumor in her biography of her husband. She cites a radio interview in which Cole described his early singing as a device to add variety to his instrumental performances. Maria Cole with Louie Robinson, *Nat King Cole: An Intimate Biography* (New York: William Morrow, 1971), p. 41.

17. Cole sold all of his rights to the royalties of "Straighten Up and Fly Right" in 1937. When the song became a million-selling hit in 1944, he attempted to regain some of his rights to the song but was thwarted. For further discussion, see Haskins, *Nat King Cole,* p. 41.

18. Ibid., p. 78.

19. Ibid., pp. 77–83.

20. "The South: Unscheduled Appearance," *Time,* April 23, 1956, p. 31. For a detailed discussion of the attack, see Brian Ward, *Just My Soul Responding: Rhythm and Blues, Black Consciousness, and Race Relations* (Berkeley: University of California Press, 1998), pp. 95–105, 130–134.

21. Police reports also mentioned that the council claimed that over one hundred and fifty men agreed to participate in the attack, but only six showed up the night of the performance. The large discrepancy between the figures casts doubt on exactly how many people were involved. Carter also asserted that rock and roll music was "the basic, heavy-beat music of Negroes. It appeals to the base in man, brings out animalism and vulgarity." "Alabama: Who the Hoodlums Are," *Newsweek,* April 23, 1956, p. 32.

22. Haskins, *Nat King Cole,* p. 139. *Newsweek,* April 23, 1956, p. 32.

23. In the essay Hughes presents his critique of Cole's actions through a dialogue with "Simple." In these dialogues Hughes participates as the rational, intellectual outsider, and his character, "Simple," represents the "genius of the black folk." See Arnold Rampersad, *The Life of Langston Hughes*, vol. 2, *1941–1967: I Dream a World* (New York: Oxford University Press, 1988), pp. 64–65. In this particular dialogue Hughes's voice acknowledges that Cole's apparent calm public acceptance of the attack was probably constructed by his white press agents. Nevertheless, "Simple" debates Hughes about Cole's decision to perform in the South under segregated conditions. Hughes, "Simple: Does King Cole Still Sing, 'Straighten Up and Fly Right'?" *Chicago Defender*, April 28, 1956, p. 10.

24. Cole biographer Leslie Gourse notes that the songwriters did not know if Cole would like the song, because he tended to avoid "special material with messages." Gourse, *Unforgettable*, pp. 191–192.

25. Bill Lane, "Nat Cole Defends Stars Who Shun Dixie Racial Picket Lines," *Chicago Defender*, May 11–17, 1963. Cole was involved in campaigns to desegregate concerts as early as 1947. See Stowe, *Swing Changes*, pp. 236–237. In 1962 Cole organized a road show entitled "Sights and Sounds: The Merry World of Nat King Cole," which featured an interracial cast of young singers and dancers. The troupe traveled throughout the country for three years from 1962 to 1965. When the troupe performed in the South, it was the first time Cole appeared in the region since the Birmingham incident of 1956. According to biographer James Haskins, the success of the show was proof to Cole that "racial relations could change and that the best tactic for promoting change was a professionalism that invited the respect of one's fellow human beings, whatever their color." Haskins, *Nat King Cole*, p. 159. See also Gourse, *Unforgettable*, p. 215.

26. Berry Gordy, *To Be Loved: The Music, the Magic, the Memories of Motown* (New York: Warner Books, 1994), p. 124.

27. Raynoma Gordy Singleton, *Berry, Me, and Motown* (Chicago: Contemporary Books, 1990), p. 53.

28. Allan Slutsky (Dr. Licks), *Standing in the Shadows of Motown: The Life and Music of Legendary Bassist James Jamerson* (Milwaukee: Hal Leonard Publishing, 1989), p. 16.

29. Ibid., pp. 81–83.

30. Mary Wilson, *Dreamgirl: My Life as a Supreme* (New York: St. Martin's Press, 1986), p. 24.

31. Ibid., p. 59.

32. Ibid., p. 28; Otis Williams with Patricia Romanowski, *Temptations* (New York: G. P. Putnam's Sons, 1988), p. 21. The perfect acoustics of the housing project architecture can be attributed to its concrete construction. Eleanor Manlove, a former tenant of the Brewster Projects, remembers, "The floors were cement, and they just left the bare cement showing. The whole place was cement—the walls, the floors. They were sort of gray. You had to have rugs." See "Discussion of Life in the Brewster Hous-

ing Projects: Gloria Manlove Hunter and Eleanor Manlove," in Elaine Latzman Moon, ed., *Untold Tales, Unsung Heroes: An Oral History of Detroit's African-American Community, 1918–1967* (Detroit: Wayne State University Press, 1994), p. 323.

33. Wilson, *Dreamgirl*, p. 14.

34. Martha Reeves with Mark Bego, *Dancing in the Street: Confessions of a Motown Diva* (New York: Hyperion Books, 1994), p. 21.

35. William (Smokey) Robinson with David Ritz, *Smokey: Inside My Life* (New York: McGraw-Hill, 1989), p. 47. For more on Motown and music education in Detroit's public schools, see Gerald Early, *One Nation under a Groove: Motown and American Culture* (Hopewell, N.J.: Ecco Press, 1995), pp. 76–78.

36. Singleton, *Berry, Me, and Motown*, pp. 12–13, 113–114; Wilson, *Dreamgirl*, pp. 50, 59.

37. Reeves, *Dancing*, p. 32; Slutsky, *Standing in the Shadows of Motown*, p. 5; Latzman Moon, *Untold Tales*, p. 240.

38. Latzman Moon, *Untold Tales*, p. 241.

39. Allan Slutsky, "Motown: The History of a Hit-Making Sound and the Keyboardists Who Made It Happen," *Keyboard*, 19, no. 5, issue 205, p. 102.

40. Slutsky, *Standing in the Shadows of Motown*, p. 21.

41. Slutsky also notes that Jamerson often alternated between playing his upright acoustic bass and his Fender electric bass, "sometimes playing his acoustic on a track and then overdubbing his electric on top of it for added punch." Ibid., pp. 12–13.

42. Ibid., p. 30.

43. Ibid., pp. 30, 41–42.

44. According to Nelson George, Diana Ross was the first black person to be hired to bus tables at Hudson's restaurant. Nelson George, *Where Did Our Love Go? The Rise and Fall of the Motown Sound* (New York: St. Martin's Press, 1985), p. 81; Reeves, *Dancing*, p. 47; Slutsky, "Motown," p. 88.

45. Rivers's poem is in the May 1965 issue of *Negro Digest*, p. 19. The Soul label existed from 1964 to 1978. Shorty Long, who had hits with "Devil in the Blue Dress," "Function at the Junction," and "Here Comes the Judge," Gladys Knight and the Pips, and Jimmy Ruffin all recorded on the label. David Bianco, *Heatwave: The Motown Fact Book* (Ann Arbor, Mich.: Popular Culture, 1988), p. 163.

46. The name changes continued after 1965. In 1969 *Billboard* changed the name again to "Soul" and then to "Black" in June 1982. Finally, in 1990, the magazine returned yet again to "Rhythm and Blues." "*Billboard* Adopts 'R&B' as New Name for Two Charts" *Billboard*, October, 27, 1990.

47. Steve Chapple and Reebee Garofalo, *Rock 'n' Roll Is Here to Pay: The History and Politics of the Music Industry* (Chicago: Nelson-Hall, 1977), pp. 236–237.

48. In the film *Malcolm X* (1992), director Spike Lee depicts a dance on the eve of Malcolm X's assassination in which young, black teenagers dance to "Shotgun"

in the same hotel where the black nationalist leader hides from the individuals following him. The urgent beat and lyrics of the song foreshadow the violence to come. See *Malcolm X*, Warner Brothers Video, 1993.

49. Gordy, *To Be Loved*, p. 209.

50. Early, *One Nation under a Groove*, pp. 60–62.

51. While there has never been a Broadway musical based on original Motown music, the 1982 musical *Dreamgirls* was loosely based on the story of the Supremes, although it had an original score. Gordy, *To Be Loved*, p. 209.

52. " 'Rock 'n' Roll': The Sound of the Sixties," *Time*, May 21, 1965, pp. 84–88.

53. Motown also marketed its music through other means beyond standard radio airplay. In 1964 several of the company's hit singles became the soundtrack of the independent film *Nothing but a Man*, directed by Michael Roemer. The film depicts the daily struggles of a young black couple, portrayed by Ivan Dixon and Abbey Lincoln, to make a life for themselves in the rural South. The film got wide distribution in early 1965 and was very popular with black audiences. Motown's participation in the project illustrates how the company marketed its music to multiple audiences simultaneously.

54. The Temptations' "My Girl" was followed by Junior Walker and the All Stars' "Shotgun," Marvin Gaye's "I'll Be Doggone," the Supremes' "Back in My Arms Again," and the Four Tops' "I Can't Help Myself." Joel Whitburn, *Joel Whitburn's Top R&B Singles, 1942–1988* (Menomonee Falls, Wisc.: Record Research Inc., 1988), p. 602. Motown songs also continued to top *Billboard*'s pop chart, but not with the frequency or duration of their dominance on the R&B chart. From January to July 1965, four of the fifteen songs to reach number one on the pop chart were from Hitsville: the Temptations' "My Girl," the Supremes' "Stop! In the Name of Love" and "Back in My Arms Again," and the Four Tops' "I Can't Help Myself." See Joel Whitburn, *The Billboard Book of Top 40 Hits* (New York: Billboard Publications, 1987).

55. In 1966 the Supremes' ability to capture Cole's market was confirmed when the group set a new house attendance record during an engagement at the Fairmont Hotel in San Francisco. At the time Florence Ballard commented, "They told us that we broke Nat King Cole's mark during our stay there. Imagine! When I was a little girl I listened to him all the time. I loved him—the way he sang, the way you could hear every word. Now we're breaking Nat Cole's records." "Supremes Are Tops," *Ebony*, 21, no. 10 (August 1966): 152–154.

56. Gordy, *To Be Loved*, pp. 221–222.

57. Robert Conot, *Rivers of Blood, Years of Darkness* (New York: Bantam Books, 1967), pp. 11–16; Jerry Cohen and William S. Murphy, *Burn, Baby, Burn! The Los Angeles Race Riot, August, 1965* (New York: E. P. Dutton, 1966), pp. 317–318.

58. Ritz, *Divided Soul*, pp. 106–107.

59. Ibid., p. 107.

60. "Martha and the Vandellas," *Ebony*, 23, no. 4 (February 1968): 83–88. Reeves, *Dancing*, p. 62.

61. Throughout my research, I have heard stories that Martha and the Vandellas' music, particularly the songs "Dancing in the Street" and "Heatwave," was banned from the radio waves in Los Angeles during the Watts uprising. I have not been able to confirm these legends as fact. On a related point, several scholars have made reference to the expression "Burn, Baby, Burn!" in their analysis of Watts. The expression was first coined by the "Magnificent Montague," a disc jockey at KGFJ, the largest black radio station in Los Angeles. Montague used the expression to introduce songs and as general banter. As he explained, "Burn, Baby, Burn!" was used to get his listeners in a receptive, hip mood and was similar to saying, "Cool it" or "What's happening?" When the violence broke out on the streets and participants appropriated the phrase as a rallying cry, Montague ceased using the expression altogether. See Cohen and Murphy, *Burn, Baby, Burn!* pp. 83–84 and Conot, *Rivers of Blood*, p. 219.

62. Ronald Snellings, "Rhythm and Blues as a Weapon," *Liberator*, 5, no. 10 (October 1965): 6–8.

63. Langston Hughes, "Black Writers in a Troubled World," Public Appearances, box 7, Langston Hughes Papers.

64. Rampersad, *Langston Hughes*, pp. 400–403. "Festival Scrapbook," *Negro Digest*, 15, no. 10 (August 1966): 85–90.

65. Albert B. Cleage Jr., "Abbey Lincoln and Black Nationalism," *Illustrated News*, December 3, 1962, pp. 3–4. Max Roach became a leading spokesperson on this topic after he released his 1960 album, *We Insist—The Freedom Now Suite*, which was quite popular in Detroit's activist circles. Interview with Grace Lee Boggs, July 12, 1994, Detroit, Michigan. See also Max Roach, "What 'Jazz' Means to Me," in Gerald Early, ed., *Speech and Power: The African-American Essay and Its Cultural Content from Polemics to Pulpit*, vol. 2 (Hopewell, N.J.: Ecco Press, 1993), pp. 50–54. Abbey Lincoln returned to Detroit in February 1963 for a "Naturally '63" fashion show at Mr. Kelley's Lounge. At the show, Lincoln promoted African fashions and natural Afro hairstyles. An early effort at the celebration of black styles and Afrocentric apparel, the "Naturally '63" meeting predates more famous campaigns to promote the concept that "Black is beautiful." For further discussion, see William L. Van Deburg, *New Day in Babylon: The Black Power Movement and American Culture, 1965–1975* (Chicago: University of Chicago Press, 1992).

66. "Freedom Now Party: Draft National Platform," *Liberator*, February 1964, pp. 4–5.

67. *Liberator*, July 1966, pp. 10–11.

68. Boone House disbanded when Margaret Danner left Detroit in 1964 to return to her native Chicago. Danner and Randall maintained their relationship as poets, however. In December 1966 Randall's Broadside Press published the book *Poem Counterpoem*. The book was a collection of poems by Randall and Danner that

were paired by theme. For more background on the project, see A. X. Nicholas, "A Conversation with Dudley Randall," *Black World*, 21, no. 2 (December 1971): 26–34.

69. Gordy, *To Be Loved*, p. 103; Melba Joyce Boyd, "Detroit's Black Unicorn: Dudley Randall and Broadside Press," unpublished manuscript presented at the American Studies Association Conference, Boston, Mass., November 1993; copy in author's possession; Nicholas, "Conversation with Randall," p. 31.

70. Nicholas, "Conversation with Randall," p. 31. For further analysis of this Broadside Series, see James Sullivan, "Real Cool Pages: The Broadside Press Broadside Series," *Contemporary Literature*, 32, no. 4 (1991): 553–572; Julius E. Thompson, *Dudley Randall, Broadside Press, and the Black Arts Movement in Detroit* (Jefferson, N.C. McFarland, 1997).

71. Dudley Randall, *Broadside Memories: Poets I Have Known* (Detroit: Broadside Press, 1975), pp. 23–24. *For Malcolm* featured the work of several Detroit poets including Oliver LaGrone and John Sinclair. Sinclair, a white poet, acted as editor of the Artist's Workshop Press in Detroit, another significant independent publishing venture. Sinclair was also a leader in the city's arts community who believed strongly in art's political influence. In his biographical sketch Sinclair writes, "like Archie Shepp said about his music, *all* my work is for Malcolm." Dudley Randall and Margaret Burroughs, eds., *For Malcolm: Poems on the Life and Death of Malcolm X* (Detroit: Broadside Press, 1967), p. 110.

72. Randall, *Broadside Memories*, p. 28.

73. *Program of the Second Annual Black Arts Convention* (Detroit: Forum 66, 1967), p. 3, Walter P. Reuther Library, Wayne State University; Betty De Ramus, "A Dead Leader, Injured Worker Star in Forum 66," *Michigan Chronicle*, July 2, 1966. Dudley Randall, "Assembly in Detroit: Report on the Black Arts Convention," *Negro Digest*, August 1966, p. 58.

74. *New York Times*, June 8, 1966, p. 26.

75. Martin Luther King Jr., *Where Do We Go from Here: Chaos or Community?* (New York: Harper and Row, 1967), pp. 25–26. For further discussion of the march, see Robert Weisbrot, *Freedom Bound: A History of America's Civil Rights Movement* (New York: Penguin Books, 1990), pp. 196–204; and David Garrow, *Bearing the Cross: Martin Luther King, Jr., and the Southern Christian Leadership Conference* (New York: Vintage Books, 1988), pp. 475–488.

76. While he did not organize Freedom Day, the Reverend C. L. Franklin supported the event and promoted it on his weekly Sunday radio broadcast. Robbie L. McCoy, "Reverend King Invites All to Attend Freedom Rally," *Michigan Chronicle*, June 18, 1966, p. 1.

77. Betty De Ramus, "Mounting Nationalism Distresses Dr. M. L. King," *Michigan Chronicle*, June 25, 1966, p. 1; See also Garrow, *Bearing the Cross*, p. 482.

78. The Black Power rallies were organized by two new groups: the Northern Student Movement (NSM) and the Afro-American Unity Movement, led by Alvin

Harrison, who came to Detroit from New York. See "Black Power Chant Links Mississippi to Detroit," *Michigan Chronicle,* July 9, 1966; and Sidney Fine, *Violence in the Model City: The Cavanagh Administration, Race Relations, and the Detroit Riot of 1967* (Ann Arbor: University of Michigan Press, 1989), p. 29.

79. In his speech Carmichael also argued, "Don't you ever apologize for any black person who throws a molotov cocktail, and don't call them riots—they're rebellions." Carol Schmidt, "Did Stokely Carmichael Miss Anyone Saturday?" *Michigan Chronicle,* August 6, 1966. See also Fine, *Violence in the Model City,* p. 26.

80. One example of the tone of this coverage was *Look* magazine's feature on Mayor Cavanagh. The cover story, entitled "Our Sick Cities and How They Can Be Cured," included a separate article, "The Mayor Who Woke Up a City," which gave Cavanagh's tenure as mayor a glowing review. See also Stanley H. Brown, "Slow Healing of a Fractured City," *Fortune,* 71, no. 6 (June 1965): 142–145, 246–262; *U.S. News and World Report,* May 23, 1966; *Wall Street Journal,* August 12, 1964; *Los Angeles Times,* February 6, 1966; and Fine, *Violence in the Model City,* pp. 33–34.

81. "Citizens and Officials Apprehensive: Can It Happen In Detroit?" *Michigan Chronicle,* July 23, 1966, p. 1.

82. "Rapport Lowers between Negro, White Detroiters," *Michigan Chronicle,* July 23, 1966; "CRC Report Cites Police Bias," *Michigan Chronicle,* July 2, 1966, p. 1.

83. For detailed discussion of the Kercheval incident, see Fine, *Violence in the Model City,* pp. 135–143.

84. Coleman Young with Lonnie Wheeler, *Hard Stuff: The Autobiography of Coleman Young* (New York: Viking Press, 1994), pp. 167–168.

85. Whitburn, *Top R&B Singles, 1942–1988,* p. 454; Whitburn, *Billboard's Top 10 Charts,* p. 54.

86. Ritz, *Divided Soul,* pp. 102–106.

87. In the speech Hughes referred to Léopold Sédar Sengor's poem "To the American Negro Troops," which includes the line, "You I salute as messengers of peace!"

5. "The Happening"

1. Mary Wilson, *Dreamgirl: My Life as a Supreme* (New York: St. Martin's Press, 1986), p. 236.

2. Ibid., p. 242.

3. Ballard also participated in national public appearances. In July 1967 the Supremes visited Vice President Hubert Humphrey in Washington, D.C. The group helped Humphrey dedicate a swimming pool at a government housing project. "The Supremes Meet H.H.H.," *Michigan Chronicle,* July 8, 1967, p. 1.

4. Joe Darden, Richard Child Hill, June Thomas, and Richard Thomas, *Detroit: Race and Uneven Development* (Philadelphia: Temple University Press, 1987), p. 57.

5. Internal memo #232, April 14, 1967, United Foundation Papers, box 23, folder 23-4, Walter P. Reuther Library, Wayne State University. "The Happening" was also the theme song for the 1967 film *The Happening*, which starred Anthony Quinn and Faye Dunaway and was directed by Elliot Silverstein.

6. *It's Happening*, 1967 United Foundation Film, United Foundation Papers.

7. For more on police brutality in the Twelfth Street neighborhood, see "Discussion on Twelfth Street Businesses: Bernard Odell and Odis Rencher," in Elaine Latzman Moon, *Untold Tales, Unsung Heroes: An Oral History of Detroit's African-American Community, 1918–1967* (Detroit: Wayne State University, 1994), p. 342.

8. Latzman Moon, *Untold Tales*, p. 363. For further discussion about the race and class dimensions of the disturbance, see Sidney Fine, *Violence in the Model City: The Cavanagh Administration, Race Relations, and the Detroit Riot of 1967* (Ann Arbor: University of Michigan Press, 1989), pp. 291, 351–353.

9. *Violence in the Model City*, p. 207.

10. Ibid., p. 233; Of the statistics cited, only the number of people arrested and killed can be confirmed. Figures for numbers of people injured and property damage vary widely depending on the source, and they often do not account for unofficial or unrecorded incidents (e.g., injuries that were not treated in a hospital or property damage that was not reported or covered by insurance). For more details, see ibid., pp. 296–301.

11. Ironically, the press quoted both Mayor Cavanagh and Governor Romney after the Watts rebellion when they proclaimed, "it can't *happen* here." The catch phrase came to haunt the city in 1967 and reverberated eerily in the Supremes' hit song. For Cavanagh's and Romney's comments, see Henry Hampton and Steve Fayer, *Voices of Freedom: An Oral History of the Civil Rights Movement from the 1950s to the 1980s* (New York: Bantam, 1990), p. 373.

12. "Supremes' Pitch Is in Tempo with the Torch Drive," *Michigan Chronicle*, August 12, 1967.

13. In its 1967 annual report, the United Foundation presented the exact figures of the Torch Drive campaign and their significance. The organization raised "a pledged total of $27,573,109 exceeding the highest goal ever set by more than $1,200,000. This was not only the United Foundation's finest accomplishment in 1967, but, in light of the conditions in this community at that time, it may well rank as the finest accomplishment this organization has ever achieved." See "The Nineteenth Annual Report of the United Foundation," United Foundation Papers.

14. "United Foundation Cites Motown Prexy," *Detroit Courier*, November 18, 1967.

15. Memorandum from Fred Campbell, "Campaign Difficulties," November 2, 1967, United Foundation Papers, box 22, folder 22-16.

16. The connection between the sentiments of the song and Detroit's shock about the rebellion can be seen in a speech given by Mayor Cavanagh several months after the event. In the speech Cavanagh discussed his feelings about how the riot had affected him personally and Detroit in general in psychological terms. He described the event as a "serious trauma . . . [t]he impact was even more severe because we as Detroiters had, perhaps, been lulled into a false sense of security. It was our belief . . . that we had made remarkable progress in achieving some measure of harmony and tranquillity . . . But the riot told us that much of what we called progress was only illusory." "Remarks by Mayor Jerome P. Cavanagh at the 22nd Annual Meeting of the National Association of Independent Insurers, 2:30 P.M., Wednesday, November 1, 1967, Americana Hotel, Bar Harbour, Florida," pp. 5–6, Jerome P. Cavanagh Papers, Archives of Labor and Urban Affairs, Wayne State University.

17. *Program of the Second Annual Black Arts Convention* (Detroit: Forum 66, 1967), Walter P. Reuther Library, Wayne State University; see also "Black Arts Convention Has 'Self Help' Theme," *Michigan Chronicle,* July 1, 1967.

18. A representative from the Cincinnati SNCC delegation also reportedly declared, "We already had our riot and we're here to show you how it's done." "Report on Riots, Civil and Criminal Disorders," *Hearings before the Committee on Government Operations,* U.S. Senate, 90th Cong., 2d sess., March 21–22, 1968, pt. 6, pp. 1415–1416; Robert Conot, *American Odyssey* (New York: William Morrow, 1974), p. 529; Fine, *Violence in the Model City,* p. 30.

19. Coleman Young with Lonnie Wheeler, *Hard Stuff: The Autobiography of Coleman Young* (New York: Viking Press, 1994), p. 22.

20. Paul Gilroy, "One Nation under a Groove: The Cultural Politics of 'Race' and Racism in Britain," in David Theo Goldberg, ed., *Anatomy of Racism,* (Minneapolis: University of Minnesota Press, 1990), p. 274. For more on the cultural politics of leisure space, see Robin D. G. Kelley, " 'We Are Not What We Seem': Rethinking Black Working-Class Opposition in the Jim Crow South," *Journal of American History,* 80, no. 1 (June 1993): 84–85.

21. For a more detailed discussion about life on Twelfth Street, see Latzman Moon, *Untold Tales,* pp. 343–347, 368–375.

22. Fine, *Violence in the Model City,* p. 155; Hubert G. Locke, *The Detroit Riot of 1967* (Detroit: Wayne State University Press, 1969), p. 26 n.

23. " 'A Known Blind Pig'—Distressing Note," *Michigan Chronicle,* July 11, 1966, editorial page; Fine, *Violence in the Model City,* p. 155; Miller Memorandum to Jacques Feuillan et al., April 14, 1967, series 10, box 46, Records of the National Advisory Commission on Civil Disorders, Lyndon Baines Johnson Presidential Library, Austin, Texas; see also "Capture and Record of Civil Disorder in Detroit, July 23–July 28, 1967," box 345, George Romney Papers, Michigan Historical Collections, Bentley Library, Ann Arbor, Michigan.

24. Fine, *Violence in the Model City,* p. 156.

25. The initial hours of the uprising had a "carnival atmosphere," which was the common pattern of urban disorders at this time. As Sidney Fine notes, participants felt "a giddy sense of release from the oppression of routine, white-dominated life in the ghetto," and as Joyce Carol Oates wrote in her novel *Them*, "[t]he pavement shook with the energy of their enchantment." Fine, *Violence in the Model City*, pp. 155–165; see also Conot, *American Odyssey*, pp. 523–525, and Locke, *Detroit Riot*, pp. 26–27.

26. Fine, *Violence in the Model City*, p. 296.

27. Louis E. Lomax, "Organized Snipers in Riot Given Help by Residents," *Detroit News*, August 8, 1967, p. 1. Three of the accused activists, Edward Vaughn, James Boggs, and Grace Lee Boggs, were not even in Detroit when the rebellion broke out. Vaughn was at a Black Power conference in Newark, New Jersey, and James and Grace Boggs were vacationing in Berkeley, California. As Fine has noted, "[t]he Lomax articles found little support among the well-informed people of Detroit . . . [Editors at the *Michigan Chronicle*] later stated that Lomax had gathered his information from a desk in the offices of the *Chronicle*, had done little investigating on his own, and had invented much of what he reported." Fine, *Violence in the Model City*, pp. 360–361; see also "Editorial on Louis Lomax," *Fifth Estate*, 2, no. 10 (36) (August 15–31, 1967): 1, 11; Hampton and Fayer, *Voices of Freedom*, p. 382; Grace Lee Boggs, *Living for Change: An Autobiography* (Minneapolis: University of Minnesota Press, 1998), p. 138.

28. Milton Henry to Jerome Cavanagh, July 25, 1967, box 393, folder 20, Jerome P. Cavanagh Papers. For more background on the Henry brothers, see Raymond L. Hall, *Black Separatism in the United States* (Hanover, N.H.: University Press of New England, 1978), pp. 129–138; Ernest Dunbar, "The Making of a Militant," *Saturday Review*, December 16, 1972, pp. 25–28.

29. "Malcolm X Society Draws Plans for Twelfth St. Area," *Michigan Chronicle*, August 19, 1967, section A, p. 8; "Malcolmite Society Lists Demands on Insurrection," *Michigan Chronicle*, August 5, 1967, p. 1.

30. Aretha Watkins, "Book Store Destroyed, Witnesses Blame Police," *Michigan Chronicle*, August 5, 1967, section A, p. 4; see also Fine, *Violence in the Model City*, p. 244.

31. Louis E. Lomax, "Lomax Sums Up: Will U.S. Listen Now?" *Detroit News*, August 10, 1967, p. 1.

32. Nelson Blackstock, *Cointelpro: The FBI's Secret War on Political Freedom* (New York: Anchor Foundation, 1988), p. 14. News coverage also noted that the bookstore was rumored to have connections with the Revolutionary Action Movement (RAM), which had been accused of planning to overthrow the government. Vaughn denied these charges saying, "I am not connected with RAM or any other group plotting the overthrow of the government. But if teaching my people pride in their true heritage and providing a place in which they can obtain this information is black nationalism, then I am a black nationalist." Watkins, "Book Store Destroyed," p. 4.

33. Hampton and Fayer, *Voices of Freedom*, p. 382.

34. For complete description of the Fox Theater performance, see Introduction, pp. 1–2. For more on Motown during the rebellion, see Berry Gordy, *To Be Loved: The Music, the Magic, the Memories of Motown* (New York: Warner Books, 1994), p. 248; "Tamla Carries On Right through Detroit Riots," *Melody Maker*, August 5, 1967; Allan Slutsky, "Motown: The History of a Hit-Making Sound and the Keyboardists Who Made It Happen," *Keyboard*, 19, no. 5, issue 205, p. 90.

35. Mickens has also recalled how her father resented the business competition that developed as large department stores began to stock recordings he had sold all his life: "My father developed this hatred against Sears and Roebuck. White society was beginning to get a piece of this black music for the first time. They were beginning to understand the marketability of black music. It drove him crazy that a person could now go to Sears and pay seventy-five cents and buy a record. He had the resentment of a person who thought, 'What are you all interested in our stuff now for?' He didn't like that. He was right." Latzman Moon, *Untold Tales*, pp. 362–364.

36. Fine, *Violence in the Model City*, pp. 271–272; " 'Swinging Time' Comes to the Fox," *Michigan Chronicle*, July 22, 1967; John Hersey, *The Algiers Motel Incident* (New York: Bantam Books, 1968), pp. 64–66.

37. For more details on the Algiers Motel incident, see Hersey, *Algiers Motel Incident*, and Fine, *Violence in the Model City*, pp. 271–290.

38. Hersey, *Algiers Motel Incident*, pp. 295–296.

39. Grace Boggs and James Boggs, "Detroit: Birth of a Nation," *National Guardian*, October 7, 1967, p. 4.

40. The early civil rights movement and black nationalist organizations have a history of using public theater to make political statements and provoke debate. The Free Southern Theater developed in the South as a traveling "freedom school" during the early 1960s. The group performed plays for school children and rural communities about the civil rights campaign and the history of race relations. See Doris Derby, Gilbert Moses, and John O'Neal, "The Need for a Southern Freedom Theatre," *Freedomways*, Winter 1964, pp. 109–112; see also Thomas C. Dent, Gilbert Moses, and Richard Schechner, eds., *The Free Southern Theater by the Free Southern Theater* (Indianapolis: Bobbs-Merrill, 1969). For black nationalists, theater was an equally provocative medium for political expression. In the late 1950s Louis Farrakhan, then Louis X, wrote the play *The Trial* for the Nation of Islam. In the play the "white man" is put on trial for the history of his crimes against black people. Mike Wallace's television documentary on the Nation of Islam, "The Hate That Hate Produced," which aired on July 10, 1959, highlighted the play to illustrate the type of antiwhite sentiments the group promoted. See C. Eric Lincoln, *The Black Muslims in America* (Grand Rapids, Mich.: William B. Eerdmans, 1994), pp. 2, 108. In Detroit black drama found its most fertile growth at the Concept East Theater, first organized by Woodie King. For more background, see "A City Survey: The Arts in Detroit." *Negro*

Digest, November 1962; and *Negro History Bulletin,* 26, no. 1 (October 1962) and 27, no. 5 (February 1964).

41. All of the trials were plagued by postponements and controversy. Ronald August's trial was first postponed from July 1968 to January 1969 because of the publication of John Hersey's book, *The Algiers Motel Incident.* Attorneys argued that the book made a fair trial impossible and also fought for a change of venue due to extensive pretrial publicity. Oakland County Circuit Court Judge William J. Beer granted the request and relocated the trial to Mason, Michigan, where he himself presided. As Sidney Fine has noted, "The population of Mason, the town where Malcolm X's father had been murdered, was 99 percent white." See Fine, *Violence in the Model City,* pp. 287–290.

42. "What Is New Detroit?" Detroit Urban League Collection, box 78, "New Detroit" folder, p. 1, Bentley Library, University of Michigan.

43. Fred Baker, Benjamin Hababee, and Frank H. Joyce, "A NEW Detroit?" *Fifth Estate,* 2, no. 10, issue 36 (August 15–31, 1967): 1, 11.

44. Ibid., p. 11; Boggs and Boggs, "Detroit: Birth of a Nation," p. 4.

45. Gary Blonston, "How Detroit's Militants Are Changing," *Detroit Free Press,* October 1, 1967.

46. "Remarks by Mayor Jerome P. Cavanagh at the 22nd Annual Meeting of the National Association of Independent Insurers, 2:30 P.M., Wednesday, November 1, 1967, Americana Hotel, Bar Harbour, Florida," Jerome P. Cavanagh Papers, Archives of Labor and Urban Affairs, Wayne State University. Cavanagh's suggestion that black Americans living in the urban North should consider returning to the rural South was not unusual; it was a product of new public policy theories that sought to end poverty in America. As historian Nicholas Lemann has documented, President Johnson set up a secret Interagency Task Force on Rural-Urban Migration near the end of his presidency. In 1969 Patrick Moynihan established a White House task force on "internal migration." And, in his 1970 State of the Union address, President Nixon declared, "We must create a new rural environment which will not only stem the migration to urban centers but reverse it." See Nicholas Lemann, *The Promised Land: The Great Black Migration and How It Changed America* (New York: Vintage Books, 1991), p. 211.

47. "People against Racism: A Conversation with the Reverend Albert B. Cleage and Frank Joyce," audio collection, Schomburg Center for Research in Black Culture, New York Public Library.

48. "Motown Prexy Tells Big Expansion Plan," *Detroit Courier,* October 28, 1967, p. 13.

49. Gordy, *To Be Loved,* p. 250; interview with Junius Griffin, July 30, 1993, notes in author's possession; interview with Esther Gordy Edwards, September 27, 1993, notes in author's possession.

50. "Motown Reveals Big Expansion and Diversification Plans," *Jet,* 33, no. 4 (November 2, 1967): 58–60; Nelson George, *Where Did Our Love Go? The Rise and*

Fall of the Motown Sound (New York: St. Martin's Press, 1985), pp. 154–155; Gordy, *To Be Loved*, p. 250.

51. "Motown Reveals Big Expansion and Diversification Plans," p. 60.

52. Comparisons between Detroit's uprising and the battles in Vietnam appeared frequently during the press coverage of the event. See Hampton and Fayer, *Voices of Freedom*, p. 383. See also news footage in "Two Societies: 1965–1968," from *Eyes on the Prize, II: America at the Racial Crossroads*, directed and produced by Sheila Bernard and Sam Pollard (Blackside Productions, 1990).

6. "What's Going On?"

1. The popular press proclaimed Franklin's reign in the world of soul music. In October 1967 *Ebony* magazine ran a lead article entitled "Aretha Franklin—'Soul Sister.' " In June 1968 *Time* magazine featured her on its cover as the "Sound of Soul." See Phyl Garland, "Aretha Franklin—'Soul Sister,' " *Ebony*, 22, no. 12 (October 1967): 47–52; "Lady Soul: Singing It Like It Is," *Time*, June 28, 1968, pp. 62–66.

2. The one song on the album that was a hit, "Today I Sing the Blues," was not a jazz arrangement and went to number ten on the rhythm and blues charts. Peter Guralnick, *Sweet Soul Music: Rhythm and Blues and the Southern Dream of Freedom* (New York: Harper and Row, 1986), p. 336.

3. Even with its musical innovations, the session ended on a sour note when the band began drinking and Franklin's husband, Ted White, objected that there were no black musicians involved. Fights ensued among the producers and musicians, and Aretha and Ted White left the next morning for Detroit before the background vocals could be added. Guralnick, *Sweet Soul Music*, pp. 341–342; Gerri Hirshey, *Nowhere to Run: The Story of Soul Music* (New York: Penguin, 1984), p. 240.

4. The origins of this expression are difficult to determine. In his book *Sweet Soul Music*, p. 345, Guralnick claims that *Ebony* magazine made the declaration, but I have not found any direct reference to this phrase in the publication. *Ebony* did publish a feature on Franklin in its October 1967 issue, but it does not include the quote. See Garland, "Aretha Franklin," pp. 47–54. In her book *Nowhere to Run*, p. 242, Hirshey writes more generally that "[s]ome blacks called a few hot months of 1967 the summer of 'Retha, Rap, and Revolt.' "

5. Rita Griffin, "Thousands Cheer Aretha Franklin at Cobo Arena," *Michigan Chronicle*, February 24, 1968.

6. For a thorough discussion of King's final year, see David Garrow, *Bearing the Cross: Martin Luther King, Jr., and the Southern Christian Leadership Conference* (New York: Vintage, 1988), chap. 11, "The Poor People's Campaign and Memphis, 1967–1968,".

7. According to Nicholas Lemann, "Johnson was furious about the report, not

least because it ruled out the possibility of a conspiracy behind the riots. He felt it put him in an impossible position—he couldn't respond to it in a way that matched the bits of angry language that had gotten into the headlines, and he certainly couldn't get through Congress the billions of dollars' worth of new government programs for the ghettos that the report recommended." See Nicholas Lemann, *The Promised Land: The Great Black Migration and How It Changed America* (New York: Vintage, 1991), p. 191. Roger Wilkins, who was working for the Johnson administration in the U.S. Justice Department when the Kerner Report was released, expressed the frustration many people felt with the president's indifference to the study's findings: "I was astonished at what a terrific job the Kerner Commission did. They worked very hard, they were serious, and they issued an extraordinary report . . . It was a mandate, had the president chosen to take it and say, 'By God, we didn't know how serious the problem was. There is racism in this society, it is deep, and since I have said that I am going to be the president who finishes what Lincoln started,' he could use that as a springboard for more social action. Instead he refused even to have the commission come over and present it to him. Basically he ignored the report, and that was the end of Johnson and me, really." Henry Hampton and Steve Fayer, *Voices of Freedom: An Oral History of the Civil Rights Movement from the 1950s to the 1980s* (New York: Bantam Press, 1990), p. 401.

8. In an interview, given on March 25, 1968, King discussed the significance of the findings of the Kerner Commission and how they provided motivation for the Poor People's Campaign. For a transcript, see "Conversation with Martin Luther King," in Clayborne Carson, David J. Garrow, Vincent Harding, and Darlene Clark Hine, ed., *The Eyes on the Prize Civil Rights Reader* (New York: Penguin Books, 1991), pp. 393–409.

9. Al Dunmore, "Motown Moving Offices to Downtown Building," *Michigan Chronicle*, March 23, 1968.

10. Ibid., "Floyd Johnson Directs Motown Modernization," *Michigan Chronicle*, April 6, 1968.

11. Some observers have speculated that Motown's move away from West Grand Boulevard emerged out of fear of the neighborhood after the 1967 unrest. While the theory might have some validity, it has never been confirmed, and Gordy representatives deny it completely. For more on the move, see Raynoma Gordy Singleton, *Berry, Me, and Motown: The Untold Story* (Chicago: Contemporary Books, 1990), p. 168.

12. William H. Chafe, *Unfinished Journey: America since World War II* (New York: Oxford University Press, 1991), p. 366.

13. Hampton and Fayer, *Voices of Freedom*, pp. 473–474; Berry Gordy, *To Be Loved: The Music, the Magic, the Memories of Motown* (New York: Warner Books, 1994), p. 250.

14. "Mrs. King Cites Gordy in Atlanta Spectacular," *Michigan Chronicle*, May 18, 1968. See also Mary Wilson, *Dreamgirl: My Life as a Supreme* (New York: St.

Martin's Press, 1986), pp. 259–261; Otis Williams with Patricia Romanowski, *Temptations* (New York: G. P. Putnam's Sons, 1988), pp. 130–132; Gordy, *To Be Loved*, p. 251.

15. Charles Fager, *Uncertain Resurrection* (Grand Rapids, Mich.: William B. Eerdman, 1969), p. 105.

16. Charlayne A. Hunter, "On the Case of Resurrection City," in Clayborne Carson, et. al., eds., *The Eyes on the Prize Civil Rights Reader,* (New York: Penguin Books, 1991), pp. 426–438.

17. From April 5 through April 11, the Detroit police made 2,074 arrests: 517 were white, 199 were women, and 189 were juveniles. According to Sidney Fine, "Detroit was able to quell its disturbance with only one death, injuries to twenty-two persons, fifty-five incendiary fires, a minimum of looting, and property damage of only a little more than $80,000." See Fine, *Violence in the Model City: The Cavanagh Administration, Race Relations, and the Detroit Riot of 1967* (Ann Arbor: University of Michigan Press, 1989), pp. 402–405.

18. Jerome P. Cavanagh, Draft of "Detroit Is Happening" speech, July 1, 1968, box 428, Jerome P. Cavanagh Papers, Walter P. Reuther Library, Wayne State University.

19. "Detroit Is Happening" brochure, box 428, Jerome P. Cavanagh Papers; "It's 'I Care about Detroit' Sunday," *Detroit Free Press*, August 8, 1969.

20. "I Care about Detroit" was written by Jimmy Clark and Jack Combs and produced by Smokey Robinson and Al Cleveland. Motown rereleased it on *Smokey Robinson and the Miracles: The Thirty-fifth Anniversary Collection* (Detroit: Motown Record Company, 1994).

21. Fine, *Violence in the Model City,* p. 406; See also "Detroit Is Happening," August 29, 1968, and "Detroit Is Happening Report: Summer 1968," box 428, Jerome P. Cavanagh Papers.

22. "Detroit Is Happening" brochure; "Detroit Is Happening Report: Summer 1968."

23. For more on Motown's various civic efforts, see Peter Benjaminson, *The Story of Motown* (New York: Grove Press, 1979), p. 105; Brian Ward, *Just My Soul Responding: Rhythm and Blues, Black Consciousness, and Race Relations* (Berkeley: University of California Press, 1998), p. 397.

24. Seven people (five blacks and two whites) were fired as a result of the wildcat strike. All except two, General G. Baker Jr. and Bennie Tate (both black), were eventually rehired. James A. Geschwender, *Class, Race, and Worker Insurgency: The League of Revolutionary Black Workers* (Cambridge: Cambridge University Press, 1977), p. 89.

25. Dan Georgakas and Marvin Surkin, *Detroit: I Do Mind Dying* (New York: St. Martin's Press, 1975), pp. 15–22; "The Split in the League of Revolutionary Black Workers: Three Lines and Three Headquarters," Dan Georgakas Collection, box 4, folder 4-11, p. 4, Walter P. Reuther Library, Wayne State University.

26. "Black Editor: An Interview," *Radical America*, 2, no. 4 (July–August 1968): 30–38.

27. Georgakas and Surkin, *Detroit*, pp. 83–84.

28. For more discussion of this strike, see the Introduction and Edward Lee, "Whoever Heard of Bongo Drums on the Picket Line?" James and Grace Lee Boggs Papers, box 5, folder 4, Walter P. Reuther Library, Wayne State University; Georgakas and Surkin, *Detroit*, pp. 129–157; Ernie Allen, "Dying from the Inside: The Decline of the League of Revolutionary Black Workers," in Dick Cluster, ed., *They Should Have Served that Cup of Coffee* (Boston: South End Press, 1979), pp. 71–109.

29. In 1968 John Watson, the editor of the *Inner City Voice*, was elected editor of the *South End*, Wayne State University's campus newspaper. Watson used the large campus paper—with a $100,000 budget and circulation of 18,000—to further the cause of DRUM. As Dan Georgakas and Marvin Surkin have written, "Watson had a bold vision of how the *South End* could be used. His term as editor proved to be one of the most successful examples in the late sixties of how a black could lead a principled coalition of black and white forces struggling within a major institution." The *Inner City Voice* continued to be published during this period, but somewhat irregularly. Georgakas and Surkin, *Detroit*, pp. 22, 55.

30. The entire article is quite short and does contain an anti-Semitic comment that Motown's only contribution to the black community was "[to save] Motown's stable of talent from Abe, Hymie and Sol [p]erhaps." John Cosby Jr., "How U Sound Motown," *Inner City Voice: Detroit's Black Community Newspaper*, 1, no. 3 (December 15, 1967): 11, Labadie Collection, University of Michigan.

31. Interestingly, the same journalist wrote both *Fortune* articles. See Stanley H. Brown, "The Motown Sound of Money," *Fortune*, 74, no. 9 (September 1, 1967): 103–108, 186, 188–189; Stanley H. Brown, "Slow Healing of a Fractured City," *Fortune*, 71, no. 6 (June 1965): 142–145, 246–262; "United Foundation Cites Motown Prexy," *Detroit Courier*, November 18, 1967; "Motown Reveals Big Expansion and Diversification Plans," *Jet*, 33, no. 4, (November 2, 1967): 58–60.

32. Nelson George, *Where Did Our Love Go? The Rise and Fall of the Motown Sound* (New York: St. Martin's Press, 1985), pp. 107, 149–150; Wilson, *Dreamgirl*, p. 258; Gordy, *To Be Loved*, p. 160.

33. David Bianco, *Heatwave: The Motown Factbook* (Ann Arbor, Mich.: Popular Culture, Ink., 1988), pp. 35–37.

34. Jack Ryan, *Recollections, the Detroit Years: The Motown Sound by the People Who Made It* (Detroit: Whitlaker Marketing, 1982), section 39.

35. Wilson, *Dreamgirl*, pp. 102–103.

36. Several Motown artists recall the meeting in their memoirs: see Wilson, *Dreamgirl*, p. 258; Singleton, *Berry, Me, and Motown*, p. 173; Williams, *Temptations*, p. 136.

37. Singleton, *Berry, Me, and Motown*, p. 170; George, *Where Did Our Love Go?* pp. 151–152.

38. Williams, *Temptations*, pp. 136–137.

39. The countersuit was officially filed on November 14, 1968, although it did not receive national publicity until December. Gordy, *To Be Loved*, pp. 263, 267–268; George, *Where Did Our Love Go?* p. 152; Wilson, *Dreamgirl*, p. 258; "New Motown Suit," *Rolling Stone*, 24 (December 21, 1968): 4; Tom Ricke, "The Story behind the Sour Notes at Motown," *Detroit Free Press*, November 22, 1968, section D, p. 8; "Prize-winning Songsmiths Sue Motown Corporation for $22 Million," *Jet*, 35, no. 9 (December 5, 1968): 58–59.

40. "Prize-winning Songsmiths Sue Motown," pp. 58–59.

41. Brown, "The Motown Sound of Money," pp. 103–108, 186, 188–189.

42. For more on the "myth" of black capitalism, see James Boggs, John Williams, and Charles Johnson, "The Myth and Irrationality of Black Capitalism," James and Grace Lee Boggs Papers, box 4, folder 15, Walter P. Reuther Library, Wayne State University.

43. Singleton, *Berry, Me, and Motown*, pp. 166–168.

44. Gordy, *To Be Loved*, p. 278. The H-D-H legal battle with Motown Records continued into the 1990s. See Richard Willing, "Motown Feud Strikes Sad Chord," *Detroit News*, February 26, 1995, section B, pp. 1, 4; and David Ashenfelter, "Songwriters Battle Gordy," *Detroit Free Press*, July 21, 1998.

45. Wilson, *Dreamgirl*, pp. 281–285.

46. For more on Ballard's downfall, see Rita Griffin, "Peace of Mind the 'Supreme' Sacrifice for Florence Ballard," *Michigan Chronicle*, November 14, 1970. In the article Griffin reported that, financially, Ballard was "broke at [the age] of 27." Ballard also commented in the interview on the ways in which she felt that Motown had stifled her. She claimed that her nickname as the "quiet one" of the group was a misnomer: "I think that the dialogue was written into the act as a hint . . . because if anything, I was outspoken. If something didn't appear right, I would mention it. It's just that people know where to hit me to get me to cooperate."

47. Wilson, *Dreamgirl*, p. 261.

48. Gordy, *To Be Loved*, p. 280.

49. Michael Jackson, *Moon Walk* (London: Heinemann-Mandarin, 1989), p. 74.

50. On November 21, 1970, Margaret Danner wrote a letter to Bertha Gordy, matriarch of the Gordy family, that expressed her gratitude about the recording "after many years of waiting." See n. 4 in June M. Aldridge, "Langston Hughes and Margaret Danner," *Langston Hughes Review*, 3, no. 2 (Fall 1984): 7–8. I have found no evidence that Bertha Gordy instigated the release in any way—although she did send Danner a copy of the album after she received Danner's letter.

51. For example, see liner notes, Stokely Carmichael, *Free Huey!* Black Forum BF452 (Detroit: Motown Record Corporation, 1970).

52. See the liner notes, *Black Spirits*, Black Forum BF456l, produced by Woodie King (Detroit: Motown Record Corporation, April 1972). Personal interview with George Schiffer, May 3, 1993, notes in author's possession. For more background on

the Elaine Brown recording, see Elaine Brown, *A Taste of Power: A Black Woman's Story* (New York: Anchor Books, 1992), pp. 304–313.

53. Terry eventually published his research as a book. See Wallace Terry, *Bloods: An Oral History of the Vietnam War by Black Veterans* (New York: Ballantine Books, 1984).

54. For example, see Black Forum advertisement, *Ebony*, April 1969, p. 21; Personal interview with Ewart Abner, March 19, 1993; notes in author's possession.

55. Gordy, *To Be Loved*, pp. 264–266.

56. Williams, *Temptations*, p. 139.

57. Bianco, *Heatwave*, p. 91.

58. Quotation from David Ritz, liner notes, *The Marvin Gaye Collection* (Los Angeles: Motown Record Company, 1990), p. 8.

59. Gordy, *To Be Loved*, pp. 145–146.

60. David Ritz, *Divided Soul: The Life of Marvin Gaye* (New York: Da Capo Press, 1991), p. 29. For further analysis of Gaye's fascination with Sinatra, see Gerald Early, "The African American and the Italian," in *One Nation under a Groove: Motown and American Culture* (Hopewell, N.J.: Ecco Press, 1995), pp. 10–28.

61. Ritz, *Divided Soul*, p. 51.

62. Gordy, *To Be Loved*, pp. 302–303. For more details about the early creative stages of the project, see Neely Tucker, "Like Getting a High-Five from God," *Detroit Free Press Magazine*, September 15, 1991; and Ritz, *Divided Soul*, chap. 15, "Sermon from the Studio," pp. 145–153.

63. "Motown Beatitudes," *Time*, October 11, 1971, p. 69. After reinstating its "Rhythm and Blues" chart in January 1965, *Billboard* magazine decided to change to the "Soul" name in August 1969. The name changed again to "Black" in June 1982, and then in October 1990 the chart became "Rhythm and Blues" once more. See "Billboard Adopts 'R&B' as New Name for Two Charts," *Billboard* magazine, October 27, 1990.

64. See liner notes, *Save the Children*, Motown soundtrack album, M800-R2 (Detroit: Motown Record Corporation, 1973).

65. Rita Griffin, "Motown's New Veep, GM Tells Firm's Future Plans," *Michigan Chronicle*, June 24, 1972, section A, pp. 1, 4; Singleton, *Berry, Me, and Motown*, p. 222.

66. The film was also nominated for best costume design, best screenplay adapted from another source, and best score. Gordy, *To Be Loved*, pp. 73, and 309–313.

67. For more on the 1969 election, see Joe T. Darden, Richard Child Hill, June Thomas, and Richard Thomas, *Detroit: Race and Uneven Development* (Philadelphia: Temple University Press, 1987), pp. 209–213; *Detroit Free Press*, Sept. 10, 1969, and September 11, 1969; *Michigan Chronicle*, August 23, 1969; Remer Tyson, "Long Struggle Led to Firm Power Base," in Scott McGehee and Susan Watson, eds., *Blacks*

in Detroit: Reprints from Detroit Free Press, (Detroit: Detroit Free Press Publications, 1980).

68. Darden et. al., *Detroit,* pp. 213–214; Georgakas and Surkin, *Detroit,* p. 69; Coleman Young, *Hard Stuff: The Autobiography of Mayor Coleman Young* (New York: Viking Press, 1994), p. 128; *Detroit Free Press,* January 4, 1976.

69. Georgakas and Surkin, *Detroit,* pp. 201–208. For the most detailed account of the STRESS controversy, see *Detroit under STRESS,* pamphlet (Detroit: From the Ground Up, 1973), in Dan Georgakas Papers, box 3, folder 3-5, Walter P. Reuther Library, Wayne State University.

70. For a more detailed analysis of the song, see Farah Jasmine Griffin, *"Who Set You Flowin'?": The African-American Migration Narrative* (New York: Oxford University Press, 1995), pp. 94–99.

71. Young, *Hard Stuff,* pp. 197–200.

72. Chafe, *Unfinished Journey,* p. 447.

73. Marji Kunz, "Diana's Show Goes On: For the Mayor and People," *Detroit Free Press,* January 3, 1974, section C, p. 1. Ross also credited her high school education at Cass Tech for helping her save the show. When Ross had to create a new stage costume by sewing a feather boa onto a new dress, she commented, "I should send a thank you note to Cass Tech. The school taught me how to do dress designing."

74. Young, *Hard Stuff,* pp. 200–201.

75. For more on corporate power in Detroit, see Lynda Ann Ewen, *Corporate Power and Urban Crisis in Detroit* (Princeton, N.J.: Princeton University Press, 1978).

76. See Herbert Koshetz, "Gains Forecast for Black Businesses," *New York Times,* June 13, 1973.

Conclusion

1. Dennis Tuttle, "Holding Viewers Is Half the Battle," *Washington Post,* January 25, 1998, Television Guide, p. 7; Johnnie L. Roberts, "'How Sweet It Is' . . . to Own All Those Fantastic Old Motown Songs," *Newsweek,* January 26, 1998, p. 70.

2. Thomas J. Sugrue, *The Origins of the Urban Crisis: Race and Inequality in Postwar Detroit* (Princeton, N.J.: Princeton University Press, 1996).

3. Charlie Gillett, *The Sound of the City: The Rise of Rock and Roll* (New York: Pantheon Books, 1983), pp. 39–41.

4. Berry Gordy, *To Be Loved: The Music, the Magic, the Memories of Motown* (New York: Warner Books, 1994), pp. 4–5.

5. For more details on these transactions, see Johnnie L. Roberts, "Pitsville, U.S.A.," *Newsweek,* December 2, 1996, pp. 49–51; Paul Farhi, "Seagram to Acquire Music Firm Polygram," *Washington Post,* May 22, 1998, section D, p. 3; Roberts, " 'How Sweet It Is,' " p. 70.

6. Sugrue, *Origins of the Urban Crisis,* p. 5.

7. Johnnie L. Roberts, "A Touch of Magic," *Newsweek*, June 15, 1998, pp. 40–43.

8. Ibid., p. 41.

9. For more on the limitations of black self-help, see Robin D. G. Kelley, *Yo' Mama's Disfunktional! Fighting the Culture Wars in Urban America* (Boston: Beacon Press, 1997), chap. 3, "Looking Backward: The Limits of Self-Help Ideology." For more on Michigan's welfare reform policies, see Larry Bivens, "Detroit Ranks Second in Requests for Food: Emergency Assistance Jumped 34 Percent in City," *Detroit News*, December 17, 1996; Lawrence W. Reed, "What Difference Has John Engler Made?" *Detroit News*, January, 26, 1997.

10. Gordy, *To Be Loved*, p. 23.

Acknowledgments

> I think throughout the whole of our lives we ought to aim at the moon, and if we fall among the stars we'll still be on high ground.
> —The Reverend C. L. Franklin, "Give Me This Mountain" sermon

I aimed at the moon when I began this project nine years ago. Fortunately for me, I fell among the stars and with the help of many have ended up on, what I believe to be, much higher ground. Several different galaxies of people offered me guidance, sources, interviews, constructive critique, and—most important—support and encouragement. First, I must thank Hazel Carby, who acted as my adviser when this book was still a dissertation. Her intellectual vision, political commitment, and generous spirit made the work a joy and sustained me in moments of doubt or exhaustion. Other members of the Yale University American Studies faculty were also important mentors. Jon Butler, Michael Denning, and Robert Stepto deserve special mention for reading early drafts, writing letters of recommendation for research fellowships, and simply sharing their ideas.

My commitment to the study of popular music and its politics has been inspired by the work of Paul Gilroy, Robin D. G. Kelley, Lawrence W. Levine, George Lipsitz, and Charles McGovern, all of whom have been spirited in their encouragement. Paul Gilroy and Robin Kelley both read early chapters of the dissertation and encouraged me over the years to complete the book. Lawrence W. Levine, George Lipsitz, and Charles

McGovern all read the entire manuscript. Their marvelously detailed comments enabled me to envision the project in new ways, and their friendship has taught me much about generosity in the academy.

My love of Detroit history has also been inspired by the work of others. Sidney Fine generously shared his own research archive from his book *Violence in the Model City*. Kevin Boyle, Michael Eric Dyson, and Jerry Herron offered their knowledge about and general enthusiasm for the Motor City. Melba Joyce Boyd and Geoffrey Jacques both enriched my understanding of poetry and its many meanings to black Detroit. Finally, Thomas Sugrue has been a wonderful mentor and friend. He also read the manuscript in its entirety. His critique and his own scholarship on postwar Detroit has been a tremendous influence on my own work.

I have had the rare opportunity and honor to have met, interviewed, and developed important relationships with individuals whose lives and work are the subject of this narrative. Grace Lee Boggs has dedicated her life to fighting injustice in Detroit through community activism and her own revolutionary thought. She shared memories, music, books, and clippings about Detroit and her vibrant life with James Boggs. Her continuing campaign to make Detroit a more humane place inspires all who meet her. The late Ewart Abner, a record industry legend at both Vee-Jay and Motown Records, was an equally influential resource and also a dear friend. Mr. Abner provided me with invaluable insights about the cultural and racial politics of the music industry. He also introduced me to Junius Griffin and George Schiffer, both of whom rounded out my picture of behind-the-scenes political activism at Motown Records. One added thanks to Junius, who cooks a mean catfish and whose own teaching on civil rights at Emory and Henry College inspires my own. I hope that this book honors the memory of "Ab" and the work that he, Junius, and George did at Motown.

Several other Motown veterans shared their memories with me. Claudette Robinson was especially gracious and also became a close friend. As Motown's first female performer, Ms. Robinson provided me with a much-needed perspective on the role of women in the Hitsville story. Also, I thank her for sharing her meticulous scrapbooks on the Miracles and other Motown artists. I am also grateful to Janie Bradford, Esther Gordy Edwards, Martha Reeves, Smokey Robinson, Georgia Ward, and Kim Weston for sharing their marvelous stories about Motown's early years. Special thanks to Detroit's own "Famous Coachman," who did not work at Motown but has kept the blues alive in Detroit since 1947. His record store on the corner of Charlevoix and Mt. Elliott is one of the few of its kind left in the country. The music still blasts out of the speakers outside, and the Coachman's warm personality welcomes anyone who steps inside. The Coachman taught me about a whole era of Detroit's musical history and reminded me that "rhythm and blues" should be called "blues and rhythm" because the blues came first.

I would like to thank the following organizations for permission to reproduce excerpts from their works: Alfred Knopf, Inc., and Harold Ober Associates for Langston Hughes's poem "Blacklash Blues," and the Broadside Press for Margaret Danner's poem "Malcolm X, A Lover of Grass Roots." The Hal Leonard Corporation has granted permission to reproduce lyrics from the following (all rights reserved, international copyright secured):

"The Happening," words and music by Lamont Dozier, Edward Holland Jr., Brian Holland, and Frank Devol, © 1967 (renewed 1995) Jobete Music Co., Inc.; and "Love Child," words and music by Deke Richards, Pamela Sawyer, Dean R. Taylor, and Frank E. Wilson, © 1968 (renewed 1996) Jobete Music Co., Inc. All rights controlled and administered by EMI April Music Inc. and EMI Blackwood Music Inc. on behalf of Jobete Music Co., Inc. and Stone Agate Music (a division of Jobete Music Co., Inc.);

"Inner City Blues (Makes Me Wanna Holler)," words and music by Marvin Gaye and James Nyx, © 1971 Jobete Music Co., Inc. All rights controlled and administered by EMI April Music Inc.;

"Living for the City," words and music by Stevie Wonder, © 1973 Jobete Music Co., Inc. and Black Bull Music c/o EMI April Music Inc.;

"Ball of Confusion (That's What the World Is Today)," words and music by Norman Whitfield and Barrett Strong, © 1970 (renewed 1998) Jobete Music Co., Inc. All rights controlled and administered by EMI Blackwood Music Inc. on behalf of Stone Agate Music (a division of Jobete Music Co., Inc.).

I received generous support and guidance from several libraries, archivists, and foundations. The Walter P. Reuther Library at Wayne State

University and its Archives of Labor and Urban Affairs proved invaluable to this study. The staff of archivists at the Reuther are among the most helpful that I have ever met. I reserve special thanks for Margaret Raucher, who went out of her way to track down sources for me and continued to mail and fax me documents as I pieced together my final chapters. The Motown Historical Museum, located in the original Hitsville, U.S.A., building on West Grand Boulevard, always welcomed me warmly. Esther Gordy Edwards is to be commended for the work she initiated to preserve Motown's rich history and share it with the public. Richard Frankensteen Jr.'s private collection of boxing memorabilia from Detroit provided me with rare data on Berry Gordy Jr.'s early boxing career. In my early research, Michael Ochs and Jonathan Hyams gave me access to the extensive collection of Motown photographs and recordings preserved at the Michael Ochs Archives. Candace Bond and David Babcock offered me a similar privilege at Motown/MCA. At Motown/Polygram photo archivist Elyse Rieder graciously assisted me as I prepared the final images for this book. Richard Warren, curator of Yale University's Historical Sound Recordings Collection, provided me with research tapes of what, I am certain, is the most extensive collection of Black Forum recordings outside Detroit or the Library of Congress.

Funds for my early research were provided by a Bordin-Gilette Research Travel Grant from the Bentley Library at the University of Michigan; a Kaiser Family Foundation Research Grant from the Walter P. Reuther Library; a John F. Enders Travel Grant from Yale University; a Yale University Dissertation Fellowship; and a summer dissertation fellowship from the Pew Program in Religion and American History. George Mason University's College of Arts and Sciences and Institute of the Arts also awarded me a Mathy Junior Faculty Fellowship, which gave me a leave to complete the final draft of the book. Many thanks also to Margaretta Fulton, my editor at Harvard University Press, who calmly guided me through the publication process, and to Elizabeth Hurwit for her meticulous manuscript editing.

I have been fortunate both at Yale and George Mason Universities to be surrounded by wonderful colleagues. At Yale, Philip Deloria, Benjamin Filene, Margaret McFadden, Carlo Rotella, and David Stowe read various incarnations of the dissertation and cheered me on with their humor and friendship. The *entire* faculty of George Mason's Department of History and Art History has been equally supportive and congenial. Special thanks to Jack Censer, department chair, and Roy Rosenzweig for his insightful reading of the manuscript. I would also like to thank my students at George Mason University for keeping me on my toes.

It is impossible to express in a sentence or two how my friends contributed to this project over the years—whether by reading a draft, sharing a dinner, or offering emotional support. I would like to acknowledge a few of the many people whose friendship helped me finish this project and reminded me that there was life beyond it: Christa and Robert Alcala, Melissa and Matthew Bail, Iris Bruno, Gretchen and John Buggeln, Paul Constantine and Ann Ferguson, Mike and Kim Fruin, John Gennari, Jim Hall, Marsha Hoem, Gail Hoffman and Michael Martin, Jim and Lois Horton, Demetri Kapetanakos, Margaret McCaffrey, Kari Miner, Laura Mitchell and Mico Loretan, Deb Raupp, Tricia Rinne, Betsy Rowe, John Stauffer, Debra Thurston, Linda Venis, and Paul Von Blum.

As a Detroit native, this project was a profound homecoming for me and renewed my appreciation for my family—both immediate and extended. I lived with my paternal grandmother, Elizabeth Smith, during my early research trips, and no one could have asked for a more lively or loving roommate. My maternal grandparents, William and Aldina Narden, welcomed me home, fed me, and continue—after over sixty-three years of marriage—to teach me about the power of love and commitment. The Johnson, Clarke, Eardley, and Peterson families also made sure that I was never hungry whenever I was in town and kept my spirits up. I would also like to thank Michael and Jan Shatusky, who warmly adopted me during my visits to Ann Arbor. My immediate family in California offered similar services whenever my research or a holiday brought me to Los Angeles. My brother Scott, my sister-in-law Christine, and the Silk and Gonzalez families offered steadfast support. Andrew, Hailey, and Jackson helped their Aunt Suzy keep her priorities straight as only children's wisdom and laughter can. Thanks also to my brother Steve, sister-in-law Dillma, and niece Pamina—my family in the Washington, D.C. area.

I am especially grateful to Douglas Fagen, who came into my life as this book entered the publication stage. He not only gave me thoughtful readings of final drafts but also was patient with me as I worked to finish the manuscript in the midst of planning our wedding. His compassion, laughter, and love inspire and sustain me every day.

I reserve my final thanks for my parents, Gerald and Caralee Smith. Their boundless love and personal integrity have been constant lodestars in my life and have given me the courage to aim at the moon in all things.

Index

Index

Gordy siblings: Anna, 65, 71, 76, 142,
237; Esther, *see* Edwards, Esther Gordy;
Fuller, 65, 67; George, 65, 67;
Gwendolyn, 65, 71, 76, 155; Loucye,
65, 67, 105, 206, 274n27; Robert,
65, 67
"Got A Job," 72–74
Graystone Ballroom, 45–48, 51, 104
Great March to Freedom, 17, 21–25, 26–28,
36, 40, 44, 51, 53, 54, 56, 77, 87, 93,
110, 176, 211, 217, 245
Great March to Freedom album, 17, 21–23,
40, 51, 77, 92, 93, 94, 137, 138, 141,
206, 216, 266n2
Gribbs, Roman S., 241
Griffin, Junius, 206–207, 216, 230, 231
Group on Advanced Leadership (GOAL),
52–53, 58, 79, 142, 195

"Happening, The," 181–182, 183, 184,
187, 189, 224, 294n11, 295n16
Hastings Street, 33, 36–37, 41, 42, 43, 44,
46, 47, 101, 186, 198–199
Henry, Milton, 40, 52, 54, 56, 79, 90, 141–
142, 145, 191, 195, 196, 201, 203, 222
Henry, Richard B., 52, 79, 142, 195, 196,
204, 222
Hitsville, U.S.A. Studios, 6, 75, 103, 123–
124, 158, 169, 213, 214, 220, 229, 230,
236, 254
Holland-Dozier-Holland songwriting team
(Brian Holland, Lamont Dozier, and
Eddie Holland), 117, 129, 155; lawsuit
of, 224–225, 226–227, 232, 233, 256
Housewives League of Detroit (HWLD), 60–
61, 66, 78, 95
Hudson, Joseph L., 203, 204, 244
Hudson's Department Store, 111, 112, 161
Hughes, Langston, 17, 94–95, 96, 107–112,
113, 115, 117, 136, 137–138, 139, 151,
172–173, 179, 190–191, 209, 230,
279n7, 281n33, 282n39, 288n23

Iacocca, Lee, 124–125, 283n65. *See also*
Ford Motor Company
Illustrated News, 38, 39, 57, 222
Inner City Voice, 221–223, 302n29

Jackson, Janet, 256
Jackson, Jesse, 42; Operation PUSH, 238–
239
Jackson, Michael, 229, 250
Jackson 5, The, 229
Jamerson, James, 47, 75, 102, 115, 155,
159, 160, 162
Jeffries, Edward, Jr., 33, 34
Jenkins, Bobo, 12, 47
Jobete Music Publishing Company, 174,
254–255
Johnson, Earvin "Magic," 256–258
Johnson, Lyndon, 135, 168, 172, 186, 196,
202, 204, 211, 212, 214, 217
Johnson, Marv, 74
Junior Walker and the All-Stars, 6, 141,
153, 162

Kaufman, Murray "the K," 127, 129–130
Kelley, George, 58, 89
Kennedy, John F., 85, 87, 152
Kercheval incident, 178–179
Kerner Commission. *See* National Advisory
Committee on Civil Disorders
King, Martin Luther, Jr.: participation in the
Great March to Freedom, 17, 21–23, 25,
27–28, 30–31, 49, 54, 55, 56, 58–59, 77,
87, 88, 92, 94–95, 217; as leader of
SCLC, 79, 146, 152, 176–177, 207, 209,
211–212, 231; assassination and funeral
of, 215–216, 218, 228
King, Coretta, 215–216
King, Woodie, Jr., 10, 231, 281n33, 297n40
King Solomon Baptist Church, 56, 58, 83,
87, 101, 112, 114, 116, 143

Lady Sings the Blues film, 240
La Grone, Oliver, 109, 110
League of Revolutionary Black Workers, 11,
222, 240
Liles, Raynoma. *See* Singleton, Raynoma
Gordy
"Living for the City," 243–244, 246
Louis, Joe, 68–69, 132
"Love Child," 232–233, 235

Madgett, Naomi Long, 109, 110, 115
Malcolm X, 56, 83–88, 92, 134, 140, 142–
143, 144–145, 153, 164, 171, 175, 176,

Index

Index